Racism and reaction

International Library of Sociology

Founded by Karl Mannheim

Editor: John Rex, University of Aston in Birmingham

Arbor Scientiae
Arbor Vitae

A catalogue of the books available in the **International Library of Sociology** and other series of Social Science books published by Routledge & Kegan Paul will be found at the end of this volume.

Racism and reaction

A profile of Handsworth

Peter Ratcliffe

Department of Sociology
University of Warwick

Routledge & Kegan Paul

London, Boston and Henley

First published in 1981
by Routledge & Kegan Paul Ltd
39 Store Street, London WC1E 7DD,
9 Park Street, Boston, Mass. 02108, USA, and
Broadway House, Newtown Road,
Henley-on-Thames, Oxon RG9 1EN
Printed in Great Britain by
Redwood Burn Ltd, Trowbridge and Esher
© Peter Ratcliffe 1981

British Library Cataloguing in Publication Data

Ratcliffe, Peter
    Racism and reaction. – (International library of
    sociology)
    1. Handsworth (Birmingham. England)
    – Race relations
    I. Title II. Series
    305.8'0424'96   DA690.H22/   80–42295

ISBN 0–7100 0696–9

To Lynne, Doris and Harry

Contents

Figures

Tables

Acknowledgments

As with most works of this nature, its completion would have been impossible had it not been for the efforts of many others. What made my task slightly unusual was that the research project on which my account is based had already been running for some two years before I formally joined the team. My first thanks must therefore go to those who designed and executed the sample design, constructed the questionnaire (as shown in Appendix 2), and recruited NOP Ltd to undertake the survey fieldwork. In addition to the team I joined in the summer of 1976, a vote of thanks must therefore go to Valdo Pons, Martin Legassick and Wyn Lewis who made important contributions to the early direction and form of the study.

I count myself fortunate indeed to have joined a team which contained so many complementary talents. John Rex, as director, steered both the theoretical and empirical dimensions of the research from its inception in 1974 with immense skill. On a personal level he not only provided the initial stimulus for me to join the team and attempt this book, but also made important critical contributions to an earlier draft of this (my first) book. To him I owe a special debt.

The importance to me of the whole team was not restricted to their undoubted academic proficiency and sensitivity to the research enterprise. They provided me with a stimulating social (as well as academic) environment. Many thanks must therefore go to Sally Tomlinson, who combined a massive capacity for work (from the beginning of the project in 1974) with an invariably pleasant disposition and smiling face, to David Hearnden who played such an important role in both fieldwork and administration, and to Val Brown who was everything a good research secretary should be. Thanks must also go to Pervaiz Nazir who was engaged in a parallel study of Pakistanis in Birmingham. Perhaps one unsung hero of the team should not go unmentioned here: Sally's black labrador-cross puppy, William. Despite his propensity for shredding research documents, he helped to keep members of the team (relatively?) sane through the often trying months.

We decided to undertake the massive task of coding the questionnaire material ourselves, for both methodological and financial reasons. This meant that a considerable team of coders was required in the summer of 1976; a team which included Alyson Burberry, Lynne Julian-Jones, Mike Stacey, Ann Oliver, Valerie Jackson and Sue Tomlinson. I am grateful for their remarkable sensitivity and stamina.

As a non-typist I can only marvel at the work of Val Brown, Olive Heaton and Iris Host, who worked tirelessly on the first two drafts of the book. I owe the existence of a final draft to Anne Love and Eunice Hodgkinson, who both had an unenviable task in dealing with my often illegible scribble. I am sincerely grateful for their efforts.

In the technical sphere I owe a debt of gratitude to our consultant cartographer, Mr M. B. Stedman, Department of Geography, University of Birmingham, who produced the maps which appear in the script. Thanks must also go to the staff of the computer unit at Warwick University, and in particular to Keith Halstead, for his help in dealing with 'bugs' in SPSS (Statistical Package for the Social Sciences).

No study of this magnitude could have been performed without considerable financial assistance. We were immensely fortunate to have the generous support of the Nuffield Foundation throughout. Of course, this support would have been to no avail without the co-operation of the people of Handsworth and the many officials who were interviewed during the life of the project. Many thanks go to this group.

My final debt is inestimable. Without the continued support of my wife, Lynne Julian-Jones, it is unlikely that this book would ever have seen the light of day. In addition to putting up with an author's variable moods (and timetable) she willingly gave up a massive amount of time to translate my unintelligible scrawl into neat and pretty prose. The book is therefore rightly dedicated to Lynne and to my parents, without whose personal sacrifices I would never have been in a position to write it.

Peter Ratcliffe

1 The sociology and politics of migration

INTRODUCTION

The data upon which this book is based represent the outcome of a major research project undertaken during the
period 1974-7. For many reasons which will become clear
in the following chapters, this was a crucial phase in the
British race relations scene, a time of high (and rising)
unemployment and an increasing sense of tension between
black minority groups and the indigenous white majority.
Not surprisingly these tensions became the focal point of
our enquiry. By talking to residents of a multi-racial
area, and to those 'outsiders' who came into contact with
local people (e.g., council officials, school teachers,
etc.) we were able to gain a fascinating though often disturbing insight into the dynamics of urban social structure. Furthermore, by supplementing this material with
data outlining the educational, work and housing experiences of a sample of individuals drawn from each of the
major ethnic groups in the area, and by examining published official statistical material, we may judge the
extent to which members of ethnic minority groups have
gained de facto equality in terms of citizenship rights.
    We chose Birmingham for our case study: a city which,
as we shall see shortly, has experienced immigration from
the New Commonwealth on a significant scale since the
early 1950s. Despite the high overall level, it is undoubtedly the case that this has resulted in certain areas
of the city bearing the brunt of this impact (e.g., in
terms of the strains on existing resources). It was
therefore decided to study in depth one such area.
Handsworth was selected as it appeared to reflect the
precise characteristics for which we were looking, both in
terms of the level of immigration and in the nature of the
racial and ethnic mix. For example, it was an area in

1

which large numbers of Asian, West Indian, Irish and native white families were living side by side.

The above will be made clear after reading the companion volume to the present work, 'Colonial Immigrants in a British City', by Rex and Tomlinson (1979). Indeed, it is quite legitimate to ask at this point why it is necessary to follow this major volume with one which ostensibly covers similar ground. However, to ask this is to be unaware of the nature and fruits of this particular piece of research: there was no space in one volume to do full justice to the wealth of material, both quantitative and qualitative, which was collated. Nor was there sufficient space to highlight the substantive links between previous empirical studies of race relations and our Handsworth research. The present book attempts to do both. In contrast, Rex and Tomlinson aimed to focus much more on the place of race relations within sociological theory in general and the relationship between black migrants and the British class structure in particular. The two books certainly converge at various points during the analysis, but, of course, it would be disturbing if they did not! However, it is to be hoped that by studying both books in conjunction, the reader will gain a clearer appreciation of the state of race relations in contemporary Britain.

The present work, then, attempts to present a systematic analysis of our empirical data in a balanced and dispassionate manner. In contrast to the book by Rex and Tomlinson, [1] two sets of figures are often given when our survey data are referred to. The reasons for this are rather technical and therefore a more detailed discussion is to be found in Appendix 1. On the other hand, it may help the reader to see the significance of this apparently cumbersome presentation if a brief outline of the reasoning is noted here.

The distinction between the two sets of figures is that one represents the unweighted raw data, whilst the other is weighted so as to take into account the fact that we are essentially dealing with a composite of two samples. These are a quota sample of 900 Handsworth householders (300 indigenous whites, 300 West Indians and 300 Asians), using a sampling scheme devised by the research team; and a supplementary group of 200 Newtown council tenants (95 West Indians, 5 Asians and 100 whites), selected purposively by the Birmingham Housing Department. The question of weightings arises because the Newtown sample, when combined with the main group of 900, effectively 'exaggerates' the presence of council tenants in general, and black council tenants in particular. Had both samples employed random sampling methods, the weighted figures

FIGURE 1 Ward map of the city of Birmingham (excluding Sutton Coldfield) indicating the survey area

only would have been given. As it is, we feel that it is
desirable to present both sets, particularly since any
differences would highlight distinctive features of the
Newtown group.

It should also be borne in mind throughout that by
focusing essentially on householders we are looking at a
group of first-generation immigrants, many of whom have
lived in Britain for fifteen years or more. Many, as we
shall see, have bought homes and raised their children
here. Their children have been educated in Birmingham and
most see themselves as British - at least in the sense
that they understandably expect the same rights as their
white classmates. Thus the perspective which the first
generation immigrant holds towards British society may be
expected to differ radically from that of his children.
[2] The outcome of this is that whilst we claim a 'dispassionate' analysis of our survey material, in gauging
the experience of being black in a white society we acknowledge Adorno's point that however 'valid' the response
of an individual, this should not lead us to the conclusion that it is equivalent to a statement of objective
truth for the society in which he lives. [3]   Therefore,
our analysis takes a critical perspective throughout in
the sense that responses are interpreted within the
context of historical and social structural considerations.

We begin our analysis with a look at the kinds of
factor which influence the level of immigration to
Britain. Later in this chapter we reflect on what immigrants now feel about their decision to come here, and,
in particular, what measure of commitment they now demonstrate towards their adopted country. The final section
deals with immigration policy and the effects which this
has on the future influx of dependants, and looks at the
potential hardship this might create among an immigrant
community such as the one which exists in present-day
Handsworth.

THE MIGRATION PROCESS

The major influx of New Commonwealth immigrants to Britain
occurred in the decade leading up to the 1962 Immigration
Act. This and subsequent controls have gradually reduced
the numbers to such an extent that in the latter half of
the 1970s new entrants are almost exclusively the dependants of families already here.

Table 1.1 confirms, as noted earlier, that most of the
black immigrant population of Birmingham in 1971 had

TABLE 1.1 Birthplace of persons resident in Birmingham: 1951,1961,1971

		1951	1961	1971
United Kingdom	England	1,007,493(90.57)	961,664(86.86)	842,625(83.04)
	Scotland	13,005	13,139	11,960
	Wales	25,457	21,560	17,280
	N.Ireland	8,251	11,379	11,375
	Other UK (including UK part not stated)	600	3,554	370
	TOTAL	1,054,806(94.83)	1,011,296(91.34)	883,610(87.08)
Remainder of British Isles	Irish Republic	26,568 (2.39)	44,798 (4.05)	39,565 (3.90)
	Ireland (part not stated)	1,530 (0.14)	2,784 (0.25)	5,300 (0.52)
Old Commonwealth	Australia	506	424	485
	Canada	909	792	725
	New Zealand	166	123	120
	TOTAL	1,581 (0.14)	1,339 (0.12)	1,330 (0.13)
New Common- wealth	(1) Africa	336 (0.03)	666 (0.06)	4,925 (0.49)
	(2) America: Guyana	26	121	170
	Jamaica	345	12,017	19,385
	Trinidad and Tobago	37	144	280
	Other	85	4,016	5,530
	TOTAL	493 (0.04)	16,298 (1.47)	25,365 (2.50)
	(3) Asia and Oceania: India	2,205	4,801	17,885
	Pakistan	1,108	5,355	17,515
	Other	606	1,796	2,250
	TOTAL	3,919 (0.35)	11,952 (1.08)	37,650 (3.71)

TABLE 1.1 (continued) Birthplace of persons resident in Birmingham: 1951,1961,1971

		1951	1961	1971
(4) Europe		309 (0.03)	402 (0.04)	390 (0.04)
	TOTAL (New Commonwealth)	5,057 (0.45)	29,369 [1] (2.65)	68,325 [1] (6.73)
Europe	France	391	319	320
	Germany	1,661	1,787	1,605
	Italy	392	945	1,000
	Poland	2,352	2,725	2,250
	Other	2,546	2,243	2,215
	TOTAL	7,342 (0.66)	8,019 (0.72)	7,390 (0.73)
Other countries and at sea		2,020 (0.18)	3,248 (0.29)	5,220 (0.51)
Birthplace not stated		13,457 (1.21)	5,604 (0.51)	3,930 (0.39)
ALL countries		1,112,361 (100.0)	1,107,187 (100.0)	1,014,670 (100.0)

Sources: 1951,1961,1971 Census County Reports for Warwickshire
1 Errors in the published Census figures produce slight inconsistencies in the data at these points.

FIGURE 2 Birmingham immigrants with both parents born in
New Commonwealth as a % of total enumerated ward population (1971 Census)

arrived within the previous twenty years. In terms of New
Commonwealth citizens, the 1951 Census showed a figure of
well under 5,000. By 1971, however, it had topped 68,000.
During this same period the overall population of
Birmingham had declined, and therefore the proportionate
increase in those of New Commonwealth origin was rather
larger than the raw data suggest. They formed a mere 0.44
per cent of the city's population in 1951 as against 6.73
per cent in 1971.

The data are presented in great detail since it is
important to bear in mind that Birmingham, in common with
a number of British cities, has a strong tradition of attracting immigrant labour, particularly from Ireland. As
was the case with black immigrants, many came to
Birmingham during the 1950s to fuel the expansionist
economy. The growth of semi-skilled and unskilled jobs
in the factories and foundries was considerable, and we
witnessed the emergence of the immigrant as 'marginal
economic man'. [4] Although the base of immigration was
extremely broad, it is specifically the black immigrant
who concerns us in the present work.

What Table 1.1 clearly confirms is that the process of
immigration from the New Commonwealth countries was by no
means an even one. Whereas migration from the West Indies
occurred mainly between the 1951 and 1961 Censuses, immigration from the Indian subcontinent was basically a phenomenon of the 1960s. Thus, Indians and Pakistanis came
to Birmingham at a time when the city's population already
contained a significant number of black immigrants. As we
shall see shortly, this is to some extent a direct product
of the immigration controls which, as noted above, were
introduced from 1962 onwards. The importance of this
point lies in the fact that the various ethnic groups are
to be found in fairly close proximity. [5] The race relations scene, then, is already rather more complex than
one which has a straightforward black-white dimension.

Handsworth is an area which throughout the nineteenth
century maintained a smart residential image. Kelly's
directory of 1864 described it as 'a fashionable suburb
... containing many of the villa residences of the
businessmen of Birmingham'. Although industrialisation
had brought with it the housing developments of rather
poorer quality, even in 1889 maps show that much of the
area was still devoted to farming. It was not until the
inter-war years that the last of these farms (Oxhill) disappeared to make way for a council estate, leaving
Handsworth Park as the only substantial area of greenery
(see Figure 3). By this time Handsworth had already lost
its residential image and the more wealthy residents had

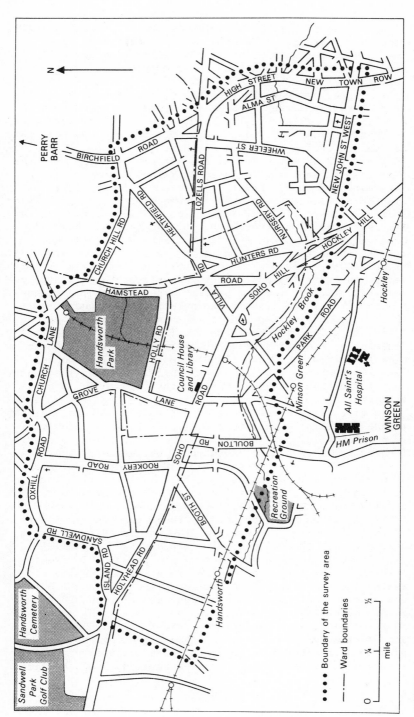

FIGURE 3 The survey area

begun to leave their large homes in order to move to newly
fashionable areas. It was this void, then, that black
immigrants in the 1950s and 1960s filled. As we shall
see, the reasons for this are both complex and interesting.

We begin, however, by focusing on the process of immigration to the survey area by concentrating on our own
survey data. In particular we draw on our interviews with
395 West Indians and 305 Asians, most of whom had come to
Handsworth during these two decades.

Table 1.2 shows in detail the pattern of entry into the
UK for this group and in so doing raises a number of
interesting issues. First, as reflected in the city
figures discussed above, the overwhelming majority of West
Indians had arrived well before the mid-1960s, whereas the
Asians tended to arrive throughout the decade. Second,
when we use the label 'Asian' we are to a large extent
talking about those born in India; a point which has considerable significance for our subsequent analysis. Similarly, the West Indians in our sample are predominantly of
Jamaican origin. For the present argument the importance
of the first issue lies in the question of whether or not
the immigrant's perception of life in Britain and the
social relationships he forms (or fails to form) are influenced by the structural factors involved in his decision to emigrate. Glass (1960), Peach (1968) and more
recently Lawrence (1974), among others, have analysed what
they termed the push-pull factors involved in the process
of migration.

In discussing the process of emigration of West Indians
to the UK, Glass argued that the major factors underlying
this movement of population were the restrictions on entry
imposed by other countries and the poor state of the home
economy. The latter factor resulted in a high incidence
of unemployment, low wages (for those able to find work),
and a lack of opportunity for advancement. This concentration on 'push' factors is echoed in Davison's work
(1962). Although unconvinced by these two pieces of work,
on the grounds that a number of the factors discussed appeared to him to be 'permissive' rather than 'dynamic'
(i.e. casual) in nature, Peach is impressed by Davison's
'extremely perceptive method' of relating per capita
wealth and the level of emigration. The argument led to
the finding that 'there was an inverse relationship between the wealth of the West Indian territories, measured
in terms of Gross Domestic Product per capita, and the
degree of emigration.' In addition to noting, however,
that this conclusion is confused by an analysis of alternative statistics to those used by Davison, Peach correct-

TABLE 1.2 Date of arrival in Britain by birthplace (weighted figures are bracketed) [3]

	West Indies				Asia			
	Jamaica %	Barbados[4] %	Other[1] %	Total %	India %	Pakistan %	Other[2] %	Total %
Before 1955	12 (14)	13 (15)	10 (9)	12 (14)	12	12	-	11
1955-9	34 (36)	53 (53)	35 (34)	35 (37)	15	29	15	17
1960-4	45 (42)	20 (16)	47 (47)	44 (41)	41	45	55	43
1965-9	6 (5)	-	4 (6)	6 (5)	26	14	5	23
1970 or later	1 (1)	-	-	1 (1)	5	-	25	6
No answer	2 (1)	13 (15)	4 (4)	2 (2)	1	-	-	1
Sample size (= 100%)	331(275)	15 (13)	49 (32)	395(320)	243	42	20	305

1 This category includes those born on other islands such as Trinidad and Tobago and those who simply said they were born in the West Indies.

2 This includes those born in East Africa as well as those from other countries in the Indian subcontinent such as Bangladesh and Sri Lanka. Care should be taken when interpreting these figures because of the small overall sample size.

3 For a technical discussion of the reasoning behind the presentation of two sets of figures, the reader is referred to Appendix 1. The major point to note from this table is that the numerical difference here reflects a phenomenon discussed in Chapter 4: that council tenants among minority groups tend to be found among the more established residents. (The unweighted figures include a disproportionately large number of council tenants.)

4 Care should be taken when interpreting these figures because of the very small sample size. The category is treated separately from the 'Other' group essentially to emphasise the over-whelming predominance of Jamaicans in the sample.

ly recognised a familiar, yet none the less important,
methodological trap. In performing correlational analyses
on sets of figures in a crucial sense abstracted from the
sphere of decision-making of individual actors in a social
scene, any imputation of explanatory significance on the
part of the variables concerned cannot have the status of
a proof of causality. Such a proof implies, in Peach's
terms, a 'dynamic' relationship. He goes on to argue that
it is clearly the case that acute poverty in itself does
not produce a high level of emigration. [6] Lawrence, on
the other hand, argues that Peach, in stressing the 'pull'
factor of the British economy, underestimates the 'push'
factors.

British politicians in the course of debating immigration control in the early 1960s, employed similar analytical tools. On 16 November 1961 R.A.B.Butler (later
Lord Butler), during a speech in support of the 1962 Immigration Act, discussed the 'striking' drop in immigration
from 30,000 in 1958 to only 21,000 in 1959. He attributed
this to what might be termed a 'lack of pull' factor
(slight economic recession in the UK) plus a 'lack of
push' factor brought about by the efforts of other governments to restrain their potential emigrants. He argued
that the effectiveness of such a control by the governments of India and Pakistan had had a constraining effect
on emigration, and later bemoaned the lack of a similar
force in the West Indies. In opposing the bill, and particularly attacking its more alarmist predictions of 'mass
immigration', 'dole scroungers' and consequent 'social
unrest', Hugh Gaitskell argued that immigration was controlled by the level of unemployment in the UK. In his
words, [7]

There has been, over the years, if the Honourable
Gentleman cares to consult the figures, an almost
precise correlation between the movement in the numbers
of unfilled vacancies, that is to say, employers
wanting labour, and the immigration figures.

As suggested earlier, it is difficult without appropriate empirical data to assess the validity of arguments
which for one thing ignore the stated views of migrants
and for another omit factors on which official statistical
data are lacking. For the former reason in particular, we
collected a great deal of interview material on the
reasons why people decided to leave their country of
origin and come to Britain. Admittedly, there are still
problems in interpreting the reconstruction of events
which in some cases may have become blurred by the passage
of time. Furthermore, remembering Adorno, these statements of 'fact' do not necessarily conform to objective

reality. They do, on the other hand, permit us a unique
view of the way in which the migrant's social world appeared to him (albeit on reflection).

We begin our empirical analysis of reasons for migration [8] by looking at our sample of Handsworth West
Indians. As Table 1.3 shows, it is possible to divide the
reasons into those which were clearly self-motivating
(e.g., the desire to travel, to better oneself, to gain
better qualifications and to look for work) and those
which seem to have been motivated by others (e.g., brought
over by their family, or sent for by their family who were
already here). The first group was probably influenced
largely by the sort of factors which Peach, Davison and
others might term macro 'push' and 'pull' factors. From
an analysis of the detailed reasons given by immigrants it
is clear that we cannot talk in terms of a single major
motivating force. West Indians were clearly reacting to a
combination of forces not all of which can be described as
being 'external' to the individual. Certainly during the
post-war period the level of economic activity in the West
Indies could not withstand the rapid population growth.
This produced an extremely high level of unemployment and
a pitifully low standard of living. On the other hand, as
was noted above, unemployment coupled with the inevitable
poverty does not in itself generate a high level of emigration.

A desperate need for labour in Britain during this
period meant that, despite the qualms of certain politicians about the desirability of attracting large numbers
of black immigrants, colonial links with the West Indies
were exploited in order to satisfy the needs of the
economy. The campaigns aimed at recruiting London Transport workers and nurses are already well documented elsewhere; e.g., by Brooks (1975), Peach (1968), Lawrence
(1974). Once again, however, the existence of effective
channels through which to sell the notion of a return to
the 'Mother Country' does not in itself explain the large
movement of labour to Britain. Indeed, as Lawrence points
out, many of his sample of West Indians in Nottingham
would have preferred to emigrate to America or Old Commonwealth countries, such as Australia, had the immigration
policies of these potential hosts permitted.

It is likely, then, that a large proportion of West
Indians in Britain today came as a result of a decision
based on a complex dynamic of 'push' and 'pull' factors.
Nor must one underestimate the importance of familial and
peer group interaction in the immigration process: 37(32)
of the West Indians in our sample said that they came to
the UK because of accounts of life in this country which

TABLE 1.3 Reasons given by West Indians [1] for coming to Britain by date of arrival (weighted figures are bracketed)

	Before 1955 %	1955-9 %	1960-4 %	1965 or later %	Total %
Economic conditions – came to look for work	33 (30)	28 (28)	25 (25)	12 (14)	27 (26)
Wanted better standard of living	4 (5)	11 (13)	5 (6)	4 (6)	7 (8)
Wanted to travel	38 (41)	28 (27)	30 (30)	12 (9)	28 (28)
Came for educational reasons	–	2 (3)	3 (3)	–	2 (2)
Came because of relatives'/friends' accounts of life in Britain	10 (11)	11 (11)	9 (9)	4 (6)	9 (10)
Family came/was brought with them	–	3 (1)	5 (4)	8 (6)	4 (2)
Family already here/was sent for	8 (7)	10 (11)	16 (16)	56 (56)	15 (15)
Other reasons	6 (7)	7 (7)	7 (8)	4 (3)	8 (8)
Sample size (= 100%)	48 (44)	139 (118)	174 (133)	25 (18)	395 (320)

1 9(7) respondents are missing from the body of the table, as they failed to answer one or both of these questions.

had been given to them by friends or members of their
family. It is extremely likely that many others were at
least influenced by similar factors.

In an earlier study by Ratcliffe (1971) one of the
major points to emerge was that the close-knit structure
of community life in the West Indies provided a firm base
for the reinforcement of newly emergent values among young
people. A mysterious kind of folklore appeared to have
been generated which not only painted an extremely ideal-
istic picture of life in Britain, but also ultimately
ascribed to emigration the role of a normative process.
The migratory tradition of West Indians, as noted by
Lawrence, may partly account for the currency of such
feelings. Undoubtedly, however, the success of the media
in transmitting government propaganda should also be regarded as having played an important role.

Among those we interviewed in Handsworth, most appeared
to have been motivated by the desire to travel, to obtain
more acceptable work, and thereby to better themselves.
These factors raised some of the issues discussed above:
namely, their migratory tradition, the lack of suitable
employment in the West Indies (especially in Jamaica), and
the belief that a better standard of living awaited them
in the UK. Table 1.3 adds an interesting further dimension to this discussion, however.

Although there was a heavy emphasis on these issues
among the early arrivals to the UK, there is a clear tendency for those who followed the major influx of immigrants during the 1950s to come here as a result of being
sent for (or at least encouraged to come) by relatives
already living here. This is perhaps as might have been
expected, given the nature of the immigration policy
heralded by the 1962 Immigration Act. Many families
feared a complete halt on immigration, resulting in relatives or dependants being 'stranded' in the West Indies.
[9]

The 'three category voucher' system introduced in 1962,
in defining clearly a status ranking of intending migrants, paved the way for stricter, more rigid controls.
It was not unexpected when in 1964 Category C vouchers
(for those without a definite job offer, and not possessing skills which were in 'short supply') were disconti-
nued. This was a severe blow to intending migrants from
the Caribbean, as the majority of would-be immigrants fell
into this group. There was a further turn of the screw in
the following year, when in July the Labour Government
placed a ceiling of 8,500 on the total number of vouchers
(Types A and B) to be issued. Furthermore, out of this
number 1,000 were reserved for Maltese.

TABLE 1.4 Reasons given by Asian respondents for emigrating to Britain by date of arrival [1]

	Before 1955 %	1955-9 %	1960-4 %	1965 or later	Total %
Came for economic reasons	55	49	37	19	36
Wanted to achieve a better standard of living	15	20	8	7	10
Wanted to travel/gain new life experiences	6	4	8	10	8
Came for educational reasons	3	4	4	5	4
Came because of relatives'/friends' description of Britain	–	2	5	6	4
Family came/was brought with them	6	10	7	5	7
Family already here/was sent for	–	6	20	32	19
Expelled from East Africa	–	–	2	16	5
Other	15	6	9	2	8
Sample size (= 100%)	33	51	130	88	305

1 The body of the table excludes 3 respondents who did not give us details of the year in which they entered Britain.

Turning to the Asians, it is often argued that this
group shares the migratory tradition of the West Indians.
In support of this, Lawrence, for example, points out that
the majority of the Asians in his sample were Punjabi
Sikhs and notes Nair's observations that: [10]
> The Punjab has borne the brunt and first impact of
> almost all the major invasions by foreign powers from
> time immemorial, this having been the traditional route
> into the sub-continent. The result has been that the
> people of the Punjab have developed an unusual capacity
> for adjustment to change which makes them one of the
> least 'rooted' communities in India, mentally, cul-
> turally and physically.

In addition, one of the results of partition in 1947 was
to create a vast army of refugees in the Punjab. The
Sikhs who migrated to the eastern Punjab had not only lost
their homes but effectively their work as well, since
they, in the main, took over land of poorer quality than
that which they had left. Given that Sikhs have no system
of primogeniture, it is not surprising to find that there
is today an acute land shortage in the region.

In our survey of Handsworth it was always unlikely that
the uniformity of origin displayed in Lawrence's sample
would be repeated. On the other hand, as will be seen
later, at least 41 per cent of the Asians interviewed were
Sikhs. Furthermore, since the majority of Sikhs live in
the eastern Punjab, it seems likely that some at least
will have been influenced by the sorts of factor mentioned
above.

As can be seen from the responses in Table 1.4, unlike
the West Indians, few Asians felt that the major impetus
for coming to Britain was a desire to travel and to start
a new life here. The major reasons were economic, and
particularly so among those who came here (reluctantly)
soon after partition. There is evidence to suggest that
many men came here initially to earn enough money to support dependants at home. The joint family system, for
example, of the Sikhs would undoubtedly act, in Peach's
terms, as a 'permissive' factor in facilitating this.

It is clear that, as with the West Indians, a fear of
the family's being forcibly separated by immigration
controls resulted in large numbers of dependants entering
Britain in the early 1960s. The balance of those coming
for reasons which might be labelled as 'self-motivating'
and those who were responding to the decisions of others
had tilted very much in favour of the latter by the mid-
1960s. In addition, by the late 1960s and early 1970s
the numbers of those of Asian origin in Britain were
swelled by the influx of refugees from East Africa,

largely products of the Kenyanisation policy and the black
racist ideology of Uganda's Idi Amin.

Apart from those Asians who felt strong ties with the
UK (for example, through direct familial connections with
the British Indian Army), it is highly likely that many
(perhaps most) of those now here would have chosen to migrate elsewhere. Many of the traditional avenues were effectively closed, notably East Africa, America and
Australia. As a result, and encouraged by commercial
entrepreneurs such as travel agents, those who, for
example, wished to escape poverty and/or the political,
social and religious tensions created by partition, found
Britain the 'obvious' choice. Lawrence argues that this
hypothesis is clearly supported by his data. There is
evidence also to suggest that many men came to Britain
without their dependants in the hope that they could amass
sufficient savings to enable them to return home with the
knowledge that they and their family would be financially
secure. Many, however, found that to achieve this state
would take considerably longer than they had anticipated.
Fearing long-term separation, many brought their dependants to the UK, and this process was hastened by the
shift in immigration policy. The problem was that those
who anticipated a relatively short stay in the UK and
hence only a temporary separation from their family, found
themselves in a Catch-22 situation. Having brought the
family here, the process of capital accumulation will in
many cases have dried up completely, and the chances of
returning home will have become very slight indeed, especially since it is extremely likely that most of the
families' possessions, including their land, will have
been sold in order to finance the trip.

REFLECTIONS ON LIFE IN BRITAIN

The above considerations are of crucial importance when
one comes to analyse the immigrant's perceptions of the
social world in which he finds himself. He will bring
with him a complex mosaic of life experiences and expectations which will inevitably influence the way he relates
to his new social scene. It matters to him, for example,
how his position within the class structure of the adopted
country compares with his previous state. In interpreting
his views, then, the sociologist needs to maintain a clear
distinction between subjectively perceived entities and
objectively defined structural attributes. At a simplistic level, we may find two Asians within our study
who are defined identically with respect to the work which

they are doing in Britain. The actor's perception of this
would perhaps differ radically, however, if, for example,
the first man had previously worked as a subsistence
farmer in the eastern Punjab, whereas the other had been
a successful businessman prior to expulsion from Uganda.

An 'explanation' of the differences in perspective in
these terms would still be at the level of 'social facts'
external to the individual, but when linked to other elements of the individual's perception of himself and his
social world would produce at least a partial picture of
his experiences. An important element of this perspective
is the 'sojourner' or 'gastarbeiter' mentality which is
concerned with the level of commitment to the adopted
society. [11] Following up this line of argument, we may
then wish to give the analysis a broader structural perspective. For example, we may ask what role the immigrant
fulfils in his adopted society. To what extent (if at
all) is his relatively weak position exploited for
economic or political purposes? What are the inner
dynamics of social fluidity and change? Throughout this
book we shall aim to develop these themes.

At present we shall concentrate on the broad structure
of immigration and examine the expectancies of and
feelings about life in Britain from the newcomers' point
of view. As in many studies, the age of those interviewed
is clearly of major importance. It is even more so in
this case, due to the influence, once again, of immigration control in the early 1960s. Before this, the majority of those coming to Britain, and now interviewed as
heads of household, had been young men in their 20s and
early 30s. Those arriving more recently tended to come
as teenagers or even younger. (Approximately 50 per cent
of all immigrants who arrived from the mid-1960s onwards
were less than 15 years of age.) The important point to
note from this is that these were the people who came to
Britain more often than not as a result of being brought
over, or more significantly, sent for. The remainder of
the Asian migrants in this period were largely those who
had suffered expulsion from East Africa.

As we saw above, the source of motivation appeared to
vary over time in a similarly radical fashion for the West
Indians we interviewed. Major differences in perspective,
then, may be expected among members of our sample. Reinforcing this is the changing nature of the British racial
climate over the last twenty years. As will be seen
later, large numbers of our sample felt that the black
immigrant was progressively becoming more of an 'outsider'. Immigration restrictions which signalled the
abandonment of the notion of free entry, combined with

TABLE 1.5 Major reason given by those West Indians who said that life in Britain is 'better' than they had expected, by year of arrival (weighted figures are bracketed)

	Economic reasons	Better standard of living	People friendly/ tolerant	Everything	Other	Sample size (= 100%)
Before 1960 %	72(68)	18(21)	-	3 (3)	8(9)	39(34)
1960 or later %	55(58)	24(21)	7(4)	10(13)	3(4)	29(24)
TOTAL	65(62)	21(21)	3(2)	6 (7)	6(7)	68(58)

TABLE 1.6 Major reason given by those West Indians who said that life in Britain is 'worse' than they had expected, by year of arrival (weighted figures are bracketed)

	Discrimi- nation/ prejudice	High cost of living Standard of living worse	Housing	Employ- ment	Life gener- ally harder	Environ- ment/ climate	Other reason or expression of general disil- lusionment	Sample size (= 100%)
Before 1960 %	18(16)	12(11)	13(11)	19(20)	9(10)	6(7)	22(25)	67 (61)
1960 or later %	14(14)	19(14)	10(12)	34(36)	7 (7)	4(5)	11(12)	97 (76)
TOTAL	16(15)	16(13)	12(12)	28(28)	8 (8)	5(6)	16(18)	164(137)

the overtly racist ideology of major politicians such as
Enoch Powell, undoubtedly contributed towards these
feelings.

Although expectancies of life in Britain can differ
radically both in nature and in intensity, it became clear
that few West Indians had been pleasantly surprised by
their experiences here. Indeed, well over 40 per cent
said that they had found things 'worse' than they had expected. The obvious question to ask at this point, then,
is 'what is it about life in Britain which West Indians
particularly liked?'

As Table 1.5 shows, only 17(18) per cent of the West
Indians we talked to felt that life in Britain was better
than they had expected. Out of this group the majority,
65(62) per cent argued that wages were better here or that
there was more regular employment than there had been back
home. This view was much more prevalent among those who
had come to Britain before the 1960s and had come specifically for economic reasons. Disillusionment with the
life which they found here was particularly high amongst
those who arrived during the 1960s. The few from this
group, 29(24) who had been pleasantly surprised by their
experiences here talked slightly less about the economic
advantages and rather more about the standard of living
compared with that in the West Indies. (They especially
mentioned such things as housing, education, the National
Health Service and transport.) Significantly perhaps,
only 2 people gave as their reason the friendliness and
tolerance which they had found here, a factor which sharply distinguishes their immigration from that, say, of
Europeans to the USA, or Jews to Israel. In the latter
case, of course, migrants had been welcomed both by
government and people as equal citizens working towards a
collective ideal, the Israeli State. In Britain immigrants are viewed in a more instrumental manner: a necessary evil in the cause of economic survival.

As we have already seen, a substantial minority of West
Indians had become disillusioned with their life in
Britain. Table 1.6 demonstrates the major dimensions of
these feelings, although it should perhaps be stressed
that these elements are by no means independent of one
another. For example, although the number of West Indians
complaining specifically about the level of racial discrimination and prejudice is fairly small at 16(15) per cent,
discriminatory practices (as will be demonstrated in subsequent chapters) are often at the root of the immigrant's
problems in relation to many features of his social world.
It is likely that those who demonstrated a general disillusionment with life and those who had found difficulty in

obtaining what they regarded as decent housing or work
would frequently fall into this category.

Large numbers of West Indians complained of difficulties in finding jobs, or at least those jobs which were
regarded as acceptable. Interestingly, although generally
seen as an important problem this seems to have been
viewed as a particularly serious one for those arriving
during the 1960s. Over one in three of the group in
Table 1.6 stressed this particular issue. Writers such as
Lawrence (1974) and Wright (1968) have discussed the ex-
ploitive relationship between many employers and their
black employees. They have also outlined the structural
forces which have resulted in discriminatory practices and
the frequent relegation of blacks to the level of replace-
ment labour; i.e., taking jobs which the indigenous population did not want (points which will be taken up in more
detail in Chapter 5).

Many West Indians in our sample were also seen as profoundly unhappy with their experiences in the housing
market, and others argued that their standard of living
was worse than that which they 'enjoyed' back home. In
addition, a significant number felt that life here is
'much harder' than they had expected, and a number of
those not specifically using these words could be identified with them. In reporting similar findings, Lawrence
argues that: [12]

This probably reflects the degree to which they had
come to believe that the lives of Europeans with whom
they had been in contact at home, or seen in films,
were typical of the whole population of countries like
Britain.

Using the now rather unfashionable concept of 'relative
deprivation' it could be argued that many West Indians,
rather than reacting to perceived deprivation with reference to their own prior state, are employing reference
points which had been generated by the homeland media and
socially reinforced in the manner discussed earlier.

If we take into account the fact that well over a half
of the 'disillusioned' West Indians gave more than one
reason for their adverse feelings about life in Britain,
almost one in four complained of racial discrimination.
Similar numbers raised issues related to housing and the
standard or cost of living, whilst over a third were dis-
appointed with job opportunities. In reporting the
findings of his research in Nottingham, Lawrence concludes
that no less than 88 per cent of his West Indians were
'surprised' by the level of prejudice and discrimination
which they had experienced in Britain. Had we asked a
more direct question specifically about discrimination,

we may well have achieved a similar result. The precise
quantitative difference is not, of course, of fundamental
significance. One conclusion is, in any case, inescapable. Many West Indians emigrating to the UK have experienced (and perceived) the disturbing effects of being defined by the host community as an unwelcome visitor, or at
most, a 'second-class' citizen. Lawrence includes a great
deal of illuminating qualitative material from his open-
ended question about expectations on arrival in the UK.
Unfortunately, he fails to analyse their significance.
For example, he reports the case of the respondent who had
to cope with the first realisation that he was 'coloured':
'As a matter of fact I did not know I was a coloured man
until the English told me so. Somebody referred to me as
a coloured person on the bus once and that was the first
time I knew who I was.' [13] This is a particularly perceptive remark, especially when one looks at the last
phrase more carefully. It encapsulates a total re-
interpretation of the individual's identity and reveals
vividly the total surprise at being regarded as an outsider, despite the obvious physical distinctiveness of
which he was aware. The individual was being unwillingly
socialised into his new role. Similarly with another respondent: 'But when I came here I quickly sensed, you
know, that there was something wrong with me.' [13] Here
the respondent (an Indian) finds himself diagnosed as
having something wrong with him; he has been ascribed the
role of 'deviant'.
    The task for the sociologist is not only to analyse the
structure of perceptions, i.e., how the actor learns and
expresses his/her self-image [14] but also to discover who
or what teaches the teachers and how (and why)? These external structural dynamics are crucial to an understanding
of multi-racial and multi-ethnic communities, and arguments throughout subsequent chapters of this book will
attempt to illuminate this particular theme.
    In expressing disillusionment with life in Britain many
of our respondents drew upon aspects of their former life
in the West Indies and reflected on their reasons for
coming to this country. For example, there was a 44-year-
old Jamaican who came to Britain in the early 1960s. His
wife and two children arrived here in 1968. Since then
two further children have been born (in Birmingham). He
originally came because he 'wanted to travel. We always
held Britain as the Mother Country. I wanted to see what
it was like. I must have been mad to come. I had a nice
house and good job (as a postman).' His bitterness, very
much in evidence by this time, was due to the fact that
    'I live in worse conditions, worse house, unhappy

atmosphere. (There are) strong feelings about
coloureds here. You are made to feel inferior. You
can't go out for a social evening; they's down on you
all the time ... no future for our kids. We are just
not liked, not wanted, every day (there are) different
issues in papers. People treat you all the same,
people are individuals - good and bad in every race.
White people are really against you, we are unhappy.'
Clearly the magnetism of the image presented of the Mother
Country and the desire for travel and to gain new life experiences were strong. Clearly for him Britain was not
the place he was led to believe it was: a place of plentiful employment and housing. Having arrived, he was
stranded through lack of funds. This disillusionment was
shared by many. One of our respondents (a 41-year-old
Jamaican woman) told us, 'A wonderful place, England was
supposed to be. When I got here, nobody wants you, no
person likes you. You have a hard time all round.
English people do not accept you.' She felt she had been
led to believe that England was a friendly, hospitable
place for newcomers - not simple a haven for the un- (or
under-) employed and those looking for good housing and a
better standard of living. On the other hand, having accepted the idealised picture of Britain, she at least had
wanted to come. Many, such as the following respondent,
had not wanted to come at all; his parents had 'sent for
him'.

'I was led to believe that blacks were not treated differently, that you could go anywhere, same as whites,
without being thought of as unacceptable. (We were)
told that streets were paved with gold - good opportunities, etc.
Because you're black you're leading a limited life.
Your colour holds you back. Can't get on in jobs as
whites do. All blacks are treated the same. People
say they're no good - all the same. I can't go socially into places with some workmates - not allowed in
certain places because I'm black - abuse and mistrust
you instead of being treated as an equal person.'
This 26-year-old Jamaican came to Britain in 1967 and is
now married to an English girl. Once again, we see the
degree of stress placed on the forms of, and the reaction
to, constraints imposed on the individual by virtue of the
'labelling' effect. There are also important comments
displaying a pessimistic view of life chances, specifically in relation to work. Perhaps the most significant
remark, however, is the one which concerns restrictions on
the nature and extent of social relationships.
This raises one of the major questions to be answered

by any study of race relations; namely, the place which
the newcomer occupies within the class structure of the
adopted society. Along with a large number of his fellow
immigrants, this Jamaican was essentially arguing that his
natural desire to participate in the social life of those
with whom he might be expected to share class interests
was severely obstructed. On the shop floor he was tolera-
ted; in the social world outside he was seen as the
'unacceptable face' of the English working class. In the
classical Marxian sense, he stands in the same position as
his white colleagues vis-à-vis the means of production.
This might lead one to argue, along the lines of the
'false consciousness' thesis, that the rather limited
membership of the working class [15] which many immigrants
have acquired militates against class solidarity and
therefore ultimately in favour of bourgeois interests.
[16]

Together with similar but more general feelings of
frustration in the realm of social life, some have come to
reject the urban industrial environment in which they now
find themselves. Among this group was another young
Jamaican who came to Britain (allegedly against his
wishes) because his parents had sent for him: 'I would be
better in my own country. I just think I would. Life
would be less complicated. You do nothing but work here.
There is no entertainment for us - nowhere that is suitable.'

In contrast to the West Indians, Asians in Handsworth
appear to be much less inclined to criticise life in
Britain. Lawrence argues that this general finding is to
be expected, given the formers' high level of identity
with Britain which 'produces high expectations and, at
least initially, a greater exposure to the kind of circumstances in which prejudice and discrimination may be encountered.' [17]

There is indeed a tendency, on the part of Asians, to
some extent because of a desire to preserve their culture,
religion and language, to be socially inward-looking. In
reducing their contact with the indigenous population they
will automatically diminish the probability of experiencing rejection. In so doing, of course, they may well
in turn increase the hostility of the host society, who
may interpret the essentially defensive formation of concentrated groups of immigrants as preparation for a future
offensive. This difference in segregational patterns of
the immigrant community of Birmingham is confirmed by
Woods (1975) who argues that while 'West Indian-born
groups are becoming less isolated from (the) majority
society ... this cannot be said for the Asian groups,

who have taken the place of the West Indians as the most
"segregated" of immigrant populations.' *[18]*

In the Handsworth sample over twice as many Asians as
West Indians, 37 per cent as against 17(18) per cent,
thought that life in Britain was 'better' than they had
expected. This could, as Lawrence suggests, be because
their expectations were considerably lower than those of
their new Caribbean neighbours. On the other hand, there
may be more subtle and technical methodological reasons
for this phenomenon (see Appendix 1). Whatever the underlying reasoning, it is clear that the more recent arrivals
to this country are, on the whole, rather more critical
than those who were among the 'first' influx of Asian immigrants in the 1960s.

A number of factors may account for this finding. More
recent immigrants were arriving here at a time which was
typified by a hardening of political attitudes against
them. Inflammatory speeches by certain politicians and a
scurrilous campaign by some sections of the media, aimed
principally at the wretched refugees from East Africa,
could hardly be expected to contribute to racial harmony.
In addition, as we have seen, many of the immigrants at
this time were young people brought or sent for by their
families. Many of these left to their own devices would
not have come here (as is suggested by their remarks).
For others, especially the refugees, Britain must have represented a great hope for the future - a new start in
life. In these circumstances disillusionment must have
struck a bitter blow.

For most of those who were pleasantly surprised by life
in Britain the major reason was an economic one. Approaching 40 per cent of the Asians in this group talked
in terms of the supply of jobs, good wages, and so on. To
those who had been accustomed to patchy, irregular
earnings, the existence of 'regular' employment was undoubtedly the major plus factor. Others (28 per cent)
spoke favourably of the standard of living or were generally uncritical about life here (16 per cent). One interesting factor which emerges here is that, as with the West
Indians, only a handful of people (6) specifically mentioned the friendliness of the white community in their
answer.

Unlike the West Indians, however, recent arrivals to
this country placed more emphasis on (what they saw as)
the favourable employment situation, and decreasing
numbers talked about having a higher standard of living
than they had expected. Furthermore, fewer of those who
had arrived since 1960 were totally uncritical or said
that 'everything' was better.

In general, many Asians seemed satisfied with life,
having at least achieved a steady job. This is understandable among certain groups of the more recent arrivals, notably the East African refugees. One such case
was a 48-year-old Indian, who, up until the time he left
Kenya, had a thriving textile business. Despite the fact
that his current job was as an unskilled labourer, he expressed satisfaction with the situation, on the grounds
that he had experienced 'no difficulty in seeking and
getting employment'. Significantly, and in sharp contrast
to the majority of Jamaicans, many Asians appeared to
employ a reference point which was directly related to
their prior life experiences. This may account for many
responses of the following form: 'The employment and education is very good. Nobody without houses or food' (25-
year-old Indian, married with two children). It would be
tempting, if rather naive, to conclude from the findings
so far reported that Asian immigrants on the whole were
extremely satisfied with their lot. One might go even
further and suggest that this was because they had surpassed their expectations in terms of the jobs and houses
they have acquired.

Indeed very few Asians (9 per cent) actually claimed
that life in Britain was worse than they had expected: a
group who were almost evenly divided between those who
argued that they were made to feel unwelcome, those who
had found difficulty in obtaining suitable employment, and
those who complained generally about the standard of
living. Some had become disillusioned when impressions of
Britain, circulated in India, had not been matched by
their subsequent experiences.

'The houses are not as good as I thought' represented
the disillusionment of a 35-year-old Indian who came here
in 1962 because 'There was no work (in India) even after
education.' His wife and children followed him here in
1968.

One 43-year-old Indian who had come here in 1961, 'to
get a good education and return home', was bitter because
'We heard by the news media about this country and when I
saw the muck in the road ... and houses was not the same
as it was shown in the news media.' 'Muck' clearly had no
place on streets that were reputedly 'paved with gold'.

There was some evidence to suggest that young Asians
tended to be especially sensitive to racial issues. Such
a conclusion should, however, remain tentative since, by
its very nature [19] our sample tends to be skewed in
favour of the older age-groups. It is perhaps significant, though, that all five of the Asians who complained
of racial conflict were young men who had come here during

the last ten years. These were men who had known no other
adult life than that which they had experienced in
Britain. They were clearly acutely aware of the racial
climate in which their children would be growing up. [20]
Among them was a 22-year-old (newly married) Indian whose
father had come to Britain alone and had subsequently sent
for him. Life in Britain had made him profoundly unhappy
because of 'problems with immigrants, fighting and
troubles with the National Front ... Enoch Powell stirring
up trouble'.

By way of conclusion, however, it should perhaps be
stressed that, among both ethnic groups, those who out-
wardly express disillusionment with life here are very
much in a minority. Furthermore, taking as an (admittedly
problematic) indicator of general contentment with life,
answers to our direct question, nearly 90 per cent of
Asians as compared with two-thirds of West Indians said
that they were satisfied with life in Britain.

This, of course, immediately provokes a rather interesting question. Why is it that Asians appear to be relatively much more contented? Is it that they are in some
tangible sense achieving a greater degree of 'success' in
terms of gaining their rights as de jure equal citizens
with members of the white majority? The evidence presented in later chapters will demonstrate that this is
true to only a very limited extent, if at all. We must
look therefore to alternative explanations.

One arises from a rather technical methodological
issue, the major discussion of which is deferred to Appendix 1. It is essentially a question both of the
greater 'cultural distance' between the Asian respondents
and (most of) their interviewers and of the relatively
greater degree of cultural insularity of the Asian communities; insularity which may appear to the researcher
as little more than defensiveness and/or an uneasy sense
of suspicion.

This insularity and its physical analogue, the high
level of geographical clustering, lead us indirectly to
the second major thesis. As we shall see later in the
book, clustering is to some extent a function of market
forces and a variety of structural constraints. [21] On
the other hand, it does also have the important 'positive'
effect of assisting the preservation of a distinctive
cultural, religious and social life. It became clear from
our research that many Asians regard this as an important
factor. Thus insularity and residential segregation may
have a positive as well as a negative dimension. A number
of the central aspects of English culture (notably sexual
and drinking activities) are seen as morally repugnant by

many Asians. [22]   Thus the maintenance of a tight-knit
community may be seen as a means of protecting their young
from the moral depravity of the outside world (predominantly white, but importantly in this respect, including
other black groups, notably the West Indians).   It is this
internalised cultural remoteness combined with the manifest external distinctiveness of the Asians which led us
to believe that 'life in Britain' was often conceptualised
as 'life within an Asian community in Britain'.   Hence the
setting up of alternative internal reference points (i.e.,
within the ethnic group) tended to have the effect of constraining forces which might otherwise have led to outward
expressions of cultural radicalism among first-generation
immigrants. [23]

If we add to this argument the possibility of an external, homeland-based reference point producing an 'exaggerated' measure of satisfaction among some Asians, our
results may be seen in a rather different light.   In any
case, as we have seen, there was a small vocal minority -
mainly young people - who were distinctly disillusioned.
In addition there was a large group of Asians (55 per
cent) who gave a wide-ranging series of non-committal (but
not uninteresting) answers when questioned about their expectancies of life here.   Many exhibited a resigned acceptance of what they found: 'I knew what to expect.'
Others had clearly modified their views: 'Things were OK
at first, but are not so good now.'   There were also those
who had emigrated so long ago that they had forgotten what
their previous life was like (and what they had felt about
the move).   Yet others, sometimes with mixed feelings, now
implicitly identified themselves as English;   for example,
those who simply said 'England is my home'.   A further
point stems from the difference in age structures (see
Chapter 2) of the two immigrant samples.   The Asian group
contained proportionally many more young people, in the
main brought here or sent for when they were still small
children.   These clearly had had few expectations about
life in Britain, and said so.

Partly because of this problem, but more generally to
enable us to look more closely at the sorts of thing which
immigrants liked about life in Britain, we asked a series
of direct questions.   As expected, these findings do not
simply duplicate the above analysis.   They are also sufficiently interesting to merit a separate discussion at
this stage.

Table 1.8 records the aspects of British life which immigrants valued most.   It would have been surprising, of
course, given the above discussion, if there had not been
a significant emphasis on economic factors.   Many had come

TABLE 1.7 Major reason given by Asians for saying that life in Britain is 'better' than they had expected, by year of entry

Year of entry	Economic reasons	Standard of living	People are friendly/ tolerant	Everything	Other	Sample size (= 100%)
Before 1960 %	26	41	3	24	6	34
1960-4 %	45	24	4	12	14	49
1965 or later %	47	20	7	13	13	30
Total %	40	28	4	16	12	113

TABLE 1.8 Aspects of British life valued most by ethnic group (weighted figures are bracketed)

	Economic climate	Standard of living	NHS/ Welfare pro- visions	Other services, e.g., education	Indivi- dual freedom	Other	Nothing	Don't know	Sample size (= 100%)
West Indian %	29(29)	10(9)	8(9)	7(8)	9(11)	10(10)	20(18)	6(7)	395(320)
Asian	2	20	9	11	10	7	9	10	305

to England to escape a situation in which they had found
extreme difficulties through unemployment, or at least
underemployment, in supporting their families. Thus, the
acquisition of regular employment, and what to many seemed
good wages, led 29 per cent of the West Indians and 22 per
cent of the Asians to answer in this way. Under the above
hypothesis (namely, that the two groups, on the whole, employed radically differing points of reference) it is perhaps not surprising that more than twice as many Asians as
West Indians (proportionately) talked favourably about
living standards in Britain. Health, welfare and educational facilities also figured as important plus points.
Among the remaining respondents it is interesting to note
that some, particularly Asians, appeared to see in the
educational system possibilities of upward social mobility
for their children. The significance of this is that it
clearly carries implications for the nature of the relationship which the immigrant has with the adopted society.
It expresses, implicitly at least, that he may hope to use
such institutions to gain a firmer foothold in the existing class structure. [24]
    Of course, veneration of the British educational system
is a cornerstone of traditional colonialist ideology;
likewise our legal system. It is perhaps not surprising
therefore that a significant number of respondents from
both groups expressed favourable attitudes towards the
level of 'individual freedom' or 'freedom' accorded to
British citizens. Naturally, belief in the existence of
an ideal may transcend individual contrary experiences.
In this case, incidents of persecution and overt discrimination, for example, may not dislodge a belief in the
'ultimate sense of fair play' often seen as a function of
the 'British character'. Furthermore, those who had experienced the harshest effects of partition or expulsion
from East Africa can perhaps be 'forgiven' for reflecting
this view. In addition, of course, there was often rather
more to the notion of freedom. To some Asians, for example, life in Britain meant a lifting (if only partial)
of the normative constraints imposed by their homeland
culture. This was particularly true of those who had
subsequently adopted an overtly 'Westernised' outlook
on life.

MIGRANTS OR SETTLERS?

Central to any study of the sociology of migration, in
particular, and of race relations in general, is the
nature and level of positive commitment which the migrant

subsequently feels towards his adopted society. Put another way, to what extent does the migrant see himself as
merely a sojourner (or temporary visitor) as distinct from
a settler? We must then analyse the answers to this in
the light of the nature of the social and physical environment from which the immigrant came, and of the treatment he has received at the hands of the adopted society.

Both of these involve a complex mosaic of interrelated
political and social structural issues. An obvious
starting point for empirical analysis might, however, be
the desire to return home or at least the level of interest shown in home news and politics. We are then in a
position to attempt to relate these levels of commitment
to the nature of the migrants' feelings and the structural
forces which generate and sustain these feelings.

As Table 1.9 shows, rather more West Indians than
Asians, 55(52) per cent as against 40 per cent, seemed to
retain an interest in the news and politics of their home
countries; a finding which, as we shall see shortly, is
mirrored even more clearly in the relative numbers of the
two groups wishing to return home. The apparent lack of
interest in their homeland on the part of first-generation
Indians and Pakistanis is particularly interesting, however, since it is directly contrary to the situation which
we would have expected on the basis of talks with representatives of important political organisations such as
the Indian Workers' Association (or at least the IWA-GB).
The impression gained here is one of a people greatly concerned with homeland political affairs; so much so, in
fact, that the lack of a similar concern for such issues
among children of Asian immigrants is usually seen as a
major 'problem'.

For both major ethnic groups, newspapers provided the
major source of up-to-date news from the homeland. Over
one in five West Indians, for example, claimed to read
newspapers aimed specifically at them (such as 'West
Indian World'). Rather fewer Asians read the various
Asian language newspapers. Given that English newspapers,
and particularly the popular press, tend to give scant
coverage of world events, those who relied on this source
of information were unlikely to have a major degree of
interest in homeland news. This applies also to those
(mainly Asians) who relied on British TV and radio.
Underlining the above point, we cannot escape the conclusion that the majority of Asians appeared to have cut
their ties with the homeland, at least at other than a
domestic, familial level.

The only other major source of news was the exchange of
letters with family and friends. For both Asians and West

TABLE 1.9 Means of contact with homeland by date of arrival and ethnic group (weighted figures are bracketed) [1]

	ASIANS					WEST INDIANS				
	Pre-1955 %	1955-9 %	1960-4 %	1965 or later %	Total [2] %	Pre-1955 %	1955-9 %	1960-4 %	1965 or later %	Total [2] %
Asian/West Indian news-papers	6	14	14	13	12	25(27)	21 (22)	20 (19)	24(26)	21 (21)
Newspapers (not specified)	12	16	15	11	14	19(20)	17 (18)	21 (20)	16(21)	19 (20)
TV/Radio	-	8	8	6	6	-	2 (3)	3 (3)	-	2 (2)
Letters	3	8	5	10	7	4 (5)	12 (9)	15 (13)	4 (*)	12 (9)
General con-versation	3	-	1	1	1	-	1 (*)	2 (1)	-	1 (*)
Not interest-ed in home news/refused	76	55	57	59	60	52(48)	47 (49)	40 (44)	56(53)	45 (48)
Sample size (=100%)	33	51	130	88	305	48(44)	139(118)	174(133)	25(18) [3]	395(320)

1 * represents a figure of less than 0.5%.
2 These totals include those respondents who failed to state their date of arrival.
3 The small sample size here should be noted.

Indians the likelihood of maintaining such contact depended to some extent on the length of time they had spent in Britain. Those who had lived here for more than twenty years only rarely mentioned letters as a major way of keeping in touch with home developments. Indeed, fewer than a quarter of the Asians in the group expressed any interest in such news. (It is perhaps not surprising that letters were seen as rather more important by those who came to Britain more recently, since the passage of time inevitably erodes some relationships. In addition some members of the migrant's family and kinsmen will either have joined him in Britain or have died in the homeland.)

Unfortunately, we did not have access to any of the letters received from or sent to the homeland by our respondents. These might have provided a fascinating insight into the relationship between the immigrant and his adopted society. They would, of course, have provided many intractable analytical problems, as discussed by Thomas and Znaniecki in their classic study of Polish émigrés in America and more recently by Lawrence in his Nottingham research. In particular, there is the problem of disentangling 'true' feelings from the desired self-image. As Lawrence points out: [25]

Despite the shock of disillusionment which figured so much in most of the interviews, very few respondents had recounted their experiences frankly to friends and relatives still in their country of origin ... the large majority of those who corresponded seemed to have avoided any reference to prejudice, discrimination or similar unpleasant aspects of life in Britain.

His respondents avoided the rather contentious issues for a variety of reasons. One was that, as many had elderly relatives at the receiving end, to have been totally frank about their experiences here would have been to run the risk of inducing a state of 'unnecessary' concern. Second, it was seen as putting the individual concerned in a bad light if he complained about his plight on the one hand and yet, by staying, implicitly submitted to the indignity. A third, and rather more devious reason, was that if the sender of the letter remained in Britain, then his stressing negative factors might be construed as an attempt to prevent the recipient from emigrating to join him.

Newspapers and television, of course, pose similar problems of interpretation for the sociologist and the intending emigrant alike. Policy decisions inevitably affect the presentation of the news, and, interestingly, in the light of the above discussion, the selection of letters to the editor.

TABLE 1.10 Percentages of immigrants who have visited
their homeland at least once since emigrating to Britain,
by year of entry (weighted figures are bracketed)

		West Indian	Asian	Sample size (= 100%)	
				West Indian	Asian
Before 1955	%	68(70)	79	47 (43)	33
1955-9	%	46(40)	84	138(117)	51
1960-4	%	43(48)	72	171(130)	130
1965 or later	%	24(22)	48	25 (18) [2]	88
TOTAL	%	46(47)	68	381(308) [1]	302 [1]

1 The table excludes those who failed to answer one or
   both of these questions.
2 It should be noted that the sample size here is very
   small.

In sharp contrast to the above findings on the degree
of 'interest' in home news, it is largely the Asians who
have actually made the long journey home. Slightly more
than two out of three have been back at least once since
first coming here, as compared with less than half of the
West Indians. If we take into account the year in which
the immigrants first arrived here, we see an expected
pattern: namely, that amongst the earlier arrivals, relatively few have not been home. This is particularly
true for the Asians. Less than one in five of those who
left their homeland within 13 years of partition have not
been back.
   The reasons for this are not difficult to discern.
Very few complete family groupings came to Britain from
the newly partitioned Indian subcontinent. Typically, as
noted earlier, the head of the family would come here, accompanied perhaps by his eldest son, or brother. This
provided in the first instance an economic unit which was
able, in theory at least, to support his dependants and
possibly to provide a base in Britain for the whole family
at a later stage.
   Setting aside immigration control problems, which, in
any case, were comparatively minor in the earlier days,
there are obvious financial reasons why large family units
did not emigrate at once. Some wished to avoid having to
uproot their entire family, selling their land and property and risking all in the move to a country with total-

ly alien culture and religions. (As Lawrence points out, few Asians identified with the label 'British'.)

For sound historical reasons, the notion of a return to the Mother Country is much more prevalent as a West Indian view of this 'new start' in life. This concept of identification is vital here. It is, in fact, at the roots of a newcomer's perception of his adopted society. The maintenance by the 'sojourner' of an instrumental orientation towards his new societal role, may, for example, induce a far greater level of tolerance of, or indifference to, adverse treatment, as a number of writers have observed; e.g., Rex and Tomlinson (1979); Lawrence (1974). This applies both in individual relationships and at a broader structural level. Returning home may enhance this perception in providing a form of safety valve. The formation in Handsworth of a 'sub-extended family' with (as we shall see later) a number of wage earners, makes it possible for members to return to their homeland, often for substantial periods of time, without breaking up this unit.

The economics of capital accumulation and the support of dependants conflict with the desire to return home, and it is therefore not surprising that relatively few of the more recent arrivals have made the trip. It may well be, of course, that to analyse the function of what may often have been brief home visits is to do little to illuminate the question of societal commitment. A more fruitful line of thought is the issue of settlement intentions. Who exactly are the people who say they wish to return home and what is it that makes them want to do so? As a first step we present (in Table 1.11) data on settlement intentions along with the least favoured aspect of life in Britain as seen through the eyes of the immigrants themselves.

Much has been written on the intentions of immigrants to settle in Britain; for example, Patterson (1963), Rex and Moore (1967), Rose (1969) and Brooks (1969,1975). Remembering that most of their findings relate to West Indians, a clear pattern does emerge; namely, that very few of those who came here did so initially with the intention of staying. The number who ultimately decided to settle, then, increased sharply with period of residence. Lawrence, for example, found that although 95 per cent of his Nottingham sample had originally seen their stay in Britain as temporary, the views of many had since changed. Only 75 per cent (78 per cent of the West Indians and 69 per cent of the Asians) now planned to return to their country of origin. To avoid problems of rationalisation during the interviews, we did not ask about 'original' in-

tentions; we base our analysis instead on a comparison of
respondents who arrived at different points in time. On
the above theory, we would expect earlier migrants to exhibit a less marked tendency (than more recent arrivals)
to wish to return.

Turning now to Table 1.11, we see that (as was the case
with Lawrence's study) there appears to be no clear relationship between settlement plans and length of residence.
Furthermore, this is the case however finely we divide the
samples by date of arrival. The major difference between
the studies lies in the massive difference in the numbers
of West Indians and Asians expressing a desire to return
to their homeland. Little more than a quarter of the
Asians wanted to leave Britain as against 65(66) per cent
of the West Indians; and less than one in five of the
latter group actually wanted to stay here. Many from both
groups were distinctly ambivalent about their position,
however. Among the Asians in particular it was clear that
a strong emotional commitment to their homeland was tem-
pered by pragmatism.

Not surprisingly, perhaps, it appears that the relationship between settlement intentions and length of residence is a spurious one. To add further weight to the
above examples, Davison (1966) found that more of the
Jamaicans in his sample wanted to go home at the end of
the second year in Britain than at the end of their first.

As with the question of why people originally came to
Britain, no single external or internal stimulus can account for our findings. It is clear that the motivation
behind this subjectively intended act has to be seen in
the light of the migrant's perception of life in Britain
for himself and his family at the present time. As the
'act' here is the statement of an intention to return, it
may to some extent be seen as a measure of identification
with Britain, and in particular with the British. Feelings of rejection, exploitation and the attendant insecurity may be mitigated by indulging in self-deception: the
'dream' of one day returning home. It may well be that
the relative social distance maintained by the Asian communities goes some way towards explaining why a group who
display a low measure of identification with Britain in
other respects demonstrate a greater commitment to life
here in the sense of a desire to settle.

It is as misleading, of course, to talk in this context
about a single 'Asian' community as it is to refer to a
single 'cause' of migration or desire to return home. The
East Africans we spoke to, for example, were extremely reluctant to criticise any aspect of British life and only
a handful (15 per cent) wished to leave. The reasons for

these findings were not too difficult to discern. Most
had come to Britain as refugees, had severed all contacts
with their 'homeland', and appeared to be comforted by the
fact that they had at least acquired a home and job in
this country.

It is perhaps only a little more difficult to account
for the fact that rather more Pakistanis (31 per cent)
than Indians (26 per cent) wished to return. [26] As we
shall see later, the jobs which the former had acquired
were often particularly poor in terms both of status and
working conditions. A number who wished to go back to
Pakistan complained specifically of the harsh and tedious
nature of their work. Thus, the complaint that 'I work
all the time ... I have no social life.' To the many who
came to Britain as peasants, speaking little or no
English, this experience no doubt came as a double blow.
As Rimmer (1972) points out, the concept of time-keeping
is of little importance in a farming community. Thus,
being constrained to work rigid (and often unsocial) hours
can have a seriously demoralising effect in itself. Added
to this, however, is the fact that those who had worked on
the land, and more often than not had owned their plot of
land (however meagre) were ill prepared for the insignificant and subordinate role they were to play in British
industry. The fact that they were still performing menial
tasks after a lengthy period in Britain could clearly be
linked to one of the two major complaints which immigrants
made of life in Britain; namely, the level of racial discrimination, and hostility (see Table 1.11). Pakistanis,
in particular, tended to feel very strongly about this
issue, about a quarter in all giving this response.
Furthermore, it was far and away the major concern of
those who wished to return to Pakistan.

These points were raised because they were by necessity
concealed in the summary Table 1.11. Returning to the
table now, we see that among both Asians and West Indians,
those who saw themselves as 'settlers' (for whatever
reason) tended to be rather reluctant to criticise aspects
of life in Britain. They were still very much in the minority, however, and especially among the West Indians.
Apart from those who complained of racial hostility, the
major complaint can perhaps be summarised best as the
British climate and the lack of availability of fresh
fruit. Though apparently trivial in a sociological sense,
this answer was interesting in that, when combined with
other qualitative data, it often reflected in a symbolic
sense an underlying mood of depression; the feeling that
the individual was trapped in a society whose social
'greyness' was amply matched by its physical attributes.

TABLE 1.11 Least favoured feature of life in Britain by settlement intentions, arrival date and ethnic origin [1]

A ASIANS

		Racial prejudice/discrimination	Weather/climate	Cost of living	Industrial way of life	Immorality/amorality	Other	Nothing	Total = 100%	Percentage of arrival cohort wishing to stay/return home
Pre-1960	Go %	20	20	5	–	5	20	30	22 [2]	24
	Stay %	9	24	2	–	2	9	53	45	54
1960-4	Go %	11	30	3	5	11	19	22	37	28
	Stay %	13	28	–	2	–	12	45	53	41
1965+	Go %	14	29	5	10	10	29	5	21 [2]	24
	Stay %	9	29	4	2	2	9	44	45	51
TOTAL	Go %	14	26	4	5	9	23	20	80	26
	Stay %	10	27	2	1	1	10	48	144	47

B WEST INDIANS (weighted figures are bracketed)

		Racial prejudice/discrimination	Weather/climate	Cost of living	Industrial way of life	Immorality/amorality	Other	Nothing	Total = 100%	Percentage of arrival cohort wishing to stay/return home
Pre-1960	Go %	16(14)	44(48)	8 (8)	7 (7)	4 (3)	7 (6)	14(15)	118(106)	63(65)
	Stay %	12(11)	41(37)	–	3 (4)	6 (4)	6 (4)	32(41)	34 (27)	18(17)
1960+	Go %	12(11)	48(50)	13(13)	4 (3)	1 (2)	9(11)	11(12)	137(104)	69(69)
	Stay %	5 (6)	45(48)	13(13)	8 (6)	–	11(10)	20(16)	40 (31)	20(21)
TOTAL	Go %	14(12)	47(50)	11(10)	5 (5)	3 (2)	8 (7)	12(13)	258(212)	65(66)
	Stay %	7 (8)	43(42)	7 (7)	5 (5)	3 (2)	10 (9)	25(27)	75 (59)	19(18)

1 The body of the table excludes those who failed to answer any of the relevant questions.
2 Care should be taken in drawing inferences here because of the small sample sizes.

In addition there was occasionally also a feeling that
they saw their needs as a minority group as inadequately
realised. Hence, in a curious yet important manner, these
types of response sometimes merged with those which had an
overtly racial dimension.

In general, the 'immigrant-settler' we met in
Handsworth can perhaps be typified as someone who has to
all intents and purposes cut his links with the homeland
and is attempting to adjust to life in a country which he
clearly realises is in many ways inhospitable. When links
are maintained it is largely at the personal level; i.e.,
keeping in touch with family and friends. The only possible exception to this 'ideal type' appears to be the
younger Jamaican who arrived during the 1960s, often at
the request of his parents. He is searching for an identity not provided by the primary community, and has in
consequence turned more and more to the homeland; as have
many of Handsworth's second-generation blacks (see Chapter
6). This group frequently read West Indian newspapers to
keep in touch with homeland news, culture and politics.

Those who lacked commitment to life in Britain, the
'sojourners', displayed in general a range of moods
stretching from bitter disillusionment or demoralisation
on the one hand, to overt hostility and alienation on the
other. To many, a return to the homeland was the only
solution to their plight. Comparatively few, even among
the Asian community, failed to express an adverse opinion
of Britain and/or British society.

As Table 1.11 shows, Asians who wished to return to
their homeland were much more likely than their 'settler'
counterparts to complain of the social and moral environment in which they and their children were living: 28 per
cent (as against 12 per cent) felt that they were the
victims of racial prejudice, that the society was morally
repugnant, or at least that the urban industrial way of
life was oppressive. Sometimes the three categories once
again could be seen to merge, and particularly among those
who abhorred the lack of respect accorded to elders.
Western industrial society was implicitly seen as weakening the traditional importance of the family unit. Thus,
the Indian who complained that 'people do not respect
their parents' could be seen through some of his subsequent responses to be making a much more fundamental point
than might appear at first sight. Further, it was implicitly argued that precisely because they as a community
wished to retain standards of moral decency that they were
being subjected to verbal and physical hostility by the
majority society.

West Indian 'sojourners' tended to place rather more

emphasis on physical rather than 'moral' entities; thus the major pre-eminence of complaints relating to the British climate, the lack of fresh fruit, and the cost of living. As with the Asians who wished to return home, there was a sizeable group who made direct reference to racial prejudice or intolerance.

The major difference between the two major ethnic groups, however, lies in the fact that among the West Indians there appears to be a very much stronger positive relationship between interest in homeland news and politics and the desire to return. Rather curiously, among those who are interested in home affairs virtually all who keep in contact via newspapers wish to re-emigrate. Only among older Indians and Pakistanis who in general arrived in Britain before 1960 does continued interest in home affairs tend to be associated with a major lack of commitment to life in Britain.

Of course, the whole question of societal commitment is extremely complex. The desire to return to one's homeland often comprises, as noted earlier, an intricate mosaic of many of the above factors. It is undoubtedly the case, however, that underlying much of this is an acute awareness, on the part of those we interviewed, of the problems which they and their children faced in negotiating the hurdles which white society had put in their way.

It is precisely these 'extra' hurdles, hurdles not placed in the way of the native working class, which lead writers such as Rex (1970) and Sivanandan (1976) to talk of a black 'under-class'. Indeed, the practical success of policies such as 'differential immigration control' and 'repatriation' depend on such a phenomenon becoming formalised and accepted as a dominant ideology among the majority white society. Many of the responses we have seen reflect the power of this particular value system. A measure of practical 'success' for the racist would be the resulting level of demand for 'voluntary' repatriation among ethnic minority groups themselves.

An unintended side effect of racialist policies, however, is the conferring of a clear social identity on black people, which, instead of promoting demoralisation and despair, actually provides a focal point for their alienation. An illustration of this phenomenon arises in the recent work of Ivan Henry. His study of West Indians in Handsworth [27] showed that most identified Enoch Powell as a racialist, and therefore an enemy. Some, however, argued further that he was useful in that 'he helps us to identify the enemy' and that 'he keeps us on our toes'. This public manifestation of the source of their alienation had thus produced a solidaristic 'us' in the

expression of their feelings. [28] Their exploitation was
perceived all the more clearly since their 'enemy' was, in
this case, the man who in the 1950s had been in the van-
guard of the immigrant recruitment drive in the Caribbean.
They had visibly become economic shuttlecocks, necessary
to fuel the expansionist economy of post-war Britain, but
undesirable when recession and the resulting social
strains became evident.

Arising from all this is a very important question: to
what extent is the verbal projection of a 'sojourner' perspective a reflection simply of alienation as distinct
from a statement of firm plans? Brooks (1975) points out,
as we have earlier, that a stated intention is by no means
equivalent to a prediction of future actions. Table 1.12
helps us to answer this question by focusing on the
present plans of those who had previously said they wished
to return home.

We can now see that, although nearly a half of the
migrants say that they would like to return home, the vast
majority have no plans at present to do so. To this group
we could well add those (mainly West Indian) who want to
return but say that they are constrained by lack of
finance. [29] A further 16 people plan to return at a
particular point in the future. These are mainly thinking
of retiring to their homelands or returning when their
'children are grown up'. [30] In all only ten West
Indians and two Asians are actually making definite plans
at present; i.e., selling their house here and/or buying
land 'at home'. With the exception of one Indian who has
been here for only a matter of months, all are established
residents (in the sense of having arrived in Britain well
over 10 years ago).

It was abundantly clear, then, that few had begun to
think in terms of concrete plans for a return. To most
the idea seemed a distant dream, a way perhaps of channel-
ling a deep sense of disillusionment and frustration with
their current position, and thereby providing a means of
coming to terms with their everyday existence. This
brings us to an interesting paradox, analogous to the
solidaristic reaction to Powell noted earlier. Whilst
theoretically enabling a large number of immigrants to
return home (i.e., those who, when asked directly, said
that they wished to return) the 'enforced repatriation
lobby' may produce a violent, and quite unintended backlash (even) from this group. By removing the means of
psychological support, i.e., by bringing 'the homecoming'
out of the realms of fantasy and firmly into that of
reality, the chance of repatriation would force blacks to
look hard at their position. Might it not for many (per-

TABLE 1.12 Details of plans to return to homeland by ethnic group (weighted figures are bracketed)

	No definite plans	Want to return but cannot afford to	Returning at particular point in future	Definite plans now	Other	Refused	Sample size (= 100%)
West Indians %	76(73)	13(14)	5 (7)	4 (4)	1 (1)	1 (1)	262(213)
Asians %	86	3	3	3	6	-	80

TABLE 1.13 Number of dependant relatives [1] by ethnic group (weighted figures are bracketed)

	None	One	Two	Three	Four or more	Total number of dependants	Sample size (= 100%)
West Indian %	53(48)	24(26)	16(17)	4 (5)	3 (4)	327(290)	395(320)
Asian %	70	13	12	3	3	183	305

1 'Dependants' here were restricted to parents, spouses and children. This is unlikely in itself to have resulted in a significant underestimation of those supported to some extent by members of our sample. These may, of course, be under- or overestimates due to misunderstandings, or perhaps due to suspicions of the researchers' motives.

haps most) be a question of being removed from a position
at the bottom of the social pile here and transposed into
a similar role in their homeland? They would also, significantly, be returning not as a result of economic self-
improvement (which many .clearly hope for) but by virtue of
handouts enforced by law and administered by descendants
of the very people who had long been their (people's)
source of economic and social exploitation. By this means
they would be stripped of what self-respect they still retained.

IMMIGRATION CONTROL AND THE DEPENDANTS ISSUE

Earlier in the present chapter we traced the shifts in
government thinking on immigration controls. This was
important in that it gave us an insight into the radically
changing climate of opinion and indeed the radically
changing relationship between the state and the immigrant
over the last 20 years. Some authors (notably Sivanandan,
1976, Birmingham CDP, 1977) have gone so far as to argue
that we have essentially moved from a free market to a
contract migrant labour system. This is central to the
present argument for two reasons.

First, for those without the right to permanent settlement, the concept of repatriation becomes largely redundant; the 'contract' enables the Home Office by means of
a negative decision (i.e., the failure to renew) to termi-
nate the person's right to stay. Second, it emphasises
the fact that, whatever the subjective feelings and intentions of the immigrants themselves, a rather more critical factor, perhaps, is how they are defined externally,
e.g., in terms of nationality, by institutions such as the
Home Office.

Except for the ideologues of the far right, who advo-
cate the forced repatriation of all blacks irrespective of
nationality status, the major focus of attempts to restrict the influx of black immigrants during the 1970s has
been the dependants of those already here. [31] As
Eversley and Sudkeo (1969) remark: [32]

> In the middle sixties the counts made under the (1962
> Commonwealth Immigrants) Act showed there was a dis-
> tinct increase in the number of arrivals in one cate-
> gory - the dependants, those who were entitled to join
> relatives already in Britain. This, in effect, means
> wives and children under 16, though in some cases older
> children and parents of pensionable age were also
> entering the country. This caused a certain amount of
> public alarm, and rather wild guesses were current as

to the potential number of further dependants who might
join the men already in this country.
In their treatment of issues of race, newspapers (and in
particular the popular dailies) have been guilty of generating, or at least giving currency to, such rumours. Perhaps even more disturbing than the scaremongering, however, is the scandalous treatment of many intending immigrants at the hands of some immigration and Home Office
bureaucrats (see CDP report, op.cit.). It came as no surprise to many when in 1979 a major scandal blew up concerning allegations (subsequently substantiated) that
Asian women had been subjected to gynaecological tests at
Heathrow Airport.

Despite the insidiousness of seeming to join the
'numbers game' in the light of this sort of behaviour (see
Chapters 2 and 3), it is, we feel, instructive to see the
size of the 'dependants problem' in relation to our sample
of Handsworth residents. Would there, for example, be a
sizeable increase (or even a 'flood') of new arrivals if
all dependants of our respondents who wished to come to
Britain were permitted (and were able) to?

A brief perusal of Table 1.13 produces a resounding
'No'. Even if every dependant, irrespective of his or
her wishes, was brought here the mean increase per family
would amount to considerably less than a single person.

Furthermore, in displaying a detailed analysis of dependants who wish to come to Britain, Table 1.14 enables
us to put 'the problem' into perspective. Less than one
in five of those listed in the previous table actually
wish to come here, and 92.4 per cent of our families had
no such dependants. Moreover, since the total size of our
immigrant sample is 3,548, [33] we are talking in terms of
a potential increase in this sector of the population of
at most 2.7 per cent. [34] There is little evidence in
our data to support the claims of some politicians that to
open the door to dependants is to invite a major increase
in the size of the minority groups. Closer inspection
reveals that almost 30 per cent of the would-be migrants
are parents of advanced age and all but one of five wives
still overseas can be assumed to be past child-bearing
age. Hence, the potential for natural increase over the
coming years would be limited to the children in this
group.

The perpetration of myths about the rates of growth in
the black population [35] does, of course, fulfil strong
conservative ideological functions, as we shall see later
in this book. It helps, for example, to foment divisions
in the working class by defining blacks as somehow geneti-
cally, socially and culturally inferior to the native

TABLE 1.14   Dependent relatives who wish to come to Britain by current country of residence

	Parents	Spouses	Children	Total	Number of families involved	% of Total
India	19	3	27	49	29	
Pakistan	4	2	13	19	7	
Bangladesh	–	–	6	6	1	
Grenada	1	–	–	1	1	
Jamaica	5	–	15	20	14	
West Indies (country not specified)	–	–	2	2	1	
ALL	29	5	63	97	53	7.6
Number of families with no dependent relatives wanting to come to Britain					647	92.4
Total sample size					700 [1]	100

1 Re-weighted figures are not present here since the two levels of weighting required complicate the presentation considerably and do not make an appreciable difference to the results.

working class. Thus, in times of stress for a capitalist economy, and particularly one with an historically entrenched class structure, such as that which exists in Britain, blacks form a convenient scapegoat (Rex, 1970). Resulting social tensions are typically interpreted by social commentators and, perhaps more significantly, by the media simply as localised outbreaks of racial conflict, and as such devoid of any broader structural significance. In presenting this external expression of alienation and frustration, blacks may then invoke the label of agitators and find that their behaviour is interpreted as justifying the initial propaganda. Furthermore, structural factors influencing the access to power ensure the maintenance of the status quo; i.e., the continued dominance of the existing value system.

SUMMARY AND CONCLUSIONS

In the first chapter we have seen something of the background of migration to Britain during the past twenty years. We have seen also how the traditional 'links with the Commonwealth' enabled this massive importation of labour to take place. Following this was the breakdown of, or rather retreat from, this colonial-style paternalism in the light of economic pressures. In this way morality and ethics were (once again) surrendered to the vagaries of economic forces. Racism, in whatever form, was then seen as a key ideological vehicle which could be used to justify the pursuance of policies creating a kind of dual 'human' market system (to be discussed in Chapters 4 and 5 in relation to housing and employment).

The practical effects of governmental policies have been considerable. The CDP Report mentioned above demonstrated clearly the human misery and suffering created by successive immigration laws. In our own study, five Asians (3 Indians and 2 Pakistanis) are still [36] separated from their spouses. Furthermore, 51 out of 63 children who want to come to Britain belong to families where both parents are already here. What is more, and Table 1.13 does not show this, 40 of these children have been separated from their parents for at least 10 years. It is true, of course, that the joint family system permits a successful adjustment to this situation, and certainly not all the children have been prevented from coming to Britain by our immigration laws. On the other hand, there was considerable evidence to suggest that these structural forces effectively compelled people to endure this separation whether they wished it or not.

Immigration policies highlight the ambiguous position black immigrants hold in British society, and certainly cannot be divorced (except in a purely technical sense) from the everyday experiences of this group.   It will be the task of the following chapters to explore these experiences in such areas as housing, education and politics, whilst retaining this notion of theoretical unity.

2 Handsworth: the changing face of an urban community

In the previous chapter we looked in some detail at the process of migration. We argued in particular that the massive movements of population from the Caribbean and the Indian subcontinent in the 1950s and 1960s could not be seen solely in terms of a return to the Mother Country in a sentimental sense. Historical and structural considerations go a long way towards explaining why this process began at the time it did, and why immigrants and their families occupy their present rather ambiguous position in British society.

What we have not yet seen is how the migration process influences, and is in turn influenced by, the changing social and cultural patterns of an urban community. It is the purpose of this chapter to do just this; to examine in some detail the sorts of area in which New Commonwealth immigrants made their homes, and the implications this held for the structure of social relations which has resulted directly and indirectly from these spatial patterns.

We begin by expanding the discussion of the early part of the last chapter. There we saw (in Table 1.1) the way in which immigration produced radical differences in the ethnic composition of the city as a whole from 1951 to 1971. Later (in Figure 2) we saw the result at ward level of this process at the beginning of the 1970s. At this point, it is illuminating to examine the way in which the spatial concentrations of the New Commonwealth population have changed, particularly since the 1961 Census.

SPATIAL CONCENTRATION OF NEW COMMONWEALTH IMMIGRANTS

As Table 2.1 demonstrates, there has been a gradual build-up of the New Commonwealth-born population of Birmingham

TABLE 2.1 Residents born in the New Commonwealth by ward (1961,1966,1971) [1]

Ward	1961 [2]				1966 [4]				1971				1971 (Total NC [5] origin)	
	No.	% of ward pop.	SI [3]	Ward pop.	No.	% of ward pop.	SI [3]	Ward pop.	No.	% of ward pop.	SI [3]	Ward pop.	% of ward pop.	SI [3] [6]
Acocks Green	355	1.2	0.44	28,874	430	1.6	0.34	27,280	723	2.7	0.40	26,978	3.6	0.40
All Saints	618	2.4	0.86	25,590	800	3.5	0.74	23,110	1,802	12.6	1.90	14,325	19.1	2.10
Aston	2,385	8.0	2.84	29,840	4,060	14.5	3.08	28,090	3,101	22.1	3.34	14,000	29.4	3.23
Billesley	88	0.3	0.12	26,880	70	0.2	0.05	29,360	136	0.5	0.07	28,262	0.6	0.07
Brandwood	190	0.6	0.23	29,616	190	0.7	0.15	27,770	328	0.9	0.14	36,088	1.0	0.11
Deritend	2,095	6.2	2.22	33,611	3,330	11.9	2.54	27,960	3,634	19.5	2.94	18,651	27.0	2.97
Duddeston	541	1.8	0.65	29,598	580	2.2	0.47	26,560	1,286	6.9	1.04	18,262	10.9	1.20
Edgbaston	2,961	11.6	4.12	25,608	3,020	11.6	2.48	25,950	2,320	8.7	3.33	26,551	9.8	1.08
Erdington	236	1.0	0.34	34,839	310	1.2	0.27	24,470	481	1.2	0.18	39,708	1.6	0.18
Fox Hollies	147	0.6	0.20	26,125	110	0.4	0.09	24,850	251	1.0	0.16	24,082	1.4	0.15
Gravelly Hill	912	3.0	1.06	30,738	1,330	4.6	0.98	29,070	2,089	7.9	1.20	26,312	11.8	1.30
Hall Green	289	1.0	0.37	27,798	270	1.0	0.21	27,040	375	1.4	0.20	27,710	1.6	0.18
Handsworth	2,826	9.3	3.30	30,467	4,610	15.6	3.32	29,620	5,954	21.4	3.24	27,771	32.1	3.53
Harborne	398	1.6	0.58	24,592	450	1.9	0.41	23,550	698	2.9	0.44	24,030	3.5	0.38
Kings Norton	254	0.9	0.32	28,610	210	0.7	0.14	32,040	380	1.2	0.18	31,973	1.4	0.15
Kingstanding	67	0.3	0.09	25,875	30	0.1	0.03	22,790	84	0.4	0.06	22,925	0.4	0.04
Ladywood	423	1.6	0.58	25,835	280	1.6	0.34	17,380	485	3.9	0.59	12,427	5.6	0.62
Longbridge	163	0.5	0.18	31,990	150	0.4	0.09	34,080	282	0.9	0.13	32,623	1.1	0.12
Moseley	1,267	4.4	1.58	28,622	1,900	6.8	1.46	27,820	2,261	8.1	1.23	27,824	11.5	1.26
Newtown	722	2.4	0.85	30,328	1,220	6.0	1.28	20,270	1,438	11.6	1.75	12,377	16.7	1.84
Northfield	171	0.6	0.21	28,599	330	1.0	0.21	33,790	252	0.7	0.11	35,182	0.8	0.09
Oscott	129	0.5	0.17	26,783	110	0.4	0.09	25,300	185	0.8	0.12	23,975	1.0	0.11
Perry Barr	112	0.4	0.15	26,949	130	0.5	0.12	23,980	358	1.5	0.22	24,316	2.3	0.25
Quinton	124	0.5	0.18	24,062	160	0.7	0.14	23,870	187	0.8	0.12	24,326	0.7	0.08
Rotton Park	1,718	5.9	2.08	29,292	3,360	12.9	2.74	26,140	3,386	17.0	2.56	19,971	26.2	2.88

Saltley	1,204	4.1	1.45	29,543	1,810	6.7	1.42	27,120	3,304	12.5	1.89	26,388	16.6	1.82
Sandwell	1,316	5.0	1.79	26,178	2,530	9.2	1.96	27,540	3,832	13.3	2.01	28,733	20.1	2.21
Selly Oak	1,745	6.2	2.20	28,240	620	2.2	0.48	27,710	888	3.3	0.50	26,595	3.9	0.43
Shard End	125	0.4	0.14	32,210	100	0.3	0.07	32,720	296	0.8	0.12	36,490	1.2	0.13
Sheldon	120	0.4	0.15	28,321	80	0.3	0.06	27,720	185	0.7	0.11	25,424	1.0	0.11
Small Heath	1,078	3.6	1.29	29,851	2,320	7.8	1.67	29,560	4,288	16.1	2.44	26,561	21.1	2.32
Soho	3,588	12.9	4.61	27,720	5,900	21.3	4.55	27,690	8,195	31.6	4.77	25,951	47.4	5.21
Sparkbrook	2,189	7.1	2.54	30,652	4,830	16.7	3.57	28,900	5,496	22.9	3.45	24,014	30.0	3.30
Sparkhill	1,226	3.8	1.37	31,950	2,710	9.2	1.96	29,460	5,273	18.8	2.83	28,112	24.1	2.65
Stechford	216	0.8	0.29	26,712	250	1.0	0.22	24,720	325	1.3	0.20	24,878	2.0	0.22
Stockland Green	207	0.8	0.28	26,393	350	1.2	0.25	29,830	372	1.3	0.20	28,290	1.8	0.20
Washwood Heath	509	1.7	0.62	29,199	730	2.7	0.57	27,500	1,831	6.9	1.04	26,632	9.2	1.01
Weoley	139	0.5	0.16	30,437	110	0.3	0.07	24,430	311	0.8	0.13	37,493	0.7	0.08
Yardley	112	0.4	0.14	28,660	90	0.3	0.07	27,180	152	0.5	0.08	28,042	0.7	0.08
TOTAL Birmingham CB	31,108	2.8	1.00	1,107,187	49,870	4.7	1.00	1,064,220	67,224	6.6	1.00	1,014,671	9.1	1.00

SI = Standardised Index.

Source: 1971 Census (Small Area Statistics) and Birmingham Central Statistical Office.

1 The 1971 figures relate first to those born in the New Commonwealth and second to those with both parents born in the New Commonwealth.

2 We are strictly talking about 'Commonwealth' rather than 'New Commonwealth' in the case of these 1961 figures, since the Birmingham Statistics Office data from which these are derived failed to separate 'the Old Commonwealth' from those born in Malta and Cyprus. The inclusion of the latter category, then, means that our figures are slightly inflated. Data on spatial concentrations, however, will only be affected to a very minor extent.

3 The 'Standardised Index' relates densities of New Commonwealth concentrations in particular wards to the appropriate overall city densities.

4 The 1966 figures are estimates based on a 10 per cent sample. One must therefore allow for sampling error in interpreting these data.

5 These figures correspond to the percentage of a particular ward's residents both of whose parents were born in the New Commonwealth.

6 The figures are sometimes marginally different from those in Figure 2, Chapter 1. This is due to the fact that 'exact' figures from the Small Area Statistics were used, no allowance being made for possible enumeration errors as was previously the case.

over the ten years covered by the three Censuses. From
well below 3 per cent [1] of the city's population in 1961
the figure rose to 4.7 per cent in 1966 and 6.6 per cent
in 1971. Furthermore, if we take second-generation immigrants into account, the percentage of Birmingham's population accounted for by this group has increased approximately threefold over the decade, to 9.1 per cent. Recent
mid-year population estimates combined with figures for
mortality and fertility of the various ethnic groups suggest that well over one in ten of the city's population is
now of New Commonwealth origin.

The obvious question to ask at this point is whether
this group has begun to disperse evenly throughout the
indigenous population or whether it has tended increasingly to settle in well-defined parts of the city. If, as
previous research suggests, immigrants to the metropolis
tend to follow this (latter) pattern, we would wish to
know why it was that these particular areas were 'chosen'.
Further, in what ways do these areas differ from those
which are ethnically more homogenous?

Tables 2.1 and 2.2 take us some of the way towards
answering these questions. The remainder of the chapter
will then extend this discussion by focusing particularly
on one area – Handsworth – which has, as we have already
noted, experienced a series of major demographic trans-
formations over the last century.

Table 2.1 answers our first question in no uncertain
terms. As Woods (1975) confirms, the settlement of New
Commonwealth immigrants has largely taken the form of a
horseshoe-shaped belt around the city centre. Following
the entry (largely of West Indians) in the 1950s, the
'immigrant areas' were already becoming clearly mapped
out. Wards such as Soho, Sparkbrook, Handsworth, Rotton
Park and Aston already had densities of New Commonwealth-
born residents more than twice the city average. In sharp
contrast, few had settled in the outer suburbs marked by
wards such as Billesley, Weoley, Kingstanding and Oscott.

It is often argued that once these residential patterns
are established further immigration not only reinforces
these patterns but also tends to result in a greater
spatial polarisation between the indigenous population and
the immigrants. Clearly the chain migration thesis discussed, among others, by Desai (1963), Banton (1972) and
Watson (1977) would suggest this outcome. True, there is
modest confirmation in the figures for Soho, Sparkbrook
and Aston. On the other hand, there is some evidence that
by 1971 the distribution of New Commonwealth residents was
beginning to look a little more diffuse. It should perhaps be stressed, however, that this does not mean that

black immigrants had moved out to the suburbs. There is
still little evidence of that. What movement there was,
was (and is) largely confined to so-called 'middle-ring'
areas.

To see why the polarisation thesis could not be expected to be borne out by the data, we need to look briefly at the state of Birmingham's housing in the late 1950s
[2] in the light of the prevailing political climate. At
this time there was already widespread concern among
council members about the shortage of housing. The
shortage was reflected in chronic overcrowding, which was
believed to be most serious in those areas in which the
'new' black population lived. This feeling was confirmed
by the publishing in May 1959 of a report by the fairly
recently-appointed Liaison Officer for Commonwealth Immigrants. In this document it was stated that there were
3,200 houses occupied by coloured people, each of which
was estimated to contain on average eleven people. Moreover, [3]

> There is ample evidence to suggest that the integration
> desired by the Council is not taking place. The immi-
> grants are living in tight pockets turning inwards to
> themselves and would seem intent on creating a 'little
> Jamaica' or the like within the City. I believe that
> this trend, unless checked, will have serious conse-
> quences.

This came at a sensitive time. Memories of the racial
disturbances in Notting Hill and Nottingham the previous
year were still very much alive; so were the speeches of
Oswald Mosley and the activities of the various extremist
groups (despite the fact that the city's mandarins prided
themselves on the comparative racial harmony of their
'patch').

The council was faced with an awkward dilemma. On the
one hand, the status quo had (for them) much to commend
it. Because the immigrants were confined to a small
region of the city they were easy to deal with 'adminis-
tratively'. Poor living conditions and overcrowding meant
that local welfare services needed to be effectively and
efficiently organised. The other major benefit for the
local authority in the almost 'reservation-like' settle-
ments, though, was the isolation of the 'problem' and
thereby the insulation from contact with blacks of the
major part of the city's population.

On the other side of the argument was the fear of the
long-term effects of ghettoisation. In addition, the high
levels of morbidity and infant mortality, particularly
among immigrants, imposed a duty on the council to do
something.

TABLE 2.2   Selected social indicators [1] by ward (1971)

Ward	Owner occupation		Private rented		Households in shared dwellings		Exclusive use of three amenities		Over 1½ persons per room		No car	
	%	SI [2]	%	SI	%	SI	%	SI	%	SI	%	SI
Acocks Green	51.6	1.22	22.2	1.14	2.7	0.68	77.5	0.99	1.5	0.52	59.4	1.03
All Saints	29.1	0.69	26.0	1.33	2.2	0.55	33.1	0.42	8.4	2.90	76.7	1.33
Aston	36.0	0.85	31.2	1.60	6.3	1.58	44.4	0.57	8.1	2.79	78.2	1.34
Billesley	38.1	0.90	5.7	0.29	0.5	0.13	70.1	0.90	1.4	0.48	52.0	0.90
Brandwood	47.4	1.12	9.1	0.47	1.3	0.33	89.9	1.15	0.9	0.31	47.7	0.83
Deritend	19.0	0.45	31.8	1.63	9.3	2.33	58.2	0.75	8.4	2.90	78.5	1.36
Duddleston	4.8	0.11	12.3	0.63	1.4	0.35	64.5	0.83	6.2	2.14	81.1	1.41
Edgbaston	27.9	0.66	44.3	2.27	11.0	2.75	74.7	0.96	3.7	1.28	55.4	0.96
Erdington	35.9	0.85	10.3	0.53	1.9	0.48	84.9	1.09	1.4	0.48	56.1	0.97
Fox Hollies	28.0	0.66	8.8	0.45	1.3	0.33	75.6	0.97	1.6	0.55	62.5	1.08
Gravelly Hill	45.3	1.07	32.0	1.64	3.3	0.83	72.7	0.93	3.9	1.34	62.9	1.09
Hall Green	72.1	1.70	14.3	0.73	3.2	0.80	88.2	1.13	0.6	0.21	40.7	0.71
Handsworth	46.1	1.09	39.4	2.02	15.6	3.90	66.4	0.85	6.6	2.28	68.9	1.19
Harborne	47.9	1.13	30.7	1.57	6.0	1.50	80.6	1.03	1.2	0.41	51.9	0.90
Kings Norton	45.3	1.07	22.3	1.14	2.0	0.50	90.1	1.15	1.0	0.34	50.7	0.88
Kingstanding	11.4	0.27	3.0	0.15	0.7	0.18	44.9	0.57	2.4	0.83	68.8	1.19
Ladywood	0.3	0.01	11.0	0.56	0.6	0.15	95.3	1.22	1.6	0.55	78.5	1.36
Longbridge	33.1	0.78	7.8	0.40	0.3	0.08	89.2	1.14	1.5	0.52	53.6	0.93
Moseley	43.4	1.03	49.6	2.54	12.9	3.23	69.8	0.89	4.2	1.45	53.7	0.93
Newtown	12.1	0.29	13.2	0.68	1.2	0.30	79.9	1.02	3.7	1.28	81.0	1.40

Northfield	46.5	1.10	11.7	0.60	0.8	0.20	94.5	1.21	1.0	0.34	46.0	0.80
Oscott	68.2	1.61	7.7	0.39	0.4	0.10	92.4	1.18	0.7	0.24	46.5	0.81
Perry Barr	81.8	1.93	9.7	0.50	0.5	0.13	96.8	1.24	0.6	0.21	41.0	0.71
Quinton	55.8	1.32	8.5	0.44	0.6	0.15	93.7	1.20	0.4	0.14	44.4	0.77
Rotton Park	28.6	0.68	40.5	2.08	12.9	3.23	41.8	0.54	9.3	3.21	75.9	1.32
Saltley	38.0	0.90	21.7	1.11	4.3	1.08	63.3	0.81	4.5	1.55	71.3	1.24
Sandwell	68.3	1.61	25.0	1.28	4.8	1.20	84.3	1.08	3.9	1.34	45.0	0.78
Selly Oak	59.8	1.41	26.1	1.34	2.3	0.58	84.2	1.08	1.1	0.38	53.5	0.93
Shard End	35.0	0.83	3.0	0.15	0.4	0.10	98.6	1.26	1.2	0.41	49.8	0.86
Sheldon	47.7	1.13	6.6	0.34	0.6	0.15	98.6	1.26	1.0	0.34	45.5	0.79
Small Heath	43.8	1.04	26.2	1.34	6.8	1.70	55.4	0.71	6.3	2.17	72.4	1.25
Soho	47.3	1.12	38.1	1.95	13.6	3.40	52.3	0.67	12.2	4.21	73.1	1.27
Sparkbrook	35.6	0.85	41.1	2.11	14.5	3.63	48.8	0.62	8.8	3.03	75.8	1.31
Sparkhill	53.6	1.27	36.9	1.89	9.0	2.25	61.4	0.79	5.1	1.76	67.0	1.16
Stechford	25.5	0.60	9.1	0.47	2.5	0.63	89.3	1.14	2.3	0.79	60.3	1.05
Stockland Green	40.1	0.95	9.7	0.50	2.1	0.53	83.2	1.07	1.2	0.41	60.0	1.04
Washwood Heath	43.1	1.02	20.4	1.05	2.1	0.53	67.7	0.87	2.3	0.79	66.7	1.16
Weoley	25.5	0.60	14.8	0.76	0.4	0.10	95.8	1.23	1.0	0.34	50.3	0.87
Yardley	50.4	1.19	5.3	0.27	0.8	0.20	86.8	1.11	1.2	0.41	48.0	0.83
TOTAL Birmingham CB	42.3	1.00	19.5	1.00	4.0	1.00	78.1	1.00	2.9	1.00	57.7	1.00

Source: 1971 Census, Small Area Statistics

1 The definitions of the indicators used are listed in the explanatory notes to the 1971 Census Small Area Statistics.

2 The 'Standardised Index' simply relates the level of phenomena at ward level to the appro- priate levels in the city as a whole.

The latter arguments finally won the day, but still
left the problem of deciding what exactly they should do.
To enforce the 1957 Housing Act wholeheartedly and attack
the overcrowding problem would have been simply to shunt
the problem to neighbouring areas and produce a massive
increase in the numbers of those to be statutorily rehoused. Predictably, the council decided to act cautious-
ly and simply monitored the problem at that time. By 1965
they had acquired legal powers to restrict the spread of
multi-occupation. This, combined with the use of council
mortgage finance and municipal housing (for those who had
satisfied the five-year residence requirement) eventually
gave impetus to the gradual spread of the ethnic minority
groups into other neighbouring middle-ring areas. As we
shall see in Chapter 4, this had the major effect of
bolstering the property market for ageing, and in many
cases, substandard housing; housing, moreover, which was
being left behind by whites who were thus enabled to migrate to greener pastures.

This brings us back, then, to the major question raised
earlier. Principally, what is the precise character of
the areas in which the black immigrants have settled in
the 1970s? To examine this we shall need to look at
Table 2.2. Before this, however, we should perhaps devote
some space to a short discussion of the reasons for se-
lecting particular indictors as 'useful'.

Although census data tell us little about the precise
quality of life enjoyed by Britain's citizens, even to the
extent of examining such issues as income and the quality
of the immediate physical environment, they do undoubtedly
provide an impressionistic overview. Indeed, the realisation that this was so prompted the local authority to
undertake a major cluster analysis of the 1966 Sample
Census data as part of their housing structure plan (see
Chapter 4). It is undeniably the case that, in terms of
'standard of living', the car-owning family who own their
own house in the suburbs can be sharply distinguished from
their (perhaps car-less) counterparts in the middle-ring
zone who share a rented house with a number of other families, lack the exclusive use of certain household amenities, and live in a state of chronic overcrowding. We
therefore focus in Table 2.2 on just such measures:
housing tenure, house sharing and amenities, overcrowding
and car ownership.

Placing the various statistical studies in the context
of the foregoing discussion we can at least gain an impression of the character of middle-ring areas such as
Soho, in comparison with 'non-immigrant' wards. As we
saw earlier, Soho is the ward with the highest volume of

New Commonwealth immigrants. It perhaps came as no surprise then that the level of private rented accommodation
is almost twice as high as in the city as a whole. This
housing sector contains much of the decaying Victorian
working-class housing which can readily be seen in the
centres of most British cities. A plus point in Soho's
favour might appear to be the slightly above average level
of home ownership;   until, that is, we realize that the
figures in themselves tell us nothing about housing quality. (Locally owned estate agents in the Soho Road have no
shortage of cheap slum or near-slum properties, aimed
almost exclusively at the immigrant market.) Looking
along the list of the remaining social indicators for Soho
we see almost total confirmation of its pathological
state: over three times the city's level of shared
dwellings, by far the worst record on overcrowding in the
city, below average level of car ownership, and a woefully
large number of families who lack or have to share at
least one of the three basic household amenities (i.e.,
bath, hot water and inside WC).

The story is repeated, to varying degrees, in each of
the other 'immigrant' wards noted earlier: Handsworth,
Sparkbrook, Aston, Sparkhill and Rotton Park. Moreover,
to complete the picture, we could well add most of the
other middle-ring wards in which there are significant
concentrations of black immigrants;   namely, Sandwell,
Deritend, All Saints, Saltley and Small Heath.

The contrast between these areas and the leafier suburbs could not be more plain. A glance at the figures in
Table 2.2 for Perry Bar, Hall Green and Oscott, for
example, underlines this point. Municipal and private
rented accommodation is scarce, the incidence of house
sharing and overcrowding is low, the vast majority of families have exclusive use of the basic household amenities
(noted above), and a comparatively large proportion have a
car.

We can conclude, therefore, that, assuming the Census
data can be taken as a fairly accurate reflection of the
average standard of living of those within a particular
ward, New Commonwealth immigrants do not seem to have
greatly benefited from their spatial 'movement' during the
1960s. Our book, of course, focuses principally on one
area of immigrant settlement - Handsworth - and we shall
return to analyse the nature of its physical environment
in much greater detail in later chapters. For the moment,
however, we concentrate on one aspect of Handsworth as a
multi-racial area: the relationship between geographical
clustering and both the internally generated cultural
norms of the settler groups and the external structural
constraints which impinge on them.

THE ETHNOGRAPHY OF A MULTI-RACIAL AREA

To the layman who lives outside the area, Handsworth tends
to mean one thing - a state of racial tension. Despite
the absence of a spectacular nationally known incident, it
is apt to become listed alongside Southall and Notting
Hill. It is the 'Babylon' of Steel Pulse's 'Handsworth
Revolution'. But we should perhaps ask ourselves at this
point how accurate this image is. Why, also, is it that
the area so often tends to be seen as a predominantly West
Indian ghetto? These are questions which relate not only
to the position of the black man in white society, but
also to the differing ways in which he defines, comes to
terms with, and expresses his ethnic identity. They also,
of course, reflect the ways in which the mass media, for
example, deal with 'the race issue'.
    Problems of race relations often become linked in the
layman's mind with heavy concentrations of blacks in inner
city areas and more generally with what has become known
as the 'numbers game'. By reducing discussions of race to
discussions of numbers, two significant results have
followed. First, great resentment has been created within
the minority communities themselves through the avoidance
of what to them are seen as the major issues, and through
the customary juxtaposition of the word 'problem' with
that of 'numbers'. (The interpretation of 'problem' in
this instance is thus heavily value-laden.) Second, the
reification of seemingly precise and incontrovertible
statistics and the apparent concern of intellectuals in
their size, defines, to some extent, what the layman sees
in his everyday life. In a way they provide inductive
support for his sense impressions. This clearly has important implications for areas of large immigrant concentrations such as Handsworth. Dour (and frequently misleading) predictions of the future size of minority
groups, such as those voiced by Enoch Powell, have already
provoked open displays of racist sentiments. His infamous
Birmingham speech of 20 April 1968 produced an immediate
'gut' reaction in the dockers of East London. This group
then gained the spontaneous support of a group of
Smithfield porters. Perhaps the most significant result
of this, however, was the fact that the mass lobby of
parliament, which was organised in support of Powell, was
given extensive coverage in the press and on television.
    In entering the demographic arena, therefore, we need
to be clear that we are entering an ideological minefield.
The 'facts' need to be faced squarely at this point, however, for two very important reasons. First, by studying
the evolution of a multi-racial and poly-ethnic settlement

TABLE 2.3   Birthplaces of 'Handsworth' residents

A   The changing scene from 1961 to 1971

	1961				1971				
	West Indies		Indian sub-continent		Total pop. = 100%	West Indies		Indian sub-continent		Total pop. = 100%
Ward	No.	%	No.	%		No.	%	No.	%	
Handsworth	2,307	(7.57)	349	(1.15)	30,467	3,291	(11.85)	2,124	(7.65)	27,771
Sandwell	1,027	(3.92)	167	(0.64)	26,178	2,086	(7.26)	1,478	(5.14)	28,733
Soho	2,749	(9.92)	732	(2.64)	27,720	2,904	(11.19)	4,776	(18.4)	25,951
Newtown	304	(1.00)	355	(1.17)	30,328	599	(4.84)	747	(6.04)	12,377
TOTAL	6,387	(5.57)	1,603	(1.40)	114,693	8,880	(9.36)	9,125	(9.62)	94,832

Source: Censuses of Population 1961,1971.

B   Birthplace of 'Handsworth' residents by ward (1971)

Ward [1]	West Indian		Indian sub-continent		Britain		Other		Total population
Sandwell	1,891	(11.7)	1,397	(8.6)	11,242	(69.5)	1,649	(10.2)	16,179 (100)
Soho 1	2,565	(12.5)	4,165	(20.2)	12,200	(59.3)	1,646	(8.0)	20,576 (100)
Soho 2	357	(7.8)	494	(10.8)	3,021	(65.9)	709	(15.5)	4,581 (100)
Handsworth	1,189	(12.3)	843	(8.7)	6,180	(63.9)	1,466	(15.1)	9,678 (100)
Newtown	518	(6.0)	678	(7.8)	6,634	(76.7)	816	(9.4)	8,646 (100)
TOTAL	6,520	(10.9)	7,577	(12.7)	39,277	(65.8)	6,286	(10.5)	59,660 (100)

Source: 1971 Census, Small Area Statistics.
The figures in brackets are the percentages of those of a given birthplace within a particular ward.

1 'Ward' now refers to that portion of a particular ward which was covered in our survey of Handsworth.

in population terms we learn a great deal about the
present position of minority groups and also about the
problems which may be faced by future generations.
Second, in so far as the 'numbers game' is a manifestation
of racist ideology, it will have a very real (though in-
direct) effect on the lives of those living in areas such
as Handsworth. We are as much concerned, therefore, with
the role of statistics and the statistician as we are with
the figures themselves.

Table 2.3A shows clearly how the ethnic composition of
the four 'Handsworth' wards changed markedly during the
1960s. Whereas in 1961 West Indians outnumbered Asians
by more than three to one, by 1971 it was the West Indians
who were in a minority. The Asian-born population increased almost sixfold over this period, and with one important exception the increase was spread fairly evenly
over the wards. Newtown (the exception) suffered a
massive decline in population between the two censuses,
this being largely due to housing clearance schemes. The
net increase in Asian population was small in comparative
terms because the council owned the vast majority of the
property remaining in 1971 (see Table 2.2). As we shall
see in later chapters, few Asians rent council property.

Perhaps the most dramatic population shift occurred in
the Soho ward. In 1961 only one in every five black immigrants was born in the Indian subcontinent. Ten years
later approximately five out of every eight were born in
this region.

If we now turn to the wards as defined in our survey
(see Table 2.3B) we see distinct similarities in the
settlement patterns of the different ethnic groups. With
the exception of Soho 1, which housed a very high proportion of Handsworth's first-generation Asian population
(55 per cent in 1971), West Indians and Asians are spread
fairly evenly throughout the wards. On the other hand,
these areas are far too large to enable us to recognise
significant clusters at street level. We shall in fact
see a little later in the present chapter that Handsworth's Muslim, Sikh and Hindu communities do tend to exhibit distinct residential patterns; patterns, moreover,
which tend to be seen by the Asians themselves as important in the maintenance of their traditional cultures.
For the present, however, we need to look rather more
closely at the structure of Handsworth's population.

Table 2.4 tells us a good deal about the effect of
changes in the ethnic balance of the area since the Second
World War. The first point to note is that although there
are quite large numbers of old people (and especially old
women) in each of the four wards, very few of these are of

TABLE 2.4 Age/sex structure of Handsworth population with particular reference to residents both of whose parents were born in the New Commonwealth (1971)

Ward	HANDSWORTH				NEWTOWN				SANDWELL				SOHO			
	New Commonwealth		Total population		New Commonwealth		Total population		New Commonwealth		Total population		New Commonwealth		Total population	
Age	Male	Female	Male	Female	Male	Female	Male	Female	Male	Female	Male	Female	Male	Female	Male	Female
0 – 4	699 (14.7)	722 (17.2)	1,399 (10.1)	1,364 (9.8)	187 (16.3)	177 (19.4)	575 (9.5)	517 (8.1)	475 (15.2)	454 (17.0)	1,211 (8.5)	1,079 (7.4)	1,149 (17.1)	1,100 (19.7)	1,761 (13.1)	1,661 (13.2)
5–14	1,277 (26.9)	1,271 (30.4)	2,535 (18.3)	2,457 (17.7)	291 (25.3)	251 (27.6)	1,052 (17.5)	1,092 (17.2)	897 (28.8)	786 (29.4)	2,585 (18.2)	2,374 (16.3)	1,718 (25.5)	1,496 (26.8)	2,711 (20.2)	2,432 (19.4)
15–24	607 (12.8)	571 (13.6)	2,044 (14.7)	1,896 (13.6)	198 (17.2)	158 (17.3)	1,003 (16.7)	890 (14.0)	466 (15.0)	409 (15.3)	2,204 (15.5)	2,081 (14.3)	1,119 (16.6)	904 (16.2)	2,124 (15.8)	1,805 (14.4)
25–34	677 (14.3)	635 (15.2)	1,757 (12.7)	1,623 (11.7)	132 (11.5)	124 (13.6)	602 (10.0)	578 (9.1)	398 (12.8)	407 (15.2)	1,593 (11.2)	1,583 (10.9)	831 (12.4)	769 (13.8)	1,593 (11.9)	1,462 (11.7)
35–44	879 (18.5)	611 (14.6)	1,850 (13.3)	1,497 (10.8)	172 (15.0)	130 (14.3)	678 (11.3)	645 (10.2)	496 (15.9)	378 (14.2)	1,775 (12.5)	1,745 (12.0)	952 (14.1)	766 (13.7)	1,618 (12.1)	1,421 (11.3)
45–54	430 (9.1)	275 (6.6)	1,626 (11.7)	1,525 (11.0)	128 (11.1)	55 (6.0)	806 (13.4)	735 (11.6)	281 (9.0)	175 (6.6)	1,946 (13.7)	1,918 (13.2)	636 (9.5)	405 (7.3)	1,490 (11.1)	1,272 (10.1)
55–64	140 (3.0)	77 (1.8)	1,462 (10.5)	1,496 (10.8)	33 (2.9)	14 (1.5)	729 (12.1)	804 (12.7)	71 (2.3)	49 (1.8)	1,656 (11.7)	1,701 (11.7)	225 (3.3)	104 (1.9)	1,167 (8.7)	1,074 (8.6)
65 or over	32 (0.7)	25 (0.6)	1,205 (8.7)	2,035 (14.6)	9 (0.8)	2 (0.2)	578 (9.6)	1,088 (17.1)	32 (1.0)	11 (0.4)	1,204 (8.5)	2,075 (14.3)	98 (1.5)	28 (0.5)	949 (7.1)	1,414 (11.3)
All ages	4,741 (100.0)	4,187 (100.0)	13,878 (100.0)	13,893 (100.0)	1,150 (100.0)	911 (100.0)	6,023 (100.0)	6,349 (100.0)	3,116 (100.0)	2,669 (100.0)	14,174 (100.0)	14,556 (100.0)	6,728 (100.0)	5,572 (100.0)	13,413 (100.0)	12,541 (100.0)

Source: Small Area Statistics, 1971 Census and Birmingham Statistics vol.18, 1973-5.

New Commonwealth origin. Of the 3,240 pensioners in the
Handsworth ward only 57 (1.8 per cent) fall into this New
Commonwealth group. We see a similar pattern in the other
wards: 0.7, 1.3 and 5.3 per cent in Newtown, Sandwell and
Soho respectively.

A glance at the other end of the age scale reveals the
second major pointer. In the Soho ward 2,249 (65.7 per
cent) of the 3,422 under-fives were of New Commonwealth
origin. The other wards tell a similar story, if slightly
less dramatically. Approximately 62 per cent of the
schoolchildren in Soho ward were black [4] as were 51 per
cent in the Handsworth ward, 34 per cent in Sandwell and
25 per cent in Newtown. [5] It is undoubtedly the case
that by the late 1970s the majority of the area's schoolchildren were descendants of the black immigrants to the
city.

We might summarise these two points, then, simply by
contrasting the age distributions of the immigrant and
indigenous sections of the ward populations; that of the
former group being skewed heavily in favour of the lower
age ranges. There is a third point, however, which should
not be forgotten. Men of New Commonwealth origin were
still (in 1971) greatly outnumbering their female counterparts and especially in the 35-54 age-range. To see why
this is so we need to reflect briefly on the recent history of Handsworth and in particular on the influence of
the post-war migration.

In the mood of rising expectations following the war,
young people began to look to the new satellite estates
springing up on the outskirts of the city. They offered
a new start (even if only in a symbolic sense), fresh air,
open spaces and greenery. These were all singularly
lacking in post-war Handsworth, an area which was already
rapidly converging towards a 'twilight zone' status. In
a very real sense then, the West Indian migrants who arrived in the 1950s began to fill a residential vacuum, as
has been suggested by Peach (1968). We thus have a
housing market situation parallel to the 'replacement-
labour' thesis. The older decaying housing vacated by the
indigenous population represented in turn the 'new start'
for the West Indian.

Importantly, also, it was in the main male immigrants
who made up the bulk of the early arrivals to Britain.
Large decaying Victorian properties had found a new lease
of life, as lodging houses (see Rex and Moore, 1967) or
flats and bedsitters. The immigrant was thereby provided
a base from which to accumulate capital. Families would
be supported in the home country, where the cost of living
was considerably lower than in Britain.

Many Asians, however, had other reasons for not wishing
to bring female kin over at that time. As Hiro argues:
[6]

An overwhelming majority of Asian settlers consider
English society morally decadent ... stories (such as
those of large numbers of unmarried mothers) in the
Indian language press in Britain confirm what Asian
settlers themselves see in parks, pubs, and streets and
on television. Apprehensive of the morally corrupting
climate many Pakistani males dread to bring their wives
and daughters to Britain.

The imbalance of the sexes is only gradually being eroded
with the uniting of families and the birth of the second
generation.

HOUSEHOLD SIZE AND STRUCTURE

We have seen something, then, of the basic demography of
Handsworth. To progress, however, beyond the overall
statistics and thereby examine the way in which people
from a number of distinct cultures have coped with life in
Britain, we need to look more closely at the lives of the
Handsworth residents we interviewed in 1976.

As might have been expected from our earlier discussion, there are marked differences in the age distributions of the British, Asian and West Indian heads of
household (see Table 2.5). Over a third of the Asians
were under 35 years of age compared with around one in
seven of the West Indians and even fewer of the British.
These differences are reflected in the median ages: for
the West Indians 44.7 (45.9), the Asians 40.6, and the
British 60.3 (61.0).

What really concerns us at this point, however, is the
difference in household structures. Is it the case, as
Krausz (1972) among others has argued, that West Indians
have in the main adopted or aspired to the Western nuclear
familial model? Further, to what extent has the Asian
forsaken the joint-family system, a central feature of
traditional culture, particularly among Sikhs? If the
joint family is indeed disappearing, the sociologist would
want to ask whether the change arose from essentially
practical considerations (e.g., overcrowding) or whether
there was a genuine desire to break with cultural and
social traditions (and, if so, why). [7]

If we begin by looking at the question of household
size (Table 2.6) we see, as might have been expected, that
there are marked differences in the patterns exhibited by
the three groups of residents.

TABLE 2.5 Age of head of household by ethnic group (weighted figures are bracketed)

	16-24	25-34	35-44	45-59	60-64	65 and over	Refused	Total sample size = 100%
West Indian %	4 (3)	12(10)	35(34)	39(42)	5 (5)	4 (4)	1 (2)	395(320)
Asian %	9	26	27	33	3	1	–	305
British %	3 (3)	11 (9)	12(11)	24(24)	13(13)	38(39)	–	400(327)

TABLE 2.6 Household size by ethnic group (weighted figures are bracketed)

	One	Two	Three	Four	Five and six	Seven to nine	Ten or more	Refused	Total sample size = 100%
West Indian %	5 (4)	12(12)	15(14)	17(16)	32(34)	16(17)	3 (2)	–	395(320)
Asian %	6	8	7	15	35	21	6	1	305
British %	22(24)	38(38)	20(20)	11(10)	7 (7)	2 (1)	1 (1)	–	400(327)

Nowhere are the divergences greater than among the smallest family sizes. According to the weighted figures, nearly a quarter of the British are living alone. These are in the main pensioners who have become widowed. In all, less than one in five of the British families is larger than three persons. By way of complete contrast we see that only a little more than one out of every five Asian families is not larger than three. In fact, 28 per cent of Asian households contain at least seven persons. As the table shows, the pattern of West Indian families lies somewhere between these two extremes.

These findings are broadly in agreement with those of a PEP research project reported in Smith (1977). Our figures for the mean household size of immigrant groups, 4.76(4.80) for the West Indians and 5.36 for the Asians, are rather higher than his (a reflection of the high concentration of these groups in Handsworth). These are, of course, well above the overall national figure, for as Smith points out: 'according to the 1971 census, the average household in England and Wales contains 2.86.' The white families in our sample, as might have been expected, produced a somewhat lower figure than this, namely 2.65(2.51). [8] Controlling for differences in the age structures of the three groups removes one important element of the variation in household size. Two major factors remain, however. First, immigrant groups have a higher (albeit declining) fertility rate than indigenous whites. Live births to West Indian parents in Birmingham fell dramatically from 1,416 in 1969 to 675 in 1973; 2,121 children were born to Indian parents in 1969, and although this rose to slightly over 2,300 the following year, the figure remained steady until 1973, [9] a period during which the population-at-risk was undoubtedly rising fairly rapidly.

Second, some immigrant groups, principally those from the Indian subcontinent, might exhibit a distinctive pattern of internal household structure. It is the latter point which, as Smith notes, accounts for much of the difference between the figures for the West Indians and Asians. The joint family, for example, represents an entity which, while correctly described as a single household (in the sense of representing a meaningful social unit) does, in fact, contain what from a Western viewpoint might be seen as a number of different families. (This raises an important definitional problem which undoubtedly has distinct methodological and ideological implications. [10]) On the basis of this proposition we would expect to find, in some cases, a large number of adults within a single household.

TABLE 2.7 Household structure by household size (weighted figures are bracketed)

A WEST INDIANS		One	Two	Three	Four	Five/six	Seven to nine	Ten or more	Total sample size = 100%
Living alone	%	100	-	-	-	-	-	-	18 (14)
Married couple (no children) [2]	%	-	100	-	-	-	-	-	29 (26)
Single person (with children) [1]	%	-	21(18)	24(17)	19(20)	28(32)	7(11)	1 (2)	68 (46)
Couple with children [2]	%	-	-	14(14)	19(18)	42(44)	21(21)	3 (3)	242(198)
Couple with children plus (relatives/friends) [2] [4] [7]	%	*	*	*	*	*	*	*	12 (12)
Three-/multi-generational family [3] [7]	%	*	*	*	*	*	*	*	3 (3)
Other	%	-	26(24)	43(48)	13(14)	13(10)	4 (5)	-	23 (21)
									395(320)

B ASIANS		One	Two	Three	Four	Five/ Six	Seven to nine	Ten or more	Re- fused	Total sample = 100%
Living alone	%	100	-	-	-	-	-	-	-	19
Married couple (no children) [2]	%	-	100	-	-	-	-	-	-	18
Single person (with children) [1] [7]	%	*	*	*	*	*	*	*	-	9
Couple with children [2]	%	-	-	8	20	44	24	3	+ [8]	210
Couple with children and relatives/ friends [2] [4]	%	-	-	-	10	29	24	33	5	21
Three-/multi- generational family [3]	%	-	-	-	-	39	33	22	6	18
Other [7]	%	*	*	*	*	*	*	*	*	10
										305

C BRITISH

		One	Two	Three	Four	Five/six	Seven to nine	Ten or more	Total sample size = 100%
Living alone	%	100	-	-	-	-	-	-	86 (79)
Married couple (no children) [2]	%	-	100	-	-	-	-	-	112 (90)
Single person (with children) [1]	%	-	47(51)	39(38)	10 (7)	4 (5)	-	-	51 (41)
Couple with children [2]	%	-	-	45(46)	29(30)	20(20)	5 (4)	1 (1)	103 (76)
Couple with children and (relatives/friends) [2] [4] [7]	%	*	*	*	*	*	*	*	4 (3)
Three-/multi-generational families [3] [7]	%	*	*	*	*	*	*	*	9 (5)
Other	%	-	43(42)	37(36)	11(12)	6 (6)	-	3 (3)	35 (33)
									400(327)

In all three tables:
1 'Single' includes widowed/separated, divorced.
2 'Married' and 'couples' include common-law 'spouse'.
3 This category includes three-/multi-generational families which also contain other relatives and/or friends.
4 'Relatives', in this case, excludes parents or grandparents. Such families fall within the category immediately below (i.e., the three-/multi-generational family).
5 'Children' are defined as aged 'less than 16'.
6 Brackets again indicate weighted figures.
7 Percentages would not be meaningful here since the sample size is so small. The overall figures are presented precisely because there are so few families in these categories.
8 + represents a figure of less than 0.5%.

We now explore in more detail the issue of household
structure and its relationship to physical numbers.
Table 2.7 enables us to look first at each of the ethnic
groups in isolation. Perhaps the major point to emerge
from Table 2.7A is that the majority of West Indian families take the form of a conventional nuclear family, i.e.,
couple plus children. Over three out of five households
were of this type. Only a handful were horizontally or
vertically extended (this is using the terminology of
Smith, 1977).

One disturbing feature to emerge from the analysis is
the very large proportion of single-parent families, corresponding to 17(14) per cent of the total. [11] As one
might have expected, the vast majority (90 per cent) of
those finding themselves in the position of supporting
(often large numbers of) children singlehanded are women.
A few had been widowed, but the overwhelming majority were
single or had suffered some form of marital breakdown.
What makes the figures all the more disturbing is that a
very high proportion of these households - 36.8 per cent
(45.1 per cent) - contained at least four children. Furthermore, it is unlikely that this is an isolated freak
result. In the course of previous research in London, the
author became aware of the high incidence of marital instability among West Indian households (Ratcliffe, 1971).
It was also apparent that the more pathological cases were
generally concentrated in pockets of the poorest housing
in what was, in any case, an area which was about to be
razed to the ground as part of a slum clearance programme.

As Smith (1977) points out, it is 'very rare indeed for
a lone parent to migrate with her children'. Most of the
children were either born here or came here as part of an
intact (nuclear) family. It is also argued that 'they
(the unsupported mothers) are therefore partly a product
of the social situation in this country rather than the
country of origin'. [12] There is a core of truth in
this, though much depends on the precise interpretation of
the word 'partly' and the term 'social situation'. The
one-parent family is by no means scarce in the West
Indies. It is a phenomenon which Krausz (1972) sees as
having distinct historical roots; in that 'traces of
slavery are still visible'. He argues further that: [13]

The rate of illegitimacy in Jamaica, for instance, is
70 per cent and this is accepted as a normal phenomenon. But those who came to Britain have definitely
moved in the direction of replacing the extended
matriarchal family with a nuclear type of family
grouping. This is giving rise in Britain to many
problems and sometimes tragic circumstances. The

relative deprived of the extended group may be left out
on a limb, or a child of an immigrant father may be
brought over to join a new family as a result of his
father's marrying another girl in Britain.

The 'social situation in this country' cannot, then, be
divorced from the structure of social relationships in the
home country and the historical legacies of colonialism.
It is not, however, suggested that the strains imposed by
a rejection of the extended family and the adoption of
what Krausz calls 'the European pattern of family life'
are the sole causes of this situation.   Structural forces
which have created the cycle of deprivation and become
manifest in terms of poor housing, poor education and
tedious, repetitive industrial work have undoubtedly
played a major part. [14]   It is, in some ways, perhaps
not surprising that the combined effects of these forces
are often greatest where the problems of adjustment to
single parenthood are potentially the most intractable.
Thus, in the current study, the mean number of children
is almost as high in the one-parent family as it is in the
two-parent situation.   In addition, the weighted figures
of 3.41 for the one-parent family and 3.51 for those with
two parents demonstrated that, as seen earlier, the number
of children per family was in both cases high, and also
concealed an element of polarisation in the distributions.
In particular, the proportion of families with four or
more children is actually slightly higher in the one-
parent family: 45 per cent as opposed to 42 per cent.

In direct contrast to this picture of familial instability, [15] the Asians exhibit a high degree of cohesiveness (at least in terms of family members remaining physically in the same household).   There are few one-parent
families, comprising only 3 per cent of the total.   In
reporting an even smaller figure (1 per cent) for the PEP
study, Smith (1977) makes the rather obvious point that
'having come to Britain comparatively recently, the Asian
women have had less time to become unsupported mothers'.
[16] He clearly realizes, however, that this is not the
major factor in accounting for the massive differential
between these two groups.   Although the relative incidence
of single parenthood (between the West Indians and Asians)
appears to be much less marked in Handsworth (approximately five to one compared with his thirteen to one) his conclusion remains valid;   namely, that this differential (in
relative incidence) 'must mainly reflect strong cultural
differences.' [17]   Where this argument is lacking is in
its failure to note the marked differences in the ways in
which these two major ethnic groups have adjusted to life
in Britain.   Many West Indians (initially at least) saw

themselves as British and wished, in Krausz's terms, to emulate 'the European pattern of family life'.

Asians, on the other hand, according to many writers such as Desai (1963) and Hiro (1973) have not thus far sought to adopt 'local' cultural norms. As has been noted earlier, many have tended to regard British society as morally repugnant, both in terms of sexual proclivities and in terms of the lack of respect shown to elders by the their children. This has resulted, if anything, in a strengthening of the internal responsibilities and obligations of family members, and especially those of the female children.

The one-parent family is an extremely rare phenomenon within the Asian community. Significantly also, none of the cases studied in Handsworth had come about as a result of illegitimacy or marital breakdown. Out of the eight cases, four were married men bringing up children in the absence of the mother, who had not yet been reunited with her family in Britain. The remainder had come about as a result of the deaths of the children's fathers. It is undoubtedly the case that there are few possibilities of extramarital sexual liaisons, given the restrictions placed on the social activities of Asian women (particularly Muslims). This fact raises an interesting point (taken up in Chapter 6) about the effects among future generations of the inevitable cultural conflict between what Hiro calls the 'liberal think-for-yourself' atmosphere of British schools [18] and the traditional culture of the homeland. As yet we can only speculate on the possible outcome of this conflict; though perhaps Hiro is correct in arguing that the most likely result of this 'culturally ambiguous' situation is the adoption by the young Asian of 'some aspects of Western culture and behaviour while retaining many of the traditional values and attitudes'. [19]

Returning to the survey data on Asian household structure (Table 2.7B) we see that the popular stereotype of the 'typical' Asian family is firmly refuted. The horizontally extended family comprising the basic nuclear unit supplemented by relatives (excluding those who are vertically related such as parents, grandparents, etc.) and/or friends is a scarce phenomenon; comprising, in fact, a mere 7 per cent of the total. In addition, the vertically extended (multi-generational) family was even more rare. Only 6 per cent of the households we studied were of this type. As these are much smaller figures than the ones quoted by Smith (1977), [20] we may strongly support his conclusion that 'it is a mistake to think that most Asians live together in large extended family units'. He argues further that:

The extended family system is far more common among
certain sections of the Asian population than among
others. Sikh households are particularly likely to
consist of extended families, and this is related to
a very high level of owner occupation among the group.
(Large enough houses could be obtained only through
owner occupation.)

There is undoubtedly some evidence that horizontally and
vertically extended families are more common among
Handsworth Sikhs than among the Hindus and Muslims. On
the other hand, the figures are not sufficiently conclu-
sive to argue that such families are 'far more common'
among Sikhs (15 per cent of such households are extended,
compared with 12 per cent of the Hindus and 10 per cent
among the Muslims). The above quote also hints at a
linkage between owner occupation and household structure.
It is unlikely, however, that Smith's assertion holds,
since, as we shall see in Chapter 4, the level of home
ownership is uniformly very high among Asians in
Handsworth. There is no evidence to suggest that household structure (or for that matter household size) is in
any statistical or substantive sense linked to housing
tenure.

Rather more difficult to assess, in terms of validity,
is the hypothesis in which Smith links socio-economic
group with household structure. It is suggested that
the extended family is largely a working-class phenomenon,
and further, that it is rare among white-collar families;
a reflection, he argues, of 'the general Westernisation of
middle-class Asians compared with the cultural confinement
of working-class Asians'. [21] By a priori reasoning it
seems likely that the middle-class Asian whose fluency in
English is rather better than that of his working-class
compatriot (and necessarily so, given his white-collar
role) might adopt certain aspects of the local culture.
After all, he does through his work tend to have a greater
degree of contact with native whites. On the other hand,
the greater economic and psychological security conferred
by a salaried job, for example, might simply mean that he
is able to avoid the problems of overcrowding suffered by
his less fortunate compatriots. [22] It may be that his
(extended) family may live in extremely close physical and
social proximity and still within a highly concentrated
and integrated Asian community. There may not, then, be
a major break with traditional cultural and social norms.
Whatever our conclusion on this particular issue, however,
it is a mistake to talk, as Smith does, about the 'looser
family structure which was the norm in the home country'.
[23] This may be a reflection of a Western value system

which idealises the nuclear family. The extension of a
household to incorporate more remote kin members in a
genealogical sense in no way implies that social roles
are more loosely defined, or that the structure is any
less tightly knit. On the contrary, mutual obligations
of family members are typically much more clearly defined
than in Western culture.

In addition to this essentially theoretical question,
there is the empirical one concerning the relationship
between occupational status and household structure among
those in the Handsworth study. It is here that we face
another major 'problem' - a 'problem', moreover, with many
dimensions. The fundamental point is that, complementing
the uniformity of tenure among Asians, we have an almost
exclusively working-class community. (Whether or not this
is a 'problem' in the sociological sense of a phenomenon
which merits explanation, will be tackled at a later point
in the book.) [24] Judging, however, by the few Asian
households whose head is in a white-collar occupation, we
have little evidence to support Smith's hypothesis.

Turning to the sample of whites, we have (in terms of
household structure) a very different picture. This
might, of course, have been expected, given the radically
different age structure of this population. Over a fifth
are old people living alone, and a somewhat larger figure
are married couples whose children have long since de-
parted. As with the West Indians, few families are of
the extended type; a mere 3(2) per cent of the total.
[25] Where these households do exist they tend to be
small and serve the joint functions of providing physical
and psychological support for elderly (usually widowed)
relatives.

The implications of these major differences in age
structure and household size and type will be seen more
clearly in subsequent chapters. A consideration of such
issues clearly provides a framework which enables us to
situate the family within a meaningful sociological context. Moreover, they help us to understand the individual's position vis-à-vis his society and the ways in
which structural forces in turn impose constraints on
his actions. In particular, for the minority groups,
there are implications for the life chances of their off-
spring in terms of access to key commodities such as education, employment and housing. In terms of the present
family, such factors have a distinct bearing on physical
and social mobility as well as on the economic or financial standing of the family.

As to economic standing, we note that among West Indian
families, for example, more than 60 per cent have at least

two wage-earners and approaching one in five have three or
more in this position. The Asians and the whites tended
to display a very similar pattern, at least on the surface. A little over a third of the Asians and approximately a third of the whites have two or more earners.
(Around one in ten of both groups have more than two in
employment.) The major differences here are not so much
the numbers who are working, but the person who is
working. Among the white (and West Indian) families where
there were two wage-earners it was usually the case that
both parents, the head of household and spouse, were
working. As we have already discussed, however, many
Asian men are unhappy about any situation where their
wives (and female kin in general) are brought into contact
with Western culture. The only case therefore where work
is acceptable is where his wife or daughter would be
working in an Asian environment. We notice then that in
Asian households it is often only the male members who
take on the role of wage-earner; for example, the head
of household plus eldest son(s) and/or a male relative
such as a brother or brother-in-law.

Understandably, economic imperatives occasionally
modify the pattern of adherence to traditional cultural
and social habits. First, as already noted, the majority
of Asian heads of household are in semi-skilled or un-
unskilled manual jobs and are thus at the bottom of the
socio-economic tree. Given the size of their families,
there is a strong incentive to increase the number of
wage-earners. Second, as we saw towards the end of
Chapter 1, a number of Asian families are incomplete and
have dependants overseas. In the absence of a clear commitment on the part of official agencies, telling them
when they will be permitted to emigrate to Britain, money
may be spent on lengthy trips to India or Pakistan. All
these circumstances impose an obligation on members of an
Asian family to earn money. Such obligations are, of
course, not new. Asian culture, in stressing the value
of the extended family, suppresses, or at least de-empha-
sises, the notion of individuality.

West Indian families in Handsworth face similar problems in terms of low-status occupations and heavy familial
obligations. Historically, the majority of those who came
to Britain from the Caribbean were drawn from the ranks of
the unskilled. What is disturbing is that (as we shall
see in Chapter 5) the majority are still in tedious, repetitive and generally undesirable work. More than three
out of every five West Indian heads of household in
Handsworth were found to have jobs which required little
in terms of acquired skills. Once again, therefore, there

is a strong incentive for a family to attempt to build up
its earning power by increasing the number of wage-
earners. This is not an easy thing to do when the national jobless total is topping the million mark [26] and
local unemployment is around 10 per cent. Nevertheless,
this was the harsh reality of the situation in the summer
of 1976 (when the fieldwork was conducted).

RELIGION, CULTURE AND SPATIAL PATTERNS

Up to this point, we have usually been talking about Asian
immigrants as if they constituted a socially and culturally homogeneous whole. This was done in order to simplify
presentation of the data and could be justified in the
light of the sort of data under discussion. In discussing
cultural aspects of settlement patterns, however, it is of
central importance to distinguish between such groups as
the Hindus, Muslims, Sikhs and possibly between less numerous ones such as the Parsees and Buddhists. Even among
West Indians, it is advisable to consider the nature of
religious affiliation in addition to island of origin when
discussing the relationship of an individual to his social
and cultural environment.
    Religion is, of course, only one element of the social
and cultural milieu within which the immigrant moves and
which he in turn modifies. The sociologist studying residents of a small urban area such as Handsworth needs to go
far beyond the conventional investigation of ethnicity as
implied by studies of family and kin-based relationships.
He needs to study the impact of the immigrant 'community'
in a number of ways. First, there is possibly the formation of a distinct local religious and cultural infrastructure. Second, he should look for the degree of
control which immigrants have over the local economy and
political institutions. Third, by adding a dynamic dimension he should assess the impact of the second and
third generation immigrant on this analysis. Finally,
in common with the overriding theme of this book, he needs
to recognise that none of this, interesting though it may
be in itself, is sociologically intelligible unless seen
within the context of historical and structural analysis.
    The principal concern of the remainder of the present
chapter is with the first of these issues; religion and
culture within the context of British urban society.
Points two and three will be dealt with exhaustively in
the final three chapters, first of all by looking at the
relationship between the immigrant and the housing and
labour markets. The final chapter then focuses on the

TABLE 2.8 Religion by country of origin (weighted figures are bracketed)

		Muslim	Hindu	Sikh	Church of England	Baptist/ Method- ist	Pente- costal/ Church of God	Roman Catho- lic	Other reli- gions	No reli- gion	Total sample size (= 100%)
Great Britain	%	–	–	–	74(71)	7 (8)	1 (2)	8 (8)	5 (5)	5 (6)	400(327)
India	%	5	38	49	3	1	–	1	1	2	243
Pakistan	%	90	2	5	–	–	–	–	2	–	42
'Other' Asian [1]	%	40	25	30	–	–	–	4	–	–	20
All Asians	%	19	32	41	3	1	–	1	1	2	305
Jamaica	%	–	–	–	19(21)	39(42)	18(17)	5 (5)	6 (6)	12(10)	331(275)
'Other' West Indies	%	–	–	–	39(40)	30(31)	11 (9)	–	6 (6)	14(13)	64 (45)
All West Indians	%	–	–	–	22(23)	38(40)	17(16)	4 (4)	6 (6)	12(10)	395(320)

1 As in Chapter 1 this term includes those born in the Indian subcontinent (but not in India or Pakistan) and those of Asian origin but born elsewhere, e.g., Africa. Care should be taken in interpreting these percentages because of the small sample size.

political infrastructure of the area, ranging from the 'party-political' (in the sense of affiliation and involvement) to the 'black-political' and 'self-help groups' such as the Indian Workers' Association, Afro-Caribbean Self-Help Organisation and the Harambee project. Throughout this analysis the emphasis will be on the social dynamics of the situation as implied by the third of the above points.

At present, then, we shall concern ourselves with the task of looking rather more closely at just who the immigrants are in our sample; at their origins, religion, culture and so on. It has been seen already (in Chapter 1) that a large majority of the 305 Asians interviewed were born in India [27] and that most of the 395 West Indians originate from the island of Jamaica. As religion is widely considered to be a major factor in the formation of clustering patterns of the Asian groups, we begin with this issue. Although West Indians are seen generally as forming systems of social relations which are colour-class and island-based rather than kin-caste and religion-based, this group are nevertheless included in Table 2.8 (largely because of the significance of 'religion' in a rather wider sense). For a similar reason, our British-born sample of 400 are also included.

As with Lawrence's (1974) Nottingham sample, a large proportion (almost a half) of the Indians interviewed were Sikhs. Apart from a handful of Muslims and Christians, all the remainder who claim to have a religion are Hindus. Since, as had been expected, over 90 per cent of those who were born in Pakistan are Muslims, we see that the three major religions of the Indian subcontinent (Islam, Hinduism and Sikhism) account for 93 per cent of our Handsworth sample. Given the central role of religion in Asian culture it is perhaps hardly surprising that only five people (all Indians) claimed to have no religion as compared with twenty of the British and forty West Indians.

It is true that the claim to a particular faith is not necessarily synonymous with the adherence to its religious principles either in theory or in practice. Many who espouse the label 'Church of England', for example, undoubtedly do so more out of a feeling for historical tradition and/or social convention than out of a reflection of current beliefs. Previous studies of religious practices in England (e.g., Martin, 1967) have demonstrated the unwillingness of those who might be described as 'lapsed Church of England' members to relinquish the label. With the exception of some village or quasi-village communities, religion, at least in terms of its outward social manifestations, plays a relatively minor

(and diminishing) role in contemporary British culture.
It is generally regarded as sufficient to simply exhibit
the label 'when required'.

To imply, however, that these religious labels may mean
little more to the Asian than they do to many 'Anglicans'
would be to deny the lasting significance of centuries of
history in the Indian subcontinent. There is unfortunately no space here to discuss the precise nature of religious conflict among the South Asian peoples (see
Community Relations Commission, 1973, for a useful intro-
ductory account). Suffice it to say that the deep divisions which led to the development of Sikhism as a break
from traditional Hinduism in the fifteenth century transcend both migration and the passage of time; similarly
the deep-rooted hostility between these groups and the
followers of Islam.

This is not to say that migration to the metropolis has
taken place without any modification of traditional religious and cultural norms. Sikhism, after all, was from
the outset a reaction against cultural rigidity and other-
worldly asceticism. Although alcohol and tobacco, for
example, are forbidden by the Holy Granth, many devout
Sikhs turn a blind eye to certain transgressions. It has
become a fact of life that many male [28] Sikhs frequent
the pubs and clubs of our major cities (including Handsworth), and as one elderly Sikh told me rather regretfully: 'Drink is strictly forbidden, but what can you do?'
Undoubtedly, however, the basic opposition to such behaviour is still very much in evidence and there are places
such as the large Indian club on the Soho Road, where prominent notices at the entrance explicitly forbid the consumption of both alcohol and tobacco.

Certain aspects of Asian culture appear even to have
been reinforced by the migration to an essentially urban
society, notably the Islamic practice [29] of purdah or
(female) seclusion. There was undoubtedly a severe sense
of social isolation felt by the Pakistani women studied by
Dahya in the Bradford of the early 1960s (Dahya, 1965).
As Banton (1972) points out: [30]

Purdah is ill-adapted to urban living. Unlike the Sikh
and Gujerati women, Pakistani women in Bradford did not
go out shopping or visiting either alone, or with women
neighbours. She went out, if she went out at all, with
her husband, who would walk a few paces ahead of her.
There was no accommodation for women at the mosque so
she could not participate in the religious life of the
community as she would in Pakistan.

Furthermore, as Khan (1977) has argued in the case of
Mirpuris: [31]

Contrary to the frequent assumption that traditional
forms of behaviour are bound to modify and become more
westernised in Britain, Mirpuri women are subject to a
stricter form of purdah (seclusion) than in the home
village ... (Mirpuri) women in Britain contribute less
to, and have less control over, the household income
due to the lack of home-centred economic activity and
the independent earning of their husbands. Besides
shopping in local Pakistani shops there are fewer
reasons to go outside and greater chance of interacting
with unrelated men.

The fundamental point is that even despite certain 're-
laxations' in the level of adherence to particular norms,
Asian 'religion' and culture are so deeply intertwined
that they jointly have a major influence on the social
scene of areas such as Handsworth. Thus the Sikh who re-
gularly visits his local pub and has dispensed with Keshes
(uncut hair) invariably retains his distinctive Sikh identity. As if to underline this point, discriminatory
treatment by whites has often resulted in a re-emergence
of unambiguous statements of ethnic identity, such as the
readoption of the turban by Sikhs in their late teens, and
early twenties (see for example the essay by the Ballards
in Watson, 1977).

In contrast to the indifference of the indigenous population to institutionalised religion, 'the church' is seen
by many to be of central importance to the West Indian in
Britain. In a detailed study of West Indian Pentecostalism, for example, Calley [32] argued that one reason for
the appeal of this church could be found in its members'
experiences of racial discrimination. The central feature
of Pentecostalism, ritual expression, contains a powerful
symbolic imagery. (On the other hand, as Calley admits,
one can take this line of argument too far.) Although the
congregations are not always exclusively West Indian, it
is from this sector of the population that most of the
congregation are drawn. [33] Because of this there is
often a specifically Caribbean flavour to such gatherings.
In the sense that they provide a source of identity it is
tempting to argue along with Banton (1972) that: 'in enabling the individual to adjust to a new situation they
contribute positively to majority-minority relations.'
[34] But here we have a contradiction. As Calley points
out, the satisfaction that a West Indian derives from belonging to the Pentecostal Church lies precisely in that
by doing so he is emphasising his divorce from 'society-
at-large'. Thus the new 'identity' might not necessarily
be one which leads to an improvement in 'majority-minority
relations'.

Having said this, there is little evidence in any case
that a large section of the Handsworth West Indian population are Pentecostalists. In our sample they are indeed
outnumbered by those who regard themselves as Anglican.
On the other hand, it is clear that the majority of West
Indians who admit to having a religion align themselves
with one of the nonconformist churches; i.e., Methodist,
Pentecostal, Baptist, Church of God, etc. Ivan Henry [35]
confirms this finding in his parallel research in Handsworth. In addition, almost one-fifth of his West Indian-
born respondents attended an Anglican church before coming
to Britain. It may well be, then, that the similar number
of Anglicans in our study are drawn largely from those who
have not changed their allegiances since coming to the UK
rather than those who have assimilated into the existing
local religious scene.

The acid test of the foregoing discussion, of course,
is the extent to which the religious label implies rather
more than the mere presentation of a religious mask. Conventionally in empirical studies, an indication of the
degree of 'religiosity' is taken to be the frequency of
attendance at a place of worship. The reasons for this
are easy to comprehend. First, it is easy to measure
(problems of reliability and validity apart). Second, an
organised religious service is not simply an occasion
where scriptures are read and their meanings internalised.
It is also a social event and is normally seen as such by
the majority of its participants. Hence, the ritualistic
elements of institutionalised religion are of great significance (although one should resist the temptation to
assume that there is in some sense a 'unity of meaning'
across the different groups, or for that matter within
groups). Despite this caveat, the general approach along
these lines can be illuminating. We have already seen
that within the Pentecostal faith there is a great emphasis on ritual; to this is added the 'social' ritual.
As Banton (1972) says of this group: 'They enjoy
dressing-up: they enjoy being the centre of attention
when they testify and preach: most of all they enjoy the
singing, the music and the good fellowship of their shared
worship.' [36] There is a strong emphasis then, on the
feeling of camaraderie, and of fellowship. In the
'dressing-up' one can detect rather more than the symbolic
shaking-off of the effects of the drab routine of everyday
(industrial) life, in rather the same way that any manual
worker might wish to dress up in a suit before going out
for an evening drink at the local. The act may be interpreted as a clear visual rejection of the conventional
'white' stereotype of the black immigrant: namely, 'his'

juxtaposition of the images 'black' and 'dirty'. In a
society where formal religious worship has been in a state
of sharp decline for a number of years, it is also a means
of conveying a message of superior spiritual purity.
These remarks apply as much to West Indian Baptists and
Methodists as to the Pentecostalists.

A major finding of Henry's study was the remarkable
change in the church-going activities of a sample in which
almost 90 per cent said that they had attended church at
least once a week in the West Indies. Only one person out
of 128 'never went to church'. It appears that the former
group now numbers less than one in five and about a third
are non-attenders. This transformation did not happen
overnight. Most continued their previous pattern of behaviour when they first arrived in Britain. Given that
this general picture is mirrored in the Pentecostal (and
other) sects, the question is whether or not it lends support to Banton's thesis that: 'In the early stages of
settlement the congregations form a buffer between the
minority and society. They help the member in difficulty
and provide a link with the homeland.' [37] The latter
implies a type of immigrant reception function for the
church, and suggests that because of this the dependency
of the individual on the institution might decline over a
period of time. It also implies, when taken with the
quotation considered a little earlier, that Pentecostalism
assumes the mantle of a community relations organisation
in helping to integrate the outsider into British society.
If this was so, then one could see the soundness of the
argument that this sect would ultimately become an accepted 'church' and very much part of the religious establishment.

Whilst accepting this conclusion, we could, however,
question the validity of the premise. We have already
seen that the church appeals precisely because it emphasises its distinctiveness from its British rivals. As
Hill (1971) argues, there is in addition a strong political force behind the growth of Pentecostalism. It may
well be that this growth will be stunted, not by the departure of West Indians duly socialised into the British
way of life, but by disillusionment resulting from a lack
of social and political (as well as spiritual) radicalism.
As is discussed in Chapter 6, the external pressures of
racism account for much of the development of black
consciousness and of groups such as the Rastafarians.
Moreover, we can draw a parallel between the wearing of
locks and a woolly hat, and the readoption of the turban
by young Sikhs.

Although more than half of Henry's sample spoke approvingly of Pentecostalism, a significant minority described it as 'corrupt and money-grabbing - just like any other business'; this being a clear reference to the requirement that members should contribute a proportion of their income to church funds. It had clearly suffered a decline in support in Handsworth over the years between the arrival of the immigrants and the present time. Interestingly, however, on the evidence of this study, it had been rather more successful in these terms than had most of the other churches and particularly the Church of England. Combining the findings of the two studies of West Indians in Handsworth (our own and that of Henry) it appears that the drift away from organised religion occurs relatively soon after coming to the UK.

Given the central position of religion within Asian culture, it is hardly surprising that this 'group' should exhibit a very much greater degree of participation in religious services than the British, for example. Amongst a largely 'Anglican' working-class urban population one would expect little such involvement. As we have already seen, the white population in Handsworth is an ageing one, the local youth having largely moved away in search of jobs and better housing. The degree of involvement in church activities for the present residents, then, will probably be influenced by two opposing factors: the usually greater commitment to religion of the aged and the lower level of physical mobility amongst such groups.

We should perhaps note at this point that in addition to the general problem of the over-reporting of religious involvement in order to win the approval of the interviewer, there are two analytical difficulties here. First, there is the issue of what is understood by the term 'place of worship', particularly by the Asian respondents. Then there is the theoretical problem of assessing the significance which each individual places on the act of attendance. It has already been noted that the social and cultural meanings vary both between and within ethnic and religious groups. The first issue is clearly the less problematic: even if some Asians include here a room set aside in their factory for (daily) worship, this will make little difference to the overall conclusions. In any case, most of the 41 per cent who attend 'at least' once a week say they do so only once and therefore this form of confusion is unlikely to occur to a significant degree. We face, then, the question of the subjective meanings attached by the individual to his act of worship (and being seen to worship); an issue which is further complicated by the fact that these meanings (and particularly their significance) are often barely (if at all) understood even by the participants themselves.

TABLE 2.9 Frequency of attendance at a place of worship by ethnic group (weighted figures are bracketed)

	At least once a week	Less often than once a week but at least once a month	Less than once a month	'Special oc- casions' only	Never	No re- ligion/ refused	Sample size (= 100%)
West Indian %	19(18)	9(11)	15(16)	30(31)	14(14)	12(10)	395(320)
Asian %	41	16	8	23	10	2	305
British %	12(13)	3 (3)	4 (5)	36(37)	39(34)	7 (8)	400(327)

A brief account of the background to West Indian church attendance has already been attempted. It has sometimes been argued that their general pattern of behaviour in this respect is beginning to move nearer to that of the indigenous population. There is certainly little evidence here to suggest that this is the case. Table 2.9 shows that approximately one in five West Indians go to a place of worship at least once a week (and Henry's findings confirm this figure). It has also been shown above that the general levels of attendance do not appear to change with length of residence; what is noticeable is a rapid change in behaviour soon after arrival in Britain. Henry's respondents in the main put the 'blame' for non-attendance on awkward shifts or the length of time they spend at work. However, a large proportion (nearly three in ten) said, interestingly, that they 'had grown out of it ... had rebelled'. One might argue that both of these reasons would be expected as 'typical' responses in studies of the indigenous population and are not specific to West Indians. This ignores one very important fact: migrants coming to the UK were not in the main youngsters. Most were in their twenties and thirties, many were approaching middle age. Thus 'growing out of' and 'rebelling' may take on a greater significance. Along the lines of previous arguments, it is likely that many saw, in their experience of organised religion in Britain, little relevance to their everyday lives within their new social milieu.

The Muslim, Hindu or Sikh in Handsworth is likely to take a very different view of organised worship. Since the first-generation Asian, at least, typically wishes to maintain the position of centrality traditionally accorded to religion, the act will take on a greater 'localised' meaning; i.e., to himself as a member of a particular religious group, family, kin-caste group, etc. Worship in the home will probably also play a much greater role in fulfilling his religious obligations than it would for most of his British or West Indian neighbours. Furthermore, attendance at a mosque or temple does not have quite the same social connotations as it has in Western or Caribbean culture. On the other hand, among Sikhs for example, presidency of the temple is a highly prized office. In fact, the kudos attached to it is often reflected in the fierce campaigns which can accompany the annual elections (Jenkins, 1971). It does, therefore, seem a little surprising that such a large number of Asians attend such a place on special occasions only (23 per cent), or never (10 per cent). Accessibility is no problem. There are a number of Sikh temples in Handsworth and in nearby areas such as Smethwick, and the important Hindu temple (the Shri Geeta Bhawa Madir) is situated on Heathfield Road. If we then discount as highly improbable a decline in religiosity, the most likely explanation is that many find their week almost totally committed to work (a thesis supported by the findings reported later in Chapter 5).

Following on from the points raised above, and given that religion and implicit social obligations vary great- ly, we now examine attendance practices rather more care- fully. Table 2.10 demonstrates the extent to which the 'public' religious behaviour of immigrant groups differs from that of the indigenous population. As expected, only a small proportion of the (largely) British-born 'Angli- cans' attend church at all frequently. Among the local white groups it is mainly the Roman Catholics, most of whom attend the Hunters Road Catholic Church of St Francis, who claim to maintain regular appearances. This particular church is a major centre for Irish activi- ty in north Birmingham and is very much more than simply a place of worship. With its regular dances and socials (in the attached hall) it has taken on very much the mantle of a community centre. This, combined with the stronger moral and social obligations typically implicit in the role of 'being a Catholic' as against, say, that of 'being an Anglican', may go some way towards explaining the observed picture.

Processes which are in some way similar are present in the case of Pentecostalism. Despite the generally low level of church attendance among West Indians, this sect proves the vital exception to the rule. A high level of commitment to religion and religious practices is expected of the member. He is not only required to support the church financially but also to adhere to a fairly strict moral code in his everyday life. Furthermore, an im- portant dimension of his faith is the act of ritual and particularly of collective ritual. It is this distinctive element which, as noted earlier, appeals to its largely working-class membership (cf. Calley, 1965). The approach is direct and emotional, and rejects the aloofness which pervades the atmosphere of many religious services. It appeals to the here and now rather than to the historical. Time and space are seen as uncritical entities. Religious events having vastly different temporal and spatial co- ordinates are transformed into current local events. Al- though relatively small in numbers (cf. Table 2.10), its members more than any other group commit a consistent amount of their time to worship. Nearly two-thirds attend church at least once a week. In fact, the vast majority

TABLE 2.10 Religion by frequency of attendance at a place of worship (weighted figures are bracketed)

		At least once a week	Less often than once a week but at least once a month	Less than once a month	'Special occasions' only	Never	No religion/ refused	Sample size (= 100%)
Muslim	%	45	15	-	32	8	-	60
Hindu	%	31	18	11	27	13	-	98
Sikh	%	48	16	9	19	8	-	126
Church of England	%	7 (8)	4 (5)	7 (8)	43(46)	36(31)	2 (3)	391(316)
Baptist/ Methodist	%	12(10)	14(16)	18(18)	34(35)	21(21)	1 (1)	180(157)
Pentecostal/ Church of God	%	65(64)	4 (5)	10 (9)	14(13)	7 (8)	-	72 (57)
Roman Catholic	%	36(35)	6 (4)	9(10)	21(20)	28(31)	-	53 (43)
Other	%	36(36)	4 (6)	9(11)	22(17)	29(31)	-	45 (36)
No religion/ refused	%	-	-	-	-	-	100.0	75 (59)

TABLE 2.11   Religious group of Asians by ward

		Sandwell	Soho 1	Soho 2	Handsworth	Newtown	Sample size (= 100%)
Muslim	%	3	20	20	33	23	60
Hindu	%	19	59	4	9	8	98
Sikh	%	21	65	4	5	5	126

of this group is made up of those who make more than a
single visit each week.

The case of the Asian religions is interesting. It may
well be that the sort of practical reasons for non-
attendance noted above might be a contributory factor in
depressing general levels of participation. A further
plausible explanation is that for many Asian peasants regular attendance at a mosque or temple might represent a
change in behaviour pattern, as many would not have had
access to such a building in their homeland. It is likely
that most Asian homes in Britain have a room with a shrine
set aside for prayer, and hence non-attendance at 'a place
of worship' does not, in itself, imply non-compliance with
religious obligations. In addition, the general level of
attendance appears to be high as compared with all but the
Pentecostalists. Perhaps the one surprising thing to come
out of Table 2.10 is the relatively low level of public
worship among the Hindus - surprising since, as pointed
out earlier, there is an important temple in Handsworth.
By way of contrast, nearly half of the Sikhs worship at
least once a week and the figure for the Muslims is only
a little smaller.

We now come to a question which has been implicit in
much of the earlier discussions: that of whether the
clustering of Asian groups appears to be related to religion and caste (and not simply to country of origin).
Table 2.11 deals with the first element of this: religion. Despite the inherent problems which the social
scientist faces in the use of arbitrary boundaries such
as those separating wards, [38] a clear pattern does
emerge here. There appear to be large concentrations of
Hindus and Sikhs in the Soho 1 ward, and most of the remainder of these two groups live in Sandwell. The
Muslims, on the other hand, display a much more dispersed
pattern of settlement. Interestingly, more than three-
quarters of this group are found in the three wards in
which few of the (predominantly Indian) Hindus and Sikhs
live. We see, then, that there is some evidence to suggest that these Asian groups do exhibit different spatial
patterns. [39] It is the Sikhs who display the most
marked tendency to concentrate in a small geographical
area. It would be a mistake to infer from this that 'religion' per se is the major determinant of these patterns.
As the groups were already concentrated in fairly distinct
geographical areas in the homeland, it may well be that
this regional distribution is simply transposed in an ap-
proximate form to the metropolis. There is, indeed, evidence to suggest that this is the case. It was often
clear that respondents were part of a highly integrated

local kin network. They sometimes reflected favourably also on the fact that their street contained a large number of fellow-Gujeratis or fellow-Punjabis. This settlement pattern undoubtedly acts as an important 'permissive' factor in the maintenance of traditional forms of social relations.

The question of the links between these patterns and caste is rather more intractable. First, by subdividing the religious groups and studying these in relation to small areas such as enumeration districts (EDs), we are dealing with very small samples; this makes it difficult to draw meaningful inferences. Second, and rather more interestingly, only half of the Asian sample were willing to label themselves as being of a particular caste. It is all the more interesting in the light of their very low refusal rates on the other questions. Many appeared genuinely baffled by the question. It is, of course, possible that the word 'caste' is simply not understood by a large number of Asians. Possible though this is, it is much more likely that many other factors were in operation here. Some writers, for example, Millar (1959) and Banton (1972), have correctly argued that, strictly speaking, only the Hindus (and possibly the Muslims) can be described as having a caste system. [40] Under this thesis our findings would not be surprising. This is misleading, however, since it would be almost inconceivable to envisage a situation where contemporary Asians had completely shaken off the socio-cultural heritage of many centuries. Although Sikhs, for example, have broken away from the traditional caste system of the Hindu, many social, economic and cultural divisions remain. These inequalities have been institutionalised in a form of social order (or social stratification) which retains many of the organic features of the caste system. Thus, Sikhs can be seen as being divided into groups, such as the high-ranking Brahmins and Khatris, the Jats (peasants) and Ramgharias or Tarkhans (craftsmen).

The interesting question for the sociologist is what happens when such groups are transposed into metropolitan society with its own (and rather different) system of stratification based on class. As noted already, first-generation Asian immigrants are largely seen as wishing to retain their traditional cultural identity. But what implications does this implicit rejection of acculturation carry for the ultimate retention of distinctions based on the notion of caste?

A number of 'castes' are linked to particular occupations such as carpentry or farming. In so far as these are areas in which few Asian immigrants are employed, one

might naively imagine that the concept would have become
redundant. This is not necessarily the case, as these
labels traditionally confer a social position which would
transcend a new occupational role and 'locally' ascribed
status. It is possible that members of the higher castes
might be loath to admit to an outsider that they were
(say) a Brahmin, in the light of their objective position
in British society (as seen in terms of such issues as employment and housing). But Banton (1972) goes as far as
to argue that: 'caste distinctions are not usually relevant to social relations in Britain'. [41] He substan-
tiates this by quoting Sharma's findings that, although a
great deal of respect is conferred on those of a high
caste, significant social encounters take place 'which
would be quite unthinkable in India' (Sharma, 1971). On
the other hand, it is extremely unlikely that many from
the lower castes will have been able to accumulate sufficient capital to enable them to emigrate to Britain, and
therefore this relative homogeneity might deceive one into
thinking that a major shift in social perspectives had
taken place. It may well be that deeply entrenched socio-
cultural values have undergone (and are still undergoing)
change within Asian communities in Britain, but it would
be a serious mistake to deduce from this that the question
of caste is unimportant. If, for whatever reason, considerations of caste do play little part in everyday social
interaction, we are witnessing something which embodies an
important unifying element; a unifying element which, as
Millar argues, is singularly lacking in the homeland. It
may well be that Hiro is correct in feeling that younger
Asians in particular are indeed becoming 'Westernised' in
important respects. Indeed, might it not be that 'caste'
for them is being replaced by 'class'?

These comments, the essence of which are followed up in
later chapters, are admittedly, firmly in the realm of
speculation. All we 'know' from the current study is that
only half of the Asians stated their 'caste'. Little can
be said definitively about the reasons for this; i.e.,
whether the matter is considered sensitive, irrelevant, or
whether, as suggested earlier, the word 'caste' is unknown
to many. True, it is possible to draw certain inferences
from the fact that few (9 per cent) actually argued that
they had 'no caste'. A similar figure refused outright;
most of the 'non-respondents' simply said they did not
know which caste they were. As might have been expected
given the historical factors noted above, Hindus were
rather more likely to answer the question than Muslims or
Sikhs.

Following up the point made towards the end of the pre-

vious paragraph, a slightly more detailed analysis was
performed. This concerned possible differences among that
group of people who, although born in the Indian subcontinent, were largely educated in Britain. We might expect
that young people would be more likely than others to
reject the notion of caste. After all, the Western view
would see it as singularly irrelevant to their life in
Britain. Interestingly, however, the Handsworth findings
lend only tentative support for this hypothesis (though
again it has to be admitted that the statement of one's
caste carries no evaluative implications; we do not know
what the notion of 'caste' means to the individual concerned).

To return to the original question of settlement
patterns, it seems likely that caste may play only a minor
part in their determination, except through the normal
operation of clustering due to chain migration (cf. Desai,
1963). (Social contacts and kin who migrate to join
fellow countrymen in Britain would undoubtedly tend to be
of the same caste.) We have seen, on the other hand, that
the three major Asian religious groups have very different
spatial distributions.

We would suggest in conclusion that whilst ethnically
distinct sub-groups exhibit a certain degree of spatial
clustering (and this information is interesting in sketch-
ing out a detailed ethnographic picture of an area such as
Handsworth), social relations are not necessarily constrained or facilitated by such patterns. The important
points for sociological analysis concern the precise
nature of these interactions between and within groups and
how the structure of social relations operates in a wider
structural context.

At the street level the 'community' appears to contain
a myriad of very distinct social groupings which rarely
have significant points of common contact. Only at a
superficial visual level do the startlingly beautiful
saris mingle with the brightly coloured hats of the young
Rastas, or the turbans with the trilby hats of the middle-
aged West Indians. Only in the same sense do greengrocers
selling Caribbean fruit blend in with the Muslim butcher
and Indian sweet centres and sari stores. Nor do traditionally 'neutral' points of social contact such as pubs
show much evidence of poly-ethnic relationships. We do
not need to be told that the white population is ageing
and in decline or that the level of black unemployment is
high (see Chapter 5). There are few whites to be seen -
mainly pensioners, yet dozens of young West Indians
hanging around outside the billiard hall and 'one-arm
bandit emporium'. Young whites and (to a lesser extent)

Asians lack a similar (or parallel) visual presence. At
the local 'political' level, organisations, as we shall
see in Chapter 6, tend to be run (in practice if not in
theory) on racial, religious or ethnic lines.

It is because of the importance which the author at-
taches to these ideas that much of what remains in this
book examines their implications. The whole of the next
chapter, for example, is devoted to an exploration of just
what the concept 'Handsworth' means to its residents. We
conclude the present chapter by providing a backdrop for
the later analysis, and in so doing tackle a major theme
noted as important earlier in the chapter: namely, the
implications of demographic analysis for the ethnic minorities.

ETHICAL AND POLITICAL IMPLICATIONS OF DEMOGRAPHIC ANALYSES

We have already remarked that the study of immigrant
numbers and concentration levels has major political implications. It could, however, be asked whether it really
has a significant influence on the everyday life of black
people living in areas such as Handsworth. In addition,
little has yet been said of the precise ways in which
demographic analysis can be used as a political weapon.

Prominent members of Birmingham City Council have frequently used demographic data to argue for a halt in immigration to the city. At a national level similar arguments have been used in debates on the immigration issue
and in forming legislation to curb the inflow of New
Commonwealth citizens. Two major issues tend to be dominant here: first, the current level of concentration of
black immigrants; and second, predicted future levels on
the basis of further immigration and fertility rates.

In a 1977 television interview, appropriately at the
scene of his 1968 speech (the Midland Hotel), Enoch Powell
once again raised the spectre of massive concentrations of
immigrants in the centre of British cities. [42] The implications are fourfold. First, this eventuality is seen
as posing a physical threat to the indigenous population,
along the lines of the US race riots. [43] In other
words, there is an implicit assumption that racial
tensions will increase. It is assumed, second, that the
larger the black population becomes, the smaller will be
the (individual) white's share of the fruits of Britain's
economic and social resources. Thus, competition (and, by
implication, unfair competition!) enters the arena. In
the field of employment, then, we find what Lawrence describes as an 'essentially Burkean notion' reflected in

the view of some of his respondents: for example, the
person who argued that, 'It's our country. I know some
blacks are born here but I still think the Englishman
should have priority.' [44] Thus, birthplace does not
necessarily confer upon the individual full rights of
citizenship. [45] Competition does not end here, of
course. The 'Englishman's' rights are also seen as being
threatened in the fields of housing and education, as will
be discussed in subsequent chapters.

Third, a major end-product of large concentrations of
(black) immigrants, living in what have been emotively
labelled 'ghetto' situations, is argued to be the 'inevitable' environmental decay. [46] Once again, therefore,
it is the black himself who is seen as the cause of social
evils. As in the case of the Victorian poor, who were
often regarded as the source of their own wretched state
by virtue of laziness, moral weakness and stupidity,
blacks are regarded as the lowest stratum of society and,
by implication, virtually beyond redemption. Hence, even
affirmative action programmes via political and social
initiatives are seen as ultimately pointless and wasteful.

Finally, the influx of those of an alien culture is
seen as a threat to the English way of life. It is assumed jingoistically that all external cultural influences
are to be rejected as inferior and are possibly, in any
case, symptoms of an uncivilised race. Such is the legacy
of a nation bred on the 'fruits' of Colonialism. However,
might these not also reflect a deep-rooted and unspoken
fear that perhaps at long last 'the sins of the fathers
will be visited upon their children'?

To a greater or lesser extent we believe that these
views inform the actions (not simply the prognostications)
of many in Britain today. This does not simply apply to
the group of working-class 'Alf Garnets' whom Lawrence saw
as Enoch Powell's major power base (a power base which has
since shifted to political organisations of the extreme
right). Much of the foregoing takes on the mantle of a
self-fulfilling prophecy. If it is assumed that blacks
form an inferior substratum or a societal 'lost cause' and
because of this no political action is taken, then dire
predictions of racial conflict will indeed be fulfilled.

Statistics can, of course, provide the ideologue with
a highly efficient means of transmitting propaganda which
masquerades as 'ultimate truth'. The figures themselves,
when presented in impressive detail, often assume the air
of incontestable facts and their sheer grandeur tends to
cloud the mind of unsuspecting recipients and veil the
intent of the presenter. To the layman an immigrant is
an immigrant is an immigrant. Hidden from him are the as-

sumptions behind what have become known colloquially as
'guestimates' and the definitional problems inherent in
immigration statistics. Confusion, even among official
government circles, amply attests to the complexity of
these issues.

In terms of current residents, for example, we must ask
whether we are referring to the population composed of
those with at least one or both parents born in the Indian
subcontinent or the Caribbean, or simply to those born in
these areas. [47] In the former cases, in particular, are
we then making any assumptions about the size of the
'enlarged' (black) population? If these assumptions involve projections on the basis of fertility we need to
query them in the light of evidence of social change such
as that outlined below. In terms of general immigration
figures, are we talking about net or gross arrivals from
overseas? The definition of 'arrival' is also complicated
by the fact that it sometimes includes those who are only
here on short-term work permits or those who come as
students with the intention of returning home when their
studies are completed. Moreover, a careful selection of
dates may also be used to maximum effect, as can the hypo-
thetical argument used by Enoch Powell in the television
interview mentioned above. Here it was suggested that
200,000 (extra) immigrants entered the country as a direct
result of the time delay in pushing the Conservative
Immigration Act of 1962 through Parliament.

Given the sort of strict controls on immigration which
are now in force, the focus of attention usually turns, if
not to an analysis of the dependency issue (as was suggested in the previous chapter), then to a comparison of
relative fertility rates. Professor Brass, in the course
of a television broadcast in which he was interestingly
introduced as a man 'with no political axe to grind'
(thereby emphasising concern with the emotive issues noted
above), argued that the 'average' West Indian (completed)
family size had declined rapidly over the past decade. By
1975 it was estimated that there were a little over two
children per West Indian family compared with a little
under two for the population as a whole. [48] A similarly
dramatic fall in fertility had occurred within Asian families, although the average number of children per family
was still approximately four. [49] This accords with the
Birmingham figures noted earlier.

One point issuing from this argument is the difference
in length of residence of these two major ethnic groups.
As we have seen, Asian immigration is a comparatively
recent phenomenon. It may well be that Asian fertility
will, within the coming decade, converge on the current

level of the remainder of the population, in line, perhaps, with the notion of 'culture lag' (Banks, 1954). The
question of why such an important modification in behaviour has already occurred, however, is probably rather
more interesting from a sociological point of view than is
the quantitative change, though the latter carries with
it, as has been suggested, major social and political implications.

Part of the explanation might be found in the shift
from a largely agrarian society to one which is heavily
industrialised. The importance of an extra pair of hands
to the subsistence farmer who depends almost totally on
manual labour is self-evident. Such social necessities
are perhaps less significant in contemporary Britain. On
the other hand, as will be seen in Chapter 5, large
numbers of our Handsworth sample were not originally
farmers (nor, incidentally, were their fathers). The
point of basic economic necessity however, remains, despite this caveat. Economic considerations (in terms of
financial support and housing) within an Asian or West
Indian family in Britain may influence them to limit their
numbers. In addition, it is undoubtedly the case that
family planning advice and support is rather more widely
available here than it is, say, in the rural Punjab (despite the policies of recent Indian governments). On the
other hand, mere availability does not imply effectiveness
in terms of reaching all sectors of our population.

A vital point in Professor Brass's argument was the
difference in age distributions of the different ethnic
groups. As seen earlier, a much larger proportion of the
indigenous population than either the West Indian or
Asian are in the older age groups. In terms of the
female population, much higher proportions of immigrants
are of child-bearing age. We would, therefore, expect
crude fertility rates [50] to be rather higher amongst
these groups. Irrespective of these facts, however, it
is nevertheless true to say that the marshalling of racist
arguments based on such demographic data is putting ever
greater pressure on our ethnic minority communities.

CONCLUDING NOTE

In this chapter we have seen how the ethnic composition of
Handsworth's population has changed over the last twenty
years or so. We have also seen a little of the changes in
the economic, religious and cultural infrastructure which
have accompanied these demographic changes.

All the evidence points to increasing concentrations of

blacks within the area, and, given the slowing down of government spending (national and local) which has taken place in 1979, the environmental prospects are not good. Continued physical decay is assured.

One would expect increased internal stress to result in a growth in cultural and political radicalism. But what do Handsworth residents themselves think of the area and how do members of the various ethnic groups feel about living in a multi-racial and poly-ethnic area? This, the subject of Chapter 3, should tell us much about the likely future of the area and its people.

3 Images of contemporary Handsworth

Much contemporary debate in the sociology of race relations in industrial societies has centred on a number of
issues. There is first the question of spatial distribution, considered in the previous chapter and by writers
such as Woods (1975). Second, following ideas developed
by urban sociologists of the Chicago school, and especially Park et al. (1923), interest has centred on the idea of
'zones of transition'. [1] This adds a dynamic historical
dimension to the (static) notion of spatiality and permits
an analysis of social change denited by more rigid, time-
bound studies of social milieux. Furthermore, when sensi-
tively applied, i.e., when one fails to be caught by the
critical fault of ecological determinism, it may also be
used to present fascinating sociological insights into the
political and social-structural forces which in part mould
contemporary society, and in part induce elements of
conflict into it. Others, such as Castells, focus on the
nature of urban social movements. A fourth approach to
the study of urban environment centres on tenure patterns
or, at a more explicitly sociological level, the relationship between differential degrees of access to the housing
market and social stratificational factors embodied in the
concept of class. [2] This and the idea of 'zonality'
will be discussed at length in Chapter 4.

The present chapter will concentrate on a much neglected area of the contemporary multi-racial scene: the
concept of urban imagery. Concerned as it is with the
theme of man's relationship with his environment (physical
and social), this analytical tool is, of course, in no
sense revolutionary. As pointed out earlier, however, the
actor's definition of his situation can be of immense
value to the sociologist in providing theoretical insights
into structural influences and constraints. It is not
argued that such an analysis can be divorced from, or sub-

97

stituted for, a study of the individual's position within
the social structure (in the broadest sense of the term)
or that it may be considered in isolation from the forms
of social relations between different sectors of society.
Indeed, it is precisely because the nature of an individual's social environment is such an important element of
the overall 'life image' that discussion of the relations
between the different racial and ethnic groups was cur-
tailed in the previous chapters. Much of the deferred
material is to be treated in some detail here.
We are not attempting in the present chapter to construct in some sense a picture of 'objective social
reality'. Our aims are rather to explore the subjective
notions implicit in the role of 'being a resident' of such
an area. In attempting to see Handsworth through the eyes
of those who are part of the local social scene, we hope,
for example, to explore the divergencies between the
theoretical notion of role ascription and the empirical
idea of role adoption. Such divergencies will be seen to
have serious implications for inter-racial harmony and
will highlight the historical and structural bases of
arguments which are at the centre of current racist
thinking.

HANDSWORTH AS A PLACE TO LIVE IN

We have already attempted to conjure up an outsider's view
of contemporary Handsworth. It is clear, however, that in
some ways the area totally belies its external image. The
label of 'slum', or more euphemistically 'twilight zone',
somehow conveys a feeling of darkness and despair which is
little in evidence. True, the physical appearance of
roads in Housing Action Areas (see Chapter 4) such as
Thornhill and Whitehall leaves a great deal to be desired.
On the other hand, it could be argued that many predominantly white working-class areas in Salford, Glasgow and
many other towns and cities are far worse. Moreover,
groups of houses with names such as 'Stoneleigh Villas'
still retain a certain elegance despite the ravages of
time. There is also clear evidence that many houses are,
in fact, being proudly looked after (and improved) by
their owners. But what do the residents themselves think
of the area?
When we explored the myriad of issues which formed the
individual's image of Handsworth, little of the questionnaire material was pre-coded. This approach has the
distinct advantage of permitting the respondent to choose
his own dimensions of experience and to indicate their

centrality to his overall perspective of life. In this
way we obtained a considerable amount of valuable qualitative material. This meant that, in addition to answers
to specific questions about the provision, for example, of
shops, transport and schools, and social environmental
factors such as quietness and public order (i.e., lack of
violence), respondents were given a free rein to express
their views about the locality in which they lived. We
now embark on an analysis of the difference in the response patterns of the three major ethnic groups and
relate these to their general feelings about racial
harmony (or, in many cases, disharmony).

The first point to make here relates to the general
mood of people in the area. Table 3.1 demonstrates quite
dramatically that white residents on the whole appear decidedly unhappy about life in Handsworth. As noted al-

TABLE 3.1   Attitudes towards life in Handsworth by ethnic
group (weighted figures are bracketed) [1]

		Like	Neither like nor dislike	Dislike	Don't know/ no answer	Total sample size (= 100%)
West Indian	%	67(63)	15(18)	16(18)	1 (1)	395(320)
Asian	%	83	5	12	* (1)	305
British	%	35(31)	18(20)	47(49)	* (1)	400(327)

1   *represents a figure of less than 0.5%.

ready, of course, we are essentially talking here about an
ageing population. The significant departure of young
whites which began in the immediate post-war period
gathered in pace during the 1960s and 1970s and it is undoubtedly the case that many of those who remain would
like to join the exodus. A closer examination of the
figures reveals that negative feelings are most common
among ageing owner-occupiers in areas with sizeable concentrations of immigrant groups, and lowest among those
living on the (largely white) Newtown council estate. [3]
Although this, taken by itself, tells us little (except by
implication) about the underlying reasons for this state
of affairs, a look at the workings of the housing market
provides some illuminating evidence which will be examined
in more detail later.

It is worth noting here, however, that, in addition to
reflecting the physical standard of housing and the gener-

al level of supply, the house pricing mechanism also takes account of prevailing social norms. It does so, in this instance, by reflecting the level of inter-racial hostility which already exists in the general population. The resulting deflation of prices in turn often has the effect of reinforcing racial tensions. The black is thus often seen not only as the cause of environmental decay (as we shall see shortly) but also as the major element in the depreciation of his (the white's) most valuable asset. Given that most blacks, as we shall see, are effectively competing at the lower end of the housing market, it is hardly surprising that it is largely decaying working-class areas which become areas of settlement. [4] The alienation of the white worker from his black counterpart is hence reinforced by the addition of this new dimension to the notion of 'the black as scapegoat'. It is for the reader to decide whether this is an integral aim of the economic system which produced it, to a large extent a concommitant factor, or simply an unintended consequence or by-product. Whatever the case, it undoubtedly has the effect of concentrating immigrant communities in localised geographical areas. An ageing white owner-occupier (in a working-class area) finding his house value thus affected has little option but to remain. For him the 'escape route' of a new mortgage is effectively blocked.

More than two in five of the whites interviewed nevertheless said they were thinking of moving out of the area. On the other hand, as was the case with many immigrants 'thinking' of returning to their homeland, there is evidence to suggest that this was more a measure of discontent than a valid predictor of future actions. Only one in ten of those thinking of moving were actually in the process of doing so; 31(14) white families [5] had applied to the council for a transfer to another area, and a further 22 had added their names to the council waiting list.

This sort of action poses a serious dilemma for local authorities committed to a policy of immigrant dispersal, as will be discussed in the following chapter. A further drifting away of whites will almost certainly heighten tensions among racial groups in the area, whichever position the council adopts. If it reserves the vacated accommodation for whites, it may find it difficult to let such property, and if it is let, the new residents may accept it reluctantly and harbour latent hostility. Local blacks may also become aware of the policy and react violently. If, on the other hand, the council specifically adopts a policy of letting such property to black families (and thus implicitly discards the notion of dispersal) this might provoke an angry reaction from present white residents. In these circumstances it is quite possible that the local authority would adopt a third stance: preserve the status quo and do nothing.

We have yet to establish, however, that the major element of discontent with life in Handsworth is a direct result of its multi-racial and multi-ethnic character. Indeed, the large difference between the weighted and unweighted figures quoted above (for the number of white council tenants wishing to move out of the area) demonstrates that a sizeable number of Newtown council residents wish to leave what is still a largely white estate. There may therefore be rather more to their feelings than, for example, a fear of black colonisation of the estate, or the increasing numbers in surrounding areas. We shall turn to this issue shortly, but first we will examine the strength of positive feelings about the area.

Although, as demonstrated by Table 3.1, the majority of whites seem dissatisfied with their lot, this is not the case for either of the immigrant groups, particularly the Asians. As many as 83 per cent of the Asians said that they liked Handsworth. To a certain extent this would have been expected from earlier analyses of this group's orientation towards life in Britain. In a material sense many have attained improvements in their standard of living by coming here. The tendency to retain traditional social and cultural values may create a view of life which discourages external material comparisons with majority society. In addition, of course, there are important elements of life experience which transcend the purely material.

In this context it is interesting to examine more closely the attitudes of the different groups towards the various facets of life in Handsworth. First of all they were asked generally about the features which they liked. As a glance at Table 3.2 indicates, the sort of answer given varies greatly between the different ethnic groups.

Clearly many were in a sense 'looking hard' for a good point about Handsworth, which perhaps accounts for the large numbers of all groups commenting favourably on the provision of amenities such as shops and public transport. What is particularly interesting is that whereas the British tended to select 'physical' attributes, both immigrant groups stressed 'social environmental' factors. Furthermore, discontent among the British seems widespread even among their 'positive' answers: 22(24) per cent, for example, claimed that there was nothing they liked, and a further 18(19) per cent expressed a mood of resigned acceptance, their commitment to the area being seen largely

TABLE 3.2 The single major positive feature of life in Handsworth by ethnic group (weighted figures are bracketed)

	Social en-vironment	Amenities	Convenient for work	Friends and/or relatives here	'Always lived here'/ 'used to it'	Other [1]	Total sample size (= 100%)
West Indian %	31(27)	25(24)	14(14)	4 (5)	8 (9)	18(20)	395(320)
Asian %	16	27	10	12	8	26	305
British %	12(13)	25(25)	11 (9)	6 (6)	18(19)	29(28)	400(327)

1 This category includes those who said there was 'nothing at all' they liked; a particularly frequent response among the British.

in terms of historical attachment. This is typified by
the comment, 'we've always lived here'. It is almost as
if it had been ordained by some supernatural force that
this is the part of the world in which they had been as-
signed a place for all time. In many cases, of course,
this undoubtedly represented a realistic appraisal of
their experiences and expectations. To someone who has
grown up within a largely working-class community, and has
built up strong emotional ties with his environment, resentment of social and physical change might surface in
this way. There are also, as noted earlier, external constraints on the individual's prospects of mobility which
can sow the seeds of latent hostility among the established white community.

Although co-victims of analogous structural forces,
blacks may present a convenient focal point for conflict.
In any society which has a history marked by class
struggles and the explicit (or, at times, implicit) acceptance of class divisions, this outcome is not unexpected. To the working-class white living in a 'twilight'
zone of a British city, there may seem to be only one
'solution' to his alienation from the more privileged
sectors of (white) society; this is, to relegate his
black neighbours to the position in the social structure
below himself - hence forming a 'new' under-class (cf.
Sivanandan, 1976; Rex and Tomlinson, 1979). The roots of
this role prescription have their ideological source in
the period of colonisation and subsequent nationalism. It
would be naive indeed for the social theorist to see the
(direct) 'cause' of racial conflict in the expression of
working-class prejudice (see below).

We have noted, then, that taken as a whole, Handsworth
whites find few positive things to say about the local
area; and where they do mention a particular issue, it
tends to relate to a 'physical' rather than 'social'
entity. [6] The West Indians, on the other hand, place
more emphasis on the social environment and in particular
on the 'friendliness' of the area. Since we discovered in
Chapter 1 that few were positively impressed by the
friendliness of their reception or subsequent treatment by
the white population, we must assume that the social relationships to which they are implicitly referring do not
usually involve local whites.

Asians also tend to select social relationships as the
most important plus factors. There is an important difference, however, between their responses and those of the
West Indians. The physical closeness of kin was often
stressed rather than a general experience of friendliness.
This might have been expected, of course, from the earlier

discussions of the Asian community in the previous
chapter. In particular, the 'area' referred to in the
question may well have been interpreted as the social
world in which the individual moves. As reflected in the
general picture of population movement and in the responses to this question, the whites are perhaps becoming
progressively isolated socially. This can be seen as resulting from the combined effect of a number of factors.
In addition to the exodus of the young and the undoubted
racial divisions, increasing age in itself exacerbates
physical and social detachment.

It is this social isolation on the part of the white
residents which manifests itself so clearly in the expression of disenchantment with life in Handsworth. Often
we found a sense of total alienation from the external
world; hostility tinged with feelings of helplessness and
despair. Naturally enough an analysis of subjective
images, however sophisticated, cannot in itself paint an
adequate picture of the multi-racial community as a whole.
For the present we confine our attention to the findings
of a set of questions which aimed to discover what people
disliked most about the area in which they lived. The
answers are summarised in Table 3.3.

As might have been expected, the major conclusions are
clear cut. There is a marked degree of consensus among
the white population that there are 'too many coloured
immigrants' in Handsworth and that these groups must take
the blame for the environmental decline of the area. Some
commentators would wish to argue that since a large majority of the white population were living in Handsworth when
the initial influx of immigrants began, judgment of historical events and processes should be left to them, and
them alone. This would involve a number of naive assumptions. One would entail the acceptance of the answers as
'statements of fact'. The respondent is thus seen as an
observer external to this particular social world and thus
devoid of value judgments. [7] To claim that there are
'too many coloureds' demonstrates a clear commitment to a
particular value stance. In an objectively defined (i.e.,
value-free) view of a social system such a statement is
devoid of meaning. [8]

Additionally there are a number of questions concerning
the notion of environmental decay. As we shall see shortly, the word 'environmental' has social as well as physical connotations. By definition, therefore, an observer
(researcher or resident) who is himself part of the social
world he is describing cannot objectively define the
notion of environmental decay in relation to the given
subject. Physical decay may to a certain extent permit

value-free analysis, but this leads us immediately to the
third area of assumption: may the 'cause' of decay be
'observed' without implicit reference to a series of value
constructs?   Even if we accept the premise that the area
has become subject to physical decay, we cannot empirically refute the hypothesis that the influx of immigrants was
merely a concommitant factor (indeed, there is much evidence to believe the latter to be the case).   Woods (1975)
suggests that Handsworth belongs to the group of areas
whose decline in social desirability began in the early
part of this century.   Many of the larger houses were occupied by wealthy professionals and businessmen who moved
out of the area when the spread of industrialisation and
its attendant requirement of small, numerous and cheap
houses for its manual labour force posed a threat to the
'social environment'.   Much of the remaining farmland, as
we saw earlier, had disappeared in this manner by the
early decades of the twentieth century.

TABLE 3.3   The major features of life in Handsworth which
members of the various ethnic groups disliked (weighted
figures are bracketed)

A   The 'most important' feature

	West Indians %	Asians %	British %
Physical decay of area	7 (8)	8	25 (27)
Too many coloureds/racial problem	5 (6)	5	35 (39)
Lack of (or poor) amenities	4 (4)	5	4 (3)
Environment	15 (14)	10	8 (7)
Vandalism/crime/violence	6 (7)	6	5 (5)
Neighbours or people in general	4 (4)	1	6 (5)
Children/delinquency	8 (8)	3	5 (3)
Other	6 (6)	2	3 (2)
Nothing	46 (43)	55	11 (10)
Don't know/refused	1 (1)	6	*(*) [1]
Total sample size (= 100%)	395 (320)	305	400 (327)

B Percentage of respondents mentioning a particular issue
[2]

	West Indians %		Asians %	British %	
Physical decay of area	21	(21)	18	35	(36)
Physical decay due to too many coloured people	4	(5)	5	36	(40)
Coloured people	3	(3)	2	21	(23)
Lack of (or poor) amenities	9	(8)	6	13	(11)
Neighbours/problem families	8	(8)	3	9	(9)
Children/delinquency	12	(13)	5	13	(10)
Vandals/crime/prostitution	10	(10)	11	19	(17)
Other	13	(13)	3	6	(5)
Nothing	46	(43)	55	11	(10)
Total sample size (= 100%)	395	(320)	305	400	(327)

1 *represents a figure of less than 0.5%.
2 A number of respondents gave more than one answer.
   Percentages therefore add up to more than 100%.

   Much of the available evidence points to a historical
re-enactment of this process of invasion and succession in
the case of the recent immigrant settlement. It is not
essential to the argument to establish whether there has
been, in Grodzin's terms, a 'tip point'. [9] We could
conceivably establish a point in time at which the white
exodus began to accelerate (though the temporal lags between successive sets of official statistics would create
analytical problems). The main point is that the replace-
ment by the urban working class of the nineteenth-century
middle-class residents of Handsworth is now seen to be
mirrored during the area's 'twilight' years by the re-
placement of the former by a new and predominantly black
or brown working class.
   The phrase 'during the area's twilight years' is in a
sense central to the present argument. Few would deny
that the survey area is in a state of physical decline.
Indeed, the local authority clearly accepts this (see
Chapter 4). There is, however, good reason for suspecting
that the perceived causal association of 'the blacks' with

this state of affairs is principally a reflection of the
level of hostility and prejudice within the white community. [10]

Although the major feature of Table 3.3 has been highlighted above, the general issue of 'social order' is also
seen as extremely important (and particularly so among the
whites). Moreover, the focus of concern appears to take
on four distinct forms. First, there are those who see
the 'problem of order' principally in terms of racial
conflict, actual or potential. A second group claims to
be disturbed by the level of vandalism, crime and (in a
few cases) prostitution in present-day Handsworth. To a
further group, youths are seen as the major problem.
Finally, there are a small number who talk in more specific terms about localised issues such as complaints
about neighbours or certain 'problem families'.

Table 3.3A clearly demonstrates the significance of the
first group. Of the white sample, 35(39) per cent regard
the volume of blacks as too great, and a large number of
these talk in terms of racial strife. Interestingly, such
comments were not exclusively the preserve of the whites.
A small number of West Indians also saw racial tensions as
the major concern. Among the Asians some agreed with the
British that there were too many blacks, i.e., West
Indians. This incidentally illustrates one point which
should not be forgotten in the discussion of relationships
between the white population and the coloured immigrants;
namely, that certain tensions exist between the various
ethnic groups which constitute the immigrants. This is
also, of course, true for the whites; a point which will
not have escaped the notice of those who have traced the
fortunes of the Irish community, for example.

We feel that it would be a mistake to suggest that
those in the three remaining response categories expressed
concerns which were, or were seen by them as being, independent of the question of race. It would be equally
wrong to claim that visions of racial conflict provided
the basis of most answers categorised in such a manner.
The validity of this argument will be partially tested in
the qualitative analysis to follow, but it is worth point-
ing out here that many respondents gave one of these 'non-
racial' answers as the secondary feature of an answer
which focused primarily on racial issues. Thus delinquency was often seen as a problem essentially concerning
'black youth', and for 'problem family' and 'neighbour'
we may sometimes, with reason, substitute the terms 'black
family' and 'black neighbour'.

Although the majority of the Asians studied appear to
be satisfied with life in Handsworth, a significant mi-

nority were disturbed by the level of violence and crime:
11 per cent mentioned this issue somewhere in their
answers. Few seemed to be worried by neighbours or by the
general issue of delinquency, a finding which might have
been predicted by our previous discussions. Given the
high level of clustering among the group as a whole, and
that of religious 'sub-communities' in particular, it is
highly likely that their neighbours will share many of
their cultural and religious values. In so far as the
latter continue to be predominantly influenced by traditional norms reinforced by the Asian community as a whole,
little conflict is to be expected. Further, on the (well
substantiated) assumption that many Asians interpret the
question specifically in terms of the Asian community (or
the Sikh, Hindu, or Muslim communities), delinquency is
hardly likely to be seen as a problem. There is a considerable body of evidence, for example, to suggest that
few Asian youths are involved in overt conflict with the
police. The major area of complaint by this group centred
on the physical environment; comparatively little overt
hostility on 'social' issues came to the surface.

As with the Asians, a central feature of West Indian
responses was the emphasis on physical decay. In contrast
to the Asians, however, approximately one out of every
eight West Indians mentioned somewhere in their reply that
'delinquency' was a serious problem, or at least, that
children were often difficult to control. This is particularly interesting since violence and crime in general
are seen by fewer people as being sufficiently serious to
be worthy of note. In addition it is often their own
children, or at least West Indian children in general, who
are the subject of attack. It is possible that much of
this concern derives from inter-generational conflict
alone. Further research in Handsworth has suggested, however, that this is a drastic over-simplification. Much of
the hostility among young second-generation blacks has
significant political and class-structural implications
(as is argued by Rex and Tomlinson (1979) and Chapter 6
of the present book). Although the West Indian father may
'see' the problem in terms of difficult children it would
be naive, we feel, to confine the discussion to this level
of analysis. For example, it seems highly likely that
lack of familial control is a 'permissive' as distinct
from a 'causal' factor.

We have already seen that a great many of the whites
used this question solely as a vehicle for airing their
feelings of hostility towards the immigrant. A further
important group noted their unhappiness about the physical
decline of the area while still linking this to the influx

of blacks. On the whole, then, physical considerations
now seem to take on a secondary role as compared with,
say, questions of 'public order'. In addition to overt
references to blacks, there is a great deal of concern
with delinquency, crime and violence. As Table 3.3B
shows, 13(10) per cent of the British sample [11] expressed their worries about the level of delinquency, and
an even larger group, 19(17) per cent, commented on vandalism, crime and violence in general. [12]

The overriding impression given by this data, then, is
an overwhelming degree of racial hostility on the part of
the white community combined with a general fear of, and
distaste for, the conflict and social tensions which are
evidenced by the sorts of issues discussed above. Very
few of the British sample (only about one in ten) found
nothing to dislike about their present life in Handsworth,
and it is the general feeling of resentment, particularly
in so far as it manifests itself in rejection of the
'newcomers', which merits further discussion.

A QUESTION OF RACIAL HARMONY

Before reflecting on the nature of racial prejudice (a
concept which appears to be central in much of the foregoing analysis) we ought perhaps to look at the general
state of race relations in Handsworth from the perspective
of those who live in the area. To do so we examine the
ways in which members of the three major ethnic groups re-
sponded to a question which asked how people of different
nationalities got on together.

Table 3.4 demonstrates just how marked were the differences in attitudes. Whereas almost two-thirds of the
Asians saw the races as living in harmony, only three out
of ten whites and much less than a half of the West
Indians agreed with this view. But perhaps the most significant factor is the very large number of whites (about
two-fifths) who argue that there are distinct (and
serious) 'racial problems'. Interestingly, the weighted
figures show a fairly marked increase in these feelings
of discontent. We can conclude from this that white
council tenants in Newtown are much more likely than
whites elsewhere to say that there are no racial problems.
It seems highly likely that the major reasons behind these
findings lie in the racial composition of the estate.
Council estimates put the number of blacks at present on
the estate as less than 10 per cent of the total. [13]
White residents, then, are living in an almost exclusively
white zone of Handsworth.

TABLE 3.4 Views concerning the present level of racial harmony by ethnic group (weighted figures are bracketed)

		Races get on well together	Races generally get on well but there are some problems	There are racial problems	Don't know/ did not answer	Sample size (= 100%)
West Indian	%	48 (43)	25 (28)	16 (18)	11 (11)	395 (320)
Asian	%	65	13	8	14	305
British	%	31 (29)	25 (25)	37 (39)	7 (7)	400 (327)

We would perhaps expect that the more recent arrivals
among the immigrant community would have become particularly aware of racial tensions. They are, after all,
young people who have sought employment and housing in a
period of rapidly worsening economic conditions. As we
have seen, they also came to Britain at a time when there
was much racial hostility on a national scale, this being
reinforced by the way in which the media generally treated
immigration issues. [14] The survey evidence offers a
considerable degree of support to this hypothesis. Among
both major immigrant groups it is predominantly those
under 35 who show the greatest awareness of racial problems. This is particularly the case among the Asians,
who, as we have seen, taken as a whole, feel that there
is a considerable degree of harmony. On the other hand,
there are dangers in reading too much into this finding
as it stands. The social and cultural isolation of much
of the Asian community leads to a rather insular view of
relationships between the different races. Attitudes to
such issues therefore tend to be rather personalised. In
other words, if the individual or the individual's kin
have not experienced 'racial problems', then such problems
are often deemed not to exist. Where social contacts between Asians and the other two major ethnic groups take
place it is likely that it would be younger Asians, especially those educated here, who would be involved. In
so far as the degree of ethnocentricity among the Asian
communities decreases in the ensuing decades, consciousness of racial tensions may become heightened.

The view which regarded the different races as 'getting
on well together' seemed to produce three major dimensions
of response. First, there were those who, as has already
been mentioned, personalised the issue. This included
members of all three ethnic groups who argued that they
had not experienced any problems or, perhaps that they had
a 'good' white (or coloured) neighbour. Few fell into the
latter category, but this group as a whole formed the vast
majority of those who felt that racial tensions were low.
A second group, and one which was relatively small numeri-
cally, reasoned that relations were harmonious because the
races didn't mix, a social variant of the Malthusian fertility principle. If people keep themselves to themselves, i.e., if social intercourse is minimised, then
conflict does not occur. A final, slightly less popular
view, was that people in Handsworth were on the whole
friendly and tolerant; that only a few caused trouble.

Where 'some problems' were admitted, most took the
fairly pragmatic stance seen above: that most people get
on well together and that it is a minority who cause

trouble. Others talked in a rather more philosophical
vein. These were the people who argued that there were
good and bad in all races, or that some problems were
caused by those who did not understand the implications of
cultural differences. The remainder almost exclusively
laid the blame for social tension firmly at the door of
the young, the blacks, or those who were unfortunate
enough to fall into both of these camps. On the whole it
was the Asian family man and the older members of the
white community, who share the cultural and social remoteness from white and black (West Indian) youth, who attacked this group.

In direct contrast to the fairly muted hostility expressed by these respondents was a sizeable minority of
the total sample who felt that relations between the different racial groups were anything but harmonious (see
Table 3.4). The most frequently expressed view here was
that some groups, such as the West Indians and Irish, are
in direct conflict. Furthermore, a large group interpreted the situation as simply a conflict between blacks
and whites. Ethnic origin is thus unimportant. The
'labelling effect' is total; it is now no longer accepted
that conflict is a localised issue, confined to small
numbers of dissidents. 'Different cultures' were seen by
many as the most significant problem, though 'culture'
here was mainly being used by whites to imply 'inferior
standards'. Blacks were attacked for lowering the respectability of the area, for not fulfilling the obligations or expectations of the 'British way of life'.

A not insignificant number of whites felt that the
problems were rooted in the arrogance of the blacks. The
causal chain was not questioned, the source of hostility
was assumed to be inherent in the 'black mentality'. A
final group simply gave a rather dour prediction for the
future: these were people who claimed to have experienced
racial conflict and who felt that 'things were getting
worse'.

RACIAL PREJUDICE: A PERSONALITY ATTRIBUTE?

A central, and sometimes implicit, feature of the current
analysis has been the concept of 'prejudice'. Some commentators (the present author excluded) have gone as far
as to imply that 'studies of race relations' and 'studies
of racial prejudice' are virtually equivalent enterprises.
It is the author's view that although any sociological
analysis of a multi-racial community presupposes an understanding of the subjective perceptions of the actors in-

volved, a broader analysis involving historical and social structural considerations is necessary. Moreover, the whole debate is so central to what follows in this book, that we devote some space to it at this point.

The study of race relations, especially in the 1950s and 1960s, appeared often to be heavily influenced by the works of Adorno and his colleagues. In their view: [15]

Although personality is a product of the social environment of the past, it is not, once it has developed, a mere object of the contemporary environment. What has developed is a structure within the individual, something which is capable of self-initiated action upon the social environment and of selection with respect to impinging stimuli, something which although modifiable is frequently very resistant to fundamental change.

This approach owes much historically to the ethology of John Stuart Mill, except that it more explicitly permits modification in the personality by the social environment (at least before the latter has developed). [16] He is, however, open to the criticism that his approach has, like Mill's, a strong element of psychologism: modes of social action can be reduced to the level of an individual's psychological, (or at least) personality, make-up. As Rex and Moore (1967) argue: [17]

Prejudice is thus held to be one aspect of the working of a disturbed authoritarian personality. It is a phenomenon to be found in a mentally disturbed minority.

More recent definitions of prejudice have often stressed the importance of 'processes within the individual'. In the words of one influential social psychologist, Marie Jahoda, for example: [18]

Prejudice is a negative unfavourable attitude towards a group or its individual members; it is characterised by stereotyped beliefs; the attitude results from processes within the bearer of the attitude rather than from the reality testing of the attributes of the group in question.

Thus, objective reality is distorted by inner processes and this distortion manifests itself in (observable) entities which are the products of, or subject to, stereotyping. Deakin, in reporting on the incidence and form of 'Racial Prejudice in Britain', [19] appears to realize, correctly in our view, that a sociologically meaningful analysis of prejudice involves social-structural issues beyond the stated attitudes of a sample of individuals. He does so by explicitly excluding Britain from the following remark: 'In a society completely free of ethnic stratification, racial hostility might be regarded as a personal observation and not a social force worthy of sociological investigation'. [20] Unfortunately, from this point onwards, he ignores the implications of this remark for a study of prejudice in Britain. In fact, in the next sentence his major concern is that, given that 'the (racial) climate is in a state of flux', there are 'limitations upon the degree of accuracy in the measurement of prejudice'. Concern with structural issues, then, is replaced by a concern with the 'accuracy' (i.e., validity) of measurement.

Other writers have adopted definitions of prejudice which do not involve any reference to the actor's definition of his situation. Oliver C.Cox, for example, sees prejudice as a 'social attitude propagated among the public by an exploiting class for the purpose of stigmatising some group inferior so that the exploitation of either the group or its resources or both may be justified'. [21] The concept is thus seen not merely in terms of something which arises independently of individual personality traits. It is seen as resulting from structural forces external to the individual's consciousness. Racial conflict in this view emanates from the manifestation of deliberately exploitative policies of the ruling class. Cox would presumably align himself with those who would support the first thesis in my discussion of housing market forces earlier in this chapter, that conflict may be seen as an aim of the economic system which produced it.

As Lawrence argues, these definitions reflect 'different theoretical positions' and not simply differences in 'terminology'. [22] He is incorrect, however, when he argues that Abrams (in Rose et al., 1969) 'does not make his theoretical position explicit', at least, that is, if we assume that Abrams and his colleagues shared a common perspective. Alan Marsh, for example, opens his re-analysis of Abrams's data [23] with Jahoda's definition of prejudice which was discussed above. Despite the early reference to structural issues, their analysis remains consistently true to the research paradigm which C.Wright Mills has termed 'abstracted empiricism'. [24] Not only is the analysis devoid of historical and structural considerations, it also bases much of the analysis on a small number of 'key' questions. The indicators of 'prejudice', as Lawrence points out, first of all stem from a rather narrow view of the substantive foci of such an issue. [25] Second, the researchers display a lack of consistency when generating the 'results' from their initial definitions of prejudice. In particular, Abrams fails to justify his as-

assertion that those who are labelled 'prejudiced' [26] display these attributes as a result of their 'irrational solutions to personality inadequacies'.

Furthermore, a similar objection should be raised to their discussion relating 'authoritarianism' to 'prejudice'. Starting from Adorno's definition of the 'authoritarian personality', he uses six questions in order to categorise people as 'high' or 'low' on the 'authoritarianism' scale. [27] Marsh argues that 'these two factors (authoritarianism and prejudice) are almost certainly related'. [28] Unfortunately, however, there is a failure in theoretical terms to link these two issues at the definitional level and also an unconvincing justification of this statement as an empirical 'fact'. An examination of his Table 2.3 [29] shows that 30 per cent of his 527 'high authoritarians' as against 39 per cent of his much smaller sample of 282 'low authoritarians' gave no hostile answers (to the test questions on 'prejudice'). There is an implicit suggestion in his report that the two concepts are causally related. If this was the case we would hardly expect this degree of 'similarity' in these results. Why, for example, do such a high proportion of high authoritarians exhibit 'no overt prejudice' (in his terms)? In addition, as Lawrence points out [30] only one third of the 10 per cent prejudiced, 24, were classified as authoritarians.

A third major criticism which may be levelled at their approach is its dependence on 'personality', i.e., the characteristics of individual members of society. Lawrence (1974) argues that: [31]

> It cannot be denied that unfavourable attitudes can arise from basic personality processes or that they may fulfil a specific irrational function for those who use them. But they arise in other, no less important ways, and can and do serve other functions.

Perhaps largely as a result of the public debate between Lawrence, Abrams and John Rowan, [32] Marsh at one point drops his veneer of methodological inhibition. In discussing his scale of prejudice he admits that: [33]

> It must be emphasised at once that this is not an absolute scale, but a relative judgment made by the social scientists concerned, in the light of their analysis. One cannot be dogmatic about the degree to which these categories correspond with reality because 'reality' in this context is ultimately dependent upon the value system in our society.

He clearly recognises a chink in his armour, but unfortunately fails to appreciate its significance and therefore takes little remedial action in his analysis. In particu-

lar, no discussion of 'value systems' [34] follows this
statement. It is crucial to realise that, borrowing a
phrase from his (or rather Jahoda's) definition of preju-
duce, 'reality testing' involves a consideration of
structural issues far beyond the subjectively interpreted
sense impression data of social actors.

Rose et al. may, finally, be criticised on the grounds
that a measure of apparent arbitrariness creeps into the
labelling of categories and the construction of their
indices. A comparison of the original publication by Rose
and associates (1969) and the abridged version by Deakin
(1970) reveals interesting differences, for example, in
the categories of prejudice. It was clearly felt that describing those who gave no hostile answers as 'tolerant'
and those who gave one hostile answer as 'tolerant-
inclined' might, in Lawrence's words, be 'potentially misleading'. These were therefore labelled as 'showing no
overt prejudice' and 'middling-prejudiced' respectively in
the revised account. Similarly, the 'prejudiced-inclined'
became the 'prejudiced', and the 'prejudiced' became
'intensely prejudiced'. This tells us a great deal about
the ability and willingness of social scientists to create,
by 'sleight of hand' an apparently different perspective.
None of the empirical details have changed, but a seemingly radical conceptual reappraisal has taken place. The
implications for the social scientist are clearly wide-
ranging. Equally important are the comments made by
Lawrence on the nature of indices; i.e., the question of
the initial measurement process and the weightings given
to particular responses in the final index. He demonstrates clearly that by imposing different assumptions on
the analysis, radically different 'conclusions' follow.
[35]

It is hoped that the reader will forgive this rather
lengthy excursus on what are essentially methodological
issues. We feel, however, that it is necessary to clarify
the ways in which our conception of prejudice and the relation between the theoretical and the empirical differ
from those we have seen. It is our opinion that, although
the incidence of racial hostility and of prejudice may be
located in the individual, the underlying causes are to be
determined not by an examination of individual personality
traits (however methodologically refined) but by a study
of the inner dynamics of social structure. Individual accounts of (for example) hostility to blacks are therefore
used to highlight structural issues rather than to tell us
something about the individual as such. In a sense we are
implicitly combining the analysis of 'those unfavourable
attitudes which involve prejudgment of groups and members

of groups regardless of how they have arisen', [36] with
the mood of Cox's position, if not a total commitment to
it.

We have not in any sense attempted to construct indices
of prejudice. To do so implies that there is some underlying theoretical rationale for constructing a uni-dimen-
sional scale from a series of multi-dimensional items.
[37] There is an important distinction also between the
sorts of question which we asked and those used in
Abrams's research. Little overt reference was made in our
questionnaire to 'other nationalities', let alone 'immigrants'. Whereas Abrams focused his questions specifically on racial issues, thereby providing a meaning structure
within which respondents were simply to be located, our
questions were much less focused. Hence the question
around which much of the discussion in this chapter
centres, asks about 'life in Handsworth' in general terms
[38] and not about a respondent's views of other nationalities. [39]

In many ways it is this methodological distinction
which makes our findings all the more disturbing. We have
seen already that (employing the weighted figures) almost
two out of five whites expressed their dislike of coloured
immigrants; indeed, this group saw blacks as the single
major 'fact of life' in Handsworth which they disliked
(see Table 3.3). This figure becomes even larger if we
include those who regard 'race' as an important but secondary concern. To those who would argue that it is a
mistake to pay much attention to these verbal expressions
of hostility, we only have to point to the recent serious
outbreaks of racial violence in the run-up to the 1977
Ladywood by-election (a by-election brought about by the
departure of Labour MP Brian Waldron to a European Commission appointment). Serious fighting accompanied a
National Front meeting in Handsworth and produced head-
lines in the local press which proclaimed 'Street Warfare
in Ladywood' and 'Police Station Siege by 400 is repel-
led'. As Layton-Henry and Taylor wrote in an article published in the week following the election: [40]

The events at Lewisham [41] and Ladywood have put race
back into the forefront of British politics.

The success of the National Front in gaining 5.7 per
cent of the total poll – probably more than 10 per cent
of the votes of non-immigrant electors – would appear
to be consistent with some kind of racial backlash
among whites.

This, combined with our own findings, paints a rather
different picture of the racial climate than that conjured

up by Abrams. As Lawrence remarks: 'taken at their face
value these (Abrams's) findings would seem to augur well
for race relations in Nottingham and elsewhere'. [42]
Press comment seemed to reinforce this optimistic view.
It was generally felt that the vast majority of whites
held attitudes which were consistent with a harmonious
system of social relations between the different racial
and ethnic groups in Britain (or at least that there was
a high degree of tolerance). Few today, we believe, would
support this thesis. In addition to the methodological
weakness of Abrams's work, which may have helped to conceal crucial elements of the race situation, there are, of
course, many factors which have contributed to the need
for a radical reassessment of this assumed state of affairs. In the decade since Abrams's survey was conducted,
and more especially after 1971, we saw a recession of
mammoth proportions: unemployment levels soared, and a
general fall in living standards was felt. The implications for the immigrant communities in economic and social
terms are particularly serious, as will be shown in
Chapter 5. Politicians, professional commentators, and
lay observers alike, cannot fail to perceive a radical
change in the importance of race as a political issue.
'Public order' has once again reared its head in the context (importantly) of inter-racial hostility. The final
chapter has therefore been devoted largely to a more detailed assessment of these 'political' issues.

As will have become evident by now, the author believes
that it is a theoretical abstraction to treat the above
issues as somehow distinct entities. Sociologists, along
with professional economists and political scientists, are
often guilty of doing just that. An adequate sociological
analysis of the position of racial and ethnic minorities
in relation to their access to housing, employment, education and political representation must be seen in a
holistic fashion. Our account throughout this and the
following chapters therefore takes on the form of a single
(if rather complex) picture in which the various features
are brought into sharper focus in sequence.

RACIAL DISHARMONY AND TERRITORIAL ATTACHMENT

For the remainder of the present chapter we examine ways
in which 'prejudice' manifests itself among Handsworth's
white population. We attempt also to explain why stated
views emerge in particular ways. Qualitative material
presented so far, for example, has suggested that many
ageing white residents have an obvious emotional commit-

ment to 'their' area;   many own property and have done for
many years.   We begin by asking whether these factors
offer any clues to the racial tension which undoubtedly
exists.

In discussing the area up to this point we have tended
to assume, implicitly at least, that we are talking about
a stable working-class white population which has over the
years been denuded of its younger members.   We have not,
however, formally established that a large proportion of
the present white residents have, in fact, lived there for
a substantial length of time.   Table 3.5 corrects this
omission.

We see immediately that the vast majority of those we
spoke to were well established 'Brummies'.   Well over 90
per cent had lived there for at least twenty years.   Furthermore, a glance at Table 3.5A shows the rather interesting picture which emerged when we asked how long they
had lived at the present address.   Even the unweighted
figures display a remarkable degree of immobility;   a
little over a half the residents having lived in their
present residence for at least ten years.   In the weighted
figures this sector of the white population rises to 63
per cent.   The contrast is particularly marked among those
who had not moved house within the previous twenty years.
It is fairly easy to see why this is the case: a large
number of the 'movers' were in fact taking up relatively
modern accommodation on the Newtown Housing Estate.

This may not in itself seem particularly significant in
terms of our overall analysis.   Such a conclusion, however, would be rather short-sighted.   We saw earlier in
this chapter that the degree of immobility heavily influenced the individuals' perception of Handsworth.   We now
know also, for example, that mobility is considerably
lower outside Newtown;   i.e., in the wards in which immigrant concentration is comparatively high (a point which
will be followed up shortly).

It is also interesting to note the areas from which the
'movers' came.   As Table 3.5B shows, approximately three
out of every five of those who had moved house in the
previous ten years came either from within the survey area
itself or from wards whose boundaries are contiguous with
the survey area.   Indeed, many of the remainder had travelled only a few miles to their new home.   Once again we
should note the difference between the weighted and unweighted figures, particularly in the 'within survey area'
category.   The larger weighted figures indicated a slight
strengthening of the 'immobility thesis' in that council
tenants from outside the area concealed to some extent the
degree of internal movement within other sectors of the
housing market.

TABLE 3.5   Residential mobility of white respondents (weighted figures are bracketed)

A

	Less than 1 year	1 year but less than 5 years	5 years but less than 10 years	10 years but less than 20 years	20 years or more	Total sample size (= 100%)
Length of residence in Birmingham %	1 (1)	2 (2)	2 (3)	3 (3)	93(91)	400(327)
Length of residence at present address %	8 (9)	19(14)	22(15)	14(17)	37(46)	400(327)

B   Area of previous address for those who have moved within the last ten years

	Within survey area [1]	Within wards contiguous with survey area [2]	Elsewhere in Birmingham (including 'area not stated')	Total sample size (= 100%)
Previous address %	38(43)	23(18)	40(40)	197(124)

1   This category includes Handsworth, Lozells and Newtown.
2   We are talking here essentially about areas such as Aston, Perry Barr, Handsworth Wood and Ladywood.

Given this lack of movement it is hardly surprising that older white residents often expressed a deep sense of emotional attachment to the area (or at least to the area as it was in their youth). A similar impression is conveyed by Rex and Moore in relation to Sparkbrook. [43]

In the same way that Asians often interpreted references to 'the area' as 'the local Asian community' (or alternatively the local Muslim, Sikh or Hindu communities) it was felt that the whites might think in slightly more localised terms than, for example, the researcher's conception of 'Handsworth'. There are indeed sound reasons for suggesting that our 'Handsworth' constitutes an amalgamation of a number of sub-areas with separate and quite distinct identities. This is so despite the fact that Soho Road, with its large number of shops, in a sense provides a sort of social focal point for the area. One result of this realisation is that we are presented with an analytical problem: we have answers couched in terms of what might be a myriad of undefined, and often indefinable, notions of 'area'. These subjective 'taken-for-granted' notions arguably bear little relation to empirically definable labels such as 'wards'. However, on reflection, it will be seen that these objections, though valid within their own terms, need not seriously concern us. For one thing wards (or some such measure) provide us with the only feasible solution in analytical terms. For another, if we take them to their logical conclusion we might produce a series of subjectively defined areas which are as numerous as the number of respondents! On the positive side, we do at least have a reaction to the actor's physical and social environment, however the latter is perceived and defined.

These matters do concern us, since a central feature of the individual's social world may well be his immediate environment. It was suggested also at the beginning of the present section that housing tenure may also be a key issue in the sense that an owner-occupier would have a vested interest in the area. [44] From these and earlier remarks, then, we might wish to advance the hypotheses (a) that overt verbal hostility to blacks is greatest in the areas in which their concentrations are heaviest; and (b) that this hostility would be particularly noticeable among, for example, owner-occupiers who had lived in the area for a long time.

Unfortunately, a detailed comparative analysis is rather difficult here, since there are few council tenants in all but the Newtown ward, and few private renters except in Soho. With the exception of Newtown, home ownership is widespread. We must therefore tread warily

and rely to some extent on the results for wards as a
whole.

Less than one in five of the Newtown residents complained of inter-racial problems or that there were 'too
many coloureds'. Significantly, in none of the other
three wards does the comparable figure drop to less than
40 per cent. In addition, fewer people in Newtown complained of the state of their physical environment, concern mainly centring on certain features of 'social' life,
and particularly on 'problems of order'. About two out of
every five respondents in the area stressed the importance
of such issues. A further 18 per cent expressed concern
at the level of vandalism, crime and violence in general,
or problems with youths in particular. The remainder complained of the unfriendliness of the area or demonstrated
hostility towards certain neighbours or 'problem' families.

It is possible that much of this might be explained in
terms of the 'localisation' of views. As most of those
interviewed in Newtown were residents of the council
estate (an estate moreover which clearly embodies some
measure of corporate identity) 'this area of Birmingham'
may well have been translated to mean 'the Newtown
estate'. Working under this assumption, the findings discussed in the previous paragraph seem more explicable.
For example, as we noted earlier, the Newtown estate is
predominantly white. It is not surprising, then, that relatively few residents regard the present volume of blacks
as a major problem. In addition, much of the housing in
the Newtown ward is post-war, and slum clearance work
since the 1950s has made considerable headway. We would
therefore expect slightly less emphasis on the physical
environment. Concern with their present quality of life,
therefore, is reflected in other local issues. In common
with many other post-war inner-city estates, elements of
'social conflict' in the broadest sense provide the major
foci of attention.

If we now compare the responses of the above group with
those of council tenants who live elsewhere in 'Handsworth', some interesting points emerge. [45] First, the
assumption concerning the subjective definition of 'area'
gains further corroborative support, as the pattern of
answers shows quite distinct differences. Second, some
doubt is cast on the suggested relationship between tenure
and hostility towards blacks. Of the non-estate council
tenants, 31 per cent express hostility towards the immigrant section of the community. This suggests that we
should perhaps not attach too much credence to the rather
naive hypothesis that council tenants per se might be

rather more disposed to accept blacks than members of
other tenure groups. To test the hypothesis we would need
to examine responses to other questionnaire items which
involve attitudes towards other races. [46] We can, however, see that overt concern about this issue appears to
be strongest among those who live in areas of high immigrant concentration. [47]

Looking now at the council group as a whole and in particular comparing the views of older, more established residents with younger families, a number of whom are recent
immigrants to the Handsworth area, we again see many differences in emphasis. Younger families, especially those
whose head is under 35, appeared to be predominantly
worried about the social and physical environment in which
their children were growing up. Less than one in ten were
concerned primarily with racial issues as such. As we
move up the age scale the picture changes somewhat. The
middle-aged seemed much more inclined to make overt references to immigrants (though this group was, in turn,
matched by a similar number who were unhappy with the
social environment in general or who complained of problem
families, unpleasant neighbours, and so on). Those who
were living out their retirement in Handsworth not surprisingly tended to be divided into two main groups: one
which was inclined to look back rather critically on the
ways in which the area had changed over the years, and
another whose members either demonstrated a resigned acceptance of their lot, or reflected a certain measure of
contentment. The first of these was the more numerous;
approximately half of the 53 over-sixty-fives specifically
complained of the influx of blacks or the general physical
decay of the area (the two often being seen as linked).

Having looked at the council tenants in detail, we now
turn to the other tenure groups. Even a cursory glance at
the figures reveals a major disparity between the volume
of racially hostile remarks generated by the owner-occupiers and private renters of Handsworth, Soho and Sandwell
on the one hand, and by the council tenants of Newtown on
the other. Making a more direct comparison between these
groups within each area is quite difficult, however,
since, as noted above, ward boundaries seem almost to be
tenure boundaries. We can, however, by grouping the
council tenants outside Newtown as before, see that a
certain tangible difference still remains. Furthermore,
there does seem to be empirical support for the initial
hypothesis that ageing well-established owner-occupiers
are particularly hostile to the ethnic minorities.

But does this, as was suggested in the initial hypothesis, suggest that 'ownership of capital' (via property)

is the key factor? Certainly it is feasible, employing a
priori reasoning, that this group is the most threatened
in financial terms by the influx of blacks. On the other
hand, of course, there are many other factors which an individual may regard as central to his 'quality of life'.
Despite this we feel it would be instructive here, to
follow up the question of ownership and in particular to
consider some of the concommitant social factors which it
embodies.

Ownership of property may, it is often argued, confer
upon the individual a sense of achievement, a general
feeling of well-being, and 'peace of mind'. In this view
then, ownership itself contains positive implications for
any measure of 'quality of life'. It is often seen also
as enabling the individual to achieve an increased measure
of mobility. Whereas the council tenant may find it difficult to move within the public sector and must always be
subject to its inbuilt constraints, the owner-occupier may
move relatively easily (within certain financial limits)
in the private housing sector. Given the recent decline
in private lettings, the renter in this market might seem
to share the fate of the council tenant.

The major problem with the above analysis is that it is
grounded on an a priori value position. It may well be
that mobility, for example, is not regarded by many white
owner-occupiers as being of importance. In addition, a
large number of factors impinge on an individual's self
image, including many which may swamp any feeling of well-
being conferred by home ownership. Tenure, and particularly tenure labels such as 'owner-occupier' and 'private
renter' may not be sociologically meaningful at the subjective level, i.e., on the level of meaning to the actors
involved. A sophisticated analysis must attempt to situate the actor within his own social world rather than that
of the researcher, and then to look at the structural
forces which impose constraints on, or redefine, his image
of society.

If the sociologist aims at such an analysis, the major
flaws in his a priori theorising may become evident. In
this instance the 'theory' would suggest that, while
owner-occupiers, realising that their 'capital' was being
devalued as a direct result of external social change,
might react in a more hostile fashion to the source of
such change than, say, a person who rents his property.
In addition, that devaluation in itself imposes con-trai
straints on mobility, thus negating one of the general
tenets of the 'home ownership ethic' which we saw above.
He might be expected to resent this restriction on his
freedom, and this resentment might again be reflected in

his hostility towards the perceived cause of this state of affairs. One conclusion which might be drawn from this is that owner-occupiers and renters in the private market share the same restrictions on mobility, but the former may react more strongly (in terms both of numbers and of vocalised ferocity) because of the additional threat to their financial well-being. [48]

It appears, however, that the data do not support this conclusion. Despite the small numbers within certain private renter groups, there seems to be little evidence that the volume of hostility towards blacks is any greater among owner-occupiers. This is also confirmed by an analysis of the qualitative data in terms of the degree of hostility towards sectors of the immigrant community. It is, indeed, a detailed perusal of this material and not a priori reasoning or tabular statistical analysis which gives a clue to some of the defects of this argument. An examination of the major components of hostility exposes a number of oversimplifications implicit in the nature of categories such as 'owner-occupier', 'private renter' and 'council tenant'. It is clear that the subjective meanings attached to these are central to any understanding of current issues. The next chapter, for example, will discuss the extent to which these categories may be successfully incorporated into a theoretical discussion of class structure within a multi-racial society. For the present, we reflect on the implications of the truism that each encompasses a group of individuals with often very different life histories in terms of both length and experience. Many will also have radically different expectations for the future and general orientations towards life.

Finally, there may be a major defect in the argument which suggests that the influx of blacks has devalued property and thus contributed towards the restriction of movement for ageing whites. As noted earlier, the ready demand for housing among the ethnic minority communities has enabled many whites to leave the area. Paradoxically, therefore, the presence of immigrants may actually have bolstered the local property market. Houses will have been sold which may otherwise have been virtually unsaleable (i.e., at any price).

We have seen that council tenants on the Newtown estate exhibit a relatively low measure of overt concern over the influx of immigrants. In contrast, both 'owner-occupiers' and those who rent in the private sector tend to place major emphasis on this issue. Given that council tenants in the areas of relatively high concentrations of immigrants demonstrate results which are closer to the pattern

for the other two groups, this factor may have considerable significance. This still leaves us with the question
of why the results of owners and private renters are
superficially similar. One reason may be that we have
underestimated the measure of immobility which typifies
members of the latter group: 79 of the 91 families involved, almost 87 per cent, have unfurnished accommodation, and a little over half of them have been living at
their present address for twenty years or more. Further,
on the basis of the rent data, [49] there seems good
reason to believe that most of these have controlled rents
and certainly a large proportion are of retirement age and
relying on state pensions. There would therefore seem to
be little chance of this group's moving to another area
should they wish to do so.

A point which is worth stressing here is that, in the
main, this group do not wish to move. It is a recurrent
theme of (often lengthy) answers, that this would be a
last resort. What does emerge, as we shall see later in
this chapter, is a feeling of smouldering resentment, that
the area in which they have lived for many years (sometimes indeed from birth) has changed radically 'since the
arrival of the coloureds'. Occasionally this resentment
is coupled with the fear of a holocaust just around the
corner. It might be argued that we are essentially talking about old people, many of whom are confined to the
house or to the street in which they live. For them,
therefore, a fear of strangers with differing cultures
could perhaps be explained in commonsense terms as 'quite
natural'.

We believe, however, that this tells only part of the
story: a 'quite natural' feeling of insecurity is
grounded in rather more significant and sinister forces.
In using oratorical skills to disseminate effectively
anecdotes which are designed to define alien cultures as
not simply different but inferior, speakers such as Enoch
Powell (and more recently National Front activists) reinforce any existing tendency towards ethnocentrism. It is
often implied that the logical outcome of the influx of
alien culture is total racial conflict, beginning with the
degradation of British cultural values which can be traced
back to the demise of the Empire and leading ultimately to
the 'end of civilisation as we know it' (with apologies to
John Cleese et al.)! At a somewhat more localised level,
much of the imagery of the old working-class residents of
Handsworth is vivid and unmistakable. The power of televised speeches and newsreels as purveyors of propagandist
rhetoric, especially when seen in terms of areas which are
already suffering a decline in physical and economic terms

is undeniable. Moreover, their 'effectiveness' is not
simply confined to older residents or for that matter to
the working class (however the latter term is conceived).
   As we have already seen, for example, equal hostility
is reflected among owner-occupiers. Indeed, if we super-
impose on the above analysis a consideration of 'social
class' via the (admittedly crude) measure of occupational
status, an interesting picture emerges. Rose et al.
(1969) and later Deakin (1970) suggested that the incidence of overt racial hostility (in verbal terms) varied
little between areas of high and low immigrant concentrations, [50] and found also that white-collar workers in
general exhibited a greater reluctance to display such
hostility than did manual workers. [51] Our data, as we
have seen, cast a certain measure of doubt on the first of
these. As to the second, we find that these groups
express similar degrees of concern: in fact, among lower-
middle-class owner-occupiers we find the greatest tendency
towards hostility. [52] This accounts for high figures on
this issue for the Sandwell ward, as it is in this ward
that the concentration of white-collar workers (and particularly non-professional or managerial workers) is the
highest. From an analysis of the wealth of qualitative
material collected on this issue, it appears that this
factor in a sense 'counteracts the effects' of low immigrant density. Many middle-class whites in Sandwell look
towards neighbouring Soho in order to 'see' the future of
their own area. There may be an element of fear, in financial terms, because of likely property depreciation;
this we cannot establish. What is certain is that they,
more than their property-owning peers in other wards,
apart possibly from Handsworth itself, express concern for
the future in terms of inter-racial strife. Many mirrored
the feelings of one 81-year-old retired clerical worker
who claimed that there are: 'too many black people - no-
one helps us to move away. There'll be racial tension in
a while; not just now'. Thus the fear of impending conflict is accompanied by a feeling of being trapped, that
they are imprisoned in their 'own area'. This man, like a
large majority of his white neighbours, has a long memory
of life in Handsworth. He has lived in his present house,
in what has now been designated a general improvement
area, for over twenty years and has disapprovingly witnessed the 'take-over by black people'.
   As noted earlier, attachment to a specific locale via
length of residence seems to be a not unimportant factor.
Three-quarters of Sandwell owner-occupiers, and almost
nine out of every ten of the comparable group in Soho,
have lived in their present house for ten years or more;

indeed, the majority of them have not moved house in the last twenty years. Only a handful have entered the survey area from other than contiguous wards, during the last decade.

It is illuminating to dwell on a few of the statements in which ageing white owner-occupiers discuss the process of social change. Consider, for example, the view of one 71-year-old widow living in a declared general improvement area in Soho with her widowed sister:

I've always liked Handsworth: it used to be a lovely area. I've lived here all my life but now it's not clean or tidy: the people are all coloured: the road is not like it used to be ... they don't keep their outsides clean. There's no real trouble but the roads are untidy now ... lots of paper and litter about.

Blacks are thus seen as offending the native cultural and social sensibilities. This and a number of similar responses seem to reflect in an important symbolic sense what local whites have come to see as a rejection of British values. The almost ritualistic cleaning of the front door step in many working-class areas of Britain is an overt expression of respectability which in some way constitutes a cultural imperative. By a failure to fulfil this 'requirement' the social equilibrium may be disturbed. This ethic, which is embodied succinctly in the notion of 'cleanliness is next to godliness', has many other ritualistic manifestations: for example, the dressing up in 'Sunday best' to attend morning services (now, as noted in Chapter 2, interestingly adopted by many West Indians), and the Sunday morning car wash of the proverbial suburbanite (the latter activity in many cases replacing the former).

It could be argued that the sorts of view noted here reflect the core element of 'prejudice'. Certainly one gains the distinct impression that immigrants are generally regarded as a single (and distinctly inferior) breed. Often the labelling is the result of only limited direct empirical evidence. Thus, the lady whose quote we considered above admitted later on in the questionnaire that 'I'm old and don't get out a lot'. The important thing to note, however, is that the values which the views represent have been inculcated over a long period by external structural forces. Members of the native working class have long been socialised into accepting uncritically that their cultural values, by definition, are superior to those of races who were 'civilised' in the colonial era by their forefathers. The media (as we noted above) then serve a vital role in reinforcing such value systems.

Powerful images reflecting perceived white (British)

superiority coupled with fears of black hostility (present
and future) featured very strongly in many responses.
Among these was a 66-year-old retired assistant technician
who lived only a few streets away from the lady discussed
above. As with many of his neighbours, he and his 60-
year-old wife (who works as a 'dinner lady' in a local
school) have lived in Birmingham for over twenty years,
and moved to Soho from nearby Winson Green about four
years ago. He spoke in rather staccato terms which reflected a great deal of bitterness. The only good thing
in the area's favour was that it was 'handy for buses. I
have only one lung and can't live where it is too hilly or
far away from a bus stop'. Once again, therefore, physical infirmity is seen as a constraining force inducing, in
part at least, a feeling of being trapped and as a result
being vulnerable to attack from hostile forces. He dislikes:

    Coloured people ... smell from greengrocery shops ...
    coloured Indian shops and rubbish in the streets ...
    litter and paper ... immigrants, muggings. I'm
    frightened to go out in the dark ... a mugging in my
    own street ... West Indians, about two months ago.
When asked for his major concern this was stated in terms
of 'coloured people ... West Indians 16-20-year-olds ...
they frighten me because of muggings'.

The dimensions of this stereotype are clear. Blacks
are in the first instance associated with dirt, litter and
odious smells; second, they are labelled as physical ag-
gressors. As we saw above, our theoretical premise pre-
dicts that culture clash at the level of 'observables'
would form a major element of the verbal accounts of local
whites. In any case similar findings have already been
well documented in studies such as Rex and Moore (1967).
[53]

The issue of physical aggression probably has even
broader general significance. It reflects much more than
the isolated fears of a man whose insecurity, grounded in
physical infirmity, advances with the years. For one
thing, these fears were expressed by many individuals,
mostly without such physical impediments. The view therefore reflects a certain measure of empirical generality.
At a more theoretical level, it is interesting both for
the form of argument it portrays and for the broader significance of its substantive content. The use of the
anecdote, whether fact or fiction, [54] is particularly
significant: an isolated event employed in such a way as
to bolster a general argument. He is, of course, in 'respectable' oratorial company in doing so. The insidious
use of one such instance, the story about excreta being

posted through a (white) constituent's letterbox, was employed with great effect by Enoch Powell in illustrating
the threat of the encroaching black peril. Further, the
assumption (or rather thesis) of the 'black as aggressor'
is a central theme of much racialist thinking. Powell in
his 'rivers of blood' speech explicitly stated this as the
(inevitable) consequence of higher concentration of blacks
in our inner cities.

Perhaps at a rather more implicit level was the allocation of the 'blame'. Blacks, and especially West Indians,
are often seen as physically powerful, assertive and ag-
gressive. It has even been suggested by some commentators
that the white reaction to the presence of such groups
results subconsciously from a virility-based inferiority
complex. Whether or not there is any validity in this
argument it is certainly the case that greater concentrations of blacks are seen as posing a threat (a) to the
British way of life, and (b) to our territorial or property rights. Clearly the argument embodied in (b), that
of territorial 'invasion and succession', carries with it,
at least by implication, an element of aggression. These
are just a few of the major themes which might form the
basis of argument for those who wish to adopt a posture of
the 'Little Englander', or (in their terms) those who wish
to restore the ethnic 'purity' [55] of the British race.

One point which should not be submerged in the analytical detail is the source of the comments which our social
actors express. It is possible that some contain an
element of facticity at the observational level. The
importance of the issues, however, lies in the nature of
the linkage between the observational and the conceptual
worlds. We argue that propaganda, in reinforcing existing
values, forms a major part of this metaphysic and, indeed,
believe that there is much to commend Cox's conviction as
to the exploitative basis of such social attitudes propagated among the public. [56] At times, in studying the
empirical manifestations of such attitudes, we gain insights into some of the ways in which these attitudes are
reinforced. Black aggressiveness is frequently 'demonstrated' on television, whether in documentary, newsreel
or theatre; whether in South Africa, urban America or
Notting Hill (or indeed Ladywood). Also crucial is the
role of the press, at national and local level, and the
police force which has the task of dealing with the very
issue of law and order which many of our respondents saw
as problematic. The response to such issues emerges in a
particularly interesting way in the case of the retired
technician whose views we discussed above. He argued very
strongly that there were inter-racial problems in Hands-

worth 'because they (the different races) can't mix, there are reports of fights in the paper every Monday night. The police warned me in the Park once that there were coloured people and mugging and we had to be careful'.

These comments are illuminating, irrespective of the extent to which they represent factual accounts of the events concerned. In the case of the local press it matters little whether there are reports of racial disturbances 'every Monday night'. What is important is that the individual has gained that impression and construes the articles as expressing a pervasive mood of hostility with implications of much broader significance than would be appropriate for acts of violent or criminal behaviour interpreted individualistically. It is clear from studying this and similar responses that such reports can have a significant effect in terms of galvanising racial stereotypes.

Comments concerning the local police, in this case taking an anecdotal form, are crucial, irrespective of source or facticity. Our retired technician clearly sees the police as protectors of the white community (hence the use of 'we') in the face of external aggression from their black 'neighbours'. It is precisely this identification of the police as a 'white organisation' which angers many blacks, and black youth [57] in particular. As we shall see in Chapters 5 and 6, the significance of this in terms of future race relations is immense. Particularly in times of high unemployment, black youths tend to find jobs even more difficult to obtain than do similarly qualified white school-leavers. [58] In such a situation many see themselves as being in the centre of a multiplicity of alienating forces. Without jobs they are much in evidence on the city's streets and thus sometimes find themselves in situations of potential conflict with the police. Personal experience of 'harassment' may then be interpreted, with some justification, as additional symbolic proof of white oppression.

THE ALLOCATION OF PUBLIC HOUSING: A STAGE FOR RACIAL CONFLICT?

There is clearly, then, a great deal of qualitative and quantitative evidence to suggest that social relations between the different racial and ethnic groups in Handsworth are not altogether harmonious. In the current discussion we have focused on the extent to which these issues were uppermost in people's minds, and particularly, in the minds of white residents. We have concentrated on those

whose major negative image of Handsworth was expressed in
such terms. It would, however, be misleading to suggest
that this encapsulates the total mood of unease. Indeed,
one important problem is raised by this analysis.

It has been argued that overt verbal hostility towards
blacks seems to be more common in areas where immigrant
concentrations are highest. This, however, does not imply
that those who live in areas of low immigrant density are
significantly more 'tolerant' and somehow more willing to
accept an influx of blacks in general, or a black neighbour in particular. [59] In common with many who live
outside the Newtown estate, residents here often complained of race relations 'problems', or sometimes said
that although all nationalities at the moment co-existed
relatively peacefully, overt conflict was not far away.

A further indicator of intolerance or 'prejudice' (as
defined earlier) relates to attitudes towards the allocation of council property. Although the broader question
of housing policies will be discussed in more detail in
Chapter 4, we feel it important in the context of the
present analysis to look at the way in which local whites
feel the different nationalities fare in the allocation
process.

We see (from Table 3.6) that on the whole the native
white population either feel that the council does not
differentiate between nationalities or say that they are
not in a position to comment on the allocation procedure.
Approaching two-thirds of the British sample falls into
this category. It is perhaps rather misleading, however,
to talk in terms of the entire sample since many of the
people concerned have had little or no direct personal
contact with the council or its officers. We are referring here, of course, to the owner-occupiers and private
renters, and particularly to those who have not been
council tenants in the recent past. Since this refers to
the vast majority of the 255 whites in the private sector
it is of some interest to note that many nevertheless saw
fit to comment upon the allocation system, over a quarter
of the owner-occupiers and more than one in three of those
in privately rented accommodation having positive views on
the current role of the council in this sphere. As Table
3.6 demonstrates, most of this group felt that there was
some form of positive discrimination in favour of black
immigrants.

There was a great deal of dissatisfaction with the
stance which the council was 'seen' to have adopted. The
prevailing mood of this section of local white opinion was
that this body was failing to perform its 'duty' ('duty'
here being implicitly defined in terms of protecting them

TABLE 3.6 Attitudes of whites towards the allocation of council housing to those of different nationalities, by tenure group

	Owner-occupiers %	Private renters %	Council tenants %
Council afraid of discriminating	4	2	8 (7)
Blacks get homes quicker	4	5	3 (4)
Blacks get priority	12	16	10 (7)
Blacks treated better/ get better housing	6	11	20 (28)
Whites fare better	1	1	4 (1)
Other [1]/D.K./no difference in treatment	74	64	55 (53)
Total sample size (= 100%)	164	91	142(100) [2]

1 Only four respondents fell into this category.
2 Bracketed figures here refer to council tenants on the Newtown estate. This form of analysis means that it is not necessary in this case to use a weighting procedure.

from an influx of coloured immigrants). It was their own council and as such was expected to act in their interests. This highlights an interesting parallelism between national and local government as seen by those who reject the notion of a multi-racial society. Both represent gatekeepers, and both are white institutions which are deemed to be abrogating their duties to white society. Nowhere is this expressed more clearly at the local level than by those respondents who argued that the council was 'afraid of discriminating against the blacks'. This may, of course, be interpreted in a number of ways. It may, for example, reflect a view that the council wish to adopt a discriminatory policy against their (the electors') wishes. This seems unlikely, however, from a closer examination of the available qualitative material. Without exception, those who gave this form of answer would agree with the respondent who argued that: 'They come first, the authorities are afraid of them because of the Race Relations Act.' The council were thus seen as having

their hands tied by legal requirements imposed upon them
by Parliament. Their actions were construed as being contrary to the interests of white society, but this did not
result in their being seen as a scapegoat. They were
usually merely regarded as potential allies compelled to
betray their white constituents by virtue of the great
power wielded by external forces.

The most frequent answers by far, however, were those
which seemed to blame the council directly for giving preferential treatment to blacks. As the table shows, there
is a certain degree of consensus among a significant minority of those in the private housing sector that blacks
either get some measure of priority in the allocation procedure or, at least, receive 'better treatment' from
council officers. We can, of course, only speculate on
the 'reasoning' behind such answers; it may be that such
'reasoning' as is present merely serves to reinforce
ascriptive racist stereotypes. Anecdotes based on personal experiences at first- or second-hand level, may play
some part in this, as may impressions gathered from the
treatment of housing issues in local and national press.
Many respondents, however, seemed to use this question
simply as a vehicle for the expression of hostility. Further, since they felt themselves to be impotent in the
fight to curtail the influx of blacks, the council as an
institution in this case formed a convenient scapegoat.

We have seen in the above discussion that it is not
simply those in council property who express views on allocation procedures. On the other hand, it is clearly the
case that such tenants were much more likely to complain
about the unfair treatment of whites than were other respondents. It may well be that these views are only a
part of a much more general dislike of the council per se.
Whatever the case, however, it is interesting to note the
degree of consensus among council tenants whether on the
Newtown estate or in non-estate property. Both groups
displayed a willingness to attack the council for demonstrating a discriminatory policy which favoured blacks.
As we shall see in the next chapter, this particular
'theory' appears to be totally unsupported by the available evidence. The important thing to note here is that
blacks were clearly regarded by many as undesirable; the
possibility of greater numbers was seen as an imminent
threat. Thus the hostility demonstrated by owner-occupiers and private renters in areas of high immigrant concentration is mirrored by hostility grounded in fears of a
similar 'fate' awaiting areas such as Newtown. The degree
of immigrant concentration appears to be a crucial issue
once again; it provides a convenient reference point. As

one 50-year-old Newtown resident remarked: 'I don't think
we have as many coloured immigrants as other areas — we
have some quite nice coloured families around.' In this,
as with some similar answers, the overriding impression is
that blacks are sometimes acceptable in small numbers.
They may even seem 'quite nice'!

Having said this, it is still the case that (even) in
the council sector more than a half of the local whites
have not used this question as a vehicle for attacking the
immigrant community. Negative factors were stressed, however, not merely from an obsession with the pathological
but because of the size of this 'minority', and because
many were looking to the future and predicting conflict,
an outcome which would undoubtedly harden the attitudes of
many of those who at present express no overt hostility.

Set against these feelings of resentment of the favourable treatment of blacks by 'white' authority are the
opinions of the blacks themselves. These reciprocal views
not surprisingly displayed a marked contrast. Only one in
ten of the West Indian sample complained that whites were
in any way treated better than their own people. The corresponding percentage of Asians was even smaller (7 per
cent). Admittedly, if we look specifically at West Indian
council tenants the figure does rise to around 15 per
cent. On the whole, however, we retain the picture of relative satisfaction and an unwillingness to engage in
verbal attacks on white society or its institutions. One
interesting point does, however, emerge if we look closely
at the Asian 'dissidents'. Almost by definition, [60] the
vast majority (16 out of 19) of these families (the ones
who felt that the whites were treated better by the
council) were themselves owner-occupiers. Could it be,
perhaps, that a number of them, at least, were people who
had tried unsuccessfully to obtain adequate council accommodation? Whatever the answer, we reach a similar conclusion in terms of overall 'satisfaction' to the one which
was noted in the case of West Indians.

CONCLUSION: A PROFILE OF RACIAL TENSIONS

In this chapter so far, we have looked at the feelings of
current residents towards life in Handsworth and have seen
in detail the measure of hostility which a large sector of
the native white population feels towards its black neighbours. The major foci were seen to be the social and physical environment of the area, but other crucial influences on ultimate 'life-chances' such as public housing allocation procedures were considered. [61] We conclude the

present discussion by adding to these a rather more sophisticated analysis of the attitudes of whites towards
the relationship between the various nationalities. This
produces a series of profiles (or clusters) of response,
thereby providing increased insight into the structural
dynamics of conflict and the attendant verbal expression
of prejudice.

We should perhaps immediately point out, however, that
there is no attempt to imitate the analysis of Rose et al.
(1969) or Deakin (1970) in the sense of constructing a
scale of 'prejudice' based on the number of hostile responses. It is clear that we are dealing with multi-
dimensional attitudinal structures. To imply, therefore,
that, say, two different combinations of hostile answers
in some tangible sense 'mean' the same thing would be to
distort the data seriously on the subjective level of
meaning. [62]

Basing our argument on three questions, interpreted for
simplicity in dichotomous terms, we look at eight distinct
response patterns. As Table 3.7 shows, these range in
type from one group, who used each of the three questions
to attack the immigrant community directly or indirectly,
to another group who made no overtly hostile reference to
blacks. [63] Even a cursory glance at the figures yields
some rather disturbing findings. First, and perhaps fore-
most, is the revelation that only one in five of the white
residents interviewed demonstrated no discernible distaste
for, or unease about, their black neighbours. At the
other extreme no less than 10 per cent argued forcefully
that (a) their major dislike of Handsworth was the
'coloureds'; (b) there were already inter-racial tensions; and (c) the council treated them (the blacks)
better than the whites in terms of housing allocation.

In a sense this group may be seen as the 'hard core' of
those who resent the influx of blacks. On the other hand,
it is misleading to regard the resentment as being largely
confined to this group. This is true for a number of
reasons outlined earlier in this chapter. First, the
majority of owner-occupiers admitted ignorance of council
policies; some perhaps felt that it was therefore an in-
appropriate question for them to answer. A second group
pointed out that although there was 'no problem' of racial
conflict at present, the eruption of violence was nevertheless only a matter of time. Thus we have a dimension
of fear which was often accompanied by the white residents' attributing the blame for this state of affairs to
the blacks. There then finally a group of respondents
who, perhaps mainly because they lived in an estate with a
low immigrant concentration, did not regard the number of
'coloureds' as a major issue.

TABLE 3.7 Summary of measures concerning race relations
in Handsworth: white residents only (weighted figures
are bracketed)

(Nominal) Group number	Response pattern	Handsworth white residents %
1	Dislike coloureds/racial disharmony/council gives preferential treatment to blacks	10 (12)
2	Dislike coloureds/racial disharmony	15 (16)
3	Dislike coloureds/council gives preferential treatment to blacks	3 (3)
4	Racial disharmony/council gives preferential treatment to blacks	12 (9)
5	Dislike coloureds	7 (8)
6	Racial disharmony	24 (27)
7	Council gives preferential treatment to blacks	9 (6)
8	No overt reference to blacks	20 (19)
	Total sample size (= 100%)	400(327)

Definition of terms used:
(a) 'Dislike coloureds' refers to that group of residents
     who gave this form of reply when asked for the main
     thing they disliked about life in Handsworth.
(b) 'Racial disharmony' includes all those who felt that
     there were at least some inter-racial problems.
(c) 'Council gives preferential treatment to blacks'
     refers to those who gave one of a number of answers,
     e.g., blacks get housing priority, are offered better
     housing, are housed quicker (than whites) or are ge-
     nerally treated better (sometimes because the council
     'are afraid of discriminating against them').

These remarks taken as a whole have a distinct bearing
on the interpretation of Table 3.7 and particularly on
groups 2,3 and 4, and to a lesser extent on groups 5,6 and
7. In particular, if we look at the second group more
closely we see, in fact, that most are indeed owner-occupiers. They had already made clear their dislike of
blacks and subsequently commented on the existence of

certain elements of racial tension; they merely refrained
from commenting upon something about which they 'knew'
little, i.e., the allocation of council housing.
     As is hinted by the wide differential between weighted
and unweighted figures, 12(9) per cent, group 4 contains a
large number of council tenants from the Newtown estate.
Then respondents often stated, in no uncertain terms, that
the council gives preferential treatment to blacks in at
least one of a number of ways, and that racial conflict is
already evident in one form or another. Given that there
are so few blacks on the estate, two things follow:
(a) The first of these two statements demonstrably contains an air of unreality, suggesting the existence of
strong anti-black sentiments; and (b) it is hardly surprising that even among 'prejudiced' individuals many decline to argue that the main thing they dislike about
their own area are the coloureds!
     The outcome of this analysis is a reinforcement of the
belief that hostility towards the immigrant is indeed
widespread. It is by no means confined to the one in ten
whose views on such matters seem to permeate their whole
outlook on life. Even among those in groups 5,6 and 7
there are many whose ideas paint an illuminating but inevitably disturbing picture of the present and future of
Handsworth. It is disturbing principally because of the
evidence of social fragmentation and even retrenchment;
hatred, fear, and racial stereotyping have become all too
much a part of their everyday image-consensus. We are
then made vividly aware of the potential outcome of years
of official neglect and the resulting urban decay.
     The conceptual worlds of social change and urban
ecology, by virtue of their very complexity, produce
fertile seedbeds for those who wish to manipulate and reinforce existing tensions. Verbal manifestations of these
forces are everywhere to be heard among the native whites.
On the other hand, similar reactions from the black communities are conspicuous by their absence: or are they?
The remaining chapters and especially the one which concludes this book will, we hope, provide at least part of
the answer.

4 Housing and race

Few would argue that the housing problems of a major city
such as Birmingham are exclusively, or even primarily, a
contemporary phenomenon. Indeed it is common for local
authorities to bemoan the paucity of the inherited housing
stock in terms both of numbers and quality. Birmingham is
no exception. In the introduction to the 'City of
Birmingham Structure Plan' (1973) produced by the department of the City Engineer, Surveyor and Planning Officer
the authors argue that: [1]
> Many of the City's present housing problems are a
> result of rapid growth during the nineteenth century.
> In the second half of the nineteenth century, the
> City's population doubled, and despite the enormous
> scale of post-war slum clearance and redevelopment,
> over 80,000 of the dwellings built before 1900 are
> still standing. Many of these dwellings are unfit or
> lacking in basic amenities.

In sheer physical terms then, their task is clearly seen
as daunting. This figure of 80,000 constitutes approximately one quarter of the total housing stock of the city.
[2]

As might have been expected, there is strong evidence
to suggest that experience of this 'housing stress' in the
widest sense is not uniformly distributed throughout the
City's population - either in geographical or in social
structural terms. The authors of the above document admit
that 'poor housing conditions are concentrated in the
inner and middle-ring wards of the city' and that 'these
areas also tend to have distinct demographic and socio-
economic characteristics'. [3]

A cluster analysis [4] of the 1966 census material
throws light on the precise nature of these 'distinct
demographic and socio-economic characteristics'. Of the
two major clusters which emerge, the first defines a

series of negative factors which in a sense might be
interpreted as indicative of a 'cycle of multiple deprivation'. They include such factors as 'low housing standard' (i.e., in terms of overcrowding and a lack of basic
amenities), 'low socio-economic status' and 'high fertility rate'. Heading the list, however, is one issue which
is of paramount importance for the current analysis: the
'level of immigrant concentration'.

The form of their discussion is brief and therefore
oversimplified. Unfortunately in aiming at a succinct
presentation they may convey a rather misleading picture
to the casual reader. Areas are ranked on the basis of
scores on the two clusters, and are then divided into
zones of types 1a, 1b and 1c: type 1a corresponding to
areas of greatest housing stress, and 1b and 1c to those
which have higher scores on the second cluster (B); [5]
which by implication includes rather more desirable, or
at least less undesirable areas of the city. It is stated
that the latter areas: [6]

> include the major concentrations of New Commonwealth
> immigrants and have a more varied socio-economic
> structure, a more mobile population and a wider variety
> of housing conditions than the '1a's. Their pattern is
> more dispersed, but they broadly form a ring around the
> redevelopment areas, and include most of the older
> housing in the City.

A cursory glance at this statement may suggest two
things;   first, that there is an association between 'New
Commonwealth immigrants' and the concepts of 'mobility'
and 'varied socio-economic status';   i.e., that black immigrants are geographically mobile and are represented in
significant numbers throughout the occupational status
hierarchy. (This latter inference will be shown in the
following chapter to be totally false.) In addition, however 'mobility' is defined, our survey suggests that, in
Handsworth at least, such movement among the black community is minimal. When it does happen it usually results
from varying degrees of necessity, rather than the realisation of a positive step towards self-improvement.

The second inference which might be drawn concerns the
position of blacks within the housing market. Whilst accepting the qualification that (even) the areas discussed
in a previous paragraph 'show signs of environmental decay
and social deprivation', one is tempted to infer that immigrants are (in relative terms) not faring too badly in
terms of housing since large numbers live outside the 1a
areas. This second (and we shall argue) false inference
arises from one of the major weaknesses of the Structure
Plan's analysis;   namely, that the level of generalisation

is too great. A large proportion of our survey area, and especially that part of the Soho ward in which immigrant concentration is heaviest, appears on their sy-map (Figure 16 in the Plan) as a 1a area. [7] Moreover, much of the area studied by Rex and Moore [8] (Sparkbrook) is similarly categorised. The tendency to oversimplify and to neglect the weaknesses of the cluster analysis technique [9] produces a nagging suspicion that post factum reasoning has been employed to gloss over the precise nature and dimensions of the problem, in particular by suggesting that things are 'going according to plan'. Nowhere is this better exemplified than in the concluding sentence of paragraph 5.2, where it is argued that: 'The close correspondence between the "1a" areas and the redevelopment areas, does, however, confirm that the city has been tackling its areas of worst housing.' [10] This being said, it is nevertheless true that, so far as the survey area is concerned, the attention of the council has in recent years been directed to improving the total physical environment. Concern therefore has not been focused totally on the 1a areas. [11] To what effect, will be seen later.

HOUSING POLICY AND THE INNER CITY

Poor housing conditions have often been cited as aggravating existing social tensions. (Indeed the cynic might argue that diffusion or repression of overt hostility remains a major, if rather implicit, theme in policy-makers' thinking.) Writing about nineteenth-century Birmingham, for example, Gill [12] noted that: 'The bad material condition of so much of the town undoubtedly had a depressing influence on moral standards.' Court records clearly show the extent to which poor housing conditions were seen as a direct cause of crimes such as vice, theft and drunkenness. However, in accord with much of Victorian morality, such ills were usually seen ultimately in terms of individual weaknesses.

It is interesting to note that today's social ills are conventionally interpreted as stemming from collective action: phrases such as 'the politics of group confrontation' have become clichés in the commentator's vocabulary. Individual acts of 'deviancy' are seen as symptomatic of 'wayward youth', 'bloody-minded unions' or 'the blacks'. The problem is, however, that these analyses remain in an important sense decontextualised; historical and social structural considerations play little part in either the determination of causes or in the nature of the proposed 'solutions'.

In contemporary Handsworth we do not have to search far
for evidence of such reactions. A recent report of street
crime in Handsworth [13] noted that the suspected culprits
lived in 'squats', but neglected to analyse the broadest
implications of this state of affairs: the problem was
instead 'seen' and discussed solely in terms of its 'observed' manifestations. A gang of approximately 200
'dreads' were deemed to be the direct cause of social
ills, by terrorising local white and Asian communitites.
Thus conflict was assumed to be the (irrational) reaction
of a disruptive element. We wish to argue that such
'layman philosophies' have a clear bearing on the way in
which solutions are sought and subsequent policies
adopted. Throughout the remaining chapters, we shall see
clear evidence of this process;   namely, the generation of
piecemeal 'solutions' to problems which are of deep structural significance.

Politicians have, on occasion, explicitly linked
housing conditions to physical and mental health. Echoing
Gill's statements, Neville Chamberlain as early as 1913
reported that: 'A large proportion of the poor in
Birmingham are living under conditions of housing detri-
mental to both health and morals.' [14] This view has,
implicitly at least, been at the heart of most subsequent
policies.

It is undeniable, of course, that whether or not action
has stemmed from feelings of civic pride, pragmatism, or
genuine social egalitarianism, positive results can be
seen. In the 1930s 8,000 of the inner-ring back-to-back
dwellings, which had long outlived their usefulness, were
demolished. A further 30,000 met a similar (and well de-
served) fate in the immediate post-war period. Most of
the remainder fall in areas which were destined to be included in Birmingham's 'Second phase redevelopment' plan,
and a major part of this clearance work has now been completed.

In the fifty years preceding 1914 different forms of
housing development grew up around the inner city. There
was the appearance of two storey artisans' terraces, which
appear mainly to have housed skilled workers. Nearby, the
wealthier professional and businessmen found family homes
in the larger semi-detached residences. Together these
constitute the middle-ring zones such as Handsworth, and
according to the 1973 Structure Plan it is these areas
which now provide the focus for proposed ameliorative
action. A result of the local implementation of certain
of the 'Inner City Initiatives' proposed by central
government has been the designation of certain 'Housing
Action' or 'General Improvement' areas. Figure 20 in the

Structure Plan [15] demonstrates clearly the way in which
(in 1972) these are largely confined to the inner and
middle-ring sectors of the city. Further, our own
Figure 4, despite relating specifically to Handsworth,
illustrates the general point that coloured immigrants
are heavily concentrated in the areas where some form of
action is deemed necessary.

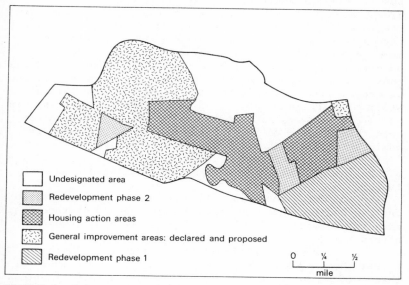

FIGURE 4   Urban renewal in the survey area 1976

ETHNIC MINORITIES AND HOUSING: AN ANALYTICAL FRAMEWORK

The central aim of the present chapter is to explore the
sociology of housing in so far as the theoretical concepts
so generated throw light on the plight of those in the
inner urban zone of a great metropolis. Central to this
is the question of degree of access to the housing market,
and, in particular, to certain types of 'preferred' [16]
housing. This, in turn requires us to examine the extent
to which (implicitly or explicitly) discriminatory practices undermine the 'equal citizenship' rights [17] of
blacks. In so doing we make much more use of our empirical material than was possible in Rex and Tomlinson
(1979).

We may be able to argue, as did the Community Relations
Commission (now the CRE) in a recent publication, that although blacks and whites are both to be found in decaying

inner-city areas: 'there can be identified clusters of
multiple deprivation in ethnic minority populations which
are not experienced together by the general population in
deprived areas.' [18] This remains to be seen; but the
crucial point is that, although necessary, this form of
analysis is not sufficient for our purposes.

As both the CRE and Smith (1977) clearly realise, a
purely internal analysis of a multi-racial and multi-
ethnic area such as Handsworth would conceal the true dimensions of the problems which face minority groups. We
have already noted that our chosen study area contains
much evidence of physical decay and that this has been
acknowledged by the local authority. It follows therefore
that much of the physical and economic deprivation will be
spread throughout the 'community'. Furthermore whites
still comprise the majority of Handsworth's residents. In
so far as in terms of certain discernible social indicators this section of the indigenous population fares as
badly as the blacks, we might conceivably ask whether
'race' is, in fact, central to a sociological analysis
of the inner city. Might not 'class' be the dominant
factor?

The following analysis will aim to show that it is, in
fact, a complex inter-relationship between these concepts,
each interpreted in its broadest possible sense, which
offers the most plausible explanatory account of social
relations and social differentiation between the ethnic
groups themselves on the one hand, and between members of
these groups and external social and economic institutions
on the other. The implications transcend the (in some
ways) arbitrary substantive categories such as housing,
employment, and education, which social scientists conventionally impose on their analyses.

Accordingly, then, 'problems' must be seen in more
global terms, the particular being used to illustrate the
general. There are, of course, different levels of
'generality'. In empirical terms it will be appropriate
to consider our survey area in relation to the city as a
whole, at least for a significant part of our analysis.
Its general population, for example, provides a convenient
yardstick against which to assess the achievement or (in
many cases) the under- or non-achievement of our sample of
West Indians, Indians and Pakistanis. [19] At a simplistic yet fundamentally important level, our survey area
is differentiable from Birmingham as a whole in the
question of ethnic composition. On this issue we are
simply noting a definitional truth. (The part is different from the whole because, given the nature of our study,
it was chosen to be so.) It is part of the process de-

scribed by Woods (1975) as 'the emergence of a "horse-shoe shaped belt" occupied by coloured immigrants from the West Indies, India and Pakistan.' [20]

In a very striking way this 'belt' is mirrored in Figure 16 of the Structure Plan. It is mirrored in that the areas of immigrant settlement are precisely those in which the level of chronic 'social need' is concentrated (though, as noted above, this is not argued by the authors of the Plan). [21] To those who have read recent reports of the CRC and PEP, [22] this comes, of course, as no great surprise. In this case, however, the close spatial similarity in part arises from a very interesting circular argument, a point illustrated neatly if we look at the operational definition of Housing Action Areas. The criteria for designation as such are twofold: first, the physical condition of the houses must be poor; and second, the area must be such that the measure of 'social need' is great. 'Social need' has in turn been defined in terms of such measures as the level of multiple occupation, the volume of immigrants, overcrowding and single-parent families. The cluster analysis which results in areas being designated roughly on this basis acts, then, as a reification of existing thinking. The fact that immigrant levels were seen as associated in a predictive sense with 'social need' presumably led to their inclusion in the model in the first place. (Having said this, it must be stressed that we are not arguing that the areas of 'social need' are in any sense illusory or hinging on definitional circularity. It is clear that the association between the various factors listed above is not merely a statistical artefact. Indeed, the nature of the linkage is fundamental to our understanding of the plight of the blacks in an urban environment such as Handsworth.)

We turn now to the theoretical component of the particular/general thesis. In looking at the distributive mechanisms inherent in housing market operations, both public and private, we are inevitably involved in an analytical enterprise which cannot meaningfully be divorced from considerations of social structure. We have already seen evidence that the housing 'cake' may not be divided into equal portions amongst the whole community. This is clearly true, for example, among different occupational status groupings within the indigenous population. What concerns us here is the possibility that there may indeed be a different (and distinctly inferior) 'cake' which is reserved for the consumption of immigrant groups. It is the conviction that this conforms with the objective reality facing these groups which led Rex and Tomlinson (among others) to the general notion of 'under-class' or

'sub-proletariat'. Thus, whereas the native semi-skilled
or unskilled worker will face certain structural constraints within the housing market institutions (e.g.,
estate agents, councils, and building societies) which
restrict his freedom of action, his black counterpart may
face a much more rigid definition of his 'action frame of
reference'. A great deal of previous research [23] has
supported this particular thesis.

What is argued, then, is that blacks may not have
acquired equal bargaining rights in the (housing) market
place, when compared with those who ostensibly share their
'class' position; for example, in the classic Marxian
sense, of their relationship to the means of production.
The 'under-class thesis' then provokes a much more fundamental question. Is it not likely that even if equal
'bargaining rights' had been achieved here, they would
mean little if blacks were systematically deprived of similar rights in the 'employment market' and more fundamentally (especially in the long run) in the 'education
market'? Thus, even at this rather simplistic level, we
have produced an analytical framework which involves an
extremely complex mosaic of class and social structural
issues.

Many attempts have been made to disentangle some of the
different elements of this mosaic; notable among these is
the discussion, initiated by Rex and Moore (1967), [24] of
the concept of 'housing classes'. Despite much subsequent
criticism, predominantly at the level of statistical reasoning and the lack of exhaustiveness in the proposed
categories, [25] the broad approach, we believe, has much
to commend it. It is an attempt to fuse the notions of
competition for, and conflict arising from, scarce housing
resources with that of 'class', the latter interpreted not
simply in terms of a measure of occupational status but
also, and more especially, in terms of an individual's position within (and degree of access to) the housing
market. Such an analysis, Rex and Moore argue, is central
to any sociological analysis of the city. They stress the
significance of Weber's position in that 'in his analysis
of the formation of classes, he gives equal consideration
to ownership of domestic property and ownership of the
means of industrial production.' [26]

We shall not proceed with a detailed discussion of this
approach or with the comments of its critics: these have
already taken up many thousands of words elsewhere, perhaps most recently in Rex and Tomlinson (1979). [27] It
will be noted, however, when the ideas in this present
work (both theoretical and empirical) illuminate the
housing class thesis. We agree in particular with the po-

sition of centrality accorded to the notion of ownership
of property. On the other hand, as noted in the previous
chapter, 'ownership' seen in theoretically enlightened
terms is not amenable to simple objective definition. It
is often argued, even if only at an implicit level, that
the fact of ownership carries with it certain value connotations; for example, a belief, however vague, in the
concept of a 'property-owning democracy'. Moreover, this
is often argued without reference to the individual or
group concerned. To adopt this line of thinking in a race
relations situation is, we believe, to commit a gross
error. Previous research, for example, has suggested that
the black immigrant, on entering a major British city,
finds himself faced by market forces which, for a variety
of structurally implicit and explicit reasons, treat him
rather differently from his white counterpart. It is
certain also that the reasons for becoming an 'owner-
occupier' are often grounded in simple pragmatism or
social obligation rather than in ideological commitment
to an 'ethic'. This complicates the 'achievement' orientation implicit in an analysis of 'housing class' which
relies in part on the nature of tenure.

A further problem is that it is difficult to demonstrate that the black owner of a large multi-occupied
house is in that position out of 'necessity'; the argument here is that the indigenous population do not want
large, and often decaying, properties in the inner-city
areas. The new black owner is thus seen as being compelled (for financial reasons) to sub-let part of his
house, sometimes at high rents, and usually to his fellow
countrymen. Rex and Moore refer to this group as: 'A
pariah group of landlords ... who will do an essential job
and take the blame for doing it'. [28] They correctly
point out the ideological ambiguities in this state of
affairs. Nevertheless, it is undoubtedly sometimes the
case that the underlying motive of some immigrants can be
explained rather differently.

First, there are the entrepreneurs whose actions may be
grounded almost solely in the profit motive. This group
is admittedly likely to be small in number, given the
shortage of capital available to the majority of those who
enter Britain. A second, and perhaps rather more significant, group is formed by those who are obliged to buy
large properties and then share or sub-let for reasons
other than ones which result solely from the differential
operation of the housing market forces. Significant among
these are Asian families which are either large at the
time of buying, or which expect to become so at a later
date, for example, through the effects of chain migration.

Thus, cultural factors involving the sort of multiplex relations noted in Chapter 2 have a distinct bearing on the analysis of immigrant housing.

It is a mistake to infer from this that any analysis based on 'social facts' is, by definition, misguided. We are arguing rather that an analysis of housing must be wary of reifying categories by implying a uniformity which is not to be found in the social world. Tenure is a crucial element of any discussion of urban sociology, but it needs to be interpreted with care and seen in relation to the sort of issues discussed above. Our analysis therefore focuses in detail on the dynamics of interaction between 'consumer' and institution by looking at residential mobility from the perspective of our immigrant groups, and examines the question of finance (both sources and level). In doing so we hope to cast some light on the access to housing of differing types and quality.

Vital here are such questions as the supply of basic amenities, the incidence of multi-occupation, the degree of overcrowding, living in a housing action area (or general improvement area), and so on. The analysis therefore looks at 'housing class' in a context not merely of tenure but also that of the range of housing 'quality' which each tenure grouping encompasses. If it is assumed that there is competition for scarce housing resources, or, employing Rex's term, 'housing-class conflict', [29] it is clear that we are talking about competition for 'desirable' housing: 'desirable' in terms of price, location and quality as well as tenure.

HOUSING TENURE IN HANDSWORTH

We begin, then, by looking at the tenure pattern among those in our sample, and for comparative purposes note the corresponding figures for the whole of Birmingham at the time of the 1971 Census. It is immediately noticeable that, unless there has been a sensational differential increase in home ownership in Birmingham as a whole since 1971, the survey area is one in which house ownership is much more common than is the case in the rest of the city. Sampling error is ruled out as an alternative explanation by checking the (weighted) [30] tenure distribution against the appropriate census material for wards. Approaching two-thirds of the weighted sample were members of this tenure group, compared with 42.3 per cent for the city as a whole. Even allowing for a similar change in market share to that which occurred between 1961 and 1966, and between 1966 and 1971, it is unlikely that in 1976

TABLE 4.1   Present housing tenure by ethnic group
(weighted figures are bracketed)

	West Indian %	Asian %	British %	Birmingham (all households) [1] %
Owner-occupiers	54 (66)	82	41 (50)	42.3
Private renters (furnished)	4 (5)	8	3 (4)	5.9
Private renters (unfurnished)	11 (14)	2	20 (24)	13.6 [2]
Council tenants	31 (15)	6	35 (21)	38.2
Tenure not stated	–	2	1 (1)	–
Total number of households (= 100%)	395(320)	305	400(327)	333,785

1   Source: 1971 Census: Warwickshire County Report.
2   This figure includes households in Housing Association
    properties.

more than 45 per cent of the city's total housing stock
was owner-occupied. [31] Birmingham, it seems, lags
behind England and Wales as a whole on this particular
index; [32] a phenomenon due in part to the desire of
many white-collar workers to commute into the city from
surrounding areas.

The difference in tenure patterns of our three major
ethnic groups is even more interesting. In terms of home
ownership, for example, we have found the differentials to
be even greater than those noted by Smith (1977). Commenting on his figures he argued that: [33]

It is remarkable that ... over a relatively short
period in this country, and in spite of the fact that
they tend to be doing inferior jobs, to be earning less
and to have larger families to support, West Indians
have achieved the same level of owner-occupation as the
white population. It is quite startling to find,
therefore, that among Asians the level of owner-
occupation is much higher than among the general population; thus three-quarters of Asian households are in
owner-occupied accommodation, compared with half of
households generally. (Figures for the general popu-

lation are derived from the 1971 Census for England and
Wales.)
It would certainly be 'remarkable' and indeed startling if
it was the case that 'owner-occupied housing' was synonymous with 'good quality housing'. As Smith himself clearly realises, this is patently untrue. He had already
pointed out [34] that although the latter relationship
usually held in terms of the 'general population', it did
not do so invariably for members of the minority groups.

As far as present-day Handsworth is concerned, it appears that fewer white residents are owner-occupiers as
compared with either of the two New Commonwealth groups.
Our estimates show that only half of the British sample
own their property as against two-thirds of the West
Indians and over four out of every five Asians.

Whatever the reasons for these findings (and they will
be discussed shortly), they have clear implications for
one facet of the Rex and Moore thesis. We refer to that
which sets out the implications for the immigrant of inherent structural constraints within housing market institutions. Using a priori reasoning they argue cogently why
the 'qualifications' required of an owner-occupier imply
that: 'As a consequence the numbers of immigrants who
succeed in entering the class of owner-occupiers is
small'. [35] It is clearly the case that one or more of
the premises on which this conclusion was based is no
longer valid, or at least that one or more has diminished
in importance over the last decade. These premises (i.e.,
qualifications for entry to the class of owner-occupier)
include such factors as 'capital', 'security and reliability of income', 'style of life - in terms of property
treatment', and 'likelihood of return to homeland'.

Undoubtedly these are simple operational canons which
could be applied by a money-lending institution in such a
way as to legitimate a form of discrimination against the
immigrant by excluding him totally from the 'property-
owning class' in the way that Rex and Moore argue. Subsequent research, however, suggests that the selective application of these rules has produced in practice a rather
more insidious form of discriminatory control of housing
resources: money is lent, but only on certain properties,
in certain locations and/or on certain financial conditions. As Lawrence (1974) remarks, research undertaken in
1967 [36] confirmed: [37]

> that coloured people were denied access to some desi-
> rable housing: that they were less likely to obtain a
> mortgage; and that even if a mortgage were granted it
> would probably require a larger than usual deposit
> and/or a higher than average rate of interest.

Lawrence's own research in Nottingham seems to provide
corroborative evidence. [38]
    We would like to argue that financial institutions
might 'relax' their 'qualifications' in three situations.
First, where they are able to minimise the risk on capital; i.e., where the required deposit is of such a magnitude that in the event of default the mortgagors are assured of holding property whose value is far in excess of
the outstanding capital. Second, where the element of
risk is compensated by a very high short-term return on
capital. The third and final case is where in the interests of turnover the agent wishes to sell property in less
desirable areas which otherwise (i.e., but for the 'immigrant market') would remain on their books indefinitely.
As with the previous two cases, the links between estate
agent and financial institutions ensure that these operations are feasible.
    One way of evading these discriminatory procedures, of
course, is to pay for the house in cash. Unlikely though
this may seem as a means of acquiring property for the
immigrant who comes to this country in order to build up
capital, it is undoubtedly a serious possibility among
members of the Asian community. Rex and Moore (1967)
argue that: 'The mutual aid system which operates in
their own (Asian) primary communities, together with the
willingness to work overtime, makes it possible for some
of them to obtain a deposit.' [39] This is indeed true,
but it underestimates the potential achievements of such
collective action. In addition, along with all the other
works so far discussed in this chapter, it ignores one
crucial point; namely, that some of the Asian religions
(and Hinduism in particular) explicitly condemn usury. A
Hindu who remains true to his faith is forbidden to have
any financial dealings with those whose business it is to
lend money for profit. Admittedly, many Asian banks do
exist, and these have to some extent ducked the issue of
usury by replacing the concept of 'interest' by one of
'commission'. It remains true, however, that the large
numbers of owner-occupiers who own their property outright
attest both to this religious obligation and to their
alternative fund-raising power. [40]
    It is often argued that the man who buys his own house
does so basically for reasons of security and social prestige or status. Undoubtedly the widespread consensus
about these issues ensures competition for scarce housing
resources. It is not surprising then to find that those
in a position to exploit the situation by creaming off the
best property available are those with the best 'qualifications'. Writers such as Smith argue quite correctly

that: 'Among the general population, the more affluent
people are, the higher their standard of housing, and the
more likely they are to be owner-occupiers.' [41] It has
generally been found, however, that the maxim does not
hold true for all immigrant groups, and this is especially
so for the Asians. For this group we find the relationship completely reversed: the lower the occupational
status of the head of household, the more likely he is to
own his own house. As Smith says: 'For a large proportion of Asians, buying their own home is not a way of
getting superior housing at a premium price (as it is for
the rest of the population) but a way of getting poor
housing cheaply.' [42] For reasons which will be discussed later, council housing is not seen as a realistic
or desirable alternative to owner-occupation, nor is private rented accommodation.

Although Smith rather overplays the importance of the
need (in language terms) rather than the desire (in
social, religious and cultural terms) and the element of
necessity (due to external structural forces) to live
amongst his fellow countrymen, he is correct in arguing
that areas of current settlement are those which are most
likely to present the most 'feasible' source of suitable
housing (in terms of size and price). As we, in our
Handsworth sample (significantly perhaps) [43] came across
few white-collar Asians, it is difficult to compare tenure
patterns across occupational groups. It is certain, however, that they could scarcely exhibit a greater propensity to buy than their blue-collar compatriots.

In the case of the West Indians studied by Smith, it
appears to be the skilled and semi-skilled who most frequently become owner-occupiers, and once again it is the
non-manual workers who are least likely to own their own
home. [44] Apart from the difference in the relative proportions of owner-occupiers among the Asians and West
Indians, the major feature which distinguishes the tenure
patterns is the comparatively large number of West Indians
in council accommodation, a point which we shall pursue
shortly. Once again, because of the significant lack of
West Indians in non-manual occupations, it is not possible
to draw meaningful conclusions about the relationship between tenure and occupation for the West Indians in the
Handsworth sample.

Returning to Table 4.1, we see a noticeable lack of
public sector housing in the survey area as against the
city as a whole. In fact, there are important historical
reasons for this. Throughout the late nineteenth and
early twentieth centuries, private housing developments
progressively swallowed up available building land. The

vast majority of this housing remains today and therefore
with the exception of Newtown council estate, and a number
of houses 'municipalised' by the local authority, public
housing is conspicuous by its absence. An issue of major
importance, however, is the massive part which private
ownership plays, and the consequent lack of rented accommodation. In the past, much of the housing stock was let
unfurnished at controlled rents, and it is largely this
property which is being progressively sold off to immigrant families on the deaths or departure of previous
tenants;   a process which lies at the roots of the present
position.

Rent controls were strengthened during the 1960s largely as a result of the public exposure of exploitative
landlordism. There were massive scandals focusing on individual cases, notably Perec Rachmann whose name was to
become synonymous with the 'evil' itself. This, combined
with legislation which aimed at providing security of
tenure, meant that many landlords, seeing the return on
their capital constrained, and fearing future punitive
measures (in their eyes), started to sell off their property by fair means or foul. [45] Thus an unintended consequence of the policies was the rapid decline in private
rented accommodation and often increased suffering in the
case of some tenants who were forced to run the gauntlet
of intimidation and abuse. As security of tenure was
strengthened, particularly in the case of unfurnished
tenancies, it is hardly surprising that it is this sector
which has diminished most sharply over the last fifteen
years or so.

It is, however, the whole problem of private rented ac-
commodation which concerns the authors of the Structure
Plan. In the course of summarising 'The Main (Housing)
Issues' they argue that: [47]

Of particular concern ... is the rapid decline in the
number of privately rented dwellings in the City (by
25 per cent over the 1961-66 period). [46] This tenure
group provides a stock of relatively cheap though frequently sub-standard accommodation for low-income
households, and for other groups of the population
(such as single persons, students and other newcomers
to the city who are ineligible for council accommodation).

It is clear that from the point of view of those who
are responsible for the local housing stock these 'frequently sub-standard' dwellings serve a useful purpose in
housing 'newcomers to the city', which, of course, includes the immigrant population. The logic of this situation is clear. To rehouse the tenants of such property

or perhaps even to use their powers of compulsory purchase
with a view to subsequent demolition or improvement, would
place a severe financial burden on the council. To do
nothing is simply to evade (by default) statutory obligations [48] and might in the meantime result, through the
tenant's departure, in a further loss to the rented stock.
To take a third (intermediate) course via improvement
grants might alleviate the plight of the tenant, at least
temporarily, and avoid major financial headaches for the
council, [49] but this would still provide no assurance
that the property would not move ultimately into the
owner-occupied sector.

Taking into account recent pressure on the public
sector borrowing requirement, inflation, and the ever-
present need to minimise increases in rates, it is hardly
surprising that the authors of the above report conclude
rather gloomily that: 'The city is still faced with a
big task in terms of home improvement and modernisation
to bring its older dwellings up to modern standards.' [50]
With regard to the private rented sector it is admitted
that: 'Despite the growing contribution of housing associations and societies to meet housing needs, it is
likely that the decline in the private rented sector has
continued in recent years.' [50] The general feeling conveyed is that this decline will continue, and certainly
nothing has happened since the publication of the Plan to
alter the position significantly.

It is clearly the case also that the movement towards
owner occupation will not, per se, increase the standard
of housing stock, and that housing associations are not
contributing significantly to the alleviation of the general shortfall in number and standard of dwellings.   In
addition, census figures show a 2.3 per cent drop in the
number of families housed by the local authority between
1966 and 1971.

As noted earlier, the level of council housing in
Handsworth is extremely low compared with that of the city
as a whole, and what accommodation there is seems on the
whole to go to whites rather than to members of the minority population, and especially the Asians. The latter
finding does not in itself imply that overt racial discrimination on the part of council employees provides the key
to the explanation. It is more likely, as argued by Smith
and Whalley, that 'minority groups could be put at a disadvantage because of the general structure of the allocation system'. [51] In the same way that financial institutions, as we have seen, operate sets of requirements for
the would-be owner-occupier, local authorities, in a situation of competition for scarce resources, have devised

measurement procedures which assess the individual's 'qualifications' for council tenancy. We do not wish to argue that the two sorts of institution are operating the same system; simply that both may work to the disadvantage of the immigrant. The point is, that, since the rules operated by finance houses are, on the whole, implicit rather than explicit, there is more latitude for the individual assessor to employ overtly discriminatory practices. Council rules and the attendant points systems (in so far as they are publicly known) usually have at least a certain superficial appearance of objectivity. Moreover, the points 'score', is seen by most (including members of ethnic minority groups) as eminently fair, even though the system as a whole clearly legitimates actions which can work (and can be seen to work) to the distinct disadvantage of the immigrant.

The British canon of 'fairness' is, of course, enshrined in the notion of the housing 'queue' or waiting list. Certain requirements, however, need to be fulfilled before an individual may join the queue, primarily some form of residence qualification. That Birmingham employ such a procedure can be seen from the quote referred to earlier. [52] 'Newcomers to the city', and therefore by implication immigrants, had therefore to find alternative accommodation for a period of at least five years.

As West Indians tended to arrive in the UK rather before the Asians, we might expect a rather larger proportion of the former to be in council accommodation. This is indeed the case among our sample, as Table 4.1 shows. It is clear, however, that length of residence is not the sole reason for the differential; if this were so we could expect, for example, that the proportions of Asian and West Indian council tenants would be rather similar among those who arrived during the same periods. A glance at Table 4.2 quickly dispels any thought that the situation is so straightforward. There are major differences in the two sets of figures. It appears that it is only among the Asians and West Indians who arrived before 1960 that the levels of council tenancy (on the more appropriate weighted figures) are approximately equal. The very fact that this occurs, however, marks a sharp divergence from the results obtained by Smith. Even among these groups (the pre-1960 arrivals) West Indian families were more than three times as likely to be in council property as the Asians. [53] Although the size of the Handsworth sample makes such fine comparisons hazardous, it appears that it is the rehousing of Asian families from demolition properties, combined with the general level of council accommodation in the area, which has con-

TABLE 4.2   Present housing tenure by date of entry to the UK (weighted figures are bracketed)

A WEST INDIANS	Before 1955 %	1955-9 %	1960-4 %	1965 and after [2] %	Total %
Owner-occupiers	73(80)	65 (76)	45 (60)	16(22)	54 (66)
Private renters (furnished)	2 (2)	4 (5)	3 (5)	12(17)	4 (5)
Private renters (unfurnished)	8 (9)	7 (8)	14 (18)	28(39)	11 (14)
Council tenants	17 (9)	25 (11)	37 (18)	44(22)	31 (15)
Total sample size [1] (= 100%)	48(44)	139(118)	174(133)	25(18)	395(320)

B ASIANS	Before 1955 %	1955-9 %	1960-4 %	1965 and after %	Total %
Owner-occupiers	73	75	88	80	82
Private renters (furnished)	6	10	7	10	8
Private renters (unfurnished)	3	-	-	5	2
Council tenants	18	12	4	2	6
Tenure not stated	-	4	2	3	2
Total sample size [3] (= 100%)	33	51	130	88	305

1   The body of the table excludes 9(7) respondents who failed to state the year in which they entered the UK.
2   As the sample size is small, care should be taken when interpreting the figures.
3   The body of the table excludes three respondents who failed to state the year in which they entered the UK.

tributed significantly to this result. As we shall see later, it is unlikely, for example, that many Asian families are moving into council properties by their own efforts.

The studies [54] are in agreement over two things: first, that the West Indian family is in general much more likely to be a council tenant than the Asian counterpart; and second, that the level of council tenancy among West Indians falls sharply with increasing length of residence. There is growing evidence, for example, that West Indians are moving out of council property and into owner-occupation. But it is dangerous to infer from this that such West Indians are in a sense improving themselves and thereby moving closer to their projected self-image on arrival in the UK (see Chapter 1). In many cases it is a question of their moving from 'patched' council property in a general improvement or housing action area to their own house in a similar area. This is certainly true for many of those in our sample who have 'achieved' this change of tenure, and it has undoubtedly illuminated a problem with the housing-class thesis. In what sense has the individual's position altered in class terms? It could conceivably be argued that he has, in fact, been 'running in order to stand still'. After all, it is quite feasible that in a few years' time the 'new' house will be compulsorily purchased by the council as part of yet another inner-city initiative. By being black and living amongst his compatriots the house-owner is, as noted earlier, defined thereby as being in 'social need'! He has not, therefore, in practical terms, achieved the measure of self-determination normally accorded to the owner of property.

There are native whites who share this position, but, as we have seen, in addition to being rather more scarce in proportional terms, they tend to differ on one major issue, that of age. Whereas most of the West Indian families have an economically active head of household and are therefore theoretically mobile, a large proportion of the whites are retired and would not normally expect to move. The point to note, therefore, is that the constraints on mobility differ radically in form.

In the realm of council housing there is an increasing amount of evidence to suggest that few blacks are found on the more popular (and higher-quality) estates. We know, for example, that even on the relatively unpopular Newtown Estate no more than one in ten of the properties is occupied by a West Indian or an Asian family. [55] Commenting on his research, Smith notes a general 'tendency for minority council tenants to group within particular es-

tates', [56] and later that 'Asian and West Indian council
tenants tend to be occupying accommodation of poorer
quality than white council tenants'. [57]

We shall return to discuss these ideas a little later
in this present chapter, and examine the whole question of
differential access to public housing. For the moment,
however, we return to Table 4.2 in order to compare the
varying patterns of tenure outside the public sector. As
far as the West Indians are concerned it seems as though
the vast majority aim ultimately to buy their own house:
certainly relatively few of those who arrived in Britain
within the last ten to fifteen years had become owner-
occupiers. Of course, we do not know from the analysis
whether the more recent arrivals differ in any important
ways from their predecessors. For example, it might be
that fewer of the younger West Indians wish to own their
own home, or perhaps that they wish to but are finding
it increasingly difficult for a variety of reasons. (Certainly without the form of primary community ties which
exist in the Asian community, problems of finance might
prove insuperable in the short to medium term.) In contrast, it is very noticeable that the vast majority of
Asian families are able to buy property within a short
space of time after arriving in Britain.

These remarks lead to very different theories about the
ways in which these two major ethnic groups approach the
housing market. West Indians, without the initial capital
to buy, and denied entry to the formal council waiting
list by residence qualifications, are in the main pushed
into the dwindling private rented sector. Interestingly,
many succeed in finding unfurnished accommodation (unlike
the Asians) and hence have stronger tenancy rights (in a
legal sense) than they might otherwise have. This state
of affairs also reflects something of the attitudes of
the different groups to the initial 'phase of settlement':
furnished tenancies take on the role of a temporary expedient, a staging-post on the way to owner-occupation.

Central to the process of Asian settlement is the
notion of 'chain migration' (as noted in Chapter 2). The
first members of a family to come here are often the
father and eldest son of the father and his brother (or
brother-in-law). On arrival they might be accepted into
the house of a kinsman or have to resort to taking rooms
in a multi-occupied house or lodging house. Since the aim
is invariably to bring the remainder of the family to
Britain within as short a time as possible, a house of
adequate size must be sought. Unfortunately, as the size
of the family tends to be larger than that of most other
immigrant groups (including West Indians), rented proper-

ty, which is usually in the form of flats, is rarely a
feasible long-term proposition. In addition, as Rex and
Moore correctly point out: [58]

Tenancies of whole houses owned by private landlords
are increasingly difficult to obtain because of the
demolition of old rented property. But even where such
tenancies are available they are rarely advertised and
friendship or kinship with the landlord or with neighbours may be an important criterion in the selection of
these tenants.

There is little to suggest that a significant proportion
of these landlords are themselves drawn from the immigrant
communities and therefore it is probably the case that
'these tenancies will not be given to coloured immigrants'. [58] Since, in the short term, council accommodation is ruled out by the residence qualification, there
is little option but to attempt to buy the cheapest property available which meets basic criteria, primarily that
of size. Containing as it does large numbers of houses
which are in local (i.e., Birmingham) terms in the lowest
price quartile, Handsworth provides a convenient 'market
place'.

These appear to be feasible modes of action for members
of the major immigrant communities in Handsworth, but the
question inevitably arises as to how far these conform to
'social reality'. Admittedly, any answers can only be
tentative. On the other hand, this does not mean that
the quest is not worthwhile, for by delving into the ways
in which individuals act, both in the deeds themselves and
their 'understanding' of them, we might, as social scientists, be in a position to gain greater insights into the
social forces which join together to enhance or constrain
action. In this instance it may help us to understand the
relations between the immigrant and the housing market if
we look at the nature of the movement between the previous
and present addresses of our Handsworth residents. (See
Table 4.3; the corresponding figures for the British
sample are included for comparative purposes.)

In the process of discussing residential patterns in
Chapter 3 it was noted that the members of the British
sample were on the whole extremely immobile in geographical terms. [59] Given the age distribution of the residents, such immobility was to be expected. With an immigrant population which is much more 'youthful' in composition, and which, by definition, is composed of people who
are accustomed to moving house, we would expect a rather
different picture. This is indeed the case, but to a
fairly limited extent: only a third (approximately) of
the Asian and West Indian families in our sample had moved

TABLE 4.3 Tenure of present and previous accommodation by
ethnic group [1] (weighted figures are bracketed)

A   WEST INDIAN

Previous tenure	Present tenure	Owner- oc- cupier %	Private renter %	Council tenant %	All %
Owner-occupier		23	5	3 (4)	10 (13)
Rented from relative		9	5	5 (2)	6 (6)
'Other' private rented		57	78	37(35)	53 (59)
Council tenant		7	–	48(54)	24 (16)
Lived with parents/ relatives		3	10	5 (2)	6 (5)
Other [4] (including tenure not stated)		1	2	2 (2)	1 (1)
Total sample size (= 100%)		91	60	121(46)	272(197)

B   ASIAN [3]

Previous tenure	Present tenure	Owner- oc- cupier %	Private renter [2] %	Council tenant [2] %	All %
Owner-occupier		33	17	25	31
Rented from relative		21	29	6	20
'Other' private rented		29	29	13	27
Council tenant		1	–	44	5
Lived with parents/ relatives		11	4	13	11
Other [5] (including tenure not stated)		4	21	–	6
Total sample size (= 100%)		150	24	16	194

C BRITISH [6]

Previous tenure	Present tenure	Owner-occupier %	Private renter %	Council tenant %	All %
Owner-occupier		43	11	2 (4)	12 (18)
Private rented [8]		35	61	23(20)	32 (37)
Council tenant		5	6	68(69)	44 (31)
Lived with parents/ relatives		14	11	6 (6)	9 (10)
Other (including tenure not stated)		3	11	1 (*) [7]	4 (3)
Total sample size (= 100%)		37	36	122(49)	197(122)

1   Excluded from the table are those who have lived at their present address for at least ten years.
2   The frequencies here are very small. Care should therefore be taken so as not to exaggerate their significance.
3   The body of this sub-table excludes four respondents who did not state their present tenure.
4   This category also includes two West Indian families who came to their present address from outside the UK.
5   This category includes twelve Asian families who came direct to their present address from outside the UK.
6   The body of this sub-table excludes two respondents who did not state their present tenure.
7   * represents a figure of less than 0.5%.
8   As only two of the British respondents rented from relatives a separate category is not reserved for them here.

within the previous five years. Table 4.3 then shows that, if we increase the time scale to ten years the figure increases to 69(62) per cent and 64 per cent for the West Indians and Asians respectively.

The significance of these findings does not emerge, however, until we compare rather carefully the people who have moved during this period with those who have not done so. In doing so we gain an intriguing impression of the temporal dynamics of an evolving multi-racial area. With the exception of two families, all the West Indians who have remained in the present house for over ten years are owner-occupiers. *[60]* These tend to be well-established family groups whose head came with the first major influx of immigrants from the Caribbean. They now mirror the pattern of geographical stability seen particularly among large sections of the native working class. Despite the shortcomings of the properties which they inhabit (a topic to be discussed shortly), they have achieved security of tenure and form part of the stable core of Handsworth families. An obvious question to ask at this point is 'To what extent will recent arrivals to this country emulate their predecessors?' Table 4.3A, whilst not providing a complete answer in itself, at least contains a number of clues.

It may be significant, for example, that amongst a group of families where only 10(13) per cent originally owned their own property, the figure has now risen to 34(46) per cent. We might infer that it is perhaps unlikely (following up a question raised earlier) that younger West Indians might differ from their older compatriots to the extent of turning their backs on owner-occupation by choice (as distinct from compulsion). Some of the younger families in the table were indeed already owner-occupiers before their most recent move. In the main, however, these families seem to have been using private rented accommodation as a temporary expedient whilst saving up the deposit to buy a house. The overwhelming majority already lived in Handsworth or its surrounding areas: a point which applies equally to those who remained in rented property. Of the present council tenants 48(54) per cent were in local authority property already, although a significant number had rented privately whilst waiting to be offered suitable council accommodation. A handful of those who had previously bought property moved against the general trend by going into rented housing - invariably as a result of the clearance schemes which were noted earlier.

It is conceivable perhaps (as was suggested in Chapter 2) that the issue of tenure is often overplayed by social scientists: might it not, in fact, be of less than prime importance to the individual immigrant family? We could point to the fact that few West Indians actually mentioned that it was a major reason for moving house. To accept this argument at face value, however, would be to misread seriously the type of situation faced by many of those whom our researchers met during the course of the study. Although the ultimate aim might be, for example, to buy a suitable property for the family, more pressing considerations often presented themselves. In addition, it is naturally the case that only those who actually did change

their tenure situation would mention it as a major driving
force. Respondents tended to argue that they had been
compelled to leave their previous house because the family
was living in a state of chronic overcrowding. Many
others were forced to leave because their property had
been condemned or because they had been evicted.

We can conlude from this that although home ownership,
and perhaps home ownership outside the 'twilight zones',
might be the dream of many, perhaps most, West Indian
families, [6] for many it is at present a question of
passive response to external pressures. All thoughts of
fulfilling their aims and expectancies must become secondary to the basic necessity of trying to find somewhere
(possibly anywhere) which might lead to a period of respite from chronic social stress. Whether or not these
families have actually improved their lot, in any sense,
is an important question which we shall defer until later.
(A priori reasoning would, however, lead us to expect that
many could scarcely do worse.) Well over a quarter of our
sample of West Indian families had been living in one
room; usually in a lodging house or bedsitter. Approaching the same figure had occupied only two rooms. When we
take into account the fact that, for many, this was not
the first 'home' they had lived in since arriving in
Britain, and that some of those who seemed to have done
better (in terms of dwelling size) were, in fact, living
in condemned property, we have a rather appalling overall
picture. We have also excluded here the 15(10) families
who were living with parents or relatives and wished to
move into a place of their own because of the stress which
this was creating.

The picture was scarcely more encouraging for the Asian
families. Excluding those who are at the moment in their
first dwelling since coming to the UK, 28 per cent of the
families had been living in one room, and a further 14 per
cent had occupied two rooms. In addition, rather more of
the Asians were sharing their home with parents or relations than was the case among the West Indians; one in
ten did so, as against (approximately) one in thirty.
When we look at the reasons given for moving, the patterns
for the two groups are, in some ways, rather similar. The
three main issues raised in relation to 'property' (as
distinct from social considerations) are still size,
tenure and demolition (or proposed demolition). The main
difference arises from their relative importance. Although size can be defined in objective terms, as having
been as serious a problem amongst both sets of families,
a much larger proportion of Asians argued that the major
reason for moving was to buy their own home - a point

which is very much in line with the sharp increase in
owner-occupation shown in Table 4.3B. A rather larger
proportion of Asian families (than West Indian) had been
living in condemned property though fewer had been rehoused in council property. Many of these families had
become owner-occupiers. Interestingly, no Asian complained that he and his family had been evicted from their previous address.

The major difference between the two ethnic groups lay
in the previous source of accommodation and the change in
the pattern of tenure since this time. We noted earlier
that even among West Indians there was a marked tendency
to buy property after spending some time in (often extremely unsatisfactory) rented accommodation. The level
of owner-occupation, however, is still small compared with
the comparable group of Asians: 31 per cent of the Asians
owned their previous property, and by 1976 over 77 per
cent had become owner-occupiers. It might be argued that
this was predictable, given the information in Table 4.2.
On the other hand, we do see that there is a distinctive
phase before owner-occupation and, in fact, many of the
'original' owner-occupiers are those who had been in the
UK for a much longer period of time and who had spent some
time in rented or shared accommodation on arrival. We may
obtain an interesting glimpse into this prior stage of
Asian settlement by looking at the new owner-occupiers.
Half of these families had rented privately; a slightly
smaller number than among the comparable West Indian
group. The major difference here, as with the Asian group
as a whole, however, is that the 'landlord' of an Indian
or Pakistani family was much more likely to have been a
relative. In fact, if we include those who described
themselves as 'living with parents or relatives' almost
a third of new owner-occupiers were previously housed in
this way. Our research also suggests that many of the remaining landlords are, in fact, friends and kinsmen (as
will be seen later).

This provides supporting evidence for previous remarks
about the 'reception' role of the primary community in the
chain migration process. When studied in conjunction with
information about the time scale within which families
were reunited, it also gives insight into an issue which
has perplexed many social scientists. In Smith's (1977)
words: [62]

Altogether outright ownership is a common form of
tenure mostly among the most disadvantaged section of
the Asian community.... It is not clear how these
people could have had enough savings to buy these properties, cheap as they were.

Indeed, among the Handsworth sample more than three out of every five Asian owner-occupiers owns his home outright, [63] and the majority are in unskilled or semi-skilled jobs.

The interesting point to which we alluded above, however, is that although 70 per cent of those families who moved house during the last ten years were complete, this number contains few of the new owner-occupiers. In following up this particular point we see that the most likely explanation is that the adult male members of the family, in migrating first, tend initially to rent property from family or friends. Given the obligation to house kinsmen it is unlikely that the rent will be anything but a purely nominal sum (if it exists at all). To behave otherwise would probably not only be seen as behaving contrary to the mutual understandings of social obligation, but would also in financial terms be rather unnecessary since the 'landlord' in the vast majority of cases owns his own home outright.

Smith is clearly sceptical of his results, on the grounds that the majority of his sample claimed to have 'found the money from savings or from working hard and doing overtime'. [62] But is this such an unlikely explanation in the light of the above discussion? A small family sub-unit (possibly one or two male wage-earners) coming to the UK ahead of other family members, enters a household containing other relations or friends and receives lodging and perhaps board for little or no outlay in money terms, 'payment' being interpreted as a future obligation to their hosts and to other members of the primary community. In this situation, by working extremely long hours (as will be confirmed in Chapter 5) the individual, or sub-unit, with little primary outlay in terms of basic living expenses, is able to amass a fairly substantial sum in a relatively short period. His only major outlay (assuming he resists the temptations of a Western-style social life) is, perhaps, money required to support kin who have not yet left India or Pakistan.

On the other hand, political realities, and the subjective interpretation by immigrants of stated and unstated intentions regarding future policies, sometimes lead to actions which disrupt the above argument. For example, someone who fears stricter immigration policies may send for his wife and/or children 'prematurely'. This has often resulted in chronic overcrowding when such families are absorbed into the primary community; but, nevertheless, absorbed they are. The basic theory remains intact, a minor modification in this case being that dependants arrive before the wage-earners have saved a suf-

ficient amount of money to acquire property. Certainly
it is the case that some borrow from friends and relatives
and that a few bring some money into Britain, as is suggested by Smith's study. What is not warranted is the implicit scepticism of the following remark: 'It seems
likely that informal pooling arrangements between friends
and relatives must have played a part, and that such arrangements are taken so much for granted that informants
did not bother to mention this.' [62]

As was the case with the West Indians, most of those
who had been at their present address for at least ten
years were owner-occupiers. One very important question
remains, and again it is one which social scientists have
failed to answer satisfactorily. It is the question of
why the level of owner-occupation among Asians is so much
higher than both that of other immigrant groups and of the
general population (or, conversely, why the level of
council tenancy among Asians is particularly low). We
believe that an understanding of the reasons for this not
only highlights sociologically important issues inherent
in the competition for scarce housing resources but also
involves discussion of the Indian or Pakistani, Hindu,
Moslem or Sikh communities vis-à-vis white (British)
society.

Smith and Whalley (1975) discuss in detail, for example, ways in which council allocation procedures can prove
'disadvantageous' as distinct from 'discriminatory',
'eligibility qualifications' and 'priority systems' being
clear examples. These are, however, procedures which
affect both West Indian and Asian alike (or at least, they
do not explain per se the massive differential in council
tenancy demonstrated by their research). More revealing
is their Item 4; the matching of the 'pool of available
accommodation' to the 'needs of minority groups'. They
argue subsequently that: [64]

For example, Asians tend to have large families, but
councils tend to have few properties with four or more
bedrooms; therefore Asian applicants will have a low
chance of being rehoused, not because of their race,
but because of their family size.

Our Handsworth study certainly confirms the general
remarks concerning the size of the Asian family. [65]   In
addition, an analysis of 1971 Census figures for the wards
in which our study was conducted shows that out of 6,059
households in council property only 935 (or 15.4 per cent)
had six or more rooms. This clearly suggests that the
supply of such large properties in the immediate locality
is small.

Although we have now gained some impressions of con-

straining factors, this is only one side of the total
question: it explains why Asians, having applied, might
not be successful. The point is, however, that comparatively few Asians do, in fact, apply for council housing.
One possible explanation is that lack of success in gaining council accommodation and the resultant belief that
the system is against them, whether or not this is seen
as racially discriminatory, might be transmitted throughout the primary community and deter would-be applicants.

A second and extremely important reason is that to
accept council property would be, in both pragmatic and
symbolic senses, to risk undermining the social obligation
to one's kinsmen. In practical terms, the council tenant
is denied, by the terms of his lease, the right to sub-let
any part of his dwelling. The mortgagee is similarly restricted, though only at a purely legalistic level, his
chances of being detected being minimal. Most Asian
owner-occupiers do not have mortgages and therefore, with
the exception of public health regulations relating to
overcrowding, are not constrained in such a manner.
Furthermore the symbolic value of ownership, and outright
ownership in particular, may be even more important. We
have already, for example, seen evidence of the desire of
Asian communitites to retain their cultural, religious and
social independence from other ethnic groups. Property
ownership provides a certain measure of immunity to external social contact and strengthens the individual's
self-image of insularity and independence in relation to
outsider groups. The existence of systems of multiplex
relations then ensures the propagation and strengthening
of such values. Suitable rented accommodation is often
scarce in areas of Asian settlement, and, in cases where
it is available, conditions of tenancy might present the
same problems as those of similar property in the public
sector.

Needless to say, the changes in tenure patterns of the
British are decidedly different. Table 4.3C shows that,
although there is a slight degree of movement towards
owner-occupation (in accordance with the national trend),
the extent of this shift is comparatively small: 12(18)
per cent to 19(30) per cent. Even then, care should be
taken not to exaggerate the significance of this change,
since the sample size is rather small. The phenomenon
appears to result mainly from a small number of young
families buying their own home after periods spent living
with parents or in private rented accommodation. As might
have been expected in a traditional working-class white
community, it is not the case, as it was with the immigrants, that those who have remained at the same address

for the last ten years are almost exclusively owner-
occupiers. Many of the older residents acquired their
unfurnished rented accommodation when such properties were
plentiful, a time, moreover, when owner-occupation was
almost exclusively the preserve of the more affluent
middle classes. It is many of these people who add to the
general picture of immobility among the white population
of Handsworth. [66]

Having traced the general movement in tenure patterns,
we now turn to look at the housing actually acquired by
current residents. In doing so we examine the question
of differential access to the housing 'cake', bearing in
mind that we are dealing with a rather minor slice of an
extremely large whole. [67] As has already been argued,
the concept of 'housing class' is both useful and perhaps
deceptively straightforward. The extent to which we may
explore it in an empirical sense is undoubtedly limited
by the bounds of our research. In the present context,
for example, we cannot establish the precise social identity of blacks who have escaped the inner-city environment
and acquired, apparently against heavy odds, more desirable property. Undoubtedly, for some the escape may ultimately be seen as illusory in terms of their subsequent
experiences. Others (as is the case with many middle-
class whites), will never even have visited an area such
as Handsworth. We believe, however, that both of these
points can be accepted without weakening our argument.

In any case, previous research has shown conclusively
that the major concentrations of blacks are almost exclusively located in 'the inner city'. [68] It is suggested, further, that these concentrations are (if anything) increasing. In the course of discussing the 'chief
areas of urban deprivation', the consultants who were com-
missioned by the Tory government in 1973 to conduct the
'Inner Area Studies' spelt out three major conclusions:
(a) that these areas contained (in 1971) one in fourteen
of the country's population; (b) that one in five of the
areas' families were in bad housing; and (c) that the
areas contained no less than one-third of the country's
black immigrants. [69] Quite understandably, sociologists
of race relations have concentrated their efforts on areas
of existing social stress and actual or potential conflict. They have done so rather than seeking to study
individuals who have broken away from the general pattern,
intellectually interesting and illuminating though this
might be (as would be the case, for example, of a social
mobility study focusing on the children of unskilled white
manual workers who subsequently enter top professions).

We need to ask ourselves at this stage one major ques-

tion: How can we approach the evaluation of 'housing
achievement'? Under the assumption that any family, irrespective of race, regards the nature and quality of his
accommodation as of prime importance, competition for
these scarce resources is assured. The fact of scarcity
is not disputed. In the official report cited earlier,
for example, Birmingham's housing deficiency in 1971 was
estimated at 13,855. [70]

Tenure, as we have already noted, is one such evaluative factor. In the present analysis we are principally
concerned with the 'ownership of capital' via property.
A sociologically informed analysis, we believe, must then
look carefully at the status of property acquired, and the
manner in which the 'capital invested' is utilised. In
terms of status we recognise that by the very nature of
our research (as noted above) we are concerned almost exclusively with property at the lower market levels.
(Indeed a cornerstone of our analysis concerns this very
point.)

Our major analytical concern at this point, then, lies
with the second dimension of the problem: the utilisation
of capital. We wish to argue that this concept embodies
four major possibilities: first, there is the acquisition
of property solely for owner-occupation, property which is
often of poor investment potential. (This is a crucial
thread of the argument since it suggests that sharp capital appreciation and the attendant financial possibility
of moving to higher-status, better quality accommodation
is rather unlikely.) This leaves three other sub-groups
of people who control capital in the form of property:
namely, those who, as noted earlier, sub-let for overt
financial gain (i.e., the entrepreneurs); those who sub-
let or share [71] their accommodation principally out of
social obligation (e.g., to close family or kin); and
those who are compelled to sub-let for reasons of financial insecurity (among whom are included the lodging-house
proprietors referred to by Rex and Moore, 1967). [72] To
the owner-occupier groups we must then add those who live
in private rented accommodation (furnished and unfurnished) and, of course, council tenants of both municipalised
and purpose-built property.

Beyond the issue of tenure there is the question of
immediate environment - important since even within an
area such as Handsworth, where the majority of houses are
situated in 'action' areas of some kind or another, differentials exist between the desirability of certain
locales. As to the property itself, it is necessary to
attempt to evaluate the quality of accommodation as seen
in terms of the provision of basic amenities, the occupa-

tional density and the existence and nature of multiple
occupation. We have, then, a complex multi-dimensional
matrix within which it is intended to locate members of
our three major ethnic groups. The significance of this
location will then be judged by reference to local and
occasionally national yardsticks. We begin with an analysis of owner-occupation in Handsworth.

OWNER-OCCUPATION IN HANDSWORTH

Within the context of the City as a whole, Handsworth is
no longer a fashionable address and has not been such for
some considerable length of time. Despite this, it is undoubtedly the case that, as was noted in the previous
paragraph (and with apologies to George Orwell), some
areas within the unequal are more equal than others. One
index of the desirability in physical terms, [73] is the
'housing area' classification, as used in Table 4.4. In
a very real sense the scale is ordinal, beginning as it
does, with redevelopment areas (i.e., those where houses
are considered unfit for human habitation – and irrevoca-
bly so) and ending with areas in which 'no action' is felt
necessary.

TABLE 4.4   'Housing area' of owner-occupation by ethnic
group [4]

	West Indian %	Asian %	British %
Redevelopment Area – phase 2	* [1]	3	3
Housing Action Area (HAA)	38	53	26
General Improvement Area – declared	38	37	46
General Improvement Area – proposed	18	6	8
'No action' area	6	1	16
Total sample size (= 100%)	212 [2]	249	165 [3]

1 * represents a figure of less than 0.5%.
2 The base figure of 211 was used here as the 'housing
   area' of one respondent was not recorded.
3 The base figure of 164 was used here as the 'housing
   area' of one respondent was not recorded.
4 Weighted figures are not needed here since the Newtown
   Council Estate is by definition excluded.

As Table 4.4 shows, only a very small proportion of our sample live in a redevelopment area (2 per cent). This is perfectly understandable at one level, since the area set aside for redevelopment, as distinct from renewal, is relatively small, as Figure 4 shows. What is less understandable, or perhaps acceptable, is that there is anyone living there at all. Most of these houses were due for demolition in the 1950s. To make matters worse, it is quite likely that, given the shift in government thinking towards 'renewal' and 'regeneration' rather than 'redevelopment', these houses may, in fact, remain. [74]

In so far as there has been consistency in housing policy during the last decade, it could be argued that the concept of amelioration by renewal has its roots, at the policy-making level, [75] in the Housing Act of 1969. This concept was put into practice in Handsworth following the setting up of the Urban Renewal Conference (later Committee) in 1972, at which juncture virtually the whole of the survey area was designated a 'General Improvement Area'. [76] This scheme was revamped when in 1974 a new Housing Act announced the birth of a new notion: that of the 'Housing Action Area'. The definition of this term has already been discussed in the present chapter: suffice it to say, in the current context, that it aimed to select from those areas which were destined neither for 'redevelopment' nor for 'no action', zones of particularly serious physical and social stress.

The 1974 Act, in theory at least, gave local authorities greater powers of compulsory improvement and (if deemed necessary) compulsory purchase, whilst occupants of houses within a Housing Action Area may receive 75 per cent grants up to a maximum of £3,700. [77] Table 4.4 illustrates very clearly the way in which members of both minority communities are heavily concentrated in these areas. [78] Almost two out of every five West Indian owner occupiers live in a Housing Action Area, as do more than a half of the comparable group of Asian families. Since a little over a quarter of the local whites are found in such areas, we have at least some supportive evidence for the 'unequal shares' thesis. Referring, once again, to the recent findings of 'Inner Area Studies' cited above, it may be that even these figures mask the 'true' extent of the differentials. Our findings also suggest that, at least in statistical terms, immigrants in general, and Asians in particular, might be much more likely to lose their homes via housing clearance, or compulsory purchase, than members of the indigenous population. The impact of this on systems of social relations could prove catastrophic, as was discussed earlier. [79]

If we look at the 'more desirable' end of the housing
spectrum, it is clear that it is white owner-occupiers who
predominate. The overriding conclusion, then, at this
level of analysis, is that 'minority' owner-occupiers tend
to be located in the least desirable sections of an area
which is itself regarded as a 'problem' in the eyes of
policy-makers. Furthermore, given the differences in age
distribution between the immigrant and white communities,
and the higher propensity to purchase property at the
bottom end of the market on the part of (particularly) the
Asians, it is likely that the position will, if anything,
polarise even further in the coming years. Even at this
admittedly elementary level, it appears that (as argued
earlier) for the immigrant community at least, 'home
ownership' is not synonymous with 'quality housing' even
in a relative sense. [80]

In October 1972 two of our survey wards, Handsworth and
Soho, contained almost a fifth of the city's houses which
were in 'Registered Multiple Occupation'. [81] If we add
to this the corresponding figures for Sandwell, the overall percentage rises to over 22 per cent. Undoubtedly
there is evidence that the level of multi-occupation is
falling. The Housing Department informed us, for example,
that Soho Ward in 1972 had 376 registered houses out of a
total stock of 7,725, compared with a figure of 432 in
1969. Similar falls were said to have occurred in the
remaining survey wards. On the other hand, the number
actually registered is still somewhat smaller than the
corresponding figure for those which nevertheless can be
described as shared dwellings (as defined, for example,
in the Population Census of 1971). [82] Whichever definition is chosen, the basic point remains: that multi-
occupation is concentrated in certain parts of the City
(see Table 2.2 in the present book). The Birmingham
Structure Plan notes that there exists a 'pattern of heavy
concentration of multi-occupied dwellings in certain areas
of the middle ring' [83] and suggests tentatively 'that
many of the newcomers to the city are housed in shared
dwellings'. [84] This final point is central to the
current analysis, since multi-occupation and overcrowding
are invariably closely related phenomena.

It is also important at this point for a somewhat different reason, and one which takes up an issue raised in
the preface to this section: that of capital utilisation.
We now have to distinguish carefully between the owner-
occupier who sub-lets part of his accommodation and one
who merely shares the living space with another house-
hold(s). The latter carries with it very different implications in terms of the nature of social relations between

TABLE 4.5   Sub-letting and sharing by ethnic group (owner-occupiers only)

SUB-LETTING

No. of rooms let	West Indian %	Asian %	British %
None/do not sub-let	94	91	96
1	1	4	1
2	2	2	1
3 or more	2	3	2
Total sample size (= 100%)	212	249	165

SHARING [1]

No. of families in dwelling	West Indian %	Asian %	British %
1	94	84	96
2	3	13	4
3	1	2	0
4 or more	2	1	0
Total sample size (= 100%)	212	249 [2]	165

1   These figures include householders who 'sub-let'.
2   The number of households in one dwelling is unknown and therefore the base figure of 248 has been used here in the body of the table.

sets of cohabitants, fundamental among these being the
notion of the 'cash nexus'. Thus in Table 4.5 we compare
the incidence of sub-letting with that of sharing (as defined in terms of the number of distinct household units
within a dwelling).

It is clear from this that, among West Indian and
British owner-occupiers at least, the two factors are
virtually synonymous. Both groups also share another
important characteristic: an extremely high level of
single family occupancy. Their profiles do diverge, however, when we come to look at the nature of multi-occupan-
cy, in the few cases which we found. In all such cases
among the British, for example, only one other family was
present. Out of the twelve shared dwellings owned by West
Indians, however, two were shared with two other households and four provided accommodation for four families.

In contrast to both the British and West Indian groups,
we see that approximately one Asian family in six shares
its house with at least one other family. Further, when
asked earlier in the questionnaire about sub-letting,
less than one in ten admitted to doing so. Working under
the empirically well substantiated assumption that some of
those who say they 'sub-let' do so without any direct
receipt of cash (in other words those who have applied a
definition of 'sub-let' which diverges from that commonly
used), we see that a sizeable number of Asian families
share their homes for reasons other than domestic economics.

In the belief that a study of this process might highlight systems of social relationships more complex than
those which would be expected under the chain migration
thesis, we now look a little more closely at those families who do share their homes. In so doing we shall see
sharp divergences between the West Indian landlords on the
one hand and their Asian counterparts on the other.

The first major point to note is that West Indians
appear to let their properties almost exclusively to their
fellow countrymen. There was, in fact, only one case in
our sample of a West Indian owner-occupier letting to an
'outsider'. This concerned one large, seven-roomed terraced house owned by a 63-year-old unemployed Jamaican.
He and his family (a wife and three young children) occupy
a four-room self-contained flat on the ground floor, and
the remainder of the house is let as three bedsitters:
the first let to two West Indians; the second to two
Africans; and the third to a single African. Interestingly, this is also perhaps the only case where rental
income as distinct from earned income appeared to play an
important role in the landlord's ability to meet his fi-

nancial commitments. The lease on the house has only
fourteen years to run and the mortgage repayments of
£56.00 per month and rates (net of rebate) of a little
over £17.00 per month seemed to impose a steep burden on
an unemployed man nearing retirement age and with a family
to support. [85] The important point about this example
is that (as implied above) it marks a distinct deviation
from the overall pattern of sub-letting (which, it will be
remembered, is itself a comparatively scarce phenomenon).

This brings us to the second major finding. It does
not appear to be the case, in Handsworth at least, that
West Indian owner-occupiers are in general 'forced' to
sub-let in order to meet the financial commitments of
ownership. Unearned income from property appears to perform a supplementary rather than a supportive role. This
should not be taken to imply that such families exude
wealth; on the contrary, most landlords we interviewed
worked full-time and displayed no major differences in
socio-economic status from their compatriots elsewhere in
the housing market. Most were in semi-skilled or unskilled factory jobs and earned wages which were at or
below the median industrial wage at the time of the
survey.

The third major feature of West Indian sub-letting is
that it is predominantly of the one room or bed-sitting-
room variety. Of the 22 families who rented property from
these landlords, no less than 18 fell into this category.
As many of them were single men, it may well be that we
are seeing the remnants of the lodging-house phenomenon
such as that documented in Rex and Moore (1967). A corollary of this leads to our fourth point: West Indian landlords in our sample have let their rooms exclusively to
adults. There were no children under 16 years of age in
any of the twelve houses concerned.

If we tie these four points together, a distinct
pattern emerges. These landlords are all well-established
residents of the UK: all have been here for over twenty
years. Some appear to have bought these large properties
many years ago and thus, despite the fact that in many
cases they are in low-paid manual occupations (if they
are working at all), few appear to be forced to let in
order to fulfil financial commitments. [86] It appears
that rented income presents for a small minority of
middle-aged West Indians, a source of additional financial
security for their retirement years. Their property also
provides what most of the tenants must hope are temporary
homes - places to stay until circumstances improve.
Whether (referring to our initial set of proposed housing
groups) we can describe West Indian landlords as 'entre-

preneurs' or perhaps even overt profiteers exploiting the
collective plight of their less fortunate countrymen, must
remain an open question. This is, however, extremely unlikely. Most appear to enter the 'landlord class' largely
as a result of wishing to fill rooms vacated by their
adult children; others have done so partly in response
to the social trauma of widowhood or divorce. That they
let almost exclusively to fellow West Indians in such circumstances is perhaps not surprising.

Among the Asian community the pattern of house sharing
takes a radically different form. To begin with, almost
half of the 'landlords' are no more than 35 years of age.
Indeed, many are still in their early twenties and are
only just beginning to build a family. Furthermore,
unlike the West Indians, joint ownership with relatives
or fellow Asians appears to be common. (Without such arrangements the chances of early home ownership probably
diminish noticeably.)

It is, however, in the nature of financing and sharing
patterns that the major differences between the ethnic
groups appear. Of the 39 Asian owner-occupiers who were
sharing their property with other families, none had a
Building Society mortgage and only three had mortgages
from Birmingham City Council. The vast majority (64 per
cent) owned their property outright and the remainder had
either borrowed money from relatives or had acquired loans
from the High Street banks or the 'fringe' banking sector.
It may well be, as Karn (1978) argues, that on the whole
Asians tend to steer clear of the more conventional (and
undoubtedly cheaper) sources of finance because of the
conditions written into contractual agreement between
borrower and lender. It is likely also that much of our
survey area is, in Duncan's terms, part of a 'housing sub-
market' within the metropolis and is thus starved of
building society finance. [87]

A few Asians were rather uneasy about discussing the
people with whom they share their house, and indeed, one
refused to do so. On the other hand, it is perhaps surprising that so many did so unhesitatingly. After all,
they were admitting in many cases to living in situations
of gross overcrowding, as we shall see, and some suspicion
of our motives might have been expected. [88] Thirty-
eight householders, then, gave the details which were
asked of them. It will be helpful for the purpose of
this analysis to separate them into three major groups:
1 Those who sub-let rooms to fellow Asians (13 cases).
2 Those who sub-let rooms to non-Asians (8 cases).
3 Those who share as distinct from 'sub-let' (17 cases).
The very existence of a significant number of people in

the second of these groups points to a major difference
between this group and the West Indians. Although, once
again, the bed-sitting-room appears to be the major
feature, it is now not all that uncommon to find a Jamaican living in a house owned and occupied on the ground
floor level by an Asian family. Out of the 15 families
renting property in group 2 above, eleven are West Indian,
most of them single adults. It is perhaps worth stressing
again that in no case did we find an Asian renting rooms
from a West Indian owner-occupier. Indeed, a number of
the West Indians expressed open hostility to the Asian
community.

On the issue of occupational densities, one factor
which is rather disturbing is that most of the Asian
tenants were also found to be living in bed-sitting-rooms,
and many of these are not single men and women but whole
or partial family units. It may be suspected that this
has a number of causes, most of which are linked to the
function of property ownership amongst Asians, and also
the operation of immigration policies. [89]

A detailed analysis of case studies reveals that, although outright ownership is common in this sample as a
whole, it is relatively scarce among groups 1 and 2, i.e.,
those who sub-let rooms. It would certainly appear likely
that rental income is used to pay off short-term bank
loans. This is not simply to give the owner security of
tenure (which in any case many do not strictly have due to
short leases and other factors such as housing policies
which are outside their control). What the outright
ownership of property does do is to give the owner a
certain financial base on which to build his future
family, either by procreation in the case of young families or unification in the case of those with members of
the family still in the Indian subcontinent and wishing to
come here. Our survey evidence confirms earlier sugges-
tions that capital accumulation, taking account of familial pooling arrangements, may well be fairly rapid; thus
explaining why so many young Asians are outright owners.

'Entrepreneurs', where they exist, appear to be largely
confined to the second category of 'sharers'. The third
group are particularly interesting in that, as far as we
can judge, the relationship between the owning family and
their cohabitants is in no way dependent on the 'cash
nexus'. In sharp contrast to the groups already discussed, outright ownership is almost universal. Only two
out of the seventeen properties in this group had loans
outstanding, and in neither of these cases was the owner
in obvious need of financial assistance via rental income.
In the first property (a small self-contained flat) was a

25-year-old Sri Lankan who taught at a local comprehensive
school. He was involved in a co-ownership scheme and paid
£57.00 per month for his flat. There were no family obligations to meet either at that time or in the near future,
and he shared his accommodation with one fellow Asian.
The second case concerns a young Indian family with a
council mortgage amounting to only a few pounds a month on
their five-roomed terraced house. It may be, of course,
that, even in the absence of apparent need, rental income
is still derived from some of these properties. A more
plausible hypothesis, however, is one which suggests that
cash relations play at most a minimal part, and that traditional social and moral obligations conventionally play
a much more significant and meaningful role.

As with the West Indians, most of these owner-occupiers
who let or share their accommodation are employed in low-
paid factory jobs (the only major exception being the
school teacher mentioned above). Where the situation
amongst the Asians is rather more disturbing is on the
level of overcrowding. Unlike the West Indian tenants (of
either landlord group) who, as we have seen, tend to be
single adults, the Asian tenants are often families with
children. Of those who rented rooms, at least eight families were living at densities of at least two persons per
room. In one case a couple and their three children occupied a single bed-sitter. Furthermore, among 'shared'
houses the situation was equally bad. These worries lead
us, then, to look more closely at the question of the
quality and type of accommodation possessed by Handsworth
residents.

We have implied throughout our analysis that the
quality of housing obtained by the black immigrant in this
country is on the whole inferior to that of his white
counterpart. Certainly many writers (e.g., Rex and Moore,
1967; Lawrence, 1974; Smith, 1977) lend support to this
hypothesis. As we have already noted, Handsworth contains
a wide variety of housing. At one end of the spectrum are
those which stand in long drab terraces ravaged by time
and neglect. At the other, there are those which still
show signs at least of an elegance which belonged to another era; an era whose passing as we have also seen many
elderly residents bitterly regret. (Ironically, of
course, these nostalgic reflections often blur the perceptions of past social distinctions which separated the
'other Handsworth' from the Handsworth they knew in their
childhood.)

We need to ask ourselves two major questions at this
point. First, whether, at the level of the survey area,
there is any evidence to suggest that the standard of

owner-occupied property differs radically between ethnic
groups. Then, second, taking a broader view, we ask
whether in the remainder of the city which, but for certain areas such as Sparkbrook, is predominantly white,
housing is of a higher quality. In order to utilise external data for comparison we use, as measures of quality,
criteria such as overcrowding and the level of possession
of basic domestic amenities.

Although in some rather obvious ways these are rather
imperfect surrogate measures of the quality of the physical environment in which families live, they do provide a
useful objective yardstick. They are also important in
that policy-makers tend to use them as indicators of their
own 'performance'. In the Structure Plan report on
housing, for example, our item 4 in Table 4.6 was regarded
as 'perhaps the best single measure of the adequacy of the
City's housing stock'. Further, in discussing changes
over the period 1966-71 and in particular the improvement
in the percentage of families with the exclusive use of
all basic amenities (from 63.6 per cent to 78.1 per cent),
they proudly argue that it 'reflects the effects of slum
clearance and redevelopment and the impact of home improvement grants'. Despite this it was admitted that:
'Nevertheless there were still in 1971 over 26,000 households with no fixed bath or shower, and 1,685 with only
shared use of an outside WC'. [90]

But on the whole the feeling conveyed is that, although
problems remain, the situation is improving rapidly.
Moreover, the area in which there is felt to be least
cause for concern is that of the owner-occupier. Certainly, as the 1971 Census figures (which are reproduced in
Table 4.6) show, only one in ten of these families lacked
exclusive use of the three basic amenities and few can be
described as living in overcrowded conditions. However,
what the figures mask are the problems of areas such as
Handsworth which share few of the relatively favourable
characteristics of the City as a whole. Since 1971 we
might realistically expect these overall (city-wide)
'measures of quality' to have shown further improvement.
Table 4.6 provides a salutary reminder that unqualified
optimism is sadly misplaced.

Many Handsworth families, and particularly those originating from the Indian subcontinent, were, even at this
simple level of analysis, seen to be living in extremely
poor housing conditions. A quarter of the Asian householders lacked exclusive use of an inside WC and 17 per
cent did not even have access to one. In addition, approximately one family in eight had no fixed bath or
shower, a figure three times higher than that for Bir-

TABLE 4.6   Measures of housing quality (owner-occupiers) by ethnic group

		West Indians %	Asians %	British %	Birmingham [1] %
Hot water supply	Sole use	96	83	94	95.1
	Shared	1	9	* [2]	1.3
	None	3	8	6	3.6
Fixed bath or shower	Sole use	97	78	90	94.1
	Shared	3	9	1	1.6
	None	* [2]	13	9	4.3
Inside WC	Sole use	97	75	88	91.0
	Shared	2	8	* [2]	1.4
	None	1	17	12	7.6
With exclusive use of all three amenities		93	70	86	89.6
Percentage of households living at densities of over 1 and up to 1½ persons per room		17	35	+ [3]	5.3
Percentage of households living at densities of over 1½ persons per room		9	11	+ [3]	2.1
Number of households (= 100%)		212	249	165	141,055

1 Source: 1971 Census, Warwickshire County Report, vol.III, Table 25.
2 * represents a figure of less than 0.5%.
3 + no British family in the sample is living at a density of more than one person per room.

mingham owner-occupiers as a whole. About one twelfth of
the Asian owner-occupiers we interviewed had no hot water
in their property. Turning to the occupational density
the grim story continues: 11 per cent of Asian householders were living at densities exceeding 1½ persons per
room, and therefore, in the words of the Structure Plan
authors 'broadly speaking, in conditions of overcrowding'.
[91] If we widen the definition slightly we see that approaching a half of our Asian sample were experiencing
densities of at least one person per room.

With these figures in mind it makes salutary reading to
make comparisons with our indigenous sample and with the
residents of the City as a whole. Even employing the less
austere definition of overcrowding, none of our British
families were found to live in such conditions. [92]
Moreover in 1971 only 7.4 per cent of Birmingham owner-
occupiers were living at a density of more than one person
per room. The first of these findings can be explained
fairly easily in that our British sample was largely an
ageing one. We have seen already that large numbers of
young whites have left Handsworth and the families which
remained tended to be of pensionable age or near pensionable age, and consequently small in size. As argued in
the Structure Plan, and confirmed by our survey, overcrowding is closely linked to family size. Large families
and particularly large poor families who have the further
disadvantage of being black in a predominantly white society might be expected to be found amongst the major
sufferers. It is precisely because of this that the
second of the above findings is rather illuminating. The
majority of owner-occupiers in Birmingham are drawn from
the native white group, and, taken as a whole, the age
distribution mirrors fairly closely that of the city's
total adult population. If we then bear in mind our
Handsworth findings and look at the Small Area Statistics
for this area, and others with high New Commonwealth immigration levels, it is difficult to escape the conclusion
that overcrowding is more likely to be a black 'immigrant'
rather than simply an 'age/family size' phenomenon.

It is undoubtedly the case that among the immigrant
families we interviewed West Indian owner-occupiers on the
face of it appeared to have found rather 'better' accommodation than the Asians in terms of household amenities and
space. Fewer families seemed to be living in overcrowded
conditions, although, as shown in Table 4.6, at the higher
levels (e.g., over 1½ persons per room) the difference is
not noticeably marked. (It should also be stressed that
strict comparison is complicated by the fact that no account is taken here of room size and household structure.)

Where differences between the two ethnic groups were substantial, however, was in the exclusive use of basic amenities. Three Asian families in ten were without exclusive access to hot water, a bath or a shower, and inside WC; whereas the comparable figures for West Indians was a mere 7 per cent: lower, in fact, than that for the City as a whole (in 1971).

This inter-ethnic group comparison should not be allowed to mask the plight of the remaining Handsworth whites. Many of these ageing residents were spending their final years in conditions which few would deny were appallingly inadequate under any of the conventional criteria. For example, one in seven white families lacked one or more of the 'modern' conveniences we have been considering. On the other hand (although it is of little comfort to the people concerned), we saw above that proportionally fewer of the indigenous population live in declining areas such as Handsworth. The point to underline here is that there is evidence to suggest that over the coming years immigrant concentrations in such areas will increase. We have good reason to expect then that differentials in the standard of living of the various ethnic communities will be further accentuated. It is precisely the fear of increasing awareness of the latter among members of immigrant groups which has provoked policy-makers into frantic activity (at least on the mental and verbal planes) over the last decade.

There is remarkably little evidence (among the first generation of Handsworth immigrants at least) to suggest that large numbers regard their present accommodation as undesirable. Perhaps for some the achievement of owner-occupier status in itself bears sufficient socio-psychological rewards. This, coupled with the apparently low expectations of many, might at least partially explain why only one in five Asians expressed dissatisfaction with any aspect of their present accommodation. Where complaints were registered these largely fell into the category of amenities and living space, which we discussed earlier. As was the case with a number of other issues, the West Indians were much more vociferous in expressing concern with their present standard of housing. It is interesting that despite the fact that in objective terms [93] this group on the whole fare rather better than the Asians, many more West Indians (41 per cent in all) complained about at least one feature of their housing situation.

There are a number of possible reasons for this phenomenon: one being the theory of higher expectations (relative to Asians) discussed in earlier chapters. A

second, and to some extent related, reason arises from the
integrationist perspective of many, perhaps most, first-
generation West Indian migrants. A greater awareness of
the objectively superior position of the majority of
whites has undoubtedly led to resentment. Finally, there
is an hypothesis which is concerned with differences in
the sort of people from the two ethnic groups who join the
'class' of owner-occupiers. As we have already seen, the
vast majority of Asians, irrespective of age and length of
residence, own their own homes; the same is not true of
West Indians.

Following up the latter point, we look more closely at
the two groups of owner-occupiers. None of the West
Indian heads of household who were under 25 years of age
owned their property and only one in five of the next age-
group (25-34) did so. This contrasts strikingly with the
corresponding figures for the Asians: 9 per cent and 54
per cent respectively. As we saw earlier in the chapter,
most West Indians typically spend a number of years elsewhere in the housing market before buying property. [94]
It was only among the middle-aged (45-59 years of age)
where the level of owner-occupation was common: approximately 70 per cent, in fact. There is some evidence to
suggest also that the West Indian owner-occupier is drawn
mainly from the group of higher wage-earners, as might
have been expected from the policies of financial institutions such as Building Societies. These factors suggest, then, that a process of individual (rather than
pooled) capital accumulation combined with the possession
of a good, secure job are central to the possibility of
his acquiring property. [95] The difficulty of overcoming
obstacles such as the sort of institutionalised discriminatory practices outlined earlier may thus further ac-
centuate any disillusionment which the individual may feel
when he comes to reflect on his 'achievement'.

As argued earlier in this chapter, it is likely that
housing tenure may be seen in an entirely different light
by the Asian community. Ownership is almost universal and
may simply serve to reinforce the sense of community, and
the desire for independence from white society and its
institutions. The above arguments lead the author to the
conclusion that satisfaction with one's housing situation
may be a function of one or more of the factors embodied
in the three hypotheses. Central to all, however, is the
individual's perception of his position vis-à-vis British
society as a whole.

We have seen that much of the property which immigrants, and particularly Asians, tend to buy is lacking
in basic amenities and is far too small for the needs of

the family. One further theory which has been advanced is
that this property also tends to be leasehold rather than
freehold, a crucial point, since it means that the individual's security of tenure is severely weakened. As Smith
(1977) has noted: [96]

> The fact in itself that a property is leasehold rather
> than freehold is a disadvantage, because it means that
> either the freehold must be purchased or the asset will
> disappear. Also, our findings show that leasehold pro-
> perties tend to be older and in a worse structural con-
> dition than freehold ones.

He also points out that the positions of Asians and West
Indians differ radically in this respect. Whereas, he
argues, 83 per cent of owner-occupiers in the general
population have freehold tenure and among West Indians the
pattern is very much the same, '21 per cent of all (Asian)
householders are owner-occupiers with leasehold tenure'.
[97] Pakistanis are singled out as the group most unlikely to own the freehold of their property.

This overall pattern seems to be broadly confirmed by
our Handsworth data, though the magnitude of the various
groups is radically different. Leasehold tenure appears
to be extremely common: 36 per cent of the families we
interviewed belonged to this group. As the majority of
the private housing stock is over fifty years old, this
was perhaps not surprising. What was a little surprising
was that over three out of every four West Indian families
owned their freehold, thereby contrasting sharply with the
figures of 66 per cent for the whites and 53 per cent for
the Asians.

This in itself provides further evidence that Asians,
at least if you exclude those who came from East Africa,
[98] appear on the whole to fare rather badly in the
private housing market. But even this masks the true
seriousness of the problem for Asian families. For one
thing, unlike whites, they tend to be much younger, and
therefore in rather greater need of a lengthy period of
security of tenure. Sadly, in Handsworth at least, it
appears that this need is not satisfied; for if we look
closely at periods which the leases have to run the following picture emerges. Whereas only a third of the
leases of local whites expire within the next twenty-five
years, the corresponding figure for the Asians is 52 per
cent.

The differences in forms of tenure between Asians and
West Indians are rather interesting and have not yet been
adequately explained by researchers. They have, we feel,
to be seen against the background of religious and cultural, rather than solely economic, considerations. As

was noted earlier in the chapter, Asians demonstrate a
great desire to own property rather than merely to rent
it. We saw that the 'problem' for some Asians who adhere
strictly to the code of behaviour required by their faith
is that they cannot borrow money from those who profit
from such a business. As a result many turn to family and
friends, for example, for financial support. Since their
families themselves are unlikely to be wealthy, they must
aim for property in the lower (perhaps lowest) reaches of
the property market. 'Short-life' houses in particular
fall into this category - a fact which probably accounts
for much of their 'popularity'.

West Indians, on the other hand, tend to wait for a
while in rented property, and when they do buy tend to do
so through the conventional channels of building society
or council mortgages. [99] We have already noted some of
the problems encountered at this stage. It is well known
that building societies in particular are extremely wary
of leasehold property, since it fails to offer adequate
security to set against their capital outlay. This, combined with the possibility of further discriminatory
practices against blacks [100] means that we would expect
to find relatively few West Indians in leasehold property.
Bearing this in mind it is not perhaps surprising that, in
contrast to the property owned by Asians, less than one in
five have short-term leases (less than 25 years) and the
mortgages on these properties, when not owned outright,
are invariably provided from council funds.

Limitation of space means that we cannot take this
analysis of owner-occupation in Handsworth a great deal
further. It would be a mistake, however, to end this
section without commenting on some extremely interesting
points which follow on from the above arguments. First,
there is the question of income [101] (both personal and
that of the family as a whole) and how this relates to the
precise form of ownership and tenure. Second, there is
the important issue concerning the percentage of disposa-
ble income consumed by house purchase commitments.

On the first point we see that, even allowing for the
problem mentioned in note 101, there is no relationship
between income and the outright ownership of property
among immigrant groups. In particular, it does not appear
to be the case that the Asians who buy property outright
are able to do so because their personal (or family)
income is particularly high. Furthermore, as there is no
discernible relationship between the former factor (i.e.,
level of outright ownership) and the date of arrival in
the UK, the theory of capital accumulation via 'third
persons' is given further empirical support. Outright

ownership amongst whites is highest among those who earn
the least, which might appear paradoxical until we realise
that the people who are in this position are almost exclusively pensioners who completed payments on their properties many years ago.

If we look now at the relationship between tenure and
outright ownership, we reach a conclusion which negates
that which might have been inferred from some of the
earlier discussions in this chapter and in the comparable
discussion in Smith (1977). It appears that, at least as
far as the Asians are concerned, there is no reason to
believe that the property which is owned outright is more
likely to be of leasehold rather than freehold tenure.
This is partly explained by the narrowness of price differentials between freehold and long-lease properties and
by the possibility that some of the freehold properties
will have been purchased via short-term loans or mortgages
rather than 100 per cent cash transactions. Whatever the
underlying reasons for this state of affairs, the fact remains that 54 per cent of the 153 Asians who owned property outright also possessed the freehold.

Turning to the second point raised above, we reach the
important conclusion that although only a handful of West
Indian and white mortgagees (2 per cent and 4 per cent respectively) spent more than a quarter of their gross
family income on repayments, [102] approximately one Asian
family in six did so. The repayments to be met by Asian
families tended also to be larger than those for the other
two groups. [103] Thus, when we take into account that
many of these families are large and the property inadequate to say the least, there is undoubtedly some cause
for concern. Whatever the reasons for this, whether it
is the use of 'fringe' bank loans rather than building
society mortgages, the length of repayment period, the
expense of some recently purchased property, or perhaps
a combination of these factors, we could argue that the
explanation is perhaps less important than the 'social
fact' itself.

To sum up, we have seen in this section that although
owner-occupation is extremely high among the Asians, the
property which they acquire appears, often, to lack the
basic amenities, and families are frequently living in
overcrowded conditions. We have also found that much of
this property is of the short-lease variety, thus undermining the individual's security of tenure. By way of a
postscript here, our Handsworth data confirm one of
Smith's (1977) findings: namely, that within the overall
'class' of owner-occupiers, Pakistanis tend to fare worst
of all. It is also the case that within the housing

market as a whole they are much more likely to be found in
rented accommodation than are East African Asians and
those who came from India itself. A little over a half of
the Pakistani families owned their current property compared with nine out of ten of the (Indian) Hindus and
Sikhs.

We have laid a considerable amount of stress, if at
times only implicitly, on the concept of security. It
must be restated, however, that much depends on the implementation of current housing policies and in particular on
the current assessment of properties within Housing Action
Areas (HAA). As Rex and Tomlinson [104] point out, there
are signs at least that there may be some resistance among
immigrants to the classification of their homes as potential demolition property. Any developments in this field
are of particular importance, of course, to the Asian communities in Handsworth, since, as we saw in Table 4.4,
they appear to be concentrated most heavily in HAAs. It
is all the more ironic, then, that hardly anyone in this
group actually knows that his family are living in such an
area. Only 5 per cent are aware of the situation and 22
per cent believe that they are not in an HAA. This ignorance is reflected, though to a lesser degree, among the
remainder of Handsworth residents. [105] With many this
can clearly be seen as resulting from confusion over terminology. Given the muddled development of thought in official circles concerning inner-city policies we can
hardly be surprised if residents think they are in a
General Improvement Area (GIA) when they are actually in
an HAA! In any case, before 1974 many of the streets
which are now designated to a part of an HAA were included
in a GIA. Even allowing for this confusion, it is still
true to say that many appear to be unaware of policies
which, though seemingly remote, nevertheless have extremely important implications for the families concerned.

COUNCIL HOUSING IN HANDSWORTH

Council housing, it is argued, confers on the individual
a security of tenure not equalled in the private rental
market, despite a tightening-up of the legal situation.
It is generally assumed further that, pound for pound,
council property offers better value for a prospective
tenant in terms of quality of accommodation and living
space. Not even the Conservatives' 'fair rents' policy,
it is argued, affects these conclusions. If we accept
this line of argument and take into account the scarcity
and expense of 'equally desirable' property in the owner-

occupier sector, competition for council property from
members of immigrant groups might be expected to be
intense.

Most local authorities in Britain undoubtedly have long
waiting lists from members of the indigenous population,
though there may sometimes be exaggerations (see Rex and
Tomlinson, 1979). Accordingly, strict allocation procedures are the norm. To lengthen these lists with the addition of newcomers, and particularly black newcomers, has
predictably led to indignation, suspicion, and outright
hostility among those who believe that their birthright
alone should secure superiority of access over less fortunate mortals. (Those who have read the latter part of
the previous chapter will have been left in no doubt that
such feelings are prevalent among many white residents of
Handsworth.)

As we have seen, the allocation procedures themselves
provide a legitimation of differential success rates among
ethnic groups. Moreover, a number of elements in the assessment process are not bound by formal rules of a purely
mechanical form, but allow more scope for the assessor's
own judgment: judgment which may or may not reflect the
feelings of those whites whose racist views we have seen.

The major aim of the following discussion is to evaluate the quality and cost of council accommodation which
Handsworth immigrants have acquired. In so doing, we look
at the council stock in Birmingham as a whole. Before
this, however, we need to question one of our basic premises. It is not self-evident that immigrants automatically concur with the view of council housing which was
expressed above. In particular, is it true that immigrants, irrespective of ethnic group, wish to rent such
properties?

To examine this we first of all look at the three major
housing groups: the owner-occupiers, the council tenants,
and the private renters. Implicit in most of our analysis
has been the view that this represents a diminishing scale
of desirability, or even (at a rather simplified level) a
scale of housing class. If we examine the survey evidence, we see that one element of this is confirmed;
namely, that owner-occupiers, although they might wish to
move to another house and to another area, would not wish
to rent property. Potential competition for local
authority housing, then, must come from those in the
private rented sector (if we restrict ourselves to a discussion of waiting-list applicants rather than transfers).

A natural starting point for this analysis is to look
at the number of those in private rented accommodation who
have applied at some stage to be considered for council

housing. During the past ten years we see that out of
the 61 West Indian families in private rented accommodation 46 (or 75 per cent) had done so. Interestingly,
though not altogether unexpectedly, out of the much
smaller number (30) of Asian families in this tenancy
group only 13 per cent had sought council accommodation.
This underlines earlier remarks about the preference of
this group for home ownership. Private renting and, in
particular, renting from family or kinsman appears to be
seen very much as the means to this end. The fact that,
in objective terms, some types of council property might
appear to be of better quality than either of the alter-
natives is largely irrelevant.

Throughout the Asian sample by far the most frequent
answer to the question which asked why they had not applied for a council house was 'I didn't need to'. It appeared that council housing was viewed as being solely for
those who were compelled to seek it; thus it was seen as
a negative rather than a positive option. There is undoubtedly an element of defensiveness here, of not wanting
to be seen as sponging off the state; an understandable
reaction when we think of the way in which the media have
treated this particular element of the 'race issue'. At
the time of the major influx of Ugandan Asians, most of
the popular daily papers gave major, if not front-page
prominence, to a story concerning a family who had been
placed in a five-star hotel by the local authority 'at
great expense to the ratepayers'. Stories such as this
are bound to reinforce a general desire for 'independence'
and financial security among the Asian community. Their
tendency to buy property, then, is not simply a question
of support for the notion of a 'property-owning democracy'
or lack of knowledge of public housing or, even the (quite
realistic) assessment of their chances of being offered
such property. If we look at the Asian families who are
in private rented accommodation it is quite clear that the
vast majority have never even considered applying for
council housing.

Competition for accommodation in the public sector,
then, appears largely to be restricted to the indigenous
population and the West Indians (at least within our
survey area). Almost two out of every five white families
in the private rented sector were found to have applied to
the council within the last decade. Interestingly, however, they had in general been 'waiting' for a much
shorter period of time than the West Indians, median
periods being approximately 18 months and $2\frac{1}{2}$ years respectively. In fact, six West Indians had since withdrawn
from the waiting list and, significantly, a further twelve
families no longer knew if they were on it!

If we look at where the families from these two groups
wanted their council accommodation, we see further evidence of a point raised in earlier chapters: the desire
of whites to leave the area. One in three white families
wished to do so. Their commitment to the area can be
gauged by the fact that only 3 out of the 35 families applied to stay in Handsworth. This pattern contrasts
sharply with the West Indian families, where 40 per cent
wished to stay and only 4 out of the total of 46 positively wished to move away. Neither group had much success in
being offered accommodation, and, in general, there was
evidence of considerable anger at the way in which their
application had been treated by the local authority. Complaints that staff were unhelpful and that 'we had to wait
too long' were common. In fact, 12 families told us that
they had not even received a reply.

It was clear that many had a strong desire to leave
their present accommodation, and an examination of their
reasons leads us to the principal issue of this section:
the question of housing quality. Of West Indian families
64 per cent said that they wanted to move because their
present accommodation was too small. A further 9 per cent
complained about the physical condition of their home
(though this was a more common feature of answers given
by the indigenous sample). Many elderly white tenants
said that they wanted to move, not because their accommodation was too small, but because it was too large for
them to look after.

Whether those we interviewed would improve their
standard of accommodation by moving into the public sector
might well depend on whether they had been allocated
purpose-built or municipalised ('patched') property. Because of this possibility we distinguish between the two
classes of housing in the following analysis.

Table 4.7 summarises the major formal quality features
of the council housing occupied by members of our Handsworth sample and includes, for comparative purposes, 1971
Census material for the city as a whole. As the reader
will notice, the figures for Asian tenants are absent.
This is a direct result of the lack of penetration of this
group into the public sector, only 19 (6 per cent) of this
group renting council property. There is some evidence,
however, that when they do obtain such accommodation it
tends to be municipalised property rather than that which
has been purpose-built. The former tends on the whole to
be of much poorer quality and less likely to have basic
amenities. This appears to apply particularly to our
small group of Asian tenants, since only 8 out of the 14
families in such accommodation have exclusive use of the

TABLE 4.7 Quality of council housing by ethnic group [1]

		West Indian		British		Birmingham [3]
		Purpose-built [4] %	Non-purpose-built %	Purpose-built [4] %	Non-purpose-built %	%
Hot water supply	Sole use	100	96	100	93	92.2
	Shared	–	–	–	–	0.4
	None	–	4	–	7	7.4
Fixed bath or shower	Sole use	100	100	100	85	92.1
	Shared	–	–	–	–	0.5
	None	–	–	–	15	7.4
Inside WC	Sole use	100	100	100	79	78.5
	Shared	–	–	–	–	0.4
	None	–	–	–	21	21.1
Percentage with exclusive use of all amenities		100	96	100	78	71.3
Percentage of households living at densities of over 1 and up to 1½ persons per room		17	44	9	2	9.5
Percentage of households living at densities of over 1½ persons per room		12	15	3	7	2.8
No. of households (= 100%)		95	27 [2]	100	42	127,610

1 Since there are only 19 Asian families in council housing (i.e., 6% of the total) – 5 in purpose-built and 14 in acquired property – this group has been omitted from the table. (See the discussion of this group in the script.)

2 Because of the small sample size the figures in this column should be interpreted with care.

3 Source: 1971 Census, Warwickshire County Report.

4 This refers, in essence, to properties on the Newtown estate.

basic amenities, and four families are living in a state
of chronic overcrowding.

Interestingly, the grim picture of the Asians is not
paralleled by similar findings among West Indians, at
least at the level of basic amenities. Only one family is
without exclusive access to hot water, inside WC and a
fixed bath or shower, and on this count at least, they
seem to fare better than local whites. [106] One factor
which may help to account for this perhaps slightly unexpected finding is that members of our indigenous sample
have often been long-term residents of ageing property
which has not yet been brought up to present-day standards. That which has been acquired and let more recently
is more likely to have basic amenities. This does not account for the basic failings of the Asian properties, and
it may simply be that West Indians tend to be more selective in the property they are willing to accept. [107] It
may well be that local authority housing is seen by the
few Asians who acquire it as a comparatively temporary
measure.

Not unexpectedly, the lettings on the Newtown council
estate satisfy the basic quality criteria as far as amenities are concerned. It should, perhaps, be stressed once
again that relatively few blacks actually live on this
estate. Moreover, the figure includes a derisorily small
number of Asians. All of which is particularly illuminating given that the contiguous areas have immigrant
levels of around 40 per cent. On the other hand, it must
be pointed out that the Newtown estate itself is not
exactly highly rated as a desirable address by the tenants
themselves; [108] as we have seen in the previous chapter
serious tensions (racial and otherwise) exist there as
they do elsewhere in Handsworth.

On the question of occupational density in council
housing a by now familiar picture re-emerges. A relatively large number of West Indian families are clearly seen
to be living in considerably overcrowded conditions. This
is not confined to the non-purpose built property. Of the
West Indian households in Newtown, 12 per cent had more
than 1½ persons per room as compared with 3 per cent among
the whites on the same estate. In the competition for
scarce public housing resources, then, West Indians appear
to have had some success, but it is rather disturbing to
find that they are failing on the very issue which is
uppermost in the minds of those of their fellow countrymen
who wish to enter this 'housing class' from the private
rented sector. We saw a little earlier that by far the
most important reason for wanting to move into council
housing was that their present accommodation was too

small. It appears, then, that they are finding access to even the less prestigious estates difficult. We can perhaps best sum up their position by saying that, apart from possibly improving their security of tenure, they will on the whole gain little by a move in this direction.

Before we look more closely at our final housing sector (the private rented market), we look at the issue of council rents and ask, in particular, whether there are major differences in the amounts paid by immigrants and their white neighbours. The simple answer appears to be 'no' or, if so, the differences are only marginal. Rent levels on the Newtown estate, as might have been expected, tend to be higher than those in the municipalised sector, the median weekly rent being £8.24 for the West Indians and £8.12 for the whites, as against £6.87 and £6.67 respectively. The slight within-sector differences can be explained, we suspect, largely by the differences in property size required by members of the two groups.

There seem to be few complaints from tenants about the rent levels; but on the other hand, one in four West Indians and 22 per cent of white tenants had had some form of dispute with the council in the previous two years. Most of the non-Newtown estate whites, as they reach their 'twilight years', along with the houses they inhabit, tend to accept their lot without much fuss. Not so their West Indian neighbours, of whom about 30 per cent have lodged official complaints about the poor physical condition of their houses.

Both groups of Newtown residents appear to be equally willing to voice concern about their housing, and among West Indians the complaints are still largely about the physical state of their accommodation. Significantly, however, among the Newtown whites an equally important concern is that of moving off the estate: 30 per cent said that they had been involved in a dispute with the local authority on the grounds that their attempts to transfer to other accommodation had been thwarted. This amply attests to the general mood of restiveness which is transmitted by individual case studies of council tenants.

The local authority in turn cannot help but recognise the danger signs: the smouldering discontent and the spasmodic but all too frequent eruption of violence and vandalism. At micro policy level the subjective devaluation of an estate poses a problem which might be tackled, for example, by the dispersion of blacks or the creation of black council estates. Few would doubt, however, that the roots of unrest go far deeper. Such is the basis of the arguments in this book and what is in many ways its companion volume (Rex and Tomlinson, 1979).

PRIVATE RENTED ACCOMMODATION IN HANDSWORTH

Although, as noted earlier, the private rented sector is
undoubtedly declining in size due largely to rent controls
[109] imposed during the last two decades, it still provides a source of accommodation for a significant sector
of the immigrant population. Its importance at this point
lies in the fact that much of this housing is of poor
quality and, compared with the public sector and owner-
occupation, often confers on the tenant little de facto
security of tenure. Moreover, for a large number of immigrants it represents the only option open to them. It
would be wrong to infer from this, of course, that immigrants comprise the majority of those who rent privately
in Handsworth. Using weighted figures we see that 28 per
cent of our indigenous sample did so, compared with 19 per
cent of the West Indians and only 10 per cent of the
Asians. However, it appears that these groups were, in
effect, using three quite distinct 'markets'.

Almost three out of every five white families rent from
individuals, as distinct from housing associations or
property companies. The landlords are almost certain to
be British and, except in the very rare case of their
being a relative, will not live on the premises. Where
they do rent property from an institution it is far more
likely to be a property agency rather than a housing association.

In sharp contrast, out of 61 West Indian families, 37
(61 per cent) rented from a housing association (such as
the Midland Area Improvement Housing Association formed
in 1967). Once again the incidence of sharing with relatives was low, only two families, in fact, doing so. On
the other hand, it is not true that the landlord is almost
exclusively of the same ethnic origin as the tenant. Out
of the 18 cases where the nationality of the landlord was
stated (and where he was not a relative) only ten were
fellow West Indians; of the remainder five were Indian,
two were Pakistanis and one was British.

As might have been expected from previous discussions
in this chapter, the Asian pattern of renting is radically
different from either of these. For one thing, no Asian
family was found to be renting property from other than an
individual. As before, it seems that Asians preserve
their independence from formal market institutions (which
tend to be run by members of the indigenous population).
It seems unlikely that discriminatory behaviour on the
part of the institutions themselves, or lack of knowledge
of them by the Asian community, provide adequate alternative explanations for this phenomenon. A second feature

which distinguishes the Asian pattern of renting is that
in nearly every case the landlord was himself Asian; the
only exception to this was one family whose landlord was
British.   One final point here concerns the relationship
between landlord and tenant.   As we have seen, renting
from members of one's family was extremely rare amongst
the West Indians and the British.   Out of the 29 Asian
families [110] who rented privately, however, no less
than 17 did so from relatives, and in most of these cases
the landlord lived on the premises.   Significantly, then,
the absentee landlord appears to be comparatively rare
among the Asian community.

One question which this pattern (in particular) raises
is whether the 'insulation' of an Asian family from direct
social and financial contact with their West Indian and
white neighbours, means that tangibly better, or at least
cheaper, accommodation is provided.   (Indeed, the answer
to the question of whether any pecuniary reward accrues to
the Asian 'landlord' would be interesting not only in the
context of the present analysis, but would also throw some
light on a discussion earlier in this chapter where we
considered the relationship between the Asian owner-occupier and tenant.)   We take these issues in order then:
first, the question of the quality of accommodation, and
second, that of rent.

Table 4.8 shows once again that in terms of basic amenities Asian families fare rather badly both in absolute
terms and in comparison with the other two ethnic groups.
[111]   Only one family in five had exclusive use of the
three basic amenities.   They also suffered more by way of
overcrowding than did the West Indians or the British:
more than a quarter were found to be living at densities
of over 1½ per room.   In fact, the situation might have
been much worse had the incidence of one-person households
(44 per cent) been lower.

The apparently 'better' accommodation of the West
Indians appears to some extent to be related to their
heavy dependence on Housing Associations.   Both our own
Handsworth data and those provided by the 1971 Census
suggest that at least in terms of basic amenities tenants
of these organisations do rather better than those in the
remainder of the private rented sector.

Most of the British families, as we have seen, rented
from private individuals;   most in fact were sitting
tenants in properties which they had occupied for over
twenty years.   It was in these houses that the provision
of basic amenities was least likely.   As in many such
areas throughout Britain, it looked as though the obligations of absentee landlords were clearly not being fulfilled.

TABLE 4.8 Quality of private rented accommodation by ethnic group

		West Indian %	Asian %	British %	Birmingham [1] %
Hot water supply	Sole use	77	27	81	68.7
	Shared	18	57	5	13.5
	None	5	17	13	17.8
Fixed bath or shower	Sole use	74	27	71	62.0
	Shared	23	57	11	19.3
	None	3	17	18	18.7
Inside WC	Sole use	75	23	66	58.8
	Shared	21	63	10	19.0
	None	3	13	24	22.2
Percentage with exclusive use of all three amenities		74	20	62	54.7
Percentage of households living at densities of over 1 and up to 1½ persons per room		5	10	1	4.2
Percentage of households living at densities of over 1½ persons per room		18	27	1	5.0
No. of households (= 100%)		61	30 [2]	91	64,845

1 Source: 1971 Census, Warwickshire County Report.
2 As the number of Asians in this form of accommodation is rather small, care should be taken in interpreting these results.

It is perhaps likely that these houses will never be improved by private capital. Assuming that they are not compulsorily purchased by the local authority, their most likely destination on the death of their present tenants will be the owner-occupier sub-market. Indeed, three out of four white households contained only one or two persons: mainly ageing widows, spinsters, or couples where both were of pensionable age. The overriding conclusion, then, is of a naturally declining white population, many of whom rent poor property. Young Asian and West Indian couples and those who are involuntarily separated from their families provide a ready demand for such houses when they ultimately come up for sale. Some, as we have seen, will pay cash accumulated through pooling arrangements; others will borrow from fringe banks where they are compelled to face often steep rates of interest but where, as Karn (1978) argues, they avoid the financial obligation of improving their property. In such circumstances further urban decay is inevitable, as is the growth of its association with the black immigrant.

It is unlikely that in objective terms an immigrant's standard of living will improve if and when he purchases property; in many ways he is simply changing his place within the lower sub-market. Few, however, have actually complained to their landlords about the state of their accommodation within the last two years: perhaps because their stay was viewed as temporary. There was little evidence of high rent levels, though the median rent paid by the West Indians (£7.23) was undoubtedly far higher than that of the whites (£4.31). This is probably due to two factors: the difference in the incidence of unfurnished (and noticeably cheaper) accommodation, and the likelihood that many of the older white residents are on controlled rents. Of West Indian families 61 per cent were in unfurnished property, compared with 85 per cent of the whites. Of the latter group 87 per cent had rents of less than £5 per week.

Once again the pattern of tenancy among the Asians was very different. For one thing the majority (28 out of the 30 families) were in furnished accommodation. More importantly, 43 per cent were living rent-free. This provides clear evidence that financial transactions, at least in the formal sense of rent, play a comparatively minor role within Asian-owned multi-occupied properties, especially where tenants are members of the owner's kinship network.

CONCLUSION

We have seen that much of the housing which black immigrants in Handsworth occupy is of poor quality and many
families are living in a state of chronic overcrowding.
What is perhaps even more worrying, however, is the
glimpse of the future which our survey data occasionally
permit. Whereas the white population of Handsworth share
many of the immigrants' housing problems, their position
differs in two major respects. First, in comparison with
the West Indians and Asians only a tiny proportion of
Birmingham's whites live in the survey area. Second, and
more important than this, is the fact that the Handsworth
white population is a declining one: declining by natural
wastage (i.e., by mortality) and by migration to other
parts of the West Midlands and elsewhere.

The combined effect of these factors is to leave a
vacuum which will undoubtedly be filled by second-generation blacks. It is also certain that without a major
input of financial resources by central and local government the area will continue to decay physically. Many
alarmist reports, such as that by John Brown (1977), have
gone further and suggested that in addition, signs of
moral and social decay already exist. We are given visions of white families fleeing the black menace; of
empty houses being used as squats by gangs of young
'dreads' who take a delight in terrorising the whites who
remain; of an 'undermanned' police force who are terri-
fied to 'walk the beat' because of the young black (West
Indian) presence. The problems, as we have said, are too
often (wrongly) located in the individual, or the identifiable social group or sub-culture such as the 'Rastafarians' or the 'Dreads'. It is, of course, easier to
attack the surface manifestations of social unrest, or
suggest solutions which assume that these manifestations
can be equated with the ultimate cause. It is much more
difficult to admit that there may be serious social
structural weaknesses which give rise to the eruption of
racial and indeed class conflict. Scapegoats, whether
those of the 'man-in-the-street' or of the policy-maker,
can serve only to intensify the conflict.

There is no evidence from our present research in
Handsworth either of 'landlordism' or of the existence of
a pariah group of immigrant lodging houses; i.e., properties such as those which were found in Sparkbrook by Rex
and Moore (1967). [112] On the other hand, the moral
ambiguities of a local authority's position, which were
highlighted in this situation, apply equally to the present one. In addition, the operation of housing or of

labour 'sub-markets' institutionalises the conflictual
systems of social relationships which reinforce feelings
of mutual hostility or suspicion. Public capital clearly
has a role to play here, i.e., in the housing market.
Good housing conditions, however, are only a part of a
highly interconnected whole. We move on now (after the
following postscript), to look at another major element
in the structure of social and class relations: the
labour market.

HOUSING CLASS: A POSTSCRIPT

It will have become clear to the reader that the 'housing
class' concept (however formulated) is exceedingly difficult to operationalise. It also tends, as Haddon (1970)
has argued, to be approached by the empirical question of
what housing has been acquired, rather than the more
theoretical question of access. This chapter has attempted to fuse the two by looking at the roles of the state
(in its national and local manifestation) and the private
sector market institutions on the one hand, and the individual (or group's) problem, achievements and aspirations
on the other. Only by analysing the problem in this
fashion can we hope to illustrate the present and likely
future fate of ethnic minority groups in urban Britain.

5 Black immigrants and the labour market

In the previous chapter we looked at the structure of
social relations in the domestic property market, and, in
particular, at the extent to which the black immigrant has
attained equal bargaining rights in the market place.
This was treated at length since the author believes that
such a discussion is central to any debate surrounding
race or class conflict in an advanced industrial (capitalist) society. The confinement of minority groups to less
desirable sub-markets (a state of affairs which we suggested has already received empirical support) denies
their members a place in the social structure alongside
members of the indigenous population. It also, of
course, in an important symbolic sense, confirms in the
minds of immigrants in general and perhaps the West Indian
community in particular, the feeling that the days of
colonialism and neo-colonialism, in spirit at least,
linger on. Current Jamaican music often reflects the ways
in which the historical experience, though internalised,
has certainly not been forgotten. In the words of Bob
Marley: [1]

> everytime I hear the crack of a whip
> my blood runs cold
> I remember on the slave ships
> how they brutalised our very souls
> today they say we are free
> only to be chained in poverty

The concept of poverty here is clearly universal: it
matters little whether the Jamaican is confined to the
slums of Kingston or those of Birmingham.

One obvious way out of literal poverty is to sell one's
labour. We devote this chapter, then, to a consideration
of the black immigrant's position in the metropolitan
economy. In particular we focus on the question noted in
general terms above; i.e., that of whether his access to

the market place is similar to that of the indigenous worker, or whether, as appears to be the case in the area of housing, he is relegated to an 'under-class' position. Whatever the outcome of this, we will still have seen only part of the racial dimension in the labour relations picture. We need to follow this analysis (subject to the limitations which our choice of methodology entailed) with a look at the systems of social relations on the shop-floor or in the office. The fact of an individual merely having obtained a foothold in the labour market tells us little, for example, about subsequent life chances.

We begin, however, with a much more fundamental question than any of those above: namely, 'To what extent do members of the black minority groups attain any access to work?' The research was undertaken at a time when both national and local unemployment was reaching the sort of levels only previously seen in the 1930s. In August 1976, 1,502,000 or 6.4 per cent of the national work-force was unemployed. At the same time, out of an estimated [2] economically active population in the Birmingham area [3] of 677,665, 7.8 per cent were without work.

Policy-makers had by this time clearly realised that it was no longer feasible to assume that the economic cycles leading to periodic booms and slumps reflected an immuta-ble scientific law, even at the level of prediction. At the very least, it was realised that the cycles might continue to increase in amplitude, thus creating a conti-nuing unemployment problem, and one which, because of its long-term structural nature, might lead to serious social unrest and possibly even a total breakdown of the social order.

Indeed, these fears must have weighed heavily on the minds of senior politicians when, on 1 January 1974, the then Labour Government set up the Manpower Services Com-mission (MSC); a body whose brief was 'to run the public employment and training services previously provided by the Department of Employment.' [4] But it was clear that more than a hint of psychology (as well as financial re-sources) lay behind this new venture. Thus: 'The main purpose of this new approach is to give responsibility to representatives of employers and workers and of local government and education interests for the management and development of the services which they use.' [5] As well as the temporary addition of jobs for young people through the Work Experience Programmes and Job Creation Schemes, there was to be a wide range of courses, training schemes and employment subsidies, the latter being despised by our EEC neighbours for their alleged effect on 'natural compe-tition' between firms. (By including in their first

annual report a section entitled 'Contingency Plans for
Higher Unemployment' the MSC clearly reflected growing
fears from outside that they, rather than industry itself,
might become the largest (perhaps the only) growth area in
the economy!)

Unfortunately, from the point of view of permanent Work
Creation, little positive assistance appears to have come
from this body: a cynic might argue that one could hardly
expect any other result from an organisation set up largely to defuse an increasingly nasty political situation.
It is undoubtedly the case that the symptoms of the
malaise have been treated rather than the root cause, and
that, even then, they have been tackled with palliatives
rather than more lasting remedies. Indeed, this lack of
willingness to do anything which might tamper significantly with the workings of the mixed economy appears to have
persisted in recent debates surrounding the destination
of the North Sea oil revenue. [6]

We are left, then, with a situation which has especially grave implications for particular sections of the work-
force. As noted by Martin and Fryer (1973), [7] the definition of a concept such as 'unemployable' shifts radically between economic booms and slumps. When the level
of aggregate demand is high: [8]

> workers who lose their jobs through changes in consumer
> preferences or technological change are relatively
> quickly reabsorbed ... (even) workers possessing poor
> sickness records find it relatively easy to obtain
> work. The major barriers to full employment are per-
> sonal and institutional barriers to mobility.

When the demand situation is reversed (i.e., when the
labour market favours the employer), the notion of employability undergoes a dramatic transformation. In this
situation it is those in the labour force whose bargaining
power is the weakest who tend to suffer most. It is precisely this question of bargaining power in a competitive
market situation which concerns us now.

EMPLOYABILITY AND MARGINALITY

It is reasonable to suppose that the four major qualities
looked for in a potential employee would be 'suitable'
age, sex, qualifications, experience and personal qualities. The young school-leaver and the person who is approaching retirement are conventionally seen by labour
market institutions as the most difficult to place: the
one principally because he/she is unsocialised (and sometimes considered unsocialisable) to the world of work;

the other because he/she is regarded as being of limited usefulness in terms of efficiency (i.e., surplus value creation) and therefore a waste of training capacity. An applicant who is lacking academic and/or trade qualifications is also in a weak situation in times of recession, as is the person who lacks appropriate job experience.

Our final category, however, is extremely nebulous and significantly so. It is also the most important in the context of our current analysis, because it is here that the personnel manager (or more generally interviewer) has more freedom to exercise his/her judgment and therefore also give vent to his/her prejudices. Applicants may be rejected not simply for 'personality' reasons, but because they are not seen as likely to 'fit in' well given the present work-force. This idea of 'fitting in' may be seen (and, judging by some convincing empirical work, [9] is seen) as constituting legitimate grounds for rejecting a potential black employee. Significantly, none of the race relations legislation to date has been able to do anything to curb this type of activity. It may well be that employers take rejection at this stage to be a far easier option than a subsequent redundancy policy affecting blacks (in which event the chance of a legal case being brought against them may be slightly higher). On the other hand, evidence has suggested that (a) the likelihood of such a case being brought is extremely small, and (b) even if it is brought the chances of the court finding in favour of the plaintiff is minimal. Indeed, such findings have provoked some to argue that the whole race relations 'machinery' is worthless [10] or, even worse, fraudulent.

Smith (1974) has found that blacks tend to apply to organisations which already have minority workers on their payroll. [11] This may, indeed, result from a realistic appraisal of their situation stemming from an internalisation of discriminatory practices. It may also reflect a desire to avoid the experience of rejection. Nevertheless, as pointed out above, this question of individual qualities is only one of the hurdles which an applicant is required to overcome. He must also prove himself suitable on grounds of age, qualifications and experience - often related phenomena. Using employment office jargon, it would appear that the most difficult person to place is the black school-leaver with no qualifications.

In the course of his highly contentious analysis of the social evils of contemporary Handsworth, Brown (1977) argues that around 25 per cent of its black youth are unemployed. [12] Moreover, the British Youth Council were also clearly aware of the problem at a national level when they noted that: [13]

The evidence of the 1971 Census showed that twice as
many West Indian youths were unemployed as the national
average, and there is no reason to suppose that the
proportions will have radically altered since then.
They go on to point out in the same paragraph that whereas
in Britain as a whole (in 1971) 8.1 per cent of men between the ages of 16 and 20 were unemployed, the appropriate figure for those of West Indian origin was 16.2
per cent. It is undoubtedly the case that in contemporary
Handsworth the figure for this group is disproportionately
high, though assessment of precise rates is ruled out because of the non-availability of statistics relating to
those who are economically active within the relevant age-
group, and because of area boundary problems. Table 5.1,
however, does show how the absolute [14] level of unemployment among local youth throughout 1977 relates to the
overall number of young workers in the Handsworth Employment Exchange Area (EEA). [15]

A number of points immediately stand out as meriting
further discussion:

1 Throughout the year the percentage of unemployed males
   who are black remains well above the 70 per cent mark,
   and among females this figure does not fall below 64.5
   per cent.
2 The major burden of this unemployment falls squarely
   on the shoulders of the West Indians.
3 The August figure shows the impact of the summer 1977
   school-leavers who had not yet found jobs. The overall
   level of unemployment rises sharply and the percentage
   share which the West Indians retain drops slightly. On
   the other hand, by tracing developments over the next
   few months we see a reversal in the original pattern
   (at least as far as the West Indians are concerned).
   They are seen to perform relatively badly in the job-
   hunting stakes. Moreover, this pattern occurred also
   in previous years.

Given the age/ethnic structure of the local population
(cf. Chapter 2), perhaps point 1 is not too surprising.
On the other hand, an extension of an earlier argument
plus evidence from a recent Department of Employment study
[16] would suggest otherwise: on this reasoning it may be
the case that blacks are suffering disproportionately from
the lack of economic activity because of the implicit re-
definition of the notion of 'unemployable' among market
institutions. (This point will be pursued further below.)
It may be also, taking up the second issue, that Asians
are seen by employers as more attractive employment pro-
positions than their West Indian neighbours: witness the
sharp relative drop in unemployment between Indian and

TABLE 5.1 Youth unemployment in the Handsworth EEA [1] by ethnic group and sex (1977)

	West Indian [4]				Indian [4]				Pakistani/Bangladeshi [4]				Total New Commonwealth [3]				Total unemployed youth [2]	
	Males	% of total males	Fe-males	% of total fe-males	Males	% of total males	Fe-males	% of total fe-males	Males	% of total males	Fe-males	% of total fe-males	Males	% of total males	Females	% of total fe-males	Males	Females
10 Feb. 1977	56	53.8	75	62.0	11	10.6	19	15.7	2	1.7	1	0.8	74	71.2	97	80.2	104	121
12 May 1977	57	55.3	55	51.4	6	5.8	13	12.1	4	3.9	nil	nil	77	74.8	69	64.5	103	107
11 Aug. 1977	195	41.6	180	48.1	94	20.0	62	16.6	26	5.5	8	2.1	334	71.2	260	69.5	469	374
10 Nov. 1977	116	51.1	96	46.6	27	11.9	31	15.0	17	7.5	5	2.4	169	74.4	137	66.5	227	206

Source: Department of Employment, Birmingham

1 This refers to the Handsworth Exchange Area. It should not be regarded as totally matching our survey area since it includes basically Handsworth, Handsworth Wood and Winson Green plus parts of contiguous areas such as Hamstead, Hockley, Sandwell, Rotten Park, Ladywood, Edgbaston, Lozells and Smethwick.

2 These figures correspond to the total numbers of workers (including non-claimants) registered at the Handsworth Careers office on the relevant day of the month (see left-hand column). It must be stressed that these figures do not give a comprehensive picture of youth unemployment as some 16-19 year olds will either not be registered at all or will be registered at the unemployment office.

3 This includes all those born in, or having at least one parent born in, the New Commonwealth or Pakistan.

4 Those born in, or having at least one parent born in, the West Indies/India/Pakistan/Bangladesh.

West Indian men between August and November 1977. It has
to be admitted that differences in qualification levels
may well be part of the reason for this and for the phenomenon embodied in point 3 (that West Indian youth tend
to take rather longer to find work than other groups).

A more feasible explanation may lie in the greater
sense of racial identity and/or political consciousness of
many young West Indians. Evidence of membership of sects
such as the Rastafarians is hardly likely to impress a
middle-class white interviewer. The wearing of 'locks' or
a 'tam' may signal a lengthy wait in the dole queue. [17]
Moreover, when questioning managers about their attitudes
to workers from minority groups, Smith (1974) found that
certain stereotypes emerged. Among these are two which
are directly relevant here. In relation to manual
workers: 'Pakistanis and Indians are thought to be equally conscientious as whites but West Indians are generally
thought to be less conscientious.' [18] The second dominant view was that: 'All three minority groups are ...
harder for management to deal with than whites; if anything, West Indians are ... harder to deal with than
Asians.' [19] Further, as potential white-collar staff,
Asians were regarded much more highly than West Indians.

As was noted in Chapter 4, it is often argued that one
of the major problems which the immigrant faces is that of
language: of straightforward verbal communication. David
Smith, for example, stresses this point in all his major
research pieces. Thus poor English is seen as a major
cause of heavy Asian concentrations in the inner cities,
difficulties in dealing with British institutions, difficulties in obtaining acceptable work, etc. Whilst there
is, of course, an element of truth in each of these sug-
gestions, we believe that over-emphasising these 'technical' problems is at best extremely misleading, and at
worst dangerously mystificatory. Put simply, it can be
used to legitimate underachievement and to suggest that a
straightforward 'technical' solution is all that is called
for: for example, more language teaching. It may well be
that Smith did not intend his work to be read in this
light: the important thing is that it has been, not just
by academics but by policy-makers. A brief but significant article in the 'Department of Employment Gazette',
[20] for example, arrives unerringly at the 'solution'
suggested above; it even includes a picture of three
Asian ladies smiling benignly at their white English
teacher 'in the canteen of an Acton firm'. (This was
presumably intended to convey the impression that the
'solution' is both practicable and palatable.)

To return to the question of youth unemployment raised

by Table 5.1, if the question of language were important
in the job market, it would be expected that West Indians
would be relatively unaffected compared with, for example,
the Asian children (even allowing for problems with Jamaican patois). By the summer of 1977 approximately
three-quarters of the West Indian school-leavers had, in
any case, been born in the UK and had presumably also been
educated here. In sharp contrast less than one out of
every five 'Indians' had been born in the UK. Thus, given
the overall findings of Table 5.1 and particularly the
extended version which compares those children who were
born here with those born overseas, it appears that, at
least as far as getting a job is concerned, the factor of
language may in itself be relatively unimportant.

The argument thus far would appear to suggest that
during periods of high employment, minority workers in the
main manage to find work (precisely what sort of work, we
shall discuss later). During periods of recession, however, these groups effectively become a marginal source of
labour and the young (especially the young West Indian)
and perhaps to a lesser extent the immigrant who is
nearing retirement, constitute the least employable of
all. Unfortunately, we have no space here to test this
thesis in detail and at regional and national level. (The
reader is referred to the article in the 'Department of
Employment Gazette' for September 1975 discussed above for
a brief justification of some of the issues raised.) [21]
Before leaving the issue, in order to look in detail at
our Handsworth survey material, we analyse the nature of
the local unemployment situation for all age-groups since
the beginning of 1974, i.e., the time when, as we saw, the
MSC was set up and the national unemployment situation
began to reach alarming proportions.

Table 5.2 shows the level of unemployment among black
minority groups in the Handsworth EEA. By following the
trends over the four years 1974-7 we can assess the marginality thesis suggested both here and by Smith (1977).
[22] Local figures have clearly risen very sharply from
a low of 1,649 in May 1974 to a high of 5,422 in August
1977, an increase of over 228 per cent. Even allowing for
the fact that the school-leavers of summer 1973 will have
mostly been absorbed into the job market by May 1974, that
the August 1977 figure included many of the year's school-
leavers, and that economic realities may have forced many
previously 'economically inactive' persons on to the job
market, the figures are disturbing. Furthermore, the
residents of Handsworth are suffering disproportionately
from the wider economic recession, it seems: in the sense
that unemployment in Birmingham has risen a little more

TABLE 5.2 Registered unemployed [1] in the Handsworth EEA by ethnic origin and sex (and overall figures for Birmingham EEA)

	New Commonwealth and Pakistan [2] (Handsworth EEA)						Total unemployed (Handsworth EEA)			Total unemployed (Birmingham EEA)	
	MALES		FEMALES		TOTAL		MALES	FEMALES	TOTAL		
	No.	% of male figure for area Col.7	No.	% of female figure for area Col.8	No.	% of total Handsworth unemployed Col.9	No.	No.	No.	No.	% of this figure who are of new Commonwealth origin
	(1)	(2)	(3)	(4)	(5)	(6)	(7)	(8)	(9)	(10)	(11)
Feb.1974	410	26.5	52	20.2	462	25.6	1,549	257	1,806	14,665	11.2
May 1974	366	26.3	80	31.4	446	27.0	1,394	255	1,649	14,918	10.5
Aug.1974	357	24.0	94	31.9	451	25.3	1,488	295	1,783	17,858	11.0
Nov.1974						No figures available					
Feb.1975	600	33.8	289	60.1	889	39.4	1,774	481	2,255	20,686	14.4
May 1975	766	33.9	313	53.1	1,079	37.9	2,258	590	2,848	25,821	14.9
Aug.1975	1,369	41.4	559	54.1	1,928	44.4	3,305	1,034	4,339	40,452	16.0
Nov.1975	1,330	39.5	485	52.6	1,815	42.4	3,363	922	4,285	39,379	16.3
Feb.1976	1,505	40.3	555	51.9	2,060	42.9	3,732	1,070	4,802	41,664	16.4
May 1976	1,463	38.6	573	53.3	2,036	41.9	3,786	1,076	4,862	39,719	16.7
Aug.1976	1,769	43.1	884	57.7	2,653	47.1	4,102	1,533	5,635	47,127	18.0
Nov.1976						No figures available					
Feb.1977	1,425	38.8	747	56.0	2,172	43.4	3,670	1,333	5,003	39,426	20.1
May 1977	1,462	42.5	600	51.0	2,062	44.7	3,438	1,177	4,615	36,635	17.1
Aug.1977	1,675	43.5	860	54.7	2,535	46.8	3,850	1,572	5,422	43,738	18.1
Nov.1977	1,141	36.3	585	46.3	1,726	39.2	3,140	1,264	4,404	36,704	16.6

Source: Manpower Services Commission, Birmingham.

1 The figures presented are aggregates of the individual sets of statistics from the careers office and unemployment exchange in Handsworth. Column 10 lists the equivalent statistics for the Birmingham EEA as a whole.

2 This category includes those born in the UK if at least one of their parents was born in the New Commonwealth or Pakistan.

slowly during the same period (193 per cent). [23] Stepping back a little further to allow a broader perspective still, we see that the overall UK picture mirrors closely that of Birmingham (with a 191 per cent increase), though the West Midlands conurbation has been affected heavily in comparison. Here there was an increase of no less than 246 per cent in the number of jobless between May 1974 and August 1977. [24]

This is not a piece of mere 'number juggling': a closer examination reveals interesting insights into the differential effects of economic recession across the community. Birmingham, as we shall see later, has an extremely high proportion of white-collar workers as compared with much of the remainder of the West Midlands region. It is likely that two things follow: first, that this sector of the community (i.e., that of the non-manual employee) has fared relatively well throughout the recession. Then, assuming that our first point is acceptable (and a more detailed appraisal of the employment statistics suggests it is), it is scarcely surprising that an inner-city area such as Handsworth should produce the figures we quoted. Indeed, both census data (discussed later) and our own survey material suggest that the social composition of this part of Birmingham is rather different from that of the city as a whole, [25] housing, as it does, only a handful of non-manual workers.

At the level of inter-area comparison, then, and using an admittedly drastic oversimplification of the effects of changes in economic activity (i.e., by confining ourselves to one factor in the change - white/blue-collar) we see that analysis of relative disadvantage is possible. We may take this approach further and ask a related but much more theoretical question: whether, within an area such as Handsworth, there are identifiable groups of workers (or would-be workers) who appear, in some sense, to be pawns in an economic game whose players are unknown to, and remote from, their everyday life.

Clearly the notions of 'marginality' and 'employability' are very closely related phenomena. Further, our arguments to date would suggest that the black immigrant and the female worker (and hence in particular the black female worker) may delineate especially disadvantaged groups. The data presented in Table 5.2 enable us to see whether there is evidence of this.

A rather simplistic first step might be to look at the growth in unemployment among the relevant groups over the four-year (or technically 3¾-year) period covered by the statistics. In doing so, we see that whereas unemployment as a whole has risen by 144 per cent, the number of blacks

out of work has increased by 274 per cent. During the
same period, female unemployment has risen by 392 per
cent, and among female blacks the figure has increased by
a staggering 1025 per cent. Thus, we now have a situation
where almost half of Handsworth's unemployed women are
black (a disturbing finding, even taking into account the
higher level of economic activity among West Indian
women).

It is apparent that there is some evidence of disadvantaged sub-groups: groups, moreover, which may be identified as possessing certain qualities (i.e., skin colour
and sex) which could define them as relatively unemployable. It remains to be established, however, whether
these groups also act as a sort of economic 'weather
vane', in the sense of reflecting, in an exaggerated form,
the worst effects of recession. Comparison of isolated
figures, such as were presented above, cannot answer this
question: we need to analyse sets of unemployment figures
over time. If, for example, black immigrants consistently
form a higher proportion of the total jobless in times of
high unemployment than they do in time of full employment,
then there is evidence of marginality. [26]

Unfortunately, there is no space here to devote to a
detailed analysis of the statistical time-series data
summarised in Table 5.2. This would entail first a graph-
ical presentation of the relationship between the proportion of immigrants in the pool of unemployed and the overall workless totals. Second, and more constructively
given the underlying hypothesis, we might perform a
sophisticated statistical decomposition of the data on
the basis of variations such as ethnic origin, sex and
area; the latter being included since, for a variety of
reasons, Handsworth may consistently suffer a disproportionately high level of unemployment.

If we do this we see that our findings clearly follow,
in broad outline at least, those of the Department of Employment, who, on a national basis, point out that:
'during the period since November 1973 when unemployment
last began an upward trend, unemployment among minority
group workers, particularly among women, has increased at
a faster rate than unemployment in general.' [27]

In particular, we gain strong support for a suggestion
that in local terms much of the high level of unemployment
may well be linked in a substantive as well as a statistical sense to the socio-economic and racial composition of
the area. Those who hold a weak bargaining position in a
competitive job market are 'marginal' in the sense of
being relatively unemployable in times of low economic
activity, and those are essentially the groups delineated
above.

EMPLOYMENT STATUS OF HANDSWORTH HOUSEHOLDERS

We turn now to look at the sample of Handsworth householders whom we interviewed in the summer of 1976, a time,
it should be remembered, when approximately 5,500 local
people were registered as unemployed. [28] Jobless rates
among black immigrants were running particularly high, so
high, in fact, that they now constituted about a half the
total for the Handsworth EEA. It is to be expected that
this picture would be reflected by those families who were
included in our study. Table 5.3 summarises our findings
in this area.

A few general points are perhaps required here before
looking at the figures in detail. The first is that because we interviewed heads of household, younger respondents (particularly those of working age) tended to be
males. Taking traditional cultural norms into account
aslo, it is not surprising that only eight Asian women
were included in our sample. On the other hand, we talked
to thirty West Indian women under the age of 35, reflecting in part the higher level of familial instability among
this group (as discussed in Chapter 2). The second point,
partly arising from this, is that care should be taken in
interpreting survey figures relating to householders,
since a literal treatment might reasonably be expected to
result in an overstatement in terms of occupational
achievement. Fortunately, we anticipated this problem and
accordingly collected a considerable amount of information
about 'economic activity' from all members of the inter-
viewee's family, material which will be discussed later in
the present chapter.

Massive differences in the ages of heads of households
account for the relatively large numbers of economically
inactive among our indigenous sample. Almost a third of
the white men had retired and a further 3 per cent (all
over 45 years of age) were off work due to long-term illness. In sharp contrast, 94 per cent of West Indian men,
and 92 per cent of Asian men are 'economically active'.
[29] As Table 5.3A shows, however, a significant number
of minority group males are unemployed. Whereas only 4
per cent of British men are unemployed, the corresponding
figures for West Indians and Asians are 8 per cent and 12
per cent respectively. [30]

Many more West Indian women than British were found to
have entered the job market, although this could largely
be explained by the differences in the respective age
distributions (only 6 per cent of the former group being
60 years of age or over compared with 60 per cent of the
latter). Further detailed comments on female employment

TABLE 5.3A   Working status by ethnic group and sex (heads of household) (weighted figures are bracketed)

| Working status | West Indian | | Asian [1] | British | | |
	Males %	Females %	Males %	Males %	Females %
In employment (full/part-time)	85 (84)	50 (49)	79	57 (56)	31 (33)
Unemployed	8 (8)	10 (13)	12	4 (5)	2 (1)
Off work through temporary illness (less than 6 months)	1 (1)	2 (3)	1	1 (*) [3]	–
Off work through illness or dis-ability (more than 6 months)	3 (3)	8 (11)	4	3 (3)	3 (4)
Retired	3 (3)	5 (3)	1	32 (33)	24 (25)
Non-working housewife and 'never worked'	NA [2]	24 (20)	NA [2]	1 (*) [3]	39 (37)
Other	* [3]	–	2	1 (2)	–
Total sample size (= 100%)	309(257)	86 (63)	297	273(215)	127(112)

1 As there are only eight female Asian householders, the figures are quoted for males only.
2 NA = not applicable.
3 * represents a figure of less than 0.5%.

TABLE 5.3B Age/sex specific unemployment rates (weighted figures are bracketed) [1]

Age of head of house-hold	West Indian Males %	Females %	Asian Males %	British Males %	Females %
16-34	6 (8)	33(46) [2]	10	13 (16)	+ [3]
35-44	7 (9)	10(11)	9	3 (*) [4]	- [2]
45-64	10 (10)	- [2]	20	6 (7)	-
All ages	8 (9)	17(20)	13	7 (8)	5 (1)
Total eco-nomically active	292(239)	54(41)	277	173(132)	43(38)

1   These are calculated as they are in the 'Department of Employment Gazette'; i.e., the number seeking work divided by the number working plus the number seeking work.

2   The sample sizes here are extremely small (i.e., 20 or less).

3   + A figure is not quoted here as there are only 11(6) British women in our sample within this age-group.

4   * represents a figure of less than 0.5%.

must therefore await analysis of the data on members of households other than the heads. Table 5.3B does indicate that where members of these two groups do enter the job market, black girls tend to face greater difficulty in finding suitable work. Even allowing for the fact that some were single and had children to support (a state of affairs which must limit employment possibilities) it is disturbing to find that 33(46) per cent of West Indian girls under the age of 35 were out of work - a finding which reinforces earlier comments in this chapter about female unemployment, since the figure is considerably higher than that for any of the comparable male groups. [31]

Reference to the age-specific unemployment rates for men of the three major ethnic groups reveals very different patterns. Moreover, the differences may well be significant in a substantive sense. Unemployment among in-

digenous heads of household, although lower overall than
for either of the other two groups, is comparatively more
serious among the 16-34 age-group. Among these men 13 per
cent are without work. Set within the context of an urban
zone where whites have an apparently high propensity to
move out (or at least a desire to move out), this could be
an important finding. It may well be that economic problems, particularly serious within inner-city and middle-
ring areas, are acting as a constraining force on certain
sectors of the population. Thus, unemployed whites might
regard the black immigrant as a scapegoat for the failures
of the economic system not simply because he is seen as
taking 'their' (the whites') jobs, but also because he is
affecting their life chances more generally.

The level of unemployment among middle-aged whites appeared to be considerably lower than the corresponding
figures for their West Indian and Asian neighbours.
Furthermore, the rate was considerably lower than among
young whites. If we look at the twenty pre-retirement
years, the rate of 6(7) per cent is less than half the
corresponding figure for the under-35s. By way of a sharp
contrast, West Indian male unemployment worsens markedly
as we move up the age scale: so much so that approximately one in ten middle-aged West Indians was out of work.
For the Asians the situation is worse: one in five Asian
men between the ages of 45 and 64 was found to be unemployed. Just how serious the overall situation is, of
course, will only be seen when we take into account other
members of the immigrant households.

. Before doing this, we look a little more closely at the
unemployed who make up the statistics we have discussed
above. Of the 71 unemployed men we interviewed, 24 were
of West Indian and 36 of Asian origin. (As there were
only 11 female heads of household who were out of work we
shall look to other members of the household to extend the
discussion of unemployment among this sector of the population.)

As might have been expected at a time of high general
unemployment, most of those who were out of work had
already spent a great deal of time on the dole. Two-
thirds of the West Indians and a half of the Asians had
already been unemployed for at least six months, and many
of these had not had work for over a year. [32] Moreover,
few rated their chances of obtaining work as very high.
On the other hand, an interesting point did arise here:
that, in general, members of the minority groups tended
to be much more pessimistic (realistic?) than their indigenous counterparts. Only 4 out of 11 whites as against
approximately 80 per cent of West Indians and 94 per cent

of Asians admitted that finding another job would be 'very
difficult'. It may well be, of course, that experience
has led many immigrants to expect rejection, [33] and the
internalisation of this reflects the inferior role to
which many have been socialised. This would in turn lead,
perhaps, to a reinforcement of their relative disadvantage
in the job market.

General conclusions are, of course, difficult to
justify where sample sizes are as small as they are in
this case. On the other hand, we may tentatively suggest
a number of results which appear to flow from detailed
case studies of the unemployed people we interviewed:

1 Relatively few of the local white unemployed had been
   made redundant, as distinct from having left their
   employer for other reasons.
2 The whites who lost their jobs appeared to be those who
   were relatively unskilled (i.e., compared with their
   employed compatriots). Indeed, if anything, skill
   levels were lower than those of jobless minority group
   members, thus lending further support to the marginality thesis, which would predict that the pool of labour
   skills would be unevenly distributed in this way between indigenous and immigrant worker.
3 Only a handful of the unemployed immigrants worked
   locally in their last job. Whereas only three of the
   British travelled beyond the immediate vicinity (i.e.,
   Handsworth and contiguous areas), two-thirds of the
   West Indians and three-quarters of the Asians did so.
   Clearly this out-commuting pattern will be central to
   later discussions of immigrant employment, since it has
   a profound influence not only on time spent away from
   home but also because it implies at a theoretical
   level: (a) a distinction between work environment and
   primary community; (b) a departure from the way in
   which sociologists have conventionally conceptualised
   'travel-to-work' patterns among working-class communities; and (c) a clear denial of the hypothesis, suggested by some, that immigrants often desire to live
   in the inner-city and middle-ring zones of the metropolis because of their nearness to the workplace.
4 Asian unemployment appears to stem from redundancies in
   one major area, that of metal manufacture. This group
   appear to have been particularly hard hit by a run down
   of labour in the foundries to the north and west of
   Birmingham. Most of this work, or at least the work
   which the Asians had been doing, was of the unskilled
   or semi-skilled variety. Although traditionally quite
   well paid, it meant enduring extremely unpleasant
   working conditions in terms of heat, physical effort

and monotony, not to mention the working of shifts.
Between a quarter and a third of our Asian workers had
previously been involved in this type of work and a
similar number had been employed in other metal industries. The nature of West Indian unemployment
cannot be summarised so easily, as their previous jobs
were spread much more evenly across the SIC Orders.
[34] Interestingly, however, very few had been involved in foundry work.

This brief analysis, then, gives us some idea of the
nature of unemployment among middle-aged immigrants in
Handsworth. In order to gain some insight into how the
younger generation is faring, however, we need to turn to
the eldest children of our respondents. (It is to be
borne in mind that at present we are concentrating on the
problem of obtaining work, whatever its precise nature.
Later in the book we shall look at how the employment
prospects of the next generation of local blacks matches
up to those of their parents and others in the city.)

Table 5.4 presents data relating to the eldest two
children who are still living within the respondent's
household. Although the information needs to be treated
with some care, since the experiences of those who have
left the family home may be somewhat different from those
who have remained, it nevertheless gives us some insight
into the forays of Handsworth youth into the world of
work. It also underlines once again the radical differences in the age distribution of our three major ethnic
groups; the incidence of children under 16 being noticeably lower among our indigenous sample.

These differences in age distribution, and the likelihood of a number of 16-year-old West Indians and Asians
being in their last few weeks at school when the interviewing took place, probably account for some of the differences between the rates of economic activity. Male
unemployment rates, on the other hand, are remarkably
stable across the three major ethnic groupings and are
noticeably higher than those for young householders (as
shown in Table 5.3B). This stability may be something of
a mirage, since it is likely that a much higher proportion
of whites have left home in search of work. [35] This is
in part a reflection of the general outward movement on
the part of local whites. It also arises to some extent
from the fact that the immigrant community, in general,
was found to lack mobility precisely because of the
structural constraints in the housing and employment
markets.

The unemployment picture among the daughters of our
Handsworth households demonstrates no such 'surface' simi-

TABLE 5.4 Economic activity and unemployment among eldest children of Handsworth respondents by ethnic group (weighted figures are bracketed) [1]

	West Indian		Asian		British	
	Males	Females	Males	Females	Males	Females
Percentage economically active [2] (aged 16 and over)	75 (73)	60 (61)	64	54	96 (93)	73 (73)
Percentage unemployed [3]	14 (14)	26 (27)	13	30	14 (13)	5 (3)
Sample sizes Under 16	213(173) [4]	203(151) [5]	199	145	64 (51) [6]	72(48)
16 and over	93 (79) [4]	96 (79) [5]	99	50	76 (58) [6]	52(40)
Total	307(253)	300(230)	298	195	140(110)	124(88)

1 The two eldest children of the heads of household are included here; but only if they are members of the present household, i.e., are living with their parents.

2 A person is defined as 'economically active' if he/she is in employment or seeking employment.

3 The number unemployed is expressed as a percentage of the number economically active.

4 and 5 In each of these cases one person refused to give the age of his child; hence the figures fail to sum to the totals stated.

6 Because of rounding errors in the weighting procedure these figures do not sum to the totals stated.

larity. It reinforces very strongly our earlier comments
about female immigrant labour. The only major difference,
in fact, was the extremely low level of unemployment among
local white girls; this in spite of a high rate of
economic activity relative to the immigrant groups. Over
one in four West Indian and Asian girls were found to be
out of work in the summer of 1976, a period of extremely
high unemployment rates for women of New Commonwealth
origin, as we saw in Table 5.2. [36]

It is clear from the unevenness in the figures for
Asians that more girls than boys have left home. Presumably (given cultural and religious obligations) this is
usually due to marriage, at which time the bride would
either set up a new nuclear family unit or join her
husband in his family's home. However, there is some evidence, for example from the imbalance in the under-16 age-
group, that the chain migration process has also played
its part here: eldest sons have come to Britain before
female siblings.

Whatever the shortcomings of this analysis, then, there
is further evidence of high levels of unemployment among
immigrant groups, particularly among women. Analysis of
economic activity and unemployment among the wives of our
sample members also confirms this picture. It also confirms the findings of Smith (1977), [37] who noted the
extremely high proportion of West Indian women who were
economically active. Our figure of around 74 per cent for
working wives matched his exactly, but relatively few of
the Asian women in our sample went out to work. This is
all the more surprising given the fact that only around
one in five of our Handsworth women were of the Islamic
faith, a group who would undoubtedly be much less likely
than other Asians to enter into public life at least via
the broader (i.e., non-ethnically based) labour market.
Altogether less than one Asian wife in four was working.

Unemployment among wives is notoriously difficult to
estimate. Certainly very few of the husbands interviewed
defined their wives as unemployed. It is perhaps likely
that, although not registered, many of those described as
housewives would, in fact, prefer to go out to work.
Whatever the actual state of affairs, our figures of 3 per
cent for West Indian wives and 5 per cent for Asians are
probably underestimates of the true extent of unemployment
among these groups. At less than 1 per cent the figure
for the wives of our indigenous sample is almost negligible (it refers, in fact, to one woman!).

On the general level of unemployment, we can conclude
that black immigrants in Handsworth appear to suffer disproportionately in times of heavy unemployment, [38] in

the sense that their share in the pool of workless increases at a faster rate than that of their white neighbours. One implication of this is that the analysis needs
to be seen in 'racial' (and not simply class) terms.
Also, importantly, this increased share cannot be explained simply in terms of the relative rise in the size
of the black work-force. Furthermore, within this pool
of 'surplus labour capacity' it is immigrant women and
youths who suffer most. All of this is of the utmost importance in the context of the future social ecology and,
in particular, the future race relations scene in areas
such as Handsworth.

A related and equally important question is whether,
having obtained work, the immigrant has achieved equality
in terms of an effective bargaining position vis-à-vis his
white counterpart, or whether he is essentially competing
for inferior (lower-status) jobs with fellow immigrants.
We turn now, therefore, to examine the role of the immigrant in the labour market.

THE BLACK IMMIGRANT AND THE 'SUB-MARKET' THESIS

With the possible exception of those who view the black
immigrant as a poacher of the native Englishmen's jobs,
most perhaps would describe him stereotypically as the
person who, by performing the sort of labour tasks local
labour found to be too unpleasant, too unrewarding financially and so on, fulfils a significant role, especially in our service industries. To argue thus is in some
way to suggest that there are indeed two distinct markets
in operation here: one for the indigenous worker and one
(distinctly inferior) 'sub-market' for the black immigrant. Many services vital to the running of the modern
metropolis would indeed collapse if there were a massive
withdrawal of black labour. Brooks (1975) for example,
discusses the vital role which West Indians play in the
running of London Transport.

A recent report from the Unit for Manpower Studies
underlines this 'dependency' on immigrant labour by
quoting important figures relating to the medical profession. In 1968, 11 per cent of all domestic staff in
British hospitals were black. Although this may seem
small it is important to realise that the overall figure
conceals many significant variations (by area). In London
teaching hospitals, for example, the figure was 37.2 per
cent, and in both north-east and north-west London more
than one in every five domestic workers was black. In
Birmingham, the area of next highest concentration, the

ratio was approaching one to nine, and immigrant labour taken as a whole comprised 17 per cent of the total domestic work-force. [39] It is not simply at this occupational level that immigrant labour is vital. Recent DHSS figures show that one in five student and pupil nurses and pupil midwives were born overseas, and that more than a half of these were recruited in their country of origin. [40] Of course, the pool of ready labour formed by the highly 'economically active' West Indian population combined with a contracting economy means that relatively few nurses now need to be recruited in the Caribbean and 'imported' to the UK. Further up the status ladder we see that more than a third of hospital doctors in employment in 1975 were from overseas, though (significantly for our later analysis) these were largely concentrated in junior posts or in unpopular specialisms. [41]

Similar analyses could be performed for other occupations in which immigrant labour is vital. Unfortunately, there is no space here to follow up this line of argument. Many writers, such as Castles and Kosack (1973), Berger and Mohr (1975), and the Department of Employment (1976) have, in any case, already done so. We cannot, however, fully understand the position of the black immigrant in the metropolis unless we study the forces which drew him to it, and his contractual relationship with the capitalist economy and its market institutions. Berger and Mohr, for example, underline clearly the ways in which this relationship is asymmetrical - its non-mutuality being exposed vividly in the notions of contract labour and (involuntary) repatriation. When we talk about the position of a black man (or woman) in British society we are as much concerned with the relationship between the individual and the state as we are with his social relations in everyday life. This necessarily involves also a discussion of ways in which blacks can seek by political means to expose the ambiguity of their position.

The remainder of this chapter will be devoted to an examination, first, of the sort of jobs which West Indians, Indians and Pakistanis in Britain are doing, both in terms of the type of industry and in terms of job status. We look, second, at changes in the pattern of jobs over time, and ask whether, for example, members of immigrant groups are achieving any tangible success in the labour market; for example, by becoming upwardly mobile in status terms. Finally, we extend the latter line of thinking by looking at work conditions and the relations between blacks and labour organisations such as the trade unions and other ethnically based bodies such as the Indian Workers Association.

OCCUPATIONAL STRUCTURE

Figures from the 1971 Census, which we shall look at in
more detail shortly, suggest that in Great Britain as a
whole a far higher proportion of New Commonwealth immigrants are employed in blue-collar occupations than
members of the general population. [42] We begin our
analysis of Birmingham, then, with an analysis of the occupational structure of the city as a whole using the same
data source (i.e., the 1971 Census). These figures are
presented in Table 5.5 along with those relating specifically to our survey wards.

As pointed out in the 'New Plan for the City', Birmingham itself houses a much higher proportion of its blue-
collar labour force than it does its professional and
managerial groups. [43] A large number of the latter commute to the central business area of the city from 'desirable' residential districts such as Sutton Coldfield in
the north, Solihull and Meriden in the south-east, and
rural Worcestershire in the south and west. The authors
of the above report clearly see this group as the life
blood of the present metropolis. Hence they argue: [44]

The importance to the city of commuters in the higher
socio-economic groups can be clearly shown. 44.4 per
cent of employers and managers working in the city and
52.4 per cent of the professional workers lived outside
the city in 1966.

Moreover this process of in-commuting by white-collar
workers is seen as an increasing trend, bringing with it
serious consequences for the manual industrial work-force
left behind in their wake.

Manufacturing industry, the major source of employment
for manual workers, has also been leaving the inner-city
area, either through the general effects of inflation and
recession or through the desire to move to more 'suitable'
sites elsewhere. For those who live in the inner-city and
middle-ring areas who are still employed, then, journeying
to work often means commuting out to the foundries of the
Black Country or the car plants of south-west Birmingham.
Large numbers, of course, are not so fortunate (?). As we
have already seen, unemployment figures are high and with
the city coffers being depleted by the lack of important
rate revenue on vacant industrial sites and the savage
cuts in rate support grants, it is hardly surprising that
the already declining inner zones of a city such as
Birmingham suffer disproportionately in such times.

As Table 5.5 shows, only 11 per cent of the city's
enumerated male residents were employed in professional
or managerial posts (SEGs 1-4), [45] and the figure rises

TABLE 5.5 Socio-economic group (SEG) [1] of economically active persons resident within Birmingham CB and the four survey wards [2] in 1971

	MALES Handsworth	Soho	Sandwell	Newtown	Birmingham
1 Employers & Managers in central & local govt., industry, commerce, etc. - large establishments	160 (2.0)	70 (0.9)	540 (6.2)	20 (0.5)	9,060 (2.9)
2 Employers & Managers in central & local govt., industry, commerce, etc. - small establishments	330 (4.0)	240 (3.0)	950 (10.8)	90 (2.3)	15,220 (4.8)
3 Professional workers Self-employed	20 (0.2)	–	60 (0.7)	10 (0.3)	1,340 (0.4)
4 Professional workers Employees	130 (1.6)	40 (0.5)	360 (4.1)	10 (0.3)	9,130 (2.9)
5 Intermediate non-manual workers	270 (3.3)	210 (2.6)	600 (6.8)	30 (0.8)	13,680 (4.4)
6 Junior non-manual workers	590 (7.2)	480 (5.9)	1,080 (12.3)	320 (8.0)	31,990 (10.2)
7 Personal service workers	90 (1.1)	60 (0.7)	40 (0.5)	50 (1.3)	2,230 (0.7)
8 Foremen/women and Supervisors - manual	220 (2.7)	160 (2.0)	240 (2.7)	90 (2.3)	11,840 (3.8)
9 Skilled manual workers	2,940 (35.9)	3,020 (37.4)	2,700 (30.8)	1,390 (34.8)	111,740 (35.6)

FEMALES	Handsworth	Soho	Sandwell	Newtown	Birmingham	TOTAL Birmingham CB
	80 (1.6)	40 (1.0)	40 (0.7)	–	1,890 (1.0)	10,950 (2.2)
	110 (2.2)	90 (2.2)	210 (3.7)	50 (2.0)	4,630 (2.5)	19,850 (4.0)
	–	–	10 (0.2)	–	240 (0.1)	1,580 (0.3)
	20 (0.4)	10 (0.2)	30 (0.5)	20 (0.8)	1,290 (0.7)	10,420 (2.1)
	340 (6.7)	210 (5.1)	960 (16.7)	100 (4.1)	16,710 (8.9)	30,390 (6.1)
	1,450 (28.5)	900 (22.1)	2,210 (38.5)	390 (15.9)	67,320 (35.8)	99,310 (19.8)
	340 (6.7)	370 (9.1)	540 (9.4)	270 (11.0)	19,310 (10.3)	21,540 (4.3)
	30 (0.6)	20 (0.5)	30 (0.5)	10 (0.4)	1,100 (0.6)	12,940 (2.6)
	330 (6.5)	460 (11.3)	240 (4.2)	220 (8.9)	10,080 (5.4)	121,820 (24.3)

TABLE 5.5 (continued)

	MALES Handsworth	Soho	Sandwell	Newtown	Birmingham
10 Semi-skilled manual workers	1,680 (20.5)	1,670 (20.7)	1,000 (11.4)	1,030 (25.8)	60,540 (19.3)
11 Unskilled manual workers	1,010 (12.3)	1,630 (20.2)	550 (6.3)	620 (15.5)	26,400 (8.4)
12 Own account workers – Non-manual	210 (2.7)	190 (2.3)	350 (4.0)	120 (3.0)	10,620 (3.4)
13 Farmers – Employers and managers	–	–	–	–	50 (*)
14 Farmers – own account	–	–	–	–	60 (*)
15 Agricultural workers	–	–	20 (0.2)	–	260 (0.1)
16 Members of Armed Forces	20 (0.2)	10 (0.1)	10 (0.1)	–	430 (0.1)
17 Those with inadequately defined occupation	510 (6.2)	300 (3.7)	270 (3.1)	220 (5.5)	9,380 (3.0)
	8,180(100.0)	8,080(100.0)	8,770(100.0)	4,000(100.0)	313,970(100.0)

FEMALES	Handsworth	Soho	Sandwell	Newtown	Birmingham	TOTAL Birmingham CB
	1,420 (27.9)	1,060 (26.0)	980 (17.1)	1,020 (41.5)	37,190 (19.8)	97,730 (19.5)
	380 (7.5)	420 (10.3)	180 (3.1)	230 (9.3)	16,580 (8.8)	42,980 (8.6)
	100 (2.0)	110 (2.7)	50 (0.9)	20 (0.8)	2,540 (1.4)	13,160 (2.6)
	-	-	-	-	-	50 (*)
	-	-	-	-	10 (*)	70 (*)
	10 (0.2)	-	-	-	190 (0.1)	450 (0.1)
	-	-	-	-	-	430 (0.1)
	480 (9.4)	390 (9.6)	260 (4.5)	130 (5.3)	8,810 (4.7)	18,190 (3.6)
	5,090(100.0)	4,080(100.0)	5,740(100.0)	2,460(100.0)	187,890(100.0)	501,860(100.0)

* represents a figure of less than 0.05%.
1 As defined in the Registrar General's Classification of Occupations 1970
2 See Figure 1

to only 25.6 per cent if we include the intermediate and
junior white-collar staff (i.e., SEGs 5 and 6). In terms
of the social composition of the city, however, this reveals only part of the total picture. The relative heter-
ogeneity of the population as a whole largely disappears
when we look at our survey wards in general, and the Soho
ward in particular. (Because of the high concentrations
of New Commonwealth immigrants this ward is the only one
which was covered completely by our sampling frame, as can
be seen in Figure 1.) Only 4.4 per cent of economically
active males in Soho were drawn from SEGs 1-4, and the
vast majority of these were employers/managers of small
establishments, i.e., were small businessmen - for example, shopkeepers and traders. A mere 12.9 per cent of
the total were in non-manual jobs. Newtown, with its
large council estate, also shows few high-status workers.
Only Sandwell, with its relatively affluent northern
sector, breaks away radically from this general pattern.
On the other hand, it is highly unlikely that this heter-
ogeneity of employment would be found among the immigrant
communities who are largely concentrated in the poorer
southern tip of the ward.

A similar picture emerges if we look at the economically active female population. Approximately three out of
every five women from the Sandwell ward are in non-manual
occupations, though it must be stressed that they are
largely employed in low-grade non-manual jobs such as
clerks, receptionists and typists. Once again in Soho and
Newtown manual occupations predominate.

Having briefly surveyed the position for members of the
general population, we now turn to the group of workers
whom we interviewed in Handsworth. The results of this
analysis are summarised in Table 5.6. As will be noticed
immediately, the data on ethnic groups have been presented
rather differently than has been customary up to this
point in the book. This step has been taken largely because previous research has shown the work experience of
Pakistani men to be rather different from that of others
of Asian origin. [46] As it happens, this change in
analytical approach appears to be totally justified by
the findings which our table reveals.

Out of thirty-six men born in Pakistan, only one has
achieved a white-collar occupation - a clerical job in a
finance office. But the contrast between the immigrant
job status distributions does not principally arise here,
since few of our non-British male sample had other than
manual jobs. The major difference lies in the level of
skills required and the type of manual job which the majority do. Over three out of five Pakistanis had semi-

skilled or unskilled occupations compared with 43(44) per
cent of the West Indians and 38 per cent of the Indians.
On the other hand, even these fairly large differences are
dwarfed when we compare the figures with the appropriate
categories of indigenous workers. Only 17(14) per cent of
our British sample were in semi-skilled or unskilled occupations, and no less than 31(35) per cent were in white-
collar jobs.

Because only one of our female Asian heads of household
was in employment we cannot say anything here about the
occupational experience of Indian and Pakistani women. We
are, however, in a position to compare the job status
profiles of the West Indian and British women. Although
the sample sizes are much smaller than those of the men,
a few interesting points do arise here. For one thing, it
seems clear that there are relatively more West Indian
women in the intermediate non-manual group. On the other
hand, there seem to be slightly fewer white women in semi-
and unskilled manual work. The latter mirrors the
findings of the male sample, though rather less spectacu-
larly: the former seems to be a reflection of the propensity of West Indian girls to enter the nursing profession.

It might perhaps be argued that sampling errors could
account for some of these observed differences (among the
male as well as the female sample). This is rather unlikely, not least because the findings appear to be well
substantiated at the national level. An analysis of the
1971 Census data conducted by the Department of Applied
Economics at Cambridge University and reported by the
Department of Employment (1976) underlines the plight of
men from the West Indies and Pakistan in particular.
Whereas 16.5 per cent of men in Great Britain as a whole
were in high-status occupations (SEG 1-4), the equivalent
figure for those born in Pakistan is 7.5 per cent and for
West Indians it is a mere 2.8 per cent. [47] Indian and
East African men appear to compare very well on this index
with the general population, principally, it seems, because of the large numbers in the medical profession [48]
and others who have acquired small businesses. Indeed, on
the latter point, it is often suggested, at least by implication, that Asians in general and East Africans in
particular are now more a 'nation of shopkeepers' than
the British!

Although it is misleading to suggest, as does Forester
(1978), [49] that it is possible to draw a clear parallel
between the success of Jewish immigrants in mastering the
intricacies of the capitalist economy and the likely
future of the present-day Asian immigrants, some of the

TABLE 5.6 Socio-economic group by birthplace and sex [1] for those heads of households who were in employment when interviewed (weighted figures are bracketed)

	West Indies		Pakistan	India	Others of Asian origin [3]	Great Britain	
	Males %	Females %	Males %	Males %	Males %	Males %	Females %
1 Employers & Managers in central & local govt., industry, commerce, etc. - large establishments	* [2]	-	-	-	-	4 (5)	-
2 Employers & Managers in central & local govt., industry, commerce, etc. - small establishments	* [2]	-	-	1	-	4 (5)	2 (3)
3 Professional workers Self-employed	-	-	-	-	-	1 (1)	-
4 Professional workers Employees	* [2]	-	-	-	-	3 (3)	-
5 Intermediate non-manual workers	1 (*) [2]	35 (40)	-	2	6	9 (11)	7 (8)
6 Junior non-manual workers	2 (2)	5 (6)	3	2	-	10 (10)	27 (28)
7 Personal service workers	1 (*) [2]	14 (15)	-	-	-	-	15 (14)

8 Foremen/women and Supervisors - manual	2 (3)	2 (*)[2]	–	1	–	8 (7)	–
9 Skilled manual workers	49 (47)	5 (4)	33	55	76	39 (39)	10 (6)
10 Semi-skilled manual workers	29 (30)	30 (24)	44	24	12	12 (10)	17 (19)
11 Unskilled manual workers	14 (14)	9 (10)	17	14	6	5 (4)	15 (15)
12 Own account workers (non-professional)	1 (1)	–	–	2	–	4 (5)	–
13-15 Agricultural workers	–	–	–	–	–	1 (*)[2]	2 (3)
16 Members of Armed Forces	–	–	–	–	–	–	–
17 Occupation inadequately defined/refused	1 (1)	–	3	1	–	–	5 (5)
Total sample size (= 100%)	263 (217)	43 (31)	36	183	17	156 (120)	41 (38)

1 As only one Asian female head of household was in employment, figures for males alone are stated.

2 * represents a figure of less than 0.5%.

3 This includes, for example, those born in Bangladesh or Sri Lanka as well as those of Asian origin who were born in (say) East Africa. Care should be taken in interpreting these figures, however, because of the very small sample size.

latter have undoubtedly stepped on to the bottom rung of
the commercial ladder. The reasons for this are perhaps
not too difficult to discern. As the Department of
Employment (1976) argues: [50]

> The tendency for a growing number of Asians to set up
> their own small businesses in industries in which the
> financial costs of doing so are relatively low (e.g.,
> retail distribution, catering and clothing) may be
> further evidence of their wish to move out of the least
> attractive jobs as well as a wish to avoid employment
> situations in which they are discriminated against.

There may, then, be a reoccurrence of the sort of process
which was evident in the field of Asian housing; namely,
a desire to restrict social relations with the indigenous
population to a minimum. Moreover, this mode of action
can possibly be interpreted as an internalisation and
implicit acceptance of discriminatory practices. Such
practices often go far beyond the refusal to offer a
person work on the grounds of colour. Even when he/she
has been accepted for employment, the job may well be at
a skill level far below that which the applicant's qualifications justify. The individual's chances of promotion
may well be generally worse than those of his white colleagues. These are all ideas which will be tested by our
own survey data shortly.

For the few who manage to accumulate enough capital to
start a business (usually by borrowing from relatives) and
who, by working around the clock, are able to expand their
business and prosper, the future may look comparatively
rosy. On the other hand, there are two important points
to bear in mind here. First, Asian businessmen often
trade almost exclusively with fellow Asians. We are
therefore talking not only about a highly restricted
market and one comprised largely of comparatively low
wage-earners, but also one which, because of immigration
policies and the falling rate of natural increase, is unlikely to grow significantly over the coming decades.
Therefore, unless the products of Asian labour are aimed
at, and accepted by, a wider market, opportunities for
growth and improved mobility in the world of business and
commerce are slight. Moreover, many newcomers will be
doomed to premature failure through the effects of competition. Our second major point is that in talking about
the Asian work-force it should not be forgotten that the
vast majority are not businessmen, successful or otherwise.

This being said, there is considerable evidence of
Asian enterprise in Handsworth. A walk along the Soho
Road reveals numerous sweet centres, grocers, butchers,

sari centres and even two cinemas run by Asians. The obvious question to ask at this point is whether West Indians are themselves making any moves to gain a foothold in the world of business and commerce. In a banner headline to a sequel to the article by Forester noted above, Phillips proclaimed that: 'Asian entrepreneurs have done well in Britain, West Indians haven't been so lucky'. [51] We would wish to argue that the first half of this statement is unacceptable without considerable qualification: the second provokes an examination of the precise social meaning and structural context of 'lucky'. The body of the article correctly points to a number of similarities in the positions of West Indian and Asian businessmen in Britain, in particular the dependence on an ethnic consumer base and the difficulty of raising capital in a fairly competitive market controlled by whites. (The latter clearly results in constraints on productive capacity and competitive weakness, since the entrepreneur is unable to respond to market forces by exploiting new areas of growth potential.) Why commercial penetration differs in the two ethnic groups is an interesting question for sociologist and economist alike; and whatever the answer, 'luck', in the everyday meaning of the term, is not it.

Initial capital accumulation is much easier among the Asian communities, given the strength of primary group ties and in particular the ability to pool money for such business ventures. This source of capital acquisition is not usually available to the would-be West Indian businessman. The lack of West Indian workshops, however, is 'explained' by Phillips in a very interesting way. The workshop is seen first of all as a means of gaining a commercial foothold without strong financial backing. Their existence depends on a ready supply of cheap labour, and West Indian labour, it is argued, 'is too expensive'. [52] It is surely naive to suggest that any major difference in observed patterns of economic activity may be laid at the door of what is presumably seen as an objective measure of 'labour cost'. If West Indians avoid the 'workshop' this is because of differences in the nature of internal social organisation of this immigrant group vis-à-vis the Asians and their radically different orientation to social and economic relations with white society. [53] Thus 'labour cost', if it is to be a sociologically meaningful term and a useful explanatory tool in this instance, needs to be seen in terms of its subjective determination grounded in social relations.

Another interesting strand of Phillips's argument is the implicit equation of the ethnically based workshop

with the 'sweat shop'. Certainly under-capitalisation
tends to imply that cheap labour is 'necessary' for the
modern business enterprise to compete successfully in a
technologically sophisticated economy. The important
point which needs to be made, however, is that if the
sweat shop phenomenon is the predominant mode of small
business organisation among Asians, then this is something
which has to be seen once again in terms of external
structural constraints in social as well as in market
terms. What we have witnessed is the creation of what
might be termed the 'pariah employer', (since the parallel
with the 'pariah landlord' is inescapable). He avoids,
often via non-union labour, any obligation to adjust his
pay rates to conform with those of unionised shops, and
thereby incurs the combined wrath of certain trade union-
ists, social scientists and politicians. And yet by providing employment for those who would be unlikely to find
it elsewhere, he does the state a service both by limiting
unemployment among minority groups and thus defusing a
situation of potential unrest, and also by limiting
pressure on the national social security coffers.

This 'economy within an economy' is seen by some
writers as a vital source of strength for members of immigrant groups. Thus a recent document published by AFFOR
[54] clearly sees as a serious 'problem' the lack of West
Indian-run businesses in Handsworth (and by implication a
similar lack in other areas of the UK where Asians and
West Indians live side by side). The internal strength of
the traditional extended family is seen here as threatened
by insuperable external forces. In the author's words:
'the protection that ... (the extended family) can offer
is considerably weakened when it is at the mercy of a
stagnant economy, and racist scaremongering in the media
and by certain political parties.' [55]

As noted earlier, however, only a tiny minority of immigrants have acquired business interests, and we therefore concentrate for the remainder of this chapter on
those who form the vast majority of immigrants in Britain.
We look first of all at the social mobility (if any) of
Asian and West Indian immigrants since their arrival in
the UK and then at the types of occupation which they now
have. On the latter point, incidentally, we shall reflect
on the immense shift in occupational roles which many will
be seen to have undergone since arriving in the metropolis
from the Caribbean, East Africa or the Indian subcontinent.

SOCIAL MOBILITY OF IMMIGRANTS FROM THE NEW COMMONWEALTH

It has already been argued that the black immigrant faces
considerable difficulties in gaining suitable employment:
suitable in the sense of that which matches his qualifications and experience. For this to be the case with
those who have recently entered the UK job market is perhaps not surprising. On the other hand, once the immigrant population has become established (in temporal
terms) one might hope that the distribution of jobs in
status terms might begin to resemble that of the indigenous population.

To see whether this is in fact the case for immigrants
from the New Commonwealth, we examine the data prepared by
the Department of Applied Economics at Cambridge University and presented by the Department of Employment (1976).
[56] This presents the socio-economic distribution of
economically active males and females born in certain New
Commonwealth countries and resident in Great Britain at
the time of the 1966 and 1971 Censuses. The figures for
all persons in Great Britain are given for comparative
purposes.

The male West Indian working population increased from
around 115,000 to almost 125,000 during this five-year
period - an increase of 8.2 per cent. During the same
period the number originating from Pakistan increased by
a half to a figure approaching 77,000, those from India by
almost 30 per cent to 138,000, and the figure for East
African-born men trebling to over 20,000. Compared with
men of Asian origin, then, the size of the West Indian
population is remarkably stable. Meanwhile the male
working population of Great Britain as a whole fell by
1 per cent to around 15,884,000.

These figures are consistent with the arguments raised
in Chapter 1 and need to be underlined here since they, by
necessity, influence our analysis of social mobility.
This is because immigration policy is clearly linked to
the demands of the British economy; and the increase,
say, in the proportion of professional men, i.e., doctors,
may be a by-product of this policy rather than an indication of improved social mobility for those already here.
We must also take into consideration the ways in which the
total pool of jobs has changed. In fact, what appears to
have happened is that the white-collar sector of the
labour force expanded considerably during the latter half
of the 1960s. Interestingly, it is almost exclusively
among the higher-status jobs that this increase has been
most noticeable. The proportions of the total male labour
force in professional and higher managerial occupations

rose from 14.3 per cent to 16.5 per cent, a numerical increase of well over 30,000.

This overall upward mobility seems largely to have bypassed the immigrant groups. Only a small proportion of West Indian men (under 3 per cent) held professional and higher managerial posts in 1971; and although the numbers of Pakistani men in these occupational groups rose considerably during the late sixties (principally due to immigration policy), the overall figure (7.5 per cent) remained small. During the same period thousands of expelled East Africans came to Britain and appear largely to have moved into skilled and semi-skilled occupations. (Earlier arrivals contained a very high proportion of men with professional skills or with business capital.) Constraints on immigration are possibly at the root of the fairly static occupational distributions for those born in India, distributions which underline the fact that the proportion of Indian men in high-status occupations is still higher than the figure for Britain as a whole. This might have been extremely significant had it not been for the fact that, as we noted earlier, for example, large numbers of Indian doctors were 'imported' to bolster the National Health Service.

It is the West Indian and, even more so, the Pakistani men who are disproportionately represented in low-status occupations. In 1966 well over 60 per cent of men born in Pakistan were in semi-skilled or unskilled occupations (compared with 23.2 per cent of the total male population). This figure had, it is true, fallen a little by 1971, but only in line with the general shift in the occupational structure. Rather more disturbing even than this is a point which appears to be common to all of these immigrant groups. This is that despite the heavy concentration in manual occupations, there were still very few signs in 1971 that blacks were being promoted into responsible positions on the shop-floor, i.e., to foremen and supervisors (a point to which we shall return shortly).

The occupational structure of the female immigrant work-force is also extremely interesting. Once again those of West Indian origin are very heavily concentrated in jobs of semi-skilled or unskilled status and only a negligible number have moved into professional or managerial posts. As to the jobs of intermediate status, nursing and other varieties of hospital work seem to present a major (and between 1966 and 1971 an increasing) source of work. In contrast, the indigenous workers who acquire non-manual occupations are much more heavily represented in clerical and secretarial work.

The period from 1966 to 1971 saw a major increase in
the level of economic activity among workers of all ethnic
groups in Britain. This holds true even in the case of
the (largely Moslem) women born in Pakistan. Here the
female work-force increased by some 115 per cent to nearly
6,000. In addition a strikingly high proportion of these
women (9.1 per cent) had achieved jobs of professional or
managerial status. On the other hand, it must be borne in
mind that this figure is, in some sense, misleading owing
to the fact that the absolute level of economic activity
among Pakistani women is still extremely low and it is
likely that among the less well educated Pakistani families in Britain, few women work. This is certainly the
evidence from our own (admittedly limited) amount of
survey data on Moslem families in Handsworth.

The immigration factor once again blurs the interpretation of the statistics, of course. On the other hand,
with or without assumptions about the effect of this
factor on the occupational structure of the Indian female
work-force, we have a dramatic worsening of status
patterns between 1966 and 1971. Whereas in 1966 approaching three quarters of Indian workers were in non-manual
occupations, by 1971 the figure had plummeted to a little
over a half. It seems likely that this has come about due
to the combination of two factors: first, more and more
Indian women wished, for a variety of reasons, to work.
This rise in 'economic activity' would tend to be accompanied by a general lowering of the average level of
formal qualifications. Second, employers, seeing a vast
untapped reservoir of labour, began in the late 1960s to
exploit this potential to the full. In this context the
rapid increase in the volume of semi-skilled female labour
is as might have been expected.

To summarise the findings of the Census data, then, we
can point to little evidence of improved social mobility
among immigrant groups: if anything, the reverse is the
case. Naturally it must be admitted that upward occupational status does not necessarily imply upward social
mobility in so far as an objective classification of occupation status tells us little about the social status
which accrues to the individual. Nevertheless, on the
assumption that social acceptance in the widest sense will
probably await the acquisition of similar occupational
roles the study of comparative occupational status
patterns is worthwhile.

Our Handsworth survey data was accordingly designed to
include information on job-history, aspirations and the
chances of promotion for immigrants and indigenous workers
alike. Being aware of the point raised earlier in the

previous paragraph, we also attempted to gauge the extent
to which black workers saw themselves as having attained
a similar status to that accorded to whites fulfilling a
similar occupational role.

We have already seen in Table 5.6 how few of the immigrant heads of household we interviewed had other than
blue-collar jobs. What this conceals is a remarkable
stability of employment. Only one in ten of those who
were working in 1976 had changed their job within the previous two years, and a much smaller number said that they
were looking for another job at the time of the interview.

This picture of stability reinforces remarks made
earlier in this book about the general geographical stability of the families studied. Most were established
Handsworth residents, and as such often gave the impression of having accepted their present situation philo-
sophically. Partly for this reason the concluding chapter
gives another perspective of Handsworth, i.e., that of its
(predominantly black) youth. These at least are free from
some of the social constraints which plagued first-generation blacks; namely, those of coping with the demands of
a new and alien society, whilst at the same time attempting to find suitable work and provide a home for their
families. These preoccupations inevitably took their
toll, especially when seen in the context of an increasingly harsh economic climate made considerably worse by
the hostility of many of British society's people and institutions.

This should not be taken to imply that the predominant
mood of middle-aged blacks in Handsworth is one of total
numbness in the face of external attack. There is evidence that some have fought for and achieved a restricted
degree of upward mobility (at least in occupational status
terms), and on a more negative note a large number express
severe reservations about their current work situation.

On the positive side, there are those who have moved to
better paid jobs or those requiring a higher skill level.
Of the sixteen West Indian men who were in skilled manual
occupations when interviewed and had changed jobs in the
last two years, twelve had made a sideways movement in
status terms, largely for an improvement in financial
rewards. The remainder had left semi-skilled or unskilled
factory work to take up these jobs. In the sphere of
white-collar work West Indian men had, of course, made
very little penetration. (In fact the sole 'beneficiary'
in this area was the man who had moved from a junior
clerical job to a management position within a large
firm.) A similar picture emerges from both the Asian and
white workers, except that the latter had been rather more
successful in achieving white-collar status.

In summary, then, we found an extremely static situation. Two thirds of our West Indian sample, for example, had been in their present job for at least five years. There was some faint evidence of upward mobility in job status terms, and, counter to this there was a handful of people changing to jobs requiring less skill than their previous one, sometimes because these enabled the individual to earn more if a large amount of overtime was worked.

One slightly encouraging pointer in terms of future generations of British-born blacks comes from an analysis of job status in relation to the source of education. What little evidence we have of householders who have received at least some of their education in this country would seem to suggest that these migrants do rather better in the job market than those who completed their schooling in the West Indies or the Indian subcontinent. On the other hand, we clearly need to beware of reading too much into these results, since only 13 male West Indians and 29 male Asians fall into the former category. In addition, the pattern of jobs acquired still does not signal a marked degree of success when compared with the achievements of native workers in Handsworth. Despite these caveats, it is perhaps worth noting that only two of the 13 West Indian men and 7 of the 19 Asians are in semi-skilled occupations. Moreover, three of these West Indians and five of the Asians are in white-collar jobs. It is perhaps not surprising that in a fiercely competitive labour market blacks who enter directly from British schools will have the edge on those who have grown up in a very different society and have worked in jobs which prepare them rather poorly for the often dehumanising demands of an advanced industrial society. This appears to us to follow from an elaboration of the supply-demand thesis of Wright (1968). [57]

As noted earlier, few of those we interviewed were actively seeking a change of job. This may, however, be no more than an internalisation of economic and social 'reality'. [58] Certainly there seemed to be a large measure of dissatisfaction with work amongst many. Approximately one West Indian in six complained of the physical conditions in which he or she was expected to work. Furthermore, although reluctance to criticise most features of their life was common among Asians, this was one issue on which they tended to agree with the West Indians. Just why this is the case will become evident when we compare the type of work undertaken by the immigrant groups. It will also become clear why relatively few indigenous workers make this type of complaint; hours

and money, in particular, are seen as equally, if not
more, important for this group.

Stability of employment might, of course, transcend
other problems associated with work, particularly with the
person whose main commitment is instrumental. We have
also noted in an earlier chapter the tendency for many immigrants to point to the mere availability of work as a
major point in this country's favour. This is hardly surprising when the reference point is not the level of employment of British whites, but the situation in their
home countries. Many of the subjects from our study would
have agreed with the West Indian sand-miller quoted by
Wright as saying: 'The job carries a lot of dirt, but I
would rather remain on it. I just love a steady job.'
[59] Our data are certainly more consistent with the
picture of labour turnover presented by Wright than that
of Banton (1955). [60] Of course, the rapidly expanding
economy of the post-war decade provided the setting for
high job mobility. As we all know, the recessions of the
early 1960s and 1970s go a long way towards explaining the
reversal.

Despite race relations legislation, the white worker
who wishes to change his job will invariably be in a
stronger position than his black colleague. The managers
interviewed by Wright were undoubtedly correct in attributing 'the low levels of labour turnover amongst coloured
workers to the difficulties in obtaining alternative employment'. [61] On the other hand, simple economic arguments based on supply and demand elucidate the permissive
conditions rather than the explanatory basis of the phenomenon. Banton's study was conducted at a time when the
number of black immigrants in Britain was relatively
small. 'Race' was not yet seen as a major problem. Politicians had yet to warn of the impending racial holocaust and the possibility of the 'British' being swamped
by those of alien cultures. [62] Furthermore, it is when
the immigrant begins to be seen as a threat to the livelihood of the native worker that we find many, as reported
by Lawrence (1974), [63] asserting their 'rights as
Englishmen'. This in turn makes it easier for the manager
to rationalise discriminatory recruitment practices.
Given the absence of truly effective legislation he can
argue that harmonious industrial relations dictate and
justify a restriction on the number of black employees.

Smith (1977) demonstrates clearly how these discriminatory procedures can in practice militate against the employment of the immigrant worker. What is perhaps more
important, however, is not that they exist, but that the
applicant knows they exist. It is not surprising that

blacks are more likely to apply for jobs in firms where a number of fellow immigrants are already employed. If no such vacancies arise it is likely that the individual will stay in his/her present job. The avoidance of encounters which would be expected to result in rejection might lead us to expect that failure to be appointed to a particular post would normally be interpreted in non-racial terms. This was not the case in our study of Handsworth. In the previous five years, one in ten of both our Asian and West Indian workers had applied for other jobs than the one which they then held. There was considerable evidence that many of the applicants interpreted their failure to gain employment as being directly due to discrimination on the grounds of colour.

What upward mobility there is available appears to depend almost exclusively on internal promotion. From all the available evidence, our own study included, the chances of this are much lower for black workers than for their white colleagues. In a sense this is almost self-evident from the data already presented: our Handsworth findings clearly replicate the pattern of occupations found by Kohler (1974) in his study of a London borough. Here he concluded that: 'There are very few black or Asian managers or clerical staff, but a concentration of black workers in semi-skilled or unskilled jobs.' [64] It was discovered also that black workers of all ages 'expressed misgivings about their prospects of promotion'. Lawrence (1974) reported similar findings; in that 96 per cent of his sample felt that 'there were ... particular kinds of jobs which immigrants had more difficulty in getting than English people with the same qualifications.' [65] These 'particular kinds of jobs' were principally those which implied supervisory responsibility or those which were of routine clerical status. This means that the immigrant often experiences occupational down-grading either in objective terms or in the sense that his (or her) expectations remain unfulfilled. Thus, as Wright (1968) argues: [66]

A large number of West Indian migrants are 'white-collar' and not manual workers. Because of the greater resistance to coloured workers in white-collar jobs, many of them may have had no alternative but to take manual jobs. Although such workers may technically be unskilled as far as manual work is concerned, to be placed in the position of having to accept such work undoubtedly represents down-grading. (Also) if the statements of West Indians concerning their own skill level ... are accepted as representing their level of aspiration, then it is apparent that the occupational

level attained falls below that expected and will probably be perceived as a down-grading.
He goes on to argue that by the same token 'Asian workers have, in general, achieved considerable occupational upgrading', and links this to the greater level of job satisfaction expressed by this group compared with West Indians. This link is, however, rather tenuous and we would take the view that this 'reluctance to criticise' is more likely to be a particular instance of the general phenomenon reported in earlier chapters of this book. It would be a mistake to conclude that Asians are, as a result, docile 'factory fodder'. Indeed, it has been argued by Sivanandan that they represent today the most militant section of the British labour force. [67] (We shall return to this point shortly.)

We turn now to look at the level and nature of internal promotion offered to members of our Handsworth sample, and then relate present job status to the qualifications (if any) held. Each respondent was asked whether he or she had been offered promotion in his or her present job, and if so, what form this took. The answers are recorded in Table 5.7. As can be seen at a glance, the major feature is the disparity between the different groups on the issue of whether promotion was offered at all. Whereas only 56 per cent of the British-born men had not been offered promotion at some time, each of the immigrant groups produced figures well in excess of 70 per cent. Furthermore, when promotion had been offered to black workers, this was almost exclusively limited to manual grades. Out of 499 male immigrants who were employed at the time of the interview only 4 (a West Indian, an East African, an Indian and a Pakistani) had been given the chance of elevation to staff/management, or non-manual supervisory status. Also significant is the fact that only the Indian had been promoted from the shop-floor. They contrast sharply with the sample of indigenous workers where 15(16) per cent had been offered promotion to the corresponding non-manual grades, and around a third of these were originally employed on the shop-floor.

We clearly have a situation which requires further scrutiny. Throughout the occupational spectrum black workers appeared to have been less successful in the promotion stakes. Even within the manual grades, great disparities existed, particularly when it came to the question of promotion to supervisory positions. This finding is by no means novel. Wright (1968) reported similar findings and elaborated in an interesting fashion the ways in which institutionalised personnel policies can produce differential career patterns among the various

TABLE 5.7 Internal promotion offered [1] by birthplace and sex (weighted figures are bracketed)

Nature of promotion	West Indies		India	Pakistan	Other Asian [3]	Great Britain	
	Males %	Females %	Males %	Males %	Males %	Males %	Females %
To more senior management position	–	–	–	–	–	8 (10)	2 (3)
To staff/management status from shop floor	–	–	1	–	–	4 (3)	2 (3)
To non-manual supervisor	* [2]	7 (7)	–	3	6	3 (3)	5 (5)
To manual supervisory post	7 (7)	5 (4)	5	–	6	22 (21)	2 (1)
From semi-skilled to skilled	4 (4)	2 (3)	4	14	6	–	–
From unskilled to semi-skilled	5 (4)	–	8	3	6	1 (1)	5 (5)
Moved to better machine	4 (4)	–	3	3	–	1 (2)	5 (5)
Other	2 (1)	9 (13)	1	–	–	4 (5)	5 (5)
No promotion offered	78 (79)	77 (73)	77	78	76	56 (55)	73 (72)
Total sample size (= 100%)	263 (217)	43 (31)	183	36	17	156 (120)	41 (38)

1 Promotion, for a variety of reasons, was not always accepted.
2 * represents a figure of less than 0.5%.
3 The definition of this term remains the same as in Table 5.6, and the same warning about the small sample applies.

racial groups within an organisation. Certain career development profiles were deemed acceptable for the black
worker, and others which might ultimately lead to a position of authority over whites were seen as unacceptable.
In order to rationalise this clearly discriminatory practice, a firm sometimes reserved certain work roles for immigrant labour. As examples of these 'differentiated'
roles in an engineering context Wright discusses the jobs
of slinger and crane-driver. These jobs, he argues: [68]

> were specially selected for the coloured workers when
> the question of promotion arose, because they were not
> jobs which would lead to a position of authority. Al-
> though of a higher grade than the ordinary labouring
> jobs, they were still in effect 'dead-end' because they
> did not lead any further. The Personnel Manager said:
> 'We have made it a policy never to employ a coloured
> man in a position such as part of a team in hot
> rolling, where in the course of events he would rise
> to a position where he would have to give orders to a
> white man.'

The managerial policy is particularly significant here,
and for two reasons. First, it is the type of action
which, if covertly applied by management might be effective in creating an occupational sub-market within a
sub-market; and might be difficult to detect by the
existing race relations legislative machinery. The covert
labelling of jobs within firms who do employ black workers
creates in theoretical terms a sub-market situation analogous to that operating in the housing market. Institutional barriers are erected to constrain the life chances
of a particular sub-group of the population and these
barriers are effectively legitimised by the affirmation
(or assumed affirmation) of members of majority society.
Furthermore, irrespective of stated trade union policy, it
is clear that there have been, and undoubtedly still are,
situations where union officials and management act in
concert on this issue (if on no other).

Sometimes (perhaps even frequently) we have a situation
such as that quoted by Wright where it is union officials
rather than management who desert the black section of
their electorate. He describes the case of Sterling Metal
Company, where: 'On one job, coloured workers were assisting white workers and one or two were so good that
management had wanted to up-grade them. However, the
union had objected and the plan was dropped.' [69] It
appears that blacks often become a kind of economic foot-
ball, bending to the needs of capital in one form or another. In the above case their productive efficiency was
recognised by management and therefore promotion was

clearly rational in economic terms. Employees in another
job in the same shop backed the promotion to skilled
status of a black worker on the grounds that his efficiency would significantly increase production and therefore
their wages. It is difficult to say how much general validity this 'rational' mode of analysis contains. But it
is not inconsistent with the system of social relations
embodied in the capitalist mode of production, and, in
particular, the dominance of the interests of capital.

The second major implication of the earlier quote is
that significant chances of promotion for black workers
would occur only in firms with a sizeable immigrant labour
force. In this case a black worker could occupy a position of authority without being in a role 'where he would
have to give orders to a white man'. The relationship between the demand for labour and the supply at the appropriate levels of skill has also played an important part
historically. Foundry work which had been seen by most in
the 1930s as a 'good job' was, in the context of the post-
war labour shortage, much less popular. Had it not been
for the fact that immigrant labour filled the vacuum left
by the indigenous work-force (who could now choose to
avoid the often harsh working conditions of the foundry),
many firms which survived would have found serious problems. Although, as Wright argues, even in these firms
most of the senior and supervisory posts still tended to
be filled by whites, management and union appear to have
had little option but to promote the more efficient of
their immigrant intake.

But what of the attempt by employers to 'explain' (the
cynic might say 'rationalise') this overall state of affairs? we have already seen that some have accused immigrants, or West Indians at least, of fecklessness. If
this is seen in terms of absenteeism, however, one would
be hard pressed to make a strong case, especially since
immigrants often possess an extremely instrumental orientation to work. Other major accusations levelled at black
immigrants are that:

(a) they suffer from language problems
(b) they lack appropriate work experience
(c) they lack ambition
(d) they lack appropriate skills and paper qualifica-
    tions, and
(e) they 'simply do not get on' with white workers (as
    is implied by the managerial policy outlined
    above).

It is illuminating to examine these in the context of
our study in Handsworth. Argument (a) is often used to
'explain' why such a large number of the Pakistani-born

labour force is employed in semi- or unskilled work. [70]
Wright argues that some immigrants were actually recruited
because they 'lacked the necessary language and literary
qualifications', [71] on the grounds that they could not
expect promotion. We might, however, be able to give a
little credence to this idea that language problems influence promotion chances if there were a marked difference
in the career profiles of, say, West Indians and Asians.
West Indians not only have fewer 'language problems';
they would also be rated higher on factor (b). Despite
this, their likelihood of being promoted appears, if anything, to be worse than that of the Asians.

On the question of 'work experience' it is clearly the
case that most New Commonwealth immigrants come from
countries where the predominant source of income is the
land. (This will be seen to be so in our Handsworth
sample.) Because of this, it is perhaps not surprising
that many mature immigrants will initially be employed on
semi-skilled or unskilled tasks when they arrive in a
heavily industrialised society such as Britain. On the
other hand, there seems to be no reason a priori (the arguments of Jenson apart) [72] why in the course of time
these same people should not progress to positions of
authority. We must remember that those we interviewed in
Handsworth had often been employed in a particular firm
for a number of years. Standardisation of the time factor
fails to assist in 'explaining', in a statistical or any
sociologically meaningful sense, why promotion patterns
between racial groups are so different. Thus it is to be
expected that many of those immigrants in our sample who
stated that promotion in their firm depended upon seniority may be in for a rude awakening.

Factor (c), that of ambition, was perhaps first raised
in an important way by the celebrated study by Stouffer.
[73] This confirmed the hypothesis that black soldiers did
less well than whites in the US army but firmly refuted
the widely held view that this could be due to a lack of
the appropriate drive and ambition. A lack of commitment
to the ethic of competition which is central to the capitalist economy might be thought of as more appropriate in
the case of the West Indian migrant who, in theory at
least, tends to approach life in a fairly relaxed philosophical manner. This ideal-typical notion does not, however, fit the picture conjured up by the answers to our
question on promotion ambitions. The proportions of West
Indian men claiming that they were not interested in promotion was at 23 per cent only slightly higher than the
corresponding figure for indigenous workers, 20 per cent.
Moreover, the number of Asian men giving this answer was

even smaller: only 15 per cent. We should, of course, be
wary of suggesting that a theory can be rigorously corroborated by reference to one, or even a few, 'face-sheet'
variables. On the other hand, answers to other questions
on promotion appear to suggest that the above figures, if
anything, underestimate the level of ambition among immigrants, and for an interesting reason. A number clearly
realised that: (i) they were in a job which was leading
nowhere; and/or (ii) they were working for a firm which
promoted only their white colleagues. As we saw earlier,
situation (i) often comes about as a direct result of
discriminatory practices at the level of management in
exactly the same way as (ii). It is extremely likely that
many black workers, seeing that they are being treated as
inferior units of labour, will internalise this process on
pragmatic grounds rather than resort to open conflict and
risk losing their livelihood (especially since they may
not be able to depend on support from their union or their
white colleagues). In this situation they may tend to
rationalise by claiming that they are really not interested in promotion. Certainly there is no evidence whatever
that blacks lack motivation to any greater degree than
anyone else. Indeed, among the sample of working women
interviewed, West Indians demonstrated a slightly higher
level of commitment to gaining promotion.

We are left then, with two of our original hypotheses:
the issue of 'qualifications for the job' and that of
'race relations on the shop floor (or in the office)'. On
the first of these we have a vast amount of empirical evidence gleaned from the educational and job histories of
each of our respondents. Unfortunately, there is only
sufficient space here to scratch the surface of these data
and we therefore simply present their major features. [74]
A comparative analysis is complicated by the fact that
some immigrants received part of their education in this
country whilst others did not. We begin, then, by looking
at the former (much smaller) group.

There were 13 West Indian and 29 Asian men who had received at least some of their schooling in the UK. Despite the problems of sample size and of historical cross-
sectional data it is instructive to compare their leaving
qualifications and final job destinations with those of
the whites. An analysis of this type shows, first, that a
much higher proportion of Asians than either of the other
two groups left school with some qualifications. On the
other hand, only two Asians out of nine who had done so,
and more especially only one out of four with 'O' levels
or above, had achieved white-collar status. These compared with figures of a little over a half and two in

three respectively for the white sample taken as a whole.
The data show, second, that the chances of a black worker
with no qualifications (academic or technical) gaining a
non-manual occupation are almost negligible in comparison
with those of local whites in a similar position.

These immigrants have been far more successful than
those who received all their formal education outside the
UK (as noted earlier in the present chapter). In age-
cohort terms, we have a fairly close match between the
samples of immigrant and indigenous workers. Unfortunately, this is where the comparison ends. Although a third
of the Asian men left school with some qualifications,
only three of these were in white-collar occupations. In
addition, we found that out of eight men with degrees or
teaching qualifications from the Indian subcontinent,
seven were employed in skilled or semi-skilled manual
work. Even allowing for Smith's quite legitimate point
relating to the difficulty of cross-national comparison
of school-leaving and further education standards [75]
(and 'language' problems), these findings carry considerable weight.

West Indian men tended to have few, if any, formal educational qualifications. What they lacked in this area,
however, they often made up for in technical or on-the-job
qualifications. In fact, rather more West Indians than
Asians had acquired such non-academic qualifications
(approximately one in three as against one in four). On
the other hand, these qualifications seem often to have
counted for nothing when it came to getting a job. Out of
27 West Indians who had successfully completed apprenticeships, 12 were employed in semi-skilled or unskilled work.
In sharp contrast, this was almost unheard of among the
indigenous sample (where only one man with a trade was
working in a job of lower than skilled status).

We can summarise the above by saying that, in general,
local white workers appeared to be in jobs whose skill
level matched (or exceeded) their qualifications. The
paper qualifications of the sample of Asian men in particular, seemed to match those of the local men. Moreover,
the level of technical and on-the-job qualifications held
by West Indians actually surpassed those of their white
neighbours. Despite these findings, it became clear that
there was a marked disparity between the status levels of
the jobs held by members of the different ethnic groups.
This leads us to the conclusion that 'lack of qualifications', as with the earlier hypotheses, fails to 'explain'
the phenomenon (and so, incidentally, does any combination
of the four hypotheses taken together).

Barring alternative theories, the failure to achieve

promotion is likely to be explained successfully only by
reference to wider structural issues reflected in the
sociology of industrial relations. At the outset the
personnel team will have discussed the implications of
employing an immigrant. He in turn may well have based
his application on the likelihood of at least being considered. (As noted before, there is some evidence to suggest that blacks tend to apply to firms who already employ
immigrant labour.) Given a buoyant source of 'suitable'
labour, as Wright correctly argues, the 'risk' of taking
on such a worker may deter the personnel department from
so doing. (This notion of 'risk' is, of course, independent of the applicant's abilities. It is usually derived
from a commonsensical view of the consensus among white
workers that, expressed euphemistically, 'the new employee
would just not fit in'.) In this view, the naive notion
that management generally reject blacks purely out of
personal dislike or prejudice is rejected. Certainly some
may be avoiding the responsibility of coping with linguistic and cultural diversity on the shop-floor, but the
overriding factor governing management's actions is the
profit motive and this implies that 'good industrial relations' are vital. In this situation many would undoubtedly take refuge in the view that a multi-racial
work-force might threaten these 'good relations'.

As we have already seen, however, in times of labour
shortage in particular, immigrants, whether English-
speaking or not, may not find it too difficult to obtain
work. Rimmer (1972) discusses the implications of their
absorption into the work-force of a number of Midlands
foundries (and incidentally into the same sorts of job in
which, as we shall see, many of our Handsworth sample are
employed). He noted, as did Wright, that immigrants often
worked in groups in a situation where social relations between themselves and the whites were minimised. On the
other hand, unlike Wright, he did not see this primarily
in terms of management's allocation of differentiated jobs
to immigrants. (This implies a conscious policy aimed at
restricting the individual's chances of advancement.) The
formation of the 'ethnic work-units' [76] are seen by
Rimmer as arising sometimes as a result of purely pragmatic reasoning: a language barrier, for example, making
some segregation necessary (in the short term at least).
As Rimmer correctly points out, there may also be 'various
social predispositions towards separation' [77] which may
or may not be independent of the question of language.
The 'social predisposition' may include an internalisation
of racial conflict, and whilst the work-units may help to
increase ethnic solidarity they will also tend to rein-

force the status quo in terms of the distribution of occupations.

Rimmer raises many interesting points in terms of the
different forms of shop-floor relations between immigrants, unions and management. Unfortunately, these
cannot be discussed further at this point. One issue of
direct relevance, however, should be mentioned briefly.
This is the element of duality sometimes attached to the
concept of promotion. The view arising, in Rimmer's
words, from '(the) norms of the traditional work culture'
is that promotion is determined by 'management's ideas
about the requisite skills and experience' of an individual. This conflicts directly with the normative structure of ethnic work-units who 'possess their own hierarchy
for promotion to better paid jobs'. [78] This situation
produced a dispute between management and work-unit in one
of the foundries studied by Rimmer. As ethnic work-units
are predominantly composed of Asian workers, this might
cast a slightly different light on the question of 'ambition for promotion' noted earlier. This notion of group
solidarity might, in particular, go some way to explaining
why Asians in our Handsworth sample tended to see promotion as something which was at least feasible.

By no means all our sample of immigrant workers were
employed in the Midlands foundries. In the next section
we look at exactly what type of work they were doing in
the summer of 1976.

THE PRESENT JOBS OF HANDSWORTH IMMIGRANTS

Before taking a detailed look at the industrial structure
of the Birmingham area and analysing the role which immigrants play in the city's economic life, it will pay us to
reflect for a moment on the social and economic milieux of
the countries they have left. It will be remembered from
an earlier chapter that some spoke of their earlier life
with a touch of nostalgia and sometimes talked of the
present in a voice tinged with a certain measure of
bitterness and regret. The longing for 'fresh fruit' and
'sunshine' had a symbolic importance far greater than that
suggested by a literal interpretation. There is an image
of greyness [79] which is Britain: a country whose
social, as well as its climatic environment, is inhospitable. A number complained bitterly of having to work 'all
the time' to support their family. Behind this there was
often a mood of hostility towards the modern factory as an
institution, its dehumanising features being seen almost
as symptomatic of Western industrial society. To see why

some conveyed this mood we need to look briefly at the
jobs which they left behind when they came to the UK.

West Indian migrants tended, on the whole, to be older
than those from the Indian subcontinent and therefore most
men (approaching 90 per cent) had gained previous work experience (in the Caribbean). Well over a third of these
had been agricultural workers, on anything from small-
holdings to the large, rich, coffee plantations of
Jamaica. Given the heat and the humidity, this can be
extremely onerous work. On the other hand, in many ways
it provides little preparation for work in the very different heat (and dust) of a Black Country foundry, and
this has been the destination of one in three of those we
interviewed in Handsworth. Nor has it, for that matter,
prepared the immigrant for working on the 'track' at
Longbridge, driving a West Midlands PTE bus, or doing
routine factory work. And this is the type of job which
most of the remainder had obtained.

After farming, the construction industry had claimed
the greatest share of the West Indian labour force. Over
20 per cent had done this type of work immediately before
coming to the UK. Despite this, only a handful were
working in the British construction industry. [80] The
remainder of the immigrants had left jobs in the sugar
refineries or in light industry. Almost irrespective of
the precise nature of their present job, perhaps the major
adjustment which Caribbean workers have had to face is the
rigidity of the working day and, in particular, the length
of time spent in the place of work without a significant
break. The obligatory siesta to avoid the midday heat of
Jamaica did at least serve to break up the working day and
help to reduce the dehumanising pressure of continual productive effort.

Many of the Asian male immigrants we interviewed were
still at school, or at least had not gained any work experience, before they came to Britain. This applies, in
fact, to 36 per cent of those who were employed at the
time of the interview. As with the West Indians, the
largest group among those who had worked before migration
were farmers. In a still largely agrarian society it is
perhaps not surprising to find that almost two out of
every five had derived his living from the land. It is
conceivable that, as Hindess (1973) has argued, some of
these might have gained some meagre industrial experience
by selling their labour to supplement the family income.
[81] Many of the 'farms', because of the lack of a system
of primogeniture, would undoubtedly have been small and of
poor quality. It is likely also that most of these immigrants were poor illiterate peasants (certainly a large

number had received little or no formal education) and by
no means all would have spoken more than a few words of
English on arrival in the UK. [82] Because of this, it is
hardly surprising that many of this group had initially
found their way into the foundries and certainly few (by
1976 at least) had graduated above jobs of semi-skilled
status. It is probably the case that the sort of recruitment procedures described by Rimmer (1972) (namely, via
contacts within the Asian community) [83] were effective
in many of their cases. Whatever the means, it is evident
that approaching 60 per cent of these ex-farmers were now
involved in the manufacture of metal.

Among the other Asian immigrants only one additional
occupational sub-group of any significance emerges. These
are the men, comprising some 16 per cent of the total, who
were employed as public servants in the Indian subcontinent. Usually these jobs would have been in the major
towns or cities and would have been viewed, irrespective
of (internal) status, as very good jobs by the peasants
whom we discussed in the previous paragraph. It is, perhaps, slightly curious that the patterns of jobs which the
two groups have acquired in Britain appear to be remarkably similar. It is not surprising, however, if we consider the situation in the context of first, the stereo-
typical view of immigrants which some employers have been
shown to hold, and second (possibly partly as a result of
this), the mismatch we have already noted earlier in the
chapter between qualifications (in the broadest sense) and
job achievement. It may well be that forms of stratification which led to radically differing occupational
patterns in India and Pakistan may well be transposed to
the workshop; for example, via stratification within the
ethnic work-unit. Our own empirical research material
cannot throw light on this question. What we can say is
that very few immigrants either from the Caribbean or from
the Indian subcontinent had experienced before migration
the type of work which they were doing in 1976. Furthermore, in many cases, especially among the Asian communities, the only contact with whites was in the factory or
workplace and this, therefore, must provide a dominant
focus for their views on Britain and her people. The
workshop, then, provides a stage; a setting where unusual
institutionalised forms of social relations take place -
relations which, as with employer and employee, usually
end at the factory gates. This air of social and cultural
duality pervaded a number of interviews, particularly
among the more forceful and articulate of the West Indian
respondents.

However distinct the work is in relation to past ex-

perience, and however restricted the forms of inter-ethnic
social relations in the workshop, this window on the world
of the majority society does nevertheless provide some
frame of reference for the migrant in his attempt to come
to terms with life in a totally alien environment.

It should be noted that, as reflected by the use of
male pronouns, we have been essentially talking here about
male migrants. As has already been seen, the level of
economic activity among Asian women, and Moslem women in
particular, is extremely low compared with their menfolk.
It is partly because of this that some researchers have
argued that the woman's problems of adjustment to life in
a totally alien society are very much more serious than
those of her male kin. In a book recently translated from
the original French, Padrun and Guyot argue that: [84]

> To an even greater degree than the men, the women are
> alienated, exploited and oppressed:
> as migrants sharing the conditions suffered by all
> migrant workers;
> as wives of migrants who have in most cases been ob-
> liged to leave their homes to follow their husbands;
> as women workers working for the lowest wages in the
> hardest and most exhausting conditions, and subjected
> to discrimination and pettiness of all kinds;
> as foreign women who have to be the guardians and de-
> fenders of the traditions of their own countries, while
> at the same time going through the cultural shock of
> adapting to life in a city;
> as women living in a male-dominated industrial society,
> and coming from societies where the man is generally
> absolute master;
> as mothers whose traditional role is to transmit the
> language, customs and religion of their country to
> their children. Yet here the children attend schools
> where only the values, language and way of life of the
> receiving country are taught.

Although the authors are principally talking here of the
wives of the 'temporary' settlers (or Gastarbeiter) in
western Europe, we believe that much of this expresses the
cluster of dilemmas facing the female immigrant in
Britain. Much recent political activity in this country
has, of course, been aimed at legitimising and perpetu-
ating the view that blacks in this country are indeed
migrants, 'guests' who have outstayed their welcome. It
is likely also that some of this ideology will have been
internalised, many within the minority communities seeing
themselves as migrants (as distinct from settlers whose
citizenship rights are identical to those of their white
neighbours).

Returning to the above quote, we might question the extent to which, judging by our evidence, immigrant women tend to do less pleasant work than that of indigenous women. More fundamentally, one might wish to argue that women, whether migrant or not, are used to some extent as a marginal source of labour. (This particular argument has already been touched on earlier in this chapter.) The analysis of job types and racial differentials is inevitably complex, since it involves an analytical separation of the black women/white women dimension, from that of immigrant/native worker (irrespective of sex). What we can say from our Handsworth data is that in terms of job status the differential between the West Indian female and her British (white) counterpart appears to be much less than between their menfolk. Indeed, the question of whether or not the white women we interviewed are deemed to have, on the whole, higher-status jobs hinges crucially on the interpretation we place on categories SEG5 and SEG6 and what (implicit) subjective weightings we give SEGs 9-11. Stated simply, West Indian girls with the appropriate qualifications are much more likely to be employed as nurses, and white girls who aim for non-manual work tend to become clerks or secretaries. It is beyond the scope of this book to analyse the relative values which 'society' places on these occupations - an adequate discourse would merit a book in itself! The office jobs are clearly seen by white school-leavers as preferable, however, and the most probable explanation for the level of immigrants in the hospital service is the economic one, resting on the notions of supply and demand, reinforced by institutional barriers which define the immigrant as 'unsuitable' for many white-collar occupations.

Within the sphere of manual work we have little evidence of a major disparity between the sorts of job done by the different groups of women. On the broader question of overall male/female status comparisons we naturally run into some fairly intractable conceptual problems. On the other hand, it does appear that in poor inner-city or middle-ring areas such as Handsworth it may well be true to say that the woman's job is often no less responsible, and may well be of higher status than that of her husband. By way of a caveat, it must be borne in mind that we have totally ignored here (out of necessity), issues such as conditions of service, work environment and, for the present, income. We have also had to ignore the question of employment among Asian women, since only one of the female heads of household whom we interviewed was working. [85] Before leaving this discussion of female employment, it is interesting to note that out of the two West Indian women in five who had gained previous working experience in the Caribbean, most appeared to have acquired 'better' jobs in Britain than the ones they had left.

To set the above discussion in a rather firmer sub-stantive context we turn now to look more carefully at the industrial structure of Birmingham and how black immi-grants fit into the general picture of employment. This is made difficult by the fact that there is not an iso-lated economic unit corresponding to Birmingham. As Sutcliffe and Smith (1974) argue: [86]

> Although a distinction can be made between Birmingham's industrial structure and that of much of the Black Country, no such boundary can be drawn between Birmingham and Smethwick, or between Birmingham and Solihull.

Even this is an oversimplification and, as we have already noted, there is evidence of a certain degree of labour outflow to the Black Country. Ultimately the choice of unit is dependent on the available statistics. Our Table 5.2 had as its reference point the Birmingham Employment Area rather than that of the West Midlands conurbation, because the former area, on balance, reflects rather more accurately the job market in which Handsworth residents move.

In historical terms, Birmingham's industrial scene has been characterised by its remarkable variety of trades. Its complexity has driven some writers such as Timmins to go so far as to argue that the task of description is 'almost insuperable'. [87] Now, more than a century after Timmins's work was completed, his statement seems to be more valid than ever. Unlike many modern cities which have lost their economic links with the past, Birmingham still retains many of the industries for which it was famous in the nineteenth century. Clearly the balance of its economy has changed with the tide of technological in-novation, but industries such as those involved in the manufacture of brass, iron and steel tubes and of bat-teries, still exist, albeit in a comparatively minor form (in terms of the proportion of the labour force employed in them). There is evidence also of the jewellery quar-ter, so vital to the wealth and prestige of Victorian Birmingham. The massive industrial plants and towering office blocks of the recent decades have come to over-shadow the traditional small business with its emphasis on the skilled man as its basic unit of labour. Over-shadowed they may be in the sense of sheer productive ca-pacity; indeed, many have been driven out of business by a combination of market forces and national industrial po-licies. On the other hand, as Sutcliffe and Smith (1974)

TABLE 5.8 Industry by birthplace [2] and sex (with industry by sex for Birmingham EEA) [6] (1971) [1] (weighted figures are bracketed)

Order	Industry [3]	West Indies Males %	West Indies Females %	India Males %	Pakistan Males %	Great Britain Males %	Great Britain Females %	Birmingham EEA Males %	Birmingham EEA Females %
I	Agriculture, forestry fishing	–	–	–	–	–	–	0.2	0.1
II	Mining and quarrying	–	–	–	–	–	2 (3)	+ [5]	+ [5]
III	Food, drink & tobacco	5 (4)	2 (3)	5	3	3 (2)	2 (3)	3.6	3.8
IV	Coal & petroleum prod.	–	–	–	–	–	–	+ [5]	+ [5]
V	Clerical & allied industries	2 (2)	–	–	3	2 (2)	2 (3)	1.4	1.0
VI	Metal manufacture	24 (25)	–	49	25	4 (4)	2 (3)	5.9	2.1
VII	Mechanical engineering	4 (5)	2 (*) [4]	7	31	8 (9)	–	6.3	3.4
VIII	Instrument engineering	1 (1)	–	–	–	1 (*) [4]	2 (3)	0.5	0.6
IX	Electrical engineering	6 (6)	14 (10)	1	6	10 (7)	15 (10)	6.5	5.3
X	Shipbuilding/ marine engin.	* [4]	–	–	–	–	–	–	–
XI	Vehicles	11 (11)	–	1	3	6 (7)	–	19.4	5.3

XII Metal goods not elsewhere specified	19 (18)	12 (10)	10	22	21 (19)	15 (10)	11.7	11.3
XIII Textiles	–	–	–	–	–	–	0.1	0.3
XIV Leather, leather goods & fur	–	–	–	–	–	–	+ [5]	0.1
XV Clothing & footwear	–	2 (*) [4]	1	–	–	5 (5)	0.1	0.8
XVI Brick, pottery, glass, cement, etc.	* [4]	–	1	–	1 (1)	–	0.6	0.3
XVII Timber, furniture, etc.	* [4]	–	1	–	1 (*) [4]	–	0.8	0.5
XVIII Paper, printing & publishing	1 (1)	–	1	–	1 (1)	–	2.0	2.0
XIX Other manufacturing industries	5 (6)	–	2	–	6 (6)	–	3.1	2.3
XX Construction	5 (4)	–	3	–	3 (2)	–	8.6	1.4
XXI Gas, elec., water	–	–	–	–	2 (2)	2 (3)	1.3	1.3
XXII Transport & com.	12 (11)	7 (7)	12	3	5 (7)	2 (3)	4.0	1.7
XXIII Distributive trades	1 (1)	5 (7)	2	–	8 (7)	5 (4)	6.7	14.2

TABLE 5.8 (continued)

Order	Industry [3]	West Indies Males %	Females %	India Males %	Pakistan Males %	Great Britain Males %	Females %	Birmingham EEA Males %	Females %
XXIV	Insurance, banking, finance & bus.	–	–	–	3	1 (2)	5 (5)	2.4	6.2
XXV	Professional & scientific services	2 (2)	40 (50)	1	–	7 (8)	27 (28)	6.2	22.4
XXVI	Miscellaneous services	1 (1)	9 (10)	3	–	5 (7)	12 (13)	4.6	9.5
XXVII	Public admin. & defence	* [4]	7 (3)	1	3	6 (7)	2 (3)	2.3	2.2
	Occupation not adequately specified	1 (1)	–	1	–	–	–	1.7	1.9
	Number of persons	263(217)	43 (31)	183	36	156(120)	41 (38)	381,765	226,345

1 Source: Department of Employment, June 1971.
2 Those of Asian origin but not born in India or Pakistan have been excluded because of the small sample size (17).
3 This classification by Industry is consistent with the Standard Industrial Classification as revised in 1968.
4 * represents a figure of less than 0.5%.
5 + represents a figure of less than 0.05%.
6 This is the same area as that defined in Tables 5.1 and 5.2.

correctly point out, the degree of dependence of the
industrial giants such as the car industry on some of
the small workshops producing components was still considerable in the immediate post-war years. [88] As might
have been expected, large-scale redevelopment of the city
centre has taken its toll on the small industrial
premises. The last few decades have also seen a significant shift away from Birmingham as primarily a large industrial centre. The service sector mushroomed dramatically during the 1960s and brought with it a major increase
in the proportion of white-collar office jobs, particularly in the new Bull Ring city centre development.

Perhaps the most recent shift in image for the city
came with the siting of the National Exhibition Centre
(NEC) on its doorstep. The way was then made clear for
Birmingham's rebirth as a major European city, perhaps
even to rival the traditional pre-eminence of the national
capital. The economic arguments for this development were
irresistible: London was becoming hopelessly congested
and was in danger of growing into a monster of Los
Angelean proportions. Its exhibition halls were ideally
suited to the tasks required of them in the latter half of
the nineteenth century. However, in the 1970s, where com-
modity markets and distribution networks are more than
ever of worldwide proportions and executive globe-trotting
is the norm rather than the exception, these centres sud-
denly seemed frustratingly inadequate. Although Birmingham had (and still has) its own internal road communication problems, its external links by road, rail and air
were, at least in UK terms, second to none. It stands at
the centre of an impressive motorway network, giving rapid
access to both the industrial centres of Northern England
and South Wales, and to what is, in some ways, its administrative alter ego, London.

It is perhaps ironic that the major immigrant settlement, which we have been studying in this book, should be
within earshot, or more accurately, almost underneath the
crossroads which are the very epitome of the new Birmingham (i.e., the Gravelly Hill interchange, more popularly
known as Spaghetti Junction). The NEC, although situated
only a few miles to the east of the city centre, appears,
with its impressive landscaping and sumptuous hotel,
worlds apart. Birmingham International Airport, and the
station especially built for the NEC, conceal from the
visitor to the showpiece the years of neglect and lack of
capital investment so evident elsewhere in the city.

It could be argued that national industrial policy had
at least slightly more coherence than did the 'inner-city
initiatives' discussed in the previous chapter. The im-

plementation of, and subsequent control over, Industrial
Development Certificates (IDCs) meant that what was seen
as a very privileged area of Britain did not take an even
greater share of the economic cake. Thus, large concerns
were prevented from becoming totally concentrated in the
Birmingham area; and, given the existence of other financial incentives, 'some of the major firms such as BMC and
Fisher and Ludlow were (persuaded) to set up production in
South Wales, Scotland and Merseyside.' [89] These moves
would have been totally inconceivable, of course, without
adequate consideration being given to the question of
transportation between plants. As we have seen, the appropriate road and rail links were at hand. Despite this
it is still argued, particularly with British Leyland (as
BMC was to become known), that the dispersal policy was
ill-conceived, and in fact had led to many of the subsequent problems from which the giant car division suffered.

As Table 5.8 shows, vehicle manufacture in 1971 swallowed up a major part of the male labour force. The
industry as a whole had contracted (in labour terms)
during the 1960s, but significantly one sector of it,
employing some 85 per cent of the workers in 1969, had
grown in importance; namely, that involved in motor car
manufacture. By the early 1970s the 'oil crisis' and the
subsequent shock waves had begun to threaten the very life
blood of the city, and much of this debate centred on
Longbridge.

Vehicle manufacture is traditionally a well-paid industry, and it would perhaps be thought that the immigrant
worker would find it fairly difficult to gain a foothold.
Indeed, few of the Asian men we talked to had done so. On
the other hand, approximately one in nine of the West
Indian men had found work in this area, and out of the 30
men interviewed, 28 worked in the car industry; a larger
proportion, incidentally, than that of Handsworth whites.
We must at the same time bear in mind the fact that the
major centre of car manufacture is in South-west Birmingham, and the relatively high proportion of West Indians
may tell us rather more about the distance they have to
travel to work than it does about their penetration into
the car industry. (Almost half of this industrial group
worked in Longbridge.)

One industry in which male New Commonwealth immigrants
are heavily over-represented is that of metal manufacture.
In proportionate terms, well over twice as many New Commonwealth immigrants as members of the total British male
labour force, work in this industry. This differential
is minor compared with the figures we obtained for Handsworth. Whereas the 1971 total for the Birmingham EEA and

the survey data for Handsworth whites indicate that the
industry employs only a very small part of the local male
work-force, the picture for the immigrant communities is
entirely different. Almost a half of the Indian men we
interviewed were involved in metal manufacture [90], along
with approximately a quarter of those from the West Indies
and Pakistan. Furthermore, it is clear from our findings
that a significant proportion of Handsworth blacks work in
the Black Country foundries. The City of Birmingham's 'A
New Plan for the City' shows that between 1960 and 1969
the metal manufacturing industry took on approximately 10
per cent extra labour. [91] Many of these were immigrants, such as those we interviewed. Undoubtedly most
were, in effect, taking jobs which, for obvious reasons,
the local whites did not want.

As seen in Table 5.8, male immigrants are heavily concentrated in routine work in the manufacturing sector, and
much more so than the city's labour force as a whole. Indigenous workers tend to be focused at the distribution
end of the production cycle and in the ancillary white-
collar jobs. In times of low unemployment other industries which tend to find recruitment difficult are those
in the service sector. (We have already seen, for
example, how Barbadian labour was 'imported' in 1956 to
solve a crisis in London Transport.) There is some evidence from our own study that West Indian and Indian men,
in particular, are employed in disproportionately large
numbers in this type of job in Birmingham.

This admittedly brief look at the city's industries
gives us a glimpse at least of the differing patterns of
employment amongst the various ethnic groups. We turn now
to look at conditions of employment and, in particular,
the questions of pay, shiftwork, the number of hours
worked per week, and commuting patterns.

The significance of shiftwork in the present context is
that, as Smith (1977) argues, it 'is intrinsically unpopular and undesirable'. He is not necessarily correct, however, when he states almost in the same breath that 'they
(shiftworkers) have made a personal choice based on the
proposition that for them the increase in pay more than
offsets the inconvenience.' [92] This appears to rest on
a crucial assumption which he implicitly rejects shortly
afterwards, that of the 'unfettered rational man'. In a
full-employment economy, and one which does not impose
restrictions (based on the structure of social relations)
that constrain the actions of individuals or groups within
that population, the wage labourer is indeed free to make
the choice which Smith suggests. However, it is a central
argument of his work and the present one (among others)

that this utopian freedom of action is, in general, not
available to ethnic minority groups. This was clearly
seen to be the case in the context of the housing market,
as noted in Chapter 4, and a similar phenomenon has been
suggested as applicable to the job market. Whether we
call this a sub-market or a secondary market as did
Bosanquet and Doeringer (1973) is, in many ways, imma-
terial. As to the level of shiftworking, Smith found
that: [93]

> It is most common among Pakistanis and least common
> among African Asians, with West Indians and Indians
> coming in the middle. Pakistanis are particularly
> likely to work night-shifts: in fact, 27 per cent of
> Pakistani men are working some kind of night-shift,
> compared with only 9 per cent of white men, a differ-
> ence of the order of three to one. Further, they are
> particularly likely to be working permanent nights.
> This pattern of working, which is very uncommon among
> the general population (accounting for only one per
> cent of white men), accounts for 8 per cent of
> Pakistanis.

Our Handsworth data are summarised in Table 5.9.

It is immediately noticeable that, although there are
some features in common with the above pattern, in particular the rarity of shiftwork among whites, important differences remain. Many of these differences are a function
of the radically different survey population and sample
designs adopted. On the other hand, they may serve to
underline the ways in which the overall pattern may change
significantly from one area of Britain to another.

The generally higher level of shiftwork among immigrants in Handsworth is likely to be a function of the
pattern both of job status and of job type and, in particular, the way in which these differ from those in Smith's
population. [94] He made the rather obvious point in relation to his own data that: 'It is not simply because
they are concentrated at the lower job levels that a
higher proportion of the minorities are working shifts.'
[95] Where he fails in his analysis is that he makes no
real attempt to say why this is the case. The point is
that certain industries involve continuous production processes. In some cases it could be argued that this is
largely the result of management decisions taken in the
interests of capital. For example, a capital-intensive
firm may become 'inefficient' if its expensive hardware
is left idle. It may be more efficient to run a plant
round the clock, even if it is not working to full capacity. In many industries it would make no sense whatever
to avoid shifts. For example, in the coal industry safety

TABLE 5.9 Shiftwork by birthplace and sex (weighted figures are bracketed)

| | West Indies | | India | Pakistan | Other Asian | Great Britain | |
	Males %	Females %	Males %	Males %	Males % [1]	Males %	Females %
Permanent nightshift	8 (8)	12 (16)	6	19	–	3 (3)	–
Occasional nightshift	27 (29)	2 (*) [2]	17	11	12	9 (11)	–
Dayshift	18 (16)	16 (17)	12	14	12	6 (4)	7 (9)
No shiftwork	47 (47)	70 (66)	65	56	76	82 (82)	93 (91)
Total sample size (= 100%)	263(217)	43 (31)	183	36	17	156(120)	41 (38)

1 The small sample size here (17) should once again be noted.
2 * represents a figure of less than 0.5%.

considerations dictate that certain staff need to be available at all times. Furnaces, the central feature of the metal manufacturing industry, cannot simply be switched on and off to confrom to a 9 till 5 routine. Other obvious examples of the need for shiftworking are the emergency services, e.g., hospitals, the fire service, the police, and so on.

Clearly, the incidence of shiftwork is lower among the white-collar labour force. On the other hand, more important here is the fact that, in many cases (as the above examples show), the willingness to work shifts is a necessary prerequisite for being appointed. Along with physical working conditions, this will be one of the criteria which might deter white workers from applying. We are not then denying that the higher wages to be gained by doing shiftwork are an incentive to the immigrant; but merely arguing that his 'willingness' to work shifts may be largely a reflection of the fact that his 'choice' of jobs may be limited.

Perhaps the most interesting feature of our Handsworth data is not the low level of shiftwork among whites, but rather the extremely high rate among West Indian men. Although smaller than the figure for Pakistani men [96] a significant number of West Indians work a permanent nightshift and well over a third are involved in this type of shift, at least on an occasional basis. Another interesting feature of the data is the relatively low level of nightshift work among Indian men.

Shiftwork among women appears to follow an occupational pattern rather more clearly than that amongst men. It appears to be almost completely the preserve of those in the nursing profession. [97] Thus West Indian women exhibit a much higher incidence of shiftwork than the British-born women we interviewed. Once again it is interesting to reflect on the comparative lack of 'demand' for nursing training and posts among white girls. In terms of pay, conditions of work and the (low) level of commitment demanded, an office job seems to present a more appealing proposition.

Clearly issues such as shiftwork, length of working week and pay are all related. In a generally poorly paid unskilled or semi-skilled job, shiftwork may be the only alternative to an unbearably long day in the factory or foundry. As Table 5.10 shows, however, many immigrants work incredibly long hours as it is. This applies particularly to Asian men: well over a quarter of this group said that they had worked at least 50 hours in the week prior to the interview. The work pattern for the West Indian and British men, on the other hand, seems rather

TABLE 5.10   Hours worked [1] by birthplace and sex (weighted figures are bracketed)

| | West Indies | | India | Pakistan | Other Asian | Great Britain | |
	Males %	Females %	Males %	Males %	Males % [2]	Males %	Females %
Less than 10 hours/ on holiday	8 (9)	2 (*) [3]	4	3	6	3 (3)	5 (2)
10 hours but less than 30 hours	1 (1)	16 (23)	1	3	-	5 (6)	24 (24)
30 hours but less than 40 hours	11 (12)	33 (26)	8	8	6	18 (17)	41 (44)
40 hours but less than 50 hours	61 (59)	44 (45)	55	56	59	54 (56)	24 (24)
50 hours or more	17 (17)	2 (3)	30	25	24	15 (15)	2 (3)
Don't know/can't remember/refused	2 (2)	2 (3)	3	3	6	4 (4)	2 (3)
Total sample size (= 100%)	263(217)	43 (31)	183	36	17	156(120)	41 (38)

1   This refers to the number of hours worked in the week prior to the interview.
2   These figures should be treated with caution because of the small sample size.
3   * represents a figure of less than 0.5%.

similar, with around one in six topping the 50-hour mark.
As Rex and Tomlinson (1979) point out, the figures for the
immigrant groups by far exceed the national level as given
by the Department of Employment. This leads us to the
conclusion that Handsworth whites, taken as a whole, also
work a very much longer than average week. The reason for
this appears to lie in the occupational structure of the
area, and in particular in the high level of blue-collar
workers.

We are left now with a whole battery of questions.
Who, in terms (other than those of country of origin) are
the people who work these incredibly long hours? Is it
true to suggest, as we did above, that shiftworkers, in
general, work a shorter week? In what ways (if any) are
industry and job status linked to hours and shiftwork?
Finally, how does income relate to these factors? There
is not sufficient space to answer these questions in
detail and to analyse the differences among the various
ethnic groups. We shall, however, present briefly our
major findings.

1 There is little evidence to suggest that shiftworking
   is associated positively with a shorter working week.
   With the notable exception of the West Indians, the
   proportion of men working 50 or more hours per week is
   rather higher among shiftworkers than among the rest
   of the work-force.

2 The analysis of job status and industry in relation to
   shiftwork yields some very complex but interesting results. Put simply, we see, as noted earlier, that some
   industries rely on the shift system to a much greater
   extent than others. The transport, metal manufacture
   and vehicle building industries in the Midlands clearly
   employ many workers under this type of arrangement.
   Accordingly, given the relatively greater concentration
   of immigrant groups in these sectors, we would expect
   them, irrespective of job status, to display a higher
   frequency of shiftworking than local whites. What we
   find on examining our data, however, is that this may
   not be the sole 'explanation' for the higher shiftworking rates among blacks. So far as we can judge from
   the small sample of whites in these same industries,
   local whites still appear to be much less likely than
   immigrants to work shifts (of any description). Further, West Indian men consistently display very much
   higher rates of shiftwork than any of the Asian groups
   in the three industries mentioned above, and these differentials are much greater than would be expected from
   a glance at Table 5.9. On the question of job status,
   it appears that among whites there is a tendency for

shiftworkers (in so far as there are any) to come from
the higher-status jobs: e.g., shiftworking is most
common among those who are in manual supervisory posts,
and non-existent among unskilled workers. Among Asian
groups there also appears to be a positive relationship
between job status and shiftworking, although here, of
course, the status 'peak' effectively ends at the
skilled worker. Once again, the West Indians clearly
break away from this pattern, with the unskilled
workers being most likely to work shifts and their
skilled colleagues least likely. It does not seem to
be the case, then, that among our Handsworth immigrants
as a whole shiftwork is used in a significant way to
boost the earnings of those in semi-skilled or unskilled jobs. Only the West Indians confirm this particular finding of Smith's (1977) research. [98] It
is, however, the case with all our immigrant groups
that the vast majority of those who work a permanent
night-shift are semi-skilled and unskilled workers in
the factories and foundries of Birmingham and the Black
Country towns.

3 We look briefly now at the influence which shiftworking
and the length of the working week have on the pay
which immigrants achieve, as compared with their white
colleagues. Among male employees as a whole, our
British-born sample tend to earn considerably more than
the immigrants. Their median wage of £58.65 compares
very well with the figure of £54.20 for the West Indian
and £53.95 and £52.86 [99] for the Indians and Pakistanis respectively. [100] Some differential would, of
course, have been expected, since the immigrants have
been seen to occupy predominantly the lower reaches of
the occupational status hierarchy. Indeed, if we look
at the manual grades, much of the differential disappears. Among skilled workers the medians of the whites
and each of the minority groups differ by approximately
£2 per week. West Indian semi-skilled and unskilled
workers earn very similar wages to those of their white
counterparts, and it is predominantly the Pakistanis
whose incomes fall behind at this stage.

These findings are interesting, first, because they indicate that despite the shorter hours and the virtual
absence of nightwork, whites in the skilled manual grades
are earning more than immigrants in similar jobs (i.e.,
jobs of the same grade). Second, it is only through
working a large amount of shiftwork that West Indians in
the semi-skilled and unskilled jobs catch up with the
British in terms of earnings. Finally, despite working
extremely long hours and performing a good deal of shift-

work, Asian skilled workers are earning no more than the
British and West Indian men. Furthermore, despite the
high incidence of nightshifts and long hours among the
Pakistani semi-skilled and unskilled, their median weekly
income of £48.75 falls well below any of the other groups.

We therefore have further confirmation that not only
are male immigrants working on the whole in jobs which are
unpopular among whites for physical and/or social reasons;
they are also doing them for markedly inferior rates of
pay. The income of female workers is difficult to analyse
because of the small sample sizes. What data we have suggest that the median earnings of the West Indian and
British women are almost identical. On the other hand,
this should be seen, as before, against the background of
the type of work done and the conditions of service in
terms of working week and shifts. If we do so we now see
that, despite a similar job status distribution, [101]
West Indian women tend to work much longer hours and do a
far greater amount of shiftwork (see Tables 5.9 and 5.10).

Beyond the questions of unsocial shifts, working conditions and the length of the working day, there are many
other factors which impinge on the desirability of particular jobs. One of these is the question of factory location, and the related issue of daily travelling time. We
have already seen earlier in the present chapter that although some immigrants have gained access to fairly
'desirable' jobs they may, often because of the nature
of social relations in the property market (cf. Chapter
4), be constrained to commute long distances to their
place of work. In this context, we raised the case of
13 West Indians who travelled from Handsworth to the
Longbridge car plant every day. The question we really
need to answer, then, is whether there is any evidence
that we have another (internal) migrant labour syndrome
among blacks, albeit on a comparatively microscopic scale?

Victorian urban systems were built on the notion of
workers' houses clustered around the factory. In-commuting was, and is, largely a middle-class phenomenon, as
was noted earlier in the case of present-day Birmingham.
There is, however, one crucial factor which distinguishes
the current metropolitan scene from its historical form.
The 'hearts' have been ripped out of many inner-city and
middle-ring areas, as capital has moved outwards to less
congested and more profitable sites. Many of the urban
working class who remain find themselves with no option
but to travel greater distances to find work. Out-commuting of manual labour is often (perhaps mainly) enforced
rather than being one of a number of choices as in the
case of the white-collar worker, a point which applies

particularly to those whose options are already limited to
poorly paid semi-skilled or unskilled work. The mechanisms of the property market ensure that this is so.
  In the case of immigrants we are in a situation of dual
constraint. First, the property market, at the very
least, reinforces any tendency there might be for certain
groups of black immigrants to cluster in particular areas
of a city. Second, existing labour market mechanisms
often have the effect of restricting the immigrant's
access to the more 'desirable' jobs. The theoretical
argument suggests that the incidence and patterns of out-
commuting will vary considerably between the various
ethnic groups, and, particularly, between black immigrants
and the white work-force.
  It would, of course, be naive to expect that there
would be a simple answer to the empirical question implied
by this argument: namely, that all blacks travel further
to work than do all whites. Indeed, the dual constraints
embody a number of elements which conflict. On the other
hand, the median commuting distance was found to be considerably higher among male West Indians in particular,
and male Pakistanis to a slightly lesser extent, than it
was among the local whites. The 'naive model' only fails
to 'work' for the Indian, and this is so for a rather important reason. As we have seen, it so happens that a
very large minority of Indians (almost a half) are employed in the manufacture of metal, and most of these jobs
are to be found in nearby Black Country boroughs. No less
than 79 per cent, in fact, work in the area covered jointly by Dudley, Smethwick, Oldbury, West Bromwich, Tipton
and Warley. A large proportion of West Indian foundrymen
also worked in this area, but a significant number travelled further afield, in particular to Walsall, Wolverhamp-
ton and Wednesbury. The local white workers were very
heavily concentrated within a zone defined by the areas
contiguous with (and including) the survey area, more than
three workers in five being employed in this zone at the
time of interview. In sharp contrast, more than half the
West Indians and Pakistanis and well over 70 per cent of
male Indians worked outside this area.
  We now have an overall picture which shows marked differences between the male and female workers of the
various ethnic groups over a wide range of issues: the
industry, its location, the level of seniority within the
firm, income, shift arrangements, length of working week,
and so on. The differences are in some ways less important in terms of what they tell us about the present
industrial scene than they are for the glimpse they permit
of the future. We are still (in 1979) in a situation of

deep economic recession, with around one and a half
million unemployed. The intense and increasing competition for jobs, even for those which were once deemed
'undesirable', must place the immigrant in an extremely
vulnerable position, and this is more true when there is
political capital to be made out of capturing 'the racist
vote'. Before following up this issue in the final chapter, however, we look briefly at the power (if any) which
the immigrant wields in the workplace and, in particular,
at the position of the trade unions.

TRADE UNIONS AND RACE

If there is one point on which our research fully corrobo-
rates a major finding of the PEP study it is when Smith
(1977) notes that 'trade union membership is, if anything,
higher among the minority groups than among the white population'. [102] It could be said that our Handsworth
sample underlines the point rather more strongly, since
87 per cent of West Indian, and 83 per cent of Asian male
workers were unionised, compared with 62 per cent of the
local whites. A similar difference applies to the female
work-force, where 61 per cent of West Indians have joined
a union as against only 39 per cent of the British-born
women.
    In many ways this is a remarkable state of affairs:
after all, working-class Asians in particular have, in
many ways, aimed to isolate themselves from majority
society. One might have thought, then, that (in the absence of a closed shop) the Indians, at least, might have
placed their sole effort behind an organisation such as
the Indian Workers Association (IWA) rather than a British
trade union. Indeed, the evidence presented already in
this chapter has given ample evidence (if any were needed)
that minority workers, despite official union policy,
cannot always rely on the local union machinery to press
their case in situations with racial overtones. To remain
outside the formal union movement would, in a symbolic
sense, represent a rejection of paternalism and the integrationist perspective. However, it might also have a
number of disturbing side effects. Depending on the level
of inter-branch solidarity, workers in some areas of low
membership might find their interests weakly represented.
Second, their overall power vis-à-vis established trade
unions has already been tested on a number of occasions,
as in the foundry dispute noted by Smith; [103] with poor
results. Third, and most importantly, this separatism on
the shop-floor might simply reinforce their current sub-

proletarian status, as is indeed suggested by our second point, since this dispute arose out of the implicit non-acceptability of Indian workers as prospective members of the GMWU.

This latter point presumably weighed heavily in the mind of Jagnohan Joshi, who spoke to our researchers in his position as the Birmingham Secretary and National Secretary of the IWA(GB). A political radical of Marxist persuasions, Joshi argued that black workers must operate within the existing trade union structure. He sees the IWA as working towards a single, unified working class, not one divided on the grounds of race, colour or creed. In terms of its formal constitution (adopted in September 1958) it is not simply an industrial pressure group, but also sees itself as a social welfare agency. This inevitably produces potential (and actual) conflict of interest between officials over and above those arising from a re-production of political divisions existing within the Indian subcontinent. [104]

While the IWA may, at times, lack precisely that which it wishes to bring to the working-class movement as a whole, i.e., unity, Indian workers have themselves, on numerous occasions, shown that they can be a force to be reckoned with. Sivanandan (1976) argues that of all the immigrant groups in Britain: [105]

Only in regard to the Asian working class was there any trouble. Their strikes at Courtaulds and Woolf's, and Mansfield Hosiery and Imperial Typewriters had threatened the system as few strikes did, for they were subsidised and supported by the community, united across divisions of labour and possessed of a genius for organisation and obstinacy against all sorts of odds (including trade union ones).

This 'trouble', he goes on to argue, did not have a cumulative effect in the sense of creating a radical social movement, largely because of a combination of 'Asian leadership and trade union racism'. If union support was ultimately lacking in these cases, it was certainly not in the major dispute involving Asian workers in 1977.

This strike over union recognition at the Grunwick Film Processing Laboratories Ltd in North London led to major trade union involvement. Not only did the local Trades Council (Brent) play an important role in supporting the local strikers and pickets, but 'flying pickets', including representatives of most of the larger trade unions, along with union leaders and politicians, were much in evidence over a period of weeks (many being arrested in scuffles with the large police contingent which was constantly in evidence). An article by Nikki Knewstub in the

'Guardian' newspaper in July and headed 'Migrants Grunwick Lesson' pointed to the 'positive' effects which the strike had in increasing the political awareness of local West Indians and Asians. Jack Dromey, secretary of the Brent Trades Council, is reported as having said that 'a flood of immigrants had been in touch with the Council to find out about joining unions' as a direct result of the Grunwick dispute. Many of these belonged to small firms with almost 100 per cent immigrant labour.

Rimmer (1972) discusses the frequent tendency for whole shops employing immigrant labour to become unionised, thereby demonstrating 'a cohesion that was not evident among the white workers and (providing) the basis for a strong shop-floor organisation'. [106] Even without this the ethnic work-units, as discussed earlier, can wield immense power if only because of their internal solidarity. Furthermore, this solidarity is not simply one which derives its strength from the conflict of class interests; it also embodies the resolve of a people who have not yet even been accorded their full rights of membership of the native working class. Except in the sense of a sub-proletarian movement, they are classless.

Much of the above applies equally to the West Indians. As we shall see in the next chapter, many of the immigrants we interviewed, with good cause, viewed politics and white politicians with cynical discontent. This view seemed also to pervade their answers to questions about the role of trade unions. For example, few of those who were not members gave reasons which implied criticism, with or without racial overtones; most were simply indifferent to the whole issue.

Looking at unionised male immigrants, most of whom were TGWU, AUEW, TASS, or GMWU members, we see that the Asians tended to feel that by far the most important role of their union was to negotiate pay rates. Male West Indians, on the other hand, seemed to put rather more emphasis on the broader and more fundamentalist notion that they existed to fight for workers' rights, and in doing so settle disputes between workers and management. No doubt the often bitter struggles of COHSE on the issue of nurses' pay influenced the female West Indian members we interviewed to argue in the main that the question of pay was the major issue.

On the question of whether the role of unions should be extended to cover things which they do not now do, few immigrants gave any positive view. In a sense, of course, this is an extremely difficult question to ask in a survey such as that which was conducted in Handsworth. Sensitive studies based in situ might be far more successful in tapping views on an issue of this complexity. [107] On the other hand, it would be incorrect, we feel, to underestimate the significance of the marked indifference which this question in particular provoked. The vast majority of West Indians and Asians alike gave no positive response to this question and those who did, usually said only that their union, for one reason or another, should be more 'efficient'.

Studies such as those by Wright (1968), Rimmer (1972) and Smith (1977) have all concluded that, although immigrants have been extremely willing to join unions, their representation within the union hierarchy is extremely weak. Usually it is in situations where, for example, we have an all-black shop that shop stewards are drawn from the immigrant labour force. Ethnic work-units can act here as electing bodies and throw up their own candidate. In most cases managements would be likely to approve of such a move, since this type of link with the work-units might prove useful in a regulative sense. Indeed, language problems might necessitate such an arrangement.

We have not discussed here, because of lack of space, many issues which merit a sociological analysis of race relations on the shop-floor; issues moreover which gain their significance in the broader context of race relations in Britain as a whole. Furthermore, we have generally tended to imply that problems of industrial conflict involving members of minority ethnic groups are exclusively of the black/white variety. This, of course, presents a drastically over-simplified picture. Regretfully, however, we must refer the reader to some of the texts cited in this chapter for a discussion of these issues.

6 Racism and the future of Handsworth

Britain in the early 1980s is, in many ways, a society at the crossroads. This much will have become plain by the arguments of earlier chapters. It will have become clear also that to apply the notion of 'one society' to Britain is somewhat of a misnomer in an increasingly important sense. Whatever Britain is at the present time, it is certainly not a unified social whole. Deep divisions exist, and what is more these divisions go far beyond the classic class conflict of a capitalist society in a state of crisis. The ultimate struggle to come (if there is to be one) may be seen by Marxist commentators as embodying many of the elements of the classic revolutionary situations, in particular the existence of a suppressed proletariat. However, our arguments have implied that it is misleading to talk of a single working class, if only for the reason that one sector of the population (itself internally disunited) has been ascribed the role of sub-proletariat. It could be argued that the latter, i.e., institutionalised racism, is largely a diversionary tactic perpetuated by the ruling class to conceal the evils of capitalism, and that ultimate unification of the working classes is inevitable, or at least, should be the aim of the committed socialist. The major purpose of this concluding chapter is to ask precisely whether this significant 'struggle' is likely to take place at all, and if it is, in what form.

Throughout this book, we have discussed conflict situations. For many blacks, as for many members of the indigenous working class, everyday life is, in itself, a never-ending series of struggles. For them the microscopic tends to blur the macroscopic, or at least renders it of secondary importance. Indeed, it is often tempting for the sociologist to study day-to-day events such as shop-floor disputes, inter-generational conflict and

street incidents as separate entities which can, in some
strange sense, be divorced from the context of larger
systems of social relations. Many 'explanations' link up,
but are essentially circular: e.g., wayward black youth
is seen by some as a problem which can be traced back to a
lack of parental control. Parental control is then argued
to be a function of the readjustment from the traditional
form of extended family among, say, the Jamaicans, to the
Western nuclear type of family. Add to these the generally higher incidence of juvenile delinquency and the circle
is completed.

Although extremely naive in its present form, this illustration nevertheless hints at an issue of great significance to the present argument. The whole concept of
'inter-generational conflict' is interesting in the sense
that it is usually seen as an essential or inevitable
feature of the process of socialisation into the adult
world - the time when youthful idealism comes face to face
with the 'real world'. Thus 'parental control' is the
institutional procedure whereby an individual learns the
rules of adult society. However, the rejection of such an
institution has particular significance in the context of
the black Briton.

In a television lecture [1] Dr Bhikhu Parekh argued
that Asian immigrants came to Britain imbued with the
values of British colonial society and that they had
largely retained their traditional deference to the white
man despite the treatment they have received here. The
young Asian child, educated in this country, was a different proposition. He/she was in the classroom alongside
white children and was not tarred with the brush of colonialism. Thus many had rejected the politics of cultural and social separatism, whether or not these were
reinforced by a deferential value system.

This stance inevitably creates a certain amount of
friction within the Asian family; but there are perhaps
some forms of inter-generational conflict which are rather
more disturbing. These arise essentially from an internalisation of racist values: a belief that they are
indeed inferior to the white man. According to Parekh,
some children spent hours scrubbing their skin in the hope
of lightening it. Others simply hoped that because of the
Westernised school clothes friends would not realise that
they were Asian. There were others who told their mothers
not to wear a sari, or were afraid to take 'English'
friends home, in case this would underline cultural
differences.

One wonders how such children might react when they
come to face situations already encountered by their

parents, i.e., those of finding a house, a job, etc., when
they may well find that merely 'aspiring to whiteness' is
not always sufficient. It is not clear how general these
values are, since they are 'private' interpretations of
the world and are thus not easily accessible to the outsider. However, the fact that they exist at all is disturbing, and it would be misleading to write them off as
simply a series of individual pathological cases, people
with some form of psychological disorder.

Clashes with parental authority can similarly arise for
reasons not directly linked to any notion of racial inferiority. Western cultural values, whether transmitted
by teachers, by white classmates, or by the media, are
often violently at odds with those of the Asians. Even if
deemed desirable, there is no way that a traditional
British compromise can solve conflicts between local white
culture (however broadly defined) and the social and cultural mores implied, for example, by the Islamic faith,
Hinduism or Sikhism. As a specific example, the whole
notion of the 'arranged marriage' has been rejected by
large numbers of Asian girls. Often, as a result, the
'inconceivable' happens: the girl leaves home. In this
situation she is, in a very real sense, hopelessly trapped
between two cultures (see Watson (1977), especially Chapter 2), often rejecting part of her cultural heritage and
not able or willing to assimilate Western values in toto.
A number of hostels have sprung up in major cities such as
Birmingham [2] and Coventry in the hope of at least providing a temporary respite for girls such as these.

As .with the Asians, inter-generational conflict among
West Indians cannot be reduced simply to problems of adjustment to alien familial roles. True, an analysis of
internal familial stress might give us an insight into the
mode of 'acting out' (i.e., the manifestations) of more
sociologically significant conflicts. Thus the labelling
of black youth as 'uncontrollable' by their parents might
be objectively true in specific cases. On the other hand,
the interesting feature of this 'uncontrollability' is
that it may well reflect on the part of black youth a rejection of the control to which the parental generation in
turn have been subjected; a pressure, moreover, to which
many seem, like their forefathers, to have succumbed.
Thus, youthful idealism is seen as grounded in historical
experience.

The physical expression of these conflict situations
has already been noted: familial disintegration and conflict, with the symbols of white authority, such as the
police, the very guardians of 'Babylon'. In many ways,
individual instances of physical conflict are, per se,

rather less important than are the underlying political catalysts (political here in its broadest sense).

To imply a universal conflict perspective would, of course, be misleading. Not all Handsworth's black youths are members of the 'visible unemployed' hanging around on street corners, in bars and outside pool halls. Not all are involved in frequent skirmishes with the police. Around 75 per cent of second-generation Handsworth blacks have found jobs; some, indeed, may well regard themselves as completely assimilated; others undoubtedly have even turned their backs on their less fortunate black brothers and sisters.

As we have seen throughout this book, first-generation immigrants have, in objective terms, tended to suffer from severely constrained life chances, even over and above those of the native working class. Despite this, they seem on the whole to have accepted their lot in the time-honoured British tradition of 'making-do'. But what of the level of political consciousness among Handsworth blacks? In particular, what forms of political expression exist and how significant are these in the broader context of contemporary race relations? If we are to attempt to understand the present and the likely future facing blacks in an advanced capitalist society such as Britain, such questions must be tackled. What follows is a discussion of race as seen through the political arena, both local and national. We consider the patterns of political allegiance among the black electorate as a whole, and also the pressure groups and ethnically based organisations acting in the interests of various sections of the immigrant community. These will be discussed with three distinct groups in mind. To begin with, there are the first-generation immigrants who, for the most part, have been members of the British electorate for a number of years. Second, there are the next generation of blacks, young men and women in their late teens and early twenties, many of them born in Britain, who have now left school and are in the labour market. Finally, there are the children who are still in our secondary schools. (In the case of this last group we focus in particular on juvenile aspirations and the likelihood of these aspirations being fulfilled.)

POLITICS AND RACE: THE FIRST-GENERATION IMMIGRANT

Most writers on politics and race relations have noted the importance of the 'immigrant vote' to the Labour Party. Rex and Moore (1967), Lawrence (1974) and Layton-Henry and Taylor (1977/78) have all discussed the tendency of the

vast majority of New Commonwealth immigrants (to some
extent irrespective of country of origin) to support the
Labour Party at the ballot box, and particularly at
General Elections. The sheer size of this 'new' electorate in itself makes it a prime target for political ma-
noeuvring among the major parties. Given even the slight
possibility of a change in the 'political ecology' of the
decaying inner-city areas, which are on the whole traditionally Labour strongholds, it is hardly surprising that
the 'immigrant vote' is seen as a worthy prize. On the
other hand, in the present situation where whites still
form a majority in all parliamentary constituencies, the
collective voice of reactionary vote is also keenly
sought. This ambiguity, seen as early as the first chapter of this book, has meant that both the major British
parties compromised themselves by their own hypocrisy.
Both, to a greater or lesser extent, have pandered to the
'conservative' climate of opinion among the indigenous
population: the 'natural' tendency for the British to
regard the outsider with suspicion. More recently, of
course, there has been an attempt in some circles to le-
gitimise the openly racist, neo-fascist ideology of the
National Front.

Before we come to analyse the contemporary climate and
in particular the 1977 Ladywood by-election, we pause to
look at the way in which the immigrant and white residents
of Handsworth said that they had voted in the past. It is
immediately clear from Table 6.1 that the allegiances of
the different ethnic groups are by no means similar. The
immigrant vote taken as a whole, however, demonstrates a
marked consistency in the form of strong Labour support,
at least in the General Election of October 1974. Indeed
it appears that the support of this portion of the
electorate may well have been crucial in returning Jenny
Lee to Westminster in 1974. The Handsworth constituency
which she won for the Labour Party with a majority of
3,896 contains the Sandwell ward, a ward which as we have
already seen has a high concentration of immigrants in its
southern sector. Our survey when looked at more closely
suggests that the generally more affluent white owner-
occupiers in this part of the ward vote fairly consistently in favour of the Tories, and the ward as a whole re-
turned three Conservative councillors in the local elections of May 1975, i.e., some eight months after the
General Election. The National Front candidate for the
parliamentary seat, despite polling a significant number
of votes (838), is unlikely to have had as important an
effect on the overall result as did the virtual 'block'
voting for Labour of the black portion of the electorate.

TABLE 6.1 Voting patterns at previous General and Local Elections [1] by ethnic group and sex (weighted figures in brackets)

| | WEST INDIAN | | | | ASIAN [3] | | BRITISH | | | |
| | Males | | Females | | Males | | Males | | Females | |
	General Election %	Local Election %	General Election %	Local Election %	General Election %	Local Election %	General Election %	Local Election %	General Election %	Local Election %
Labour	67(67)	29(27)	50(53)	27(26)	70	59	39(36)	22(22)	30(28)	10 (8)
Conservative	3 (3)	4 (3)	5 (6)	2 (2)	3	3	33(38)	26(31)	33(37)	26(29)
Liberal	* [4]	1 (*)	2 (2)	1 (*)	*	1	9 (6)	7 (4)	6 (5)	3 (2)
National Front	–	–	–	–	–	–	*	1 (1)	–	–
Voted other [2]	8 (9)	6 (7)	5 (5)	3 (4)	14	11	2 (2)	*	2 (2)	2 (2)
Did not vote	17(16)	55(57)	35(32)	64(68)	8	22	16(15)	41(39)	28(27)	57(58)
Not eligible	1 (1)	1 (1)	2 (1)	2 (1)	1	1	–	1 (1)	–	1 (1)
Refused/can't remember [5]	5 (5)	3 (3)	1 (*)	–	3	3	1 (2)	2 (2)	1 (1)	1 (1)
Sample size (= 100%)	309(257)		86(63)		297		273(215)		127(112)	

1 'General Election' refers to the October 1974 election.
2 This refers to people who said that they had voted for a party other than those listed, and those who could not remember (or refused to tell us) which party they did vote for.
3 Figures are not presented for Asian females since we interviewed a total of only eight women in this group.
4 * represents a figure of less than 0.5%.
5 Refers to those who refused to answer the question or couldn't remember whether or not they had voted.
6 It is interesting to note that at both General and Local Elections support for Labour is consistently strongest among Pakistanis and weakest among East African Asians.

The parliamentary constituency of Ladywood is a very
different proposition, containing as it does the Soho
ward, along with All Saints, Rotten Park and Ladywood
itself. Judging by our survey evidence, blacks in the
Soho ward, at least, voted massively in favour of the
Labour candidate, Brian Walden, in October 1974. [3]
That, combined with the traditional support of a section
(although proportionally very much smaller) of the indigenous working class, ensured his comfortable majority of
9,739. Perhaps not surprisingly, the local elections in
1975 produced a clean sweep for Labour in the Soho ward
(the three councillors including the Chairman of the Urban
Renewal Committee).

It is illuminating to look rather more closely at the
figures in Table 6.1. On a general view we see a major
degree of polarity in terms of support for the major parties. Whereas the Tories capture only a handful of votes
from both immigrant groups, they gain a substantial minority of the votes of local whites. Further, in the
light of past election results, it may well be that a
significant number of local whites have moved away from
their traditional allegiance to the Labour Party. Nor is
it stretching the imagination too far to suggest that the
issue of race may well have influenced many into making
this decision. Few, in 1976 at least, seemed to have been
prepared to support the ultra-right, i.e., the National
Front. On the other hand, it is only in the last year or
so that the Front appear to have assumed the role of, and
been accepted by many as, a 'respectable' political force.
Some of our white respondents may therefore have concealed
their true sympathies. The position by 1978 may have been
rather different: in two by-elections, at Walsall North
and at Stetchford (both fairly close to Handsworth in
geographical terms) the Front had beaten the Liberals into
fourth place. As Layton-Henry argues, when it came to the
subsequent by-election at Ladywood: [4]

Front leaders were pleased with the opportunity of
building on their previous successes and continued
their strategy of posing as a respectable constitution-
al party that would win through the ballot box. They
were delighted to be described as the fourth party in
England and described themselves as the third party in
the West Midlands.

One feature frequently noted by other commentators, and
largely confirmed by our own data, is the relatively high
turnout rate of immigrants. The 'Guardian' of 20 August
1977, referring to the Asian and West Indian voters of
Ladywood, talked of 'their tradition of greater electoral
enthusiasm than their indigenous neighbours'. [5]

Lawrence (1974) estimates that as far back as the 1966 election 87.9 per cent of the Indians and Pakistanis who were registered to vote in the central Nottingham constituency did so. This compared with 70.8 per cent for the West Indians, and 68.3 per cent for the local whites. The author goes on to point out, however, that the local registration among black immigrants was extremely low - less than 75 per cent, in fact. [6] Despite this, it is likely that, as with trade union membership, greater awareness of British political institutions has significantly reduced the numbers of those who are effectively disenfranchised in the latter half of the 1970s. Membership of trade unions and propensity to vote do not, of course, per se, tell us anything about the level of political consciousness among blacks. There may still be more than a glimmer of truth in the view of Katznelson that 'the only resource uniformly available to West Indian, Indian and Pakistani immigrants in Britain has been the vote.' [7] On the other hand, as we have seen, industrial muscle does not depend solely on decisions via the ballot box, and many immigrants, and in particular Asian workers, have demonstrated an ability to make their grievances felt. Furthermore, important alliances between IWAs and antifascist organisations such as the Anti-Nazi League promise to represent a major new political force in the 1980s.

It could be argued also that white workers themselves often feel powerless in the face of the economic and political forces which control their daily lives. They also have few alternative 'resources' through which to channel their feelings of discontent. One of the reasons often used to explain the apathy of white voters (and in particular white working-class voters) is that they feel 'it doesn't really matter how I vote'. Thus, the failure to vote is a form of legitimate (though ineffective) dissent. Whatever the underlying reasons, approximately one in five of the white householders we interviewed did not cast a vote at the General Election of October 1974. This was, in turn, matched by a similar figure for the West Indians. In sharp contrast only 8 per cent of the Asian men said that they had not voted and, at the local elections of 1976, despite the massive display of apathy from the West Indians and the whites, approaching four Asians in five cast a vote.

One way of looking at the figures is from the point of view of the parties themselves. The Labour Party may derive considerable satisfaction from the knowledge that the immigrant vote thus far appears to have gone largely in their favour. [8] They have also, it appears, largely avoided the loss to other parties of anything like an

equivalent number of whites. The endemic problem for the
Labour Party of 'getting out the vote' also appears to be
less serious for constituencies with large concentrations
of working-class Asian voters. When we talk about these
past voting patterns, at least so far as actual elections
are concerned, we are essentially talking about first-
generation immigrants. Few British-born blacks would have
been eligible to vote in the 1974 General Election. The
problem, noted by Lawrence, of having to translate election messages into Punjabi, Urdu and Hindi [9] to ensure
electoral support from the Asian communities, will not be
the major one facing Labour in future elections. On the
other hand, the apathy and cynicism of many working-class
whites with traditional Labour sympathies have already, it
appears, been mirrored by a similar phenomenon among West
Indians - and West Indian youth in particular.

The 'similarity' is likely to be illusory, however.
The cynicism of the black youths interviewed in a BBC
election programme on the day of the 1978 by-election in
Lambeth, for example, revealed a total rejection of any
symbols of white authority. The local MP, of whatever
political hue, could not represent them - and this would
be the case even if that MP happened to have a black face.
For those who view the political scene in such a manner
the seeds of the politics of confrontation have been well
and truly sown. The economic oppression suffered by those
in the industrial desert lands of the inner cities, for
many blacks in particular, undoubtedly evokes fearful
recollections of their historical legacy. This is not
mere conjecture or idle scaremongering. Indeed, the fear
of a breakdown in social order far wider-reaching than
that involving West Indian youth, has already provoked
near-panic reactions from politicians of all the major
parties. [10]

We return to this argument shortly to analyse the implications for areas such as Handsworth. Before doing so,
however, we move on to consider briefly a second series of
questions which are raised by the voting figures we have
seen: for example, from whom do the different parties
derive their electoral support? What degree of commitment
do voters show towards the party ideologies? And, finally, what is it about a particular party which appeals to
individual voters from the various sectors of the electorate?

On the first of these questions it is sometimes argued
that blacks, in voting overwhelmingly for the Labour
Party, are doing so because they see themselves as supporting the party of the working class. Since the majority of blacks are in manual occupations, the argument goes,

the higher propensity of blacks to vote in this way is
hardly surprising. Certainly a few of Lawrence's interviewees explained their own behaviour in this way, but the
assumption of a direct link between voting pattern and occupational status is hopelessly naive. Among our West
Indian and Asian householders, the pattern of voting was
similar throughout the job status range. [11] This, and
the finding that voting patterns do not differ tangibly if
we control for the age factor, find support in the recent
research in Ladywood referred to above. [12] It is only
among native whites that the slightly less naive model,
linking job status and age to voting behaviour, appears
to fit the evidence moderately well. Even then it only
does so for a rather spurious (if interesting) reason.
    We have already noted the way in which the character of
Handsworth has continually changed throughout the twentieth century and in particular since the Second World War.
If we look, for example, at the group of Handsworth whites
who have lived in the area throughout the post-war period
we see a group of retired white-collar workers and skilled
tradesmen who bought their homes when the area was still
(in the words of one respondent) 'a peaceful respectable
suburb'. It is perhaps not surprising that these retired
'suburbanites' turned to the Conservative Party as a possible means of restoring some semblance of the status quo.
Moreover, it was still widely believed that Labour was the
party of immigration and that the Tories would 'get rid of
the wogs'.
    In terms of commitment to the political parties, the
first thing which can be said is that the general level of
party membership was extremely low: only 17 per cent of
the total sample were party members. Furthermore, membership was particularly rare among the immigrant communities. Of those we interviewed, only one West Indian and
four Asians were actually card-carrying members (all of
the Labour Party). Among the whites, 14 were found to be
party members: 6 Conservative and 8 Labour supporters.
It appears, then, that direct involvement with local party
politics is extremely low, and that few blacks in particular have seen fit to use the formal party-political machinery to voice grievances. This might to some extent
reflect lack of effort on the part of existing party members to recruit new blood from the ranks of the immigrant
communities. However, it is also likely that there is a
certain measure of reluctance to join political movements
which, in general, fail to reflect a powerful self-image
on the part of black workers. Thus identification with
the politics of the shop-floor, which has led to relatively high levels of trade union membership among immigrants,

is not reflected in a similar measure of formal involvement in the broader political sense - at least within the
existing party-political structure.

In asking the question 'Which of the parties do you
think does most for people like you?' we were aiming to
assess the degree of general identification with a political party.   Interestingly, it revealed a widespread
cynicism, much more widespread, in fact, than the 'failure
to vote'.   Even among the Asians 18 per cent answered
'none of them', and a further 27 per cent gave a non-
committal 'don't know'.   Admittedly, the question is
rather difficult to answer, and the interpretation of the
phrase 'people like you' is problematic in the sense that
its interpretation can vary depending on the respondent's
self-image.   On the other hand, the researchers held the
view that feelings of remoteness from the legislative
machinery and the resultant lack of control over their
life chances were indeed largely interpreted in ethnic
terms, at least as far as the immigrant respondents were
concerned.   Approaching a third of the whites felt that
their interests were generally ignored by the national
parties, and the neglect by policy-makers of areas such
as Handsworth (as well as the question of immigration)
seems to have influenced their answers.

As implied above, West Indians seemed to interpret the
question as relating to the West Indian community as a
whole.   Once again, a large proportion (approaching 30 per
cent) expressed disenchantment with the political parties.
Significantly, among all ethnic groups and in particular
the West Indians, the willingness to vote for a particular
party did not necessarily imply a conviction that the
party had his/her interests at heart.   Overall the lack of
consistent commitment is reflected, not so much by a
higher incidence of 'cross voting' (i.e., voting for different parties at the General Election of 1974 and the
local election of 1976), as by the failure to vote at all
on one (or both) of these occasions. [13] Moreover, the
greater fickleness of the West Indian vote is probably of
more significance in substantive terms than seen merely as
a 'problem' for the Labour Party at election times.   In
other words, the failure to vote seems to be grounded in
cynicism and a feeling of being alienated from the party
system, at least as much as it is simply an indication of
temporary disillusionment or the feeling that the extra
vote would not affect the overall result.

It is always difficult to gauge the reasons why individuals vote as they do.   Even in the case of the whites,
which we discussed earlier, it is only possible to give a
general indication of the motives behind certain types of

voting behaviour. Certainly there is a likelihood of some voting of a 'habitual' type, based on a negative commitment and predicated on prior actions rather than on a rational assessment of current events. The traditional working-class Labour vote does exist, as does the white-collar Tory equivalent.

It is likely, however, that the Labour Party has lost some of those whose vote it could have relied upon in previous years, owing to its failure to address itself in concrete terms to the problems of the urban working class. In some cases racism has undoubtedly filled this void and has produced, in electoral terms, a 'swing' to the political right. As far as the immigrant groups are concerned, there is clearly little evidence of the 'deferential' vote and in some ways they seem to have assumed the mantle of previous (white) residents in political terms. The notion that the Labour Party exists to fight for the rights of the working man and is able to communicate with the trade unions appears to have been effectively communicated to black workers. There is also evidence that organisations such as the IWAs have on occasion taken an important hand in furthering this message. [14]

The Tory Party appears to have had little success in shaking off its imperialist image and, given the recent public statements on race and immigration, this image could only have been confirmed. Apart from some rather injudicious speeches from members of the Conservative right, the overriding impression conveyed by the major parties, however, is one of conciliation and integration. Most politicians would accept both the logic and the outcome of the predictions made by Layton-Henry (1978). Commenting after the Ladywood by-election, he argued that: [15]

> It cannot be long before immigrant voters form the majority of the electorate in areas like Handsworth and Ladywood, and they are certain to use this strength, to demand a share of local political patronage including parliamentary nominations.

Whilst few would deny that more vigorous attempts will be made by subsequent generations of blacks to gain rights of equal citizenship, it is by no means certain that they will use the existing political machinery to do so.

LEWISHAM AND LADYWOOD: THE AFTERMATH

In many ways the events of August 1977 may prove to have marked a watershed in British race-relations history. Prior to the events of Lewisham and Ladywood, there had

been isolated incidents of open conflict. Many blacks
will still remember the so-called 'race riots' of Notting
Hill and Nottingham. There had also been speeches made,
and political campaigns fought, specifically on the 'race
issue'. But the open flaunting of racist propaganda and
incitement to racial violence marked a distinctly new and
horrifying dimension. It also provided a severe jolt to
those who had previously assumed that we were heading towards a period of racial harmony to be followed by the
total integration of immigrants into the economic and
political (if not cultural and religious) life of Britain.
The mass conflict perspective, as distinct from that of
the isolated skirmish, had gained a foothold in the public
consciousness.

Its coming had been heralded by a number of writers,
among them Mullard. His book 'Black Britain', written in
1973, launches a scathing attack on the 'liberal' policies
and pronouncements of both politicians and the existing
race relations 'industry'. It accuses organisations such
as the Community Relations Commission and the Race Relations Board (now amalgamated as the Commission for Racial
Equality, CRE) of adopting a 'holier than thou' attitude
which not only lost them the support of blacks, but also
drove blacks 'into organising their own race groups'. [16]
'Their chief job,' the author argues, 'has been the prop-
ping-up of racism by maintaining the status quo.' [17]
Whether or not we accept Mullard's interpretation of
events and in particular his evaluation of the driving
force behind the creation of militant black organisations
is, except in an academic sense, irrelevant. What is of
prime importance is that such organisations exist, and
that the sort of feelings which prompted Mullard's book
appear to be strengthening among the black communities.
(The previous chapters of the present study aimed, in
part, to explain why this is the case.)

There is, however, much more to Mullard's emotive
rhetoric than the expression of despair from a member of
an oppressed racial group; he is talking above all as a
black Englishman, and moreover one who has been denied his
full rights of citizenship. He and his fellow British-
born blacks do not, as Parekh rightly argues, judge their
experience of life in Britain by the colonial or neo-
colonial yardstick, as some of their parents may have
done. [18] Their frame of reference will be based on the
experiences of their classroom colleagues and their general perceptions of life opportunities.

Before going on to look at the work experience of the
children of our interviewees, [19] we pause to consider a
number of points which are germane to the above discus-

sion. In terms of an overall theoretical perspective we
have said little so far about the notions of 'integration'
on the one hand and 'conflict' on the other. It often appears to be assumed that one can simply map out a number
of points on a continuum and thus locate individuals, community organisations and/or political bodies at some point
along the integration-conflict scale. This approach ob-
viously has great aesthetic appeal on account of its simplicity. Unfortunately, of course, it is hopelessly simplistic. It is not denied that we can distinguish between
an organisation where objectives are integration and as-
similation whatever the 'cost' in terms of human dignity,
and a body which adopts an uncompromising posture grounded
in the politics of confrontation. What we are suggesting
is that, in general, the important distinctions are essentially not differences of degree but differences of
kind. [20]

Bearing this in mind, it will be illuminating at this
point to examine the stances which various political or
quasi-political bodies adopt and then to attempt to assess
the response of those at whom their attention is directed.
Few would argue that the dominant (stated) theme of the
major political parties is one of striving towards racial
harmony. There is also little doubt that these messages
of goodwill are received with more than a hint of cynicism
by members of the immigrant community. Discussions of
'race relations' at national levels have repeatedly dis-
solved into discussions of the 'immigration issue'. Even
the Labour Party felt itself constrained by public opinion
[21] to play the 'numbers game', as we saw in the first
chapter. Thus, immigrants have good reason to assume a
rather apprehensive stance towards both the major parties.
Both, in turn, have brought into being Acts of Parliament
which have created hardship and despair for countless
families whose members have been kept apart by immigration
quotas. Both have presided over government-sponsored race
relations machinery which to many has seemed largely inef-
fectual. It is hardly surprising then, that 'new' bodies
such as the CRE fail to be received with unbounded joy by
the immigrant community. Many blacks rightly feel cheated
of their full rights of citizenship. Even more significantly, the second generation may be less charitable to
the authorities which have failed them, and there is already clear evidence (as noted earlier) that many youngsters resent the loss of dignity and self-respect stemming
from their parents' complicity.

It remains to be established, however, that past legislation and its attendant enforcement machinery have in
fact been ineffective in the way this argument suggests.

One could argue, of course, that any legislation which attempts to attack the roots of racist ideology is doomed to
failure, since this ideology is an integral feature of
western capitalism, and certainly no law can prevent
people from holding certain views. What it can do, however, is to minimise the harmful manifestations of those
beliefs; hence the focus on discriminatory practices in
public places: work, housing, etc. Given that in the
Handsworth of the late 1970s we have confirmed the
findings of earlier researchers (namely, that discrimination in many forms still exists), there is some justification for arguing that legislation has not been totally
effective. As Smith (1977) argues, one side-effect has
been that discriminatory practices seem to have become
more covert. [22] One consequence of this is that such
instances are much more difficult to detect, and once detected the case has to be established in a court of law.

Smith goes on to point out that whatever the failings
of the 1968 Act, it at least provided a public statement
of commitment to the cause of racial equality. The problem was, however, that the statement carried little conviction; and the cynic might argue that had it been more
than, at best, a goodwill gesture, the legal back-up would
have been made rather more effective. Furthermore, as
Smith later admits, only a minority of the immigrants
interviewed by PEP had even heard of the Race Relations
Board (RRB) and there was also 'evidence of a certain reluctance to make a complaint among a substantial proportion of Asians and West Indians.' [23] The author concludes that: [24]

They are right to be cautious because it is extraordi-
narily difficult to prove that discrimination has occurred in particular cases especially since the Board
has no power to subpoena documents or witnesses.

As Mullard argues, the dice were from the outset very
heavily loaded in favour of the defendant. [25] Employers
and businessmen were undoubtedly one group of individuals
who were well aware of both the law and the RRB, and many
found means of avoiding falling foul of this piece of
legislation.

The present author recalls one incident vividly. Only
a few months after the 1968 Act had been passed I took a
factory job in Manchester: a job which I had found by
walking up to the factory gates and asking to see the
personnel manager. I was later surprised to find that
although there was no clear evidence of vacancies (i.e.,
by means of the usual gate sign) there was, in fact, a
serious shortage of labour. I was then asked if I knew
any other people who wanted work. Surprised by the ap-

parent suggestion that labour was in short supply I asked
(rather naively in retrospect) why they didn't advertise
at the local Labour Exchange. The answer, given the foregoing discussion, was predictable: 'I couldn't do that,
lad; we'd get a bus-load of wogs round and we'd get taken
to the Race Relations Board if we didn't take 'em on.'

The Act could be dodged in many ways; and employers,
for example, must have soon realised that the chances of
being taken to court were minute; and also that, even if
they were, the odds were that they wouldn't be convicted.
There was also an added bonus - some very useful publicity
could be gained during the lengthy hearings! In short
then, the Act was, in practical terms, a disaster and
moreover an insult to the intelligence and dignity of
black people. The whole exercise was little more than a
palliative. Beyond providing jobs for race relation boys,
it did little more than create a large, inefficient bureaucratic organisation [26] whose main function was to
be seen to be 'doing something about the race problem'.
It is hardly surprising, then, that politically conscious
blacks would reject this 'con trick' and look elsewhere to
solve their problems. [27]

Eight years after the passing of this Act we were
rather overdue for 'a new strategy'. [28] The cover was
now wearing rather thin and not surprisingly it was felt
that the body which had been established initially to enforce the requirements of the 1965 Act (the RRB) should be
disbanded. The new amalgamated body, the CRE, was duly
entrusted with the task of providing the muscle behind the
1976 Race Relations Act. Perhaps the single most important change of principle from previous race legislation
was the fact that the focus of attention shifted from the
individual claimant to the bodies which were suspected of
discriminatory practices. In addition, the complaints-
based procedure was scrapped: the Commission now had the
power to institute investigative procedures whether or not
a formal complaint had been lodged, and had the authority
to subpoena documents and witnesses.

These changes mean that the new body will, in theory at
least, become rather more effective. It was clearly ludi-
crous to regard discriminatory practices as a collection
of isolated cases. Moreover, as we have already seen, of
those who had heard of the RRB [29] most said that they
would not take a complaint to this body. It is also
likely that, in practice, the number would be fewer still.
Individual complaints are now taken directly to the
courts, thus avoiding the painfully laborious bureaucratic
machinery involving the submission of a case to the Conciliation Committee. The claimant also had no redress if

this committee decided in its 'pre-opinion' letter that no
discrimination had occurred. Should the Committee decide
that discrimination had been proven they were bound to attempt to reach a 'settlement' between the parties and an
'assurance' from the discriminating person or body that
the instance would not reoccur. Only if this failed was
the issue taken to a court of law. In the first four
years of operation, for example, 4,026 complaints were
made; of these 685 cases were proven (in the eyes of the
Board) but only 15 reached the County Courts. When one
bears in mind that a complaint is unlikely to be brought
to the Board in the first place unless it has some sub-
stance, this does not appear to be a particularly enviable
record.

It might have been more impressive had the 'assurances
of good behaviour' been reinforced by subsequent investi-
gations by the Board. Fortunately this checking mechanism
has also been built into the new Act. As Smith (1977)
states: [30]

> Where discrimination has been proved, the Commission
> will be empowered to serve a non-discrimination notice;
> that is, it can require the organisation to change the
> discriminatory practices and it can later require the
> organisation to show that it has complied with the
> notice.

The Act has also made provision for the investigation of
some forms of activity which, although not openly discriminatory, do at least put the immigrant at a disadvantage.
For example, there is the issue of council house allocation.

We should perhaps ask ourselves at this point whether
we can assume that the fate of black citizens is now in
good hands. Certainly the new approach has much to commend it, and in theory the CRE has the potential to succeed where earlier attempts have failed. Its success,
however, hinges on a number of matters beyond the quality
and tenacity of its staff. It depends crucially on the
level of resources which it obtains and on the directions
in which these resources are channelled. It depends also
on the way in which potential conflicts of interest on the
part of individual Commissioners are solved.

The initial traumatic upheavals caused by the merging
of two disparate organisations appear now to have been, if
not forgotten, at least suppressed. It is still too early
to assess fully the work which they have done to date.
Recent conversations with a member of the Commission's
investigative staff leave us with something of a question
mark hanging over the resource issue. There are undoubtedly concerns over the shortage of staff and other re-

sources, and this is likely to mean that even some rather
disturbing cases of alleged discrimination are unlikely to
be investigated in the forseeable future.

It would be tragic if this institution was to fail in
the manner of previous ones simply for lack of financial
backing. [31] Furthermore, if the CRE is not seen by the
new generation of black Englishmen and women as effectively serving their interests, their alienation from the official race relations machinery will increase. Indeed the
mood, if not the words, of Mullard were echoed in a conversation which one of our researchers had some four years
ago with the then Senior Community Relations Officer for
Birmingham. Having expressed the view that the West
Indians were well represented on the local Community
Relations Committee, he went on to express concern that:
'We seem to be having a separatist move from some West
Indian groups: integration seems to have gone by the
board for the time being.'

As is reflected by this statement, the approach of the
CRC had been extremely 'low key', stressing integration
and racial harmony. On the other hand, black organisations such as Harambee clearly felt (and feel) stifled by
the overriding aura of paternalism. National and local
finance is fine: but at what personal cost to recipient
groups? In an article welcoming government funding of
'self-help' groups the local evening paper exposed the
dilemma of blacks striving for a measure of independence
and dignity. In a 'Birmingham Evening Mail' editorial of
14 May 1976, carrying the headline 'Tolerance and Self-
help', West Indians were urged to 'take a fuller part, and
as individuals in their own community, tackle their own
social problems and discipline their young hooligans.'
Thus problems are seen as internal to the black community
and funding is seen as a means of instituting black control agencies. Having donated the cash, the national
conscience is presumably clear. Little wonder then that
Harambee workers tend to feel that 'the City politicians
have tried to use the big stick to force the association
to alter its policies'. Little wonder either that they
regarded with suspicion an offer of an urban aid grant in
1976 which carried the condition that all property bought
should be in the name of the local authority.

The basic ideology of the Harambee project is summed up
by its title, meaning 'working together'. This does not,
however, imply working with the white man on the white
man's terms. Its aim is to restore the dignity of blacks,
and its philosophy is influenced by Pan-Africanism and
African Socialism with infusions of 'black power' ideology. In terms of policy it is very much grounded in the

problems of blacks in the inner city rather than in other-
worldly asceticism. Thus the dream of a mass exodus to
Africa is rejected in whatever guise - Ethiopian, Black
Nationalism, etc. The emphasis is very much on education.

Vacation schools have been held since 1970 and the
local authority has permitted schools to be used for this
purpose. Black kids have been seen to display evidence of
an internalised 'failure syndrome' even before they have
left secondary school. Moreover, as the report of the
1975 summer school noted, 'They display the symptoms of
alienation. They baffle their teachers at school and in-
furiate their parents.' To counteract the culturally specific content of the secondary school curriculum, the
extra schools aim to teach basic subjects within a framework which make them more intelligible and of more direct
relevance to children with an equally important cultural
heritage.

The overriding approach, then, is based on the rejection of paternalism in whatever form. It does not, however, see the white man, per se, as an enemy. As with the
IWA and other Asian bodies such as the Pak-Kashmiri and
Bangladeshi Workers Associations they incorporate a welfare function as a major part of their day-to-day activities. Their shop and advice centre were opened in Grove
Lane in 1974, legal advice and representation by qualified
lawyers being available to those who needed them. Also in
common with the Asian groups, Marxist philosophy is
central to much of their thinking, thus capitalism rather
than the white man is regarded as the fundamental 'enemy'.
Thus 'integration' would be interpreted as integration of
the working class irrespective of colour, race and creed.
By the same token, 'conflict' represents the ultimate conflict between the proletariat and the oppressive forces of
capitalism, not the day-to-day hassles with Birmingham
City Council!

There are now some signs that Harambee is becoming
'institutionalised' or, in Althusserian terms, 'incorporated'. There are also fears among some of its workers
that it will become just another social work organisation.
This will inevitably influence the future of Handsworth
since many of the more militant young blacks will turn to
other groups as a solution to their 'dilemma'. Many already have. One possible 'solution' would be that offered
by the Afro-Caribbean Self-Help organisation (ACSHO). To
this group the possibility of a large-scale confrontation
with whites is accepted as inevitable. It is a body,
moreover, which refuses to have any contact with white
society and bases its ideology on Pan-Africanism and, in
particular, the belief that 'the black man's destiny is

Africa'. Indeed, links have been forged with political
movements in Africa and a few powerful personalities are
emerging: people who may prove to be future leaders of a
radicalised West Indian youth.

It is, however, the Rastafarian movement which perhaps
has generated the most public debate. This is in some
ways inevitable in a society which is traditionally in-
tolerant and extremely suspicious of those whose external
appearance seems to be rather strange. Certainly the
wearing of 'locks' and woolly hats and the adoption of a
form of patois [32] which is virtually unintelligible to
the non-cognoscenti, represent in a symbolic form a total
rejection of the normative ethos. As noted earlier, the
'Rasta' has become equated with the evil in our midst - an
evil which goes far beyond the smoking of ganja (mari-
juana) and the apparently menacing appearance. He [33]
stands accused of the 'classical' crimes of rape and pil-
lage; of mugging old (white) ladies in the street and of
enticing young girls to their squalid dens of immorality
and vice (their squats). He is the Sunday papers' dream,
the mugger, rapist, junkie, squatter and thief all rolled
into one; and what is more, he's black. To the local
press he is also frequently seen in a similar light. In
a major article following Brown's (1977) report on the relationship between young blacks and the police, Frederick
Whitehead wrote in an unashamedly sensationalist manner
about what he called 'The stark truth on Handsworth.'
Brown's report, he writes: [34]

> acknowledges [35] that a hard core of around 200 young
> West Indians [later to be described as young thugs
> wearing their hair in 'dreadlocks'] are terrorising a
> large part of old Handsworth. It reveals starkly that
> the majority of victims of street attacks and robberies
> are defenceless white women and some Asians who are
> often afraid to report the crimes.

The 'thugs' live, we are told, mostly in 'pads' which are:
provided (largely at public expense) by well-meaning
charitable housing trusts such as COPEC. These con-
verted houses (my old home may be one of them) are
tailor-made Fagin's dens. No less than twenty-two of
them are known to the police, and girls as young as 13,
14 and 15 have been found there among the Rastafarian
males.

The Rastafarian, then, is seen as the perpetrator of
all the evil mentioned earlier and of a few 'new' misde-
meanours. He is also now a sponger off the state and
(horror of horrors!) he is the desecrator of white man's
property: in this case symbolised by the home (significantly not simply the house) of the author of the article.

The 'home' itself is described in lyrical terms, a place
of moral purity, peace and tranquillity in those halcyon
days before Handsworth became, in Whitehead's words, an
'ally of putrefaction'.   The public conscience as well as
its purse is seen as having been raped.   Both 'public' and
'state' become innocent victims of an external alien
force.   Thus the article provides a classic example of the
ideological stance which this book has aimed to expose.
Given his (Whitehead's) definition of the 'problem', the
proposed solution is predictable.   The state defends
itself and the public by increasing the size of its police
force and the 'bolt holes' (Whitehead's term) are closed;
i.e., liberal do-gooders in the form of charitable housing
organisations are prevented from consorting to help the
aliens.   Let us now leave this inflammatory rhetoric
behind, and unlike Whitehead, look at the Rastafarian as
a fellow member of the human race.

It is perhaps rather easier to define the origins and
the stated destiny of the movement than it is to understand the politics of the Rasta in the British urban context.   As Barrett (1977) argues: [36]

> The Rastafarian cult is a messianic movement unique to
> Jamaica.   Its members believe that Haile Selassie,
> Emperor of Ethiopia, is the black Messiah who appeared
> in the flesh for the redemption of all blacks exiled in
> the world of white oppressors.   The movement views
> Ethiopia as the promised land, the place where black
> people will be repatriated through a wholesale exodus
> from all western countries where they have been in
> exile (slavery).

Despite its roots in slavery the movement itself is
founded on the notion of peace and harmony among peoples.
On the other hand, for the young black (as for the young
working-class white in an area such as Handsworth) the
hope of some distant utopia (however 'inevitable') is not
always enough.   The 'reality' of living in 'Babylon' especially when seen in the context of '400 years of slavery' [37] helps to engender a mood of hostility which is at
odds with other-worldly asceticism.

The parallel with working-class whites was drawn for a
very important reason.   Despite the total rejection of any
conventionally perceived integrationist perspective, we
have recently seen a fascinating attempt to fuse two
streams of cultural symbolism.   It has been the concerted
reaction of politically conscious whites and blacks to the
forces of racism which has produced this apparently paradoxical situation.   In opposing ultra-right neo-fascist
organisations such as the National Front, the politically
broad-based Anti-Nazi League has sought to marshal support

from 'youth' as a whole via contemporary pop culture. We
have, therefore, seen meetings on stage of punk (or new
wave) and reggae during anti-fascist demonstrations.
Whether punk music in the form of, for example, the relatively sophisticated Tom Robinson Band has really communicated its underlying political message among working-class
youths remains a moot point. [38] Reggae, on the other
hand, has had a major impact among young West Indians
throughout the country, whether or not they would regard
themselves as Dreads or Rastas.

It may well be, then, that the powerful cultural identity generated by the message of reggae music and distinctive dress and language may galvanise West Indian youth
and at the same time further broaden the Rastafarian movement and give it a coherent political strategy. Political
divisions may, of course, have the opposite effect and
produce a total fragmentation of what is already an extremely complex movement, embodying as it does many disparate factions (in Britain at least). Unfortunately,
lack of space necessarily limits our discussion at this
point. [39] (We shall, however, briefly return to these
issues later when we come to discuss the views of the West
Indian youths we talked to.)

Until now, we have said little about the political
(with both a small and large 'p') orientation of Asian
communities, apart from noting their current electoral
support for the Labour Party. In fact, much of the cynicism of formal 'race industry' organisations, such as the
Birmingham CRC which was evident in the case of West
Indians, appears to be mirrored by the Asians. Certainly
there were full-time Asian officials who saw their jobs as
representing the interests of 'their' community. Unfortunately, however, they seemed as remote from the average
Asian worker as many of the 'native' organisations seem
from the ordinary English worker. Furthermore, our interviews with representatives of Asian organisations suggest
that the CRC and in particular its Asian officials are regarded with a mixture of indifference and contempt:
indifference by those who regard them as of no importance,
and contempt by those who regard them (in Mullard's sense)
as 'white' blacks, servants of the City Council and ene-
mies of their own people.

Individual problems, then, are unlikely to be transmitted directly to the CRC. They are much more likely to be
taken (if at all) to the Asian Resource Centre or one of
the Workers Associations noted earlier (the IWA, Pak-
Kashmiri Workers Association or the Bangladeshi Workers
Association). The WAs see themselves as providing for the
general welfare of the Asian communities and not simply as

bodies who deal with employment problems. That being
said, they do nevertheless have a strong commitment to
representing not only the interests of Asian workers, but
also of the working class in general (as we have already
seen). The President of the IWA told us that in terms of
employment one of the major problems facing Asian workers
was the question of obtaining work which matched the individual's qualifications. He added significantly that 'Our
children are not going to be satisfied with this'. On a
more general point he regarded a major task to be one of
'educating' union officials to act in the interests of the
working class as a whole, and looked to the IWA's good relations with the West Indian Workers Federation and the
Pak-Kashmiri Workers Association to create unity among immigrant groups on this point. Our researcher did, however, gain the impression that the unity between the IWA
and their West Indian counterpart was not all it might
have been, at least to the extent that the Indians regarded themselves as rather superior in terms of both
skill and intellect.

There was an overwhelming feeling of respect for
British educational institutions: a feeling which, incidentally, appears to be reflected in the interest which
Asian parents tend to take in their children's education
and in the qualifications which the children in turn are
obtaining. However, the IWA was aware that education,
though certainly important, was not in itself sufficient.
It acknowledged that unity among immigrant worker groups
needed to be matched by a willingness on the part of the
British trade union movement and managements to accept
black workers on equal terms. It also explicitly endorsed
a point which was made in the previous chapter; namely,
that unions and managements often colluded on issues such
as 'the number of coloureds employed', 'promotion policies', etc.

Another significant point in terms of the success of
the local IWAs in carrying the support of future generations of Asian workers was the fact that it kept records
on firms which were suspected of discriminatory policies.
If this material were consistently channelled to the CRE
and pressure brought to bear on them to start investigative proceedings, it (the IWA) might become a stronger
political force. As with other black organisations such
as Harambee, failure to achieve at least the status of an
efficient pressure group may mean that the Asian youngsters will turn to more radical organisations to provide
solutions to their problems. Other organisations such as
the Bangladeshi Workers Association appear to be rather
scornful of the extent to which other Asian organisations

concentrate their activities on issues of welfare:
travel, completion of tax forms, burial arrangements, etc.
According to their President it was felt that they should
exert overt political pressure to achieve the unification
of the whole of the British working class. They clearly
realised that, although this process of 'integration'
would in itself create severe factional conflicts within
the British trade union movement, it was a necessary prerequisite in the light of their ultimate goal, providing
as it would a base from which the 'major conflict' could
be launched.

Another body which, in the words of its organiser,
Ranjit Sondhi, is struggling 'to raise the political
consciousness of local Asian people' is the Asian Resource
Centre (ARC). The Birmingham CRC is (once again) seen as
'a waste of time' because of its remoteness from the ordinary Asian family. Modelled on the Harambee project, the
ARC sees its welfare function as extremely important. On
the other hand, this is in some ways a means to an end.
Sondhi acknowledges that one of his major tasks is to
overcome the reluctance of older Asians to enter the
struggle against discrimination. As a young man (in his
late twenties) and educated at an English Public School,
one might have thought that he too would have been remote
from his clients, many of whom are illiterate or semi-
literate. This does not, however, appear to be the case.
In fact, his background gives him the decisive advantage
of being able to communicate with Asian schoolchildren and
to some extent enables him to understand the problems of
inter-generational culture conflict. This leads him to
give unequivocal support to the recently created hostel
(noted earlier) which is largely for victims of what he
calls 'the conservative forces necessary for the maintenance of the extended family system and all that goes with
it'.

He is the only full-time paid member of staff at the
ARC and clearly realises that much of their future work
depends on a reliable and significant source of financial
support. They have so far been able to obtain funds from
the Cadbury Trust, but would like to enlist the additional
support of an organisation such as the CRE. This could
bring with it serious problems, not least since it may
ultimately impair their relations with the IWA, which are
at the moment said to be very good. To become tarred with
the brush of paternalism and to be restricted to a totally
integrationist policy would almost certainly do this.

It is likely that many young blacks, in seeking a more
radical political solution, will turn to one of the existing left-wing parties such as Socialist Unity or the

Socialist Workers (SWP). Both these put up candidates at
the 1977 Ladywood by-election, and both figured very pro-
minently in the campaign, if not in the final poll. The
major feature of their stance was violent opposition to
the National Front, and it is clear that the major intention was to mobilise the immigrant vote on the grounds of
the growing threat which the ultra-right represented.
Layton-Henry (1978) correctly points out that the Labour
Party was extremely worried about the possibility of
losing immigrant votes for a number of reasons: first,
their position on immigration policy had been exposed as
ambiguous; second, they had consistently failed to nomi-
nate any Asian or West Indian for local council posts;
and third, their party election agent had been accused by
Raghib Ahsan, the Socialist Unity candidate, of neo-
fascist sympathies and had been rapidly dropped as a
result.

The significance of these leftist groups in areas such
as Handsworth goes far beyond their present 'ballot-box
appeal'. Nevertheless, it is interesting to note that
Raghib Ahsan achieved, in Layton-Henry's words, 'a credit-
able vote of 534' [40] when Socialist Unity candidates had
tended to have a derisorily low level of support in the
previous elections which they had contested. One explanation is that Ahsan won the votes of those immigrants who
were impressed by their confrontation of the forces of the
ultra-right. Though plausible, this fails to explain the
almost total failure of the SWP, who took an equally significant role in confronting the neo-fascists at both the
Lewisham march and the National Front election rally at
Boulton Road School on the edge of the Ladywood constituency. A second hypothesis is implicitly suggested by
Layton-Henry when he argues that 'the most intriguing
question that emerges from this analysis is the possibility of the development of ethnic voting'. [41] Raghib
Ahsan was not only a local man with an efficient back-up
from his party machine, he was also an Asian and might
therefore have been expected to gain support from this
section of the electorate. Similarly James Hunte, the
independent West Indian candidate, may have picked up a
large proportion of his 336 votes from his compatriots.
It would be misleading to suggest, however, that the prime
motive of voters for these two candidates was essentially
similar, or that the motive was primarily ethnic in
character.

We would argue that the two cases were radically dis-
similar. James Hunte was a well-known local man and it is
likely that he did indeed capture the votes of a sizeable
number of politically moderate West Indians who were dis-

enchanted with the major parties (and in particular with the local Labour Party). However, it is likely that had a West Indian or Asian candidate stood as (for example) a Tory, he/she would not have obtained even the level of support which Hunte achieved. We would suggest, therefore, that to talk about ethnic voting in isolation from other political issues is rather naive. The most likely explanation for the 'success' of Ahsan is that he, along with Hunte and Gordon (the SWP candidate), captured his share of the votes of disenchanted Labour voters. More important than this is the fact that he was not simply a local Asian man who had exposed the neo-fascist links of an important Labour Party worker, he was also someone who represented a well-organised Marxist group which may well have captured the votes of the increasingly politically conscious and militant faction of the Asian working class. Moreover, he like many of his fellow party members had begun to communicate successfully at grass roots level, in particular by demonstrating the links between institutionalised racism, on the one hand, and the class relations involved in the capitalist mode of production on the other. Whether this increasing radicalism of the party political scene will in fact materialise depends on a mass of disparate factors, not least on the experiences of second-generation blacks. The remainder of this chapter, then, is devoted to a discussion of that part of our research in Handsworth which concerned itself with the children of our immigrant respondents.

BLACK YOUTH - BLACK FUTURE?

We have already seen (in Chapter 5) the major employment problems facing young people leaving school in the latter half of the 1970s. We noted also that a great deal of research had shown that black children seemed to be facing particularly serious difficulties. The importance of this in the present context is that it is the 'visible black unemployed', black youths hanging around the street at all hours of the day, who are the focus of much attention, particularly from the police. It is in this context where much of the physical confrontation between these two groups occurs. Black youths often feel, with some justification, that they are the victims of rather liberal interpretations of 'crimes' such as 'loitering with intent', 'behaviour likely to cause a breach of the peace', etc. [42]

Certainly, unemployment is a major factor in an increasingly tense political climate; but what of the black

youth who have jobs? What kind of work are they doing and
how does this compare with that of their parents? Table
6.2 presents at least part of the answer. We are looking
here at the next generation of Handsworth householders:
the two eldest children of our respondents who were still
living at home and were between the ages of 16 and 24 in-
clusive. [43] Large numbers were, in fact, around the
ages of 16 and 17, and many of them were therefore still
at school when their parents were interviewed. This is
not without importance in itself, since many were undoubtedly staying on at school in the hope of gaining some
qualifications. In addition there were those who were
enrolled at the local college of further education,
amounting, among the minority groups, to 10 West Indians
(5 boys and 5 girls) and 12 Asians (7 boys and 5 girls).
Though smaller in number, there were some who had achieved
places in the higher education sector. (Because of demographic factors such as the older age structure of the
sample of local white children, only a handful of this
group were still in full-time education.)

If we exclude those who are economically inactive from
Table 6.2, a number of points emerge. First, unemployment
is seen to be even more serious among immigrants than was
at first thought. Over one in four of the economically
active Asians, along with approximately one in five of the
West Indians, were out of work. It might be argued that
the figure for the local white children was relatively
small because they had spent, on average, longer in the
job market. However, a more important factor is the possibility of 'hidden unemployment' among minority groups
(i.e., black children waiting to leave school and having
little chance of employment; or perhaps staying on at
school as an alternative to the dole queue).

The second point to be made is that, as with their
parents, relatively few West Indians and Asians have obtained white-collar occupations. Admittedly it is conceivable that this is not quite as serious a problem as it
appears. For one thing, very few of the 'immigrant'
children were born and educated in the UK. It may very
well be therefore that their younger brothers and sisters
will be more successful in the job market. A further
moderating point would be that other research, for
example, the OPCS Young People's Employment Study, has
demonstrated the tendency for job status distributions of
West Indians and whites to converge over a period of a few
years. [44] Against these 'optimistic' arguments, however, one could point to the distinct likelihood that many
of the more successful young whites in Handsworth will
have joined the general outflow of whites from the area.

TABLE 6.2 Occupational status of males and females between the ages of 16 and 24 [1] by ethnic group (weighted figures in brackets)

Registrar General's classification	WEST INDIAN		ASIAN [2]		BRITISH	
	Males %	Females %	Males %	Females %	Males %	Females %
I & II Professional Managerial and Intermediate Non-manual	–	–	–	–	2 (*) [4]	3 (4)
III NM. Routine non-manual	10(12)	27(31)	6	15	19(23)	33(36)
III M. Skilled manual	31(30)	1 (1)	16	–	37(34)	13 (7)
IV & V. Semi-skilled & unskilled	22(19)	12(12)	23	23	26(29)	20(25)
Unemployed	10(10)	15(16)	10	15	9 (6)	5 (4)
Economically inactive [3]	27(29)	44(39)	44	48	7 (9)	28(25)
Sample size (= 100%)	91(77)	91(74)	81	48	43(35)	40(28)

1 This refers to the two eldest children in a family still living at home and between the stated ages.

2 The sample sizes are too small here to separate the children into those of Indian and those of Pakistani or Bangladeshi origin.

3 This consists mainly of those who are still at school (see text) but it does also include those who are at college and those who are not seeking work for other reasons.

4 * represents a figure of less than 0.5%.

Given the generally lower mobility of young blacks, therefore, Table 6.2 may understate the level of local job
status differentials.

Whatever we might say about the present job relativi-
ties among ethnic groups, one point is clear. For the
black children who have actually got a job, their prospects, in a purely objective sense, look a little bright-
er than those of their parents. A detailed comparison of
the jobs held by the two generations suggests that, although many young blacks work in the same industry (and
often in similarly unpleasant work) as their parents, a
fairly high proportion have already aspired to the same,
or higher status in the job hierarchy. Whether they will
continue to progress in career terms and win posts in competition with whites remains to be seen.

One of the rather worrying aspects about the situation
is the apparent rapidity of the dual-market effects discussed earlier. It looks as though the many sources of
reinforcement may well be no less strong than they were
when the first generation began looking for jobs. We may
be witnessing simply a change in the nature (rather than
the frequency) of reinforcement. Black parents, in the
light of their own experience, may well channel youngsters
into the sorts of job which they feel are accessible to
their children. Teachers and Youth Employment Officers
(YEOs) may also at times be guilty of underestimating
their abilities. There is some evidence to suggest that
immigrants are less likely to be entered for 'O' and 'A'
level examinations (or even CSEs) than their white colleagues, irrespective of potential. [45] YEOs subject to
the many structural pressures discussed by Fowler,
Littlewood and Madigan (1977) may slot immigrants into the
'holes of least resistance'. [46] The oft-repeated rationalisation that immigrants' aspirations are 'too high'
may be seen as 'objectively valid' in terms of paper qualifications. Where this explanation fails, however, is in
defining as a valid measure of ability the possession of
paper qualifications, when the likelihood of gaining such
qualifications is itself a function of the teacher's definition of ability!

In order to throw some light on these and other issues
concerning the experiences of young immigrants, our research team interviewed a random sample of 25 West Indians
(14 boys and 11 girls) and 25 Asians (13 boys and 12
girls) between the ages of 16 and 21 from the total number
of children in this age-group in the families of our
original immigrant sample. [47] With the exception of two
Asian boys who wanted to go to university, all had left
school before their eighteenth birthday. [48] Indeed,
three-quarters of these had left at 16.

The experiences of the two groups whilst at school were markedly different, as were the qualifications with which they emerged. None of the West Indians had progressed beyond CSEs, and there appeared to be a distinct mood of dissatisfaction with the interest which the teachers had shown in them. Only a third felt that their teachers had given them consistent encouragement throughout secondary school. Many, along the lines of the earlier argument, said that their teachers had effectively prevented them from studying 'O' level examinations which they thought that they could have passed. A fundamental problem seemed to be the vicious circle sometimes created by the combined alienatory effects of school environment and curriculum. Black children had often reacted against authority, in the form of the teacher and the institution itself, by 'messing about'. This in turn produced indifference on the part of some teachers and outright hostility and vindictiveness on the part of others. Some children described teachers in terms which suggested both open physical conflict and the perception of staff as symbols of an oppressive force. For example: 'Some teachers were army-major types - gave us the cane. I put a chair over the French teacher's head' (West Indian boy). Half of the West Indian children we interviewed left school with no paper qualifications at all, and less than one in four felt that the YEOs who interviewed them had been any help.

Asians were equally sceptical about the 'advice' of the YEOs and the 'ethnic stereotyping' appeared sufficiently blatant at times for the children to become aware that their hopes of meaningful communications were limited. Thus, the West Indian boy who told us: 'They took up self-judgment. They saw me doing a particular job - a labouring job.' and the Asian boy who said: 'When I had my interview with the Careers Officer, I told him I wanted to go on to study and he kept trying to persuade me to get a job.' As with white children, aspirations may indeed be unrealistic at times, but the significance here lies in the fact that those whom we interviewed seemed to imply that they saw these instances as yet another way in which their identity and potentiality were being suppressed by white society.

In terms of school-leaving qualifications, the Asian youths seemed to do rather better than the West Indians, although approximately the same proportions (a half) had left with no formal qualifications. Asian boys in particular seemed to be keen to gain 'O' and 'A' level passes. In fact, three boys had passed 'A' levels, and at the other end of the scale only five had left without taking any examinations. This keenness to gain qualifications is

reflected in their job aspirations: almost a half of the
Asian boys were aiming for scientific or other professional occupations. If the two boys who are at present
science undergraduates at Aston University (in Birmingham)
complete their courses, they at least stand a good chance
of achieving their ambitions. Judging by their present
jobs, it is unlikely that any of the others will do so.
As with their West Indian contemporaries, many had faced
serious difficulties in finding work of any kind and often
had to settle for second, or even third, best. Of course,
in a tight job situation many white youths would also face
similar problems. On the other hand, it is clear from our
interviews that most of these black youths had had to go
it alone in trying to find work, and that when faced with
white personnel staff many (realistically) assessed their
chances of employment as slim.

For those in work at the time of interview, many in
what were regarded as totally unsuitable jobs, the chances
of self-improvement appear slim. As we have already
noted, UK unemployment in the foreseeable future is unlikely to drop much below the 1½ million mark. This makes
job changing more difficult. Of those who had changed
their job since leaving school most were either unemployed
when interviewed [49] or had not moved to anything significantly better. In the absence of positive assistance
from the local careers service or Labour Exchange, many
had drifted into the same types of job as their parents.
For example, one West Indian boy working as a labourer described his job as 'dirty and hard. It really kills you.
It's hot and greasy.' A large number found themselves in
dead-end jobs and resented the fact. We recall the views
of the IWA President who said that children of Asian immigrants would not be willing to suffer the same jobs as
their parents. Many clearly are not, and, what is more
significant, the roots of the 'cycle of deprivation' which
is now threatening to encircle them are becoming exposed.
In describing their position in work and in British society as a whole, a few actually used the word 'exploited'. Many more clearly felt the same, whilst not verbal-
ising their feelings in such explicit terms.

Outside the work situation many had radically different
views from their parents on the climate of race relations:
76 per cent of the West Indian and 44 per cent of the
Asian children admitted that there were at least 'some
problems' leading to disharmony. When the parents of the
same children were interviewed some six months or so previously the corresponding figures had been 40 per cent and
20 per cent respectively. It is unlikely that the time
lag between the two interviews would markedly effect

answers to this question. A much more plausible reason
would be a greater sensitivity to these problems on the
part of children who have grown up alongside their local
white contemporaries. They realised that these problems
would have to be faced through the coming years. Some
seemed to feel that the older generation of immigrants
had largely withdrawn from the battle to gain equal citizenship rights. Most conveyed the impression of a group
living under siege conditions, under attack from politicians (such as Enoch Powell), the police and white society
in general.

An internalisation of activities such as 'Paki-bashing'
has led to other feelings of insecurity among Asians,
feelings expressed clearly by one boy who argued that
'whites mock Asians'. The apparent timidity of Asians has
sometimes, in a violent environment, led to inter-racial
conflict within immigrant groups. Thus, West Indians
have, on occasions, sought and won the respect of white
youth by their display of brute force in exposing the alleged physical weakness of Asians. It was this type of
activity which led one girl in particular to argue that
'West Indians are uncivilised'. These threats to both
their ethnic identity and their physical prowess have had
the effect of reinforcing the views of many leading figures in the Asian communities: views which, at least
implicitly, define the West Indians as intellectually inferior. As noted earlier, discussions with IWA officials
confirmed this theory. Ironically, of course, this undermines their own stated objective, i.e., the unification of
the working class. The theoretical significance of our
findings, then, lies in the implicit fragmentation of the
sub-proletariat: a mirror image, in symbolic terms at
least, of the parallel phenomenon among the native working
class.

It might be objected here that we are omitting to discuss the youths who did not see signs of racial conflict
in Handsworth. These, like the older generation, tended
to look upon the issue in relation to their own experiences. Lack of personal conflict was perceived to be evidence of a general phenomenon. The main point to be
stressed here is that the children who took this view were
rather few in number; less than 30 per cent of the whole
sample. Furthermore, we must bear in mind that we are
dealing here with youths who are still living at home with
their parent(s). We have accordingly excluded by definition those who, for example, have totally rejected the
world of the first-generation immigrant; in particular
those variously dismissed as immune to the pressures of
'socialisation', e.g., 'militants', 'troublemakers', etc.

The 'conservative face' of some might also reflect the fact of being interviewed by white researchers. Certainly an attempt to win the approval of their interviewer is consistent with the presentation, by some, of the classic integrationist perspective. Hence the views of one West Indian girl, who disassociated herself from some of her male compatriots:

'They are too strong-headed ... the kids who wear hats with stripes - they're living in the past, back in slavery - they're stupid. They all want to stick together.'

Having said this, she realised that she was wrongly criticising her own people and qualified her statement before returning to reflect on the white 'stereotype' of the Rasta: [50]

'I don't know how to explain it - there's nothing wrong with that but I don't like the way they carry themselves. They look dirty with their trousers half-way up their legs.'

Similarly, among the Asians, there were a few who criticised their own community on the grounds of their insularity. For example, there were the Asian boys who made the following remarks:

'Asians stick together too much. English people have left the area.'

'Cohesiveness of Indian culture is a bad thing - especially arranged marriages.'

The radical difference between the ethnic groups in terms of open conflict with the police is reflected in one of the most interesting findings of the youth study. Whereas 64 per cent of the Asian youths said that the police treated black people fairly, only 24 per cent of the West Indians gave a similar response. The views of the two groups are more interesting still if we consider simultaneously their views on the recruitment of black policemen and policewomen. West Indians were, on the whole, much less enthusiastic about this suggestion. Those who were opposed tended to take the view that such people would be 'traitors' to their own kind. To them, 'the police' represented their white oppressors irrespective of their race, colour or creed. Those recruited would become 'white' blacks, imbued with the ideology of their white colleagues.

'If they join, they will act like their white comrades act. I've seen black police kicking black girls. They get brainwashed.'

This statement by a West Indian girl gives some impression of the strength of feeling generated by this question.

A little over a half of the West Indians did, however, think that the suggestion was a good one, largely on the grounds that police harassment would decrease. For example:

'A coloured cop would be there to make sure the white cop doesn't treat black people rough - we'd respect the police a bit more.'

'There wouldn't be so much unfair treatment and prejudice against black people.'

The belief in the high frequency, even commonplace nature, of police violence against blacks was widespread among these and other West Indians we interviewed. Some put these feelings more strongly: 'They (the police) are hooligans. They are like vandals walking the streets.' Thus the commonsense terms defining deviant types are employed in a reflexive manner to apply to the police themselves.

The Asian youths we interviewed tended to see 'police/black' relations as essentially 'police/West Indian' relations. Hence, one of the overwhelming majority who approved of immigrant policemen and policewomen said that 'West Indians would take more notice of black police'. Significantly the remainder thought that Asian police would be a good idea because they would be useful in a largely pragmatic sense. For example: 'They would help communicate with Asian families who can't speak English', and 'A coloured policeman would help with communications.' Interestingly, only a few Asians questioned the authority of the police to behave as they did at present.

Both ethnic groups were extremely unhappy about the present state of race relations in Britain as a whole. In fact, only 30 per cent felt that matters were actually improving. Economic pressure, cultural differences, white racism: all were seen as contributing to a radical worsening in relations. Furthermore, almost a half of the sample felt that black people ought to organise to protect themselves if attacked, and many clearly felt this to be a distinct possibility. One Asian boy pointed out that a vigilante group of his fellow countrymen had, indeed, already been formed.

Despite these ominous factors, a large number of Asians saw their future being spent in Handsworth. Family and cultural ties, together with an understandable measure of apprehension and fear, all seemed to contribute towards this. Altogether half of the Asian children, compared with approximately four out of five of their parents, said that they had no intention of moving out of the area. Included in this number were some who felt that the time

had come for there to be a much greater degree of social
mixing between black and white communities. Significantly, none went so far as to suggest that a greater degree
of inter-marriage might be a good thing for race relations. [51]

Whether these changes will come to pass, and if so how
quickly, is as yet uncertain. It is undoubtedly the case
that stated opinions alone present insufficient evidence
to answer a question of this nature. However, when one
finds that a sizeable minority of both groups had no
friends from a different ethnic background than him/her-
self, 'integration' in any form, pluralist or otherwise,
appears unlikely. Furthermore, when groups such as the
Rastafarians and the Pan-Africans are growing in strength,
as more and more West Indian youths search for a meaningful identity in a hostile and oppressive society, and when
Asians consider forming vigilante groups to protect themselves from whites and West Indians alike, we can expect
at best a 'cold war' situation - at worst outright and
worsening inter-racial violence.

The future of those who are still in our secondary
schools does not look particularly encouraging. As has
been argued consistently throughout this book, much will
depend on the degree of access which blacks achieve in
relation to crucial commodities such as housing and employment. But what do they and their parents expect of
the future? To assess this we asked a whole battery of
questions of those in the main sample who had children of
school age. These related largely to their eldest boy and
girl at school.

Perhaps the major point to emerge was the value which
parents, irrespective of ethnic group, placed on the con-
tinuation of education after secondary school. Approximately two-thirds of West Indian parents, and as many as
85 per cent of Asians, hoped that their eldest son would
continue his education after school. Although parents
often said that it was largely up to him to decide on a
career, it was clear from the remainder that the jobs they
had in mind were usually considerably more prestigious
than their own. Many Asians clearly hoped that their sons
would enter the professions, and amongst these Indian
fathers seemed especially to favour the medical profession. It is likely that this latter group were acutely
aware that here was an occupation which had already admitted many of their countrymen and therefore could be seen
as a realistic aspiration. Assuming that at least some of
their children achieve the ambition set for them, we may
well see as a consequence little radical transformation in
the broad job distribution of this group.

West Indian parents tended to set their sights rather
lower, perhaps reflecting the role which their generation
had played in the labour market. The main emphasis,
therefore, was placed on the importance of their sons
acquiring good, steady well-paid jobs. With both groups
there appeared to be little major disagreement between
parents and their children on this issue. [52]

Continuing education was also seen to be important for
their eldest daughters, but much more so in the case of
West Indians. As some of the Asian girls in our youth
study had told us, they were not expected, by custom, to
work. Economic pressures have undoubtedly played an important part in transforming attitudes, so much so that
even among Asians, three out of every five parents hoped
that their daughter would continue her education after
school. This was invariably seen as a prerequisite for
finding a rewarding career. What was striking about the
choice of careers given by both sets of immigrant parents
was that, with a few (minor) exceptions, they were all
white-collar jobs. Few, however, saw their girls in prestigious professional occupations. Most hoped that they
would slot into the 'traditional' sectors of the female
labour market; i.e., that they would find jobs as
teachers, nurses, office workers, bank clerks, etc. Among
West Indians the nursing profession was chosen, largely
one suspects because it was seen as a feasible proposition
for black girls; and indeed there was some evidence of
mothers hoping that their daughters would follow in their
footsteps in this respect.

Once again the aspirations of the children themselves
were seen as largely conforming to their parents' wishes.
There was one major exception. Out of 132 West Indian
girls who were said to have made up their minds on a
career, 64, i.e., almost a half were said by their parents
to want to become nurses. However, in only 26 of these
cases did their parents positively agree with this choice
of career. Often these mothers were nurses themselves, as
was suggested above. The interesting thing here is that
in so far as it is meaningful to talk about a female
ethnic job market, certain of the existing parameters are
seemingly being reinforced by the children themselves as
much as by their parents. This is made even more significant if we bear in mind the finding of our youth survey
which suggested that black children largely relied on
their own resources in deciding on a career and finding
work, rather than, say, using the job market institutions
such as the Careers Service, and Labour Exchange. It may
well be that black girls often limit their job horizons in
order to conform to their perceptions of the present immigrant job market.

During the coming decades the destiny of these young black citizens will be determined. In the process they will undoubtedly face many of the structural constraints which have been discussed throughout this book. In political terms, much will depend on the success of policy-makers in tackling overt racialism rather than simply defusing situations of actual or potential racial conflict. Those of us who are firmly committed to the cause of racial equality, not just in Britain, but world-wide, will hope that the often gloomy predictions which this book has made of life in the remaining decades of this century are proved utterly false.

Appendix 1 Research methodology

It is conventional at this point in a book devoted to an analysis of a particular piece of sociological research, to say something about the way in which the empirical work was done. There are good reasons for this. How else, after all, could the outsider obtain a glimpse of the data collection process and thereby come to his own (necessarily somewhat tentative) conclusions as to the degree of creditability to place on the research findings? The case for such a discussion in the present context might, however, seem rather less evident since Rex and Tomlinson (1979) have already outlined the major features of the research design in their own work (see Rex and Tomlinson, 1979, pp.321-6).

Despite this, there are a number of reasons why we believe a discussion of research methodology is an essential ingredient in this account. For one thing, our analysis of the state of race relations in Handsworth is much more heavily dependent on the survey element of the study (and necessarily so, given the author's brief), than was the account presented by Rex and Tomlinson. We need, therefore, to devote rather more time to a justification of the use of such an approach in the context of race relations research.

Second, we have adopted a rather unusual style of data presentation. Researchers conventionally publish weighted or unweighted figures, but not both. We need to discuss why such an apparently cumbersome form of analysis was considered desirable.

Finally, there are numerous points in the book where essentially methodological points were raised. For the sake of clarity, we tended to devote little space to each of them as they arose. We noted, for example, the problem of acquiescence among first-generation Asians and the general implications of confining the main sample to

first-generation immigrant householders in the inner city.
Clearly, however, a coherent overview is essential since
only by approaching the discussion in this holistic
fashion can we appraise the final worth of the research.

Each of these problems will be tackled in turn, but
first of all we must ask why it was that the research took
the form it did. This involved principally the question:
'why a survey?'.

WHY A SURVEY?

It would be thoroughly misleading, of course, to suggest
that the research team saw the ultimate goal solely, or
even principally, in terms of a single end product;
namely, 'the survey analysis'. Although, to the outsider,
the feverish activity and bureaucratic endeavour involved
in coding and checking a mountain of questionnaires seems
an all-consuming activity this was only one component of
the wider research enterprise. As Rex and Tomlinson
(1979, p.322) correctly point out, a large number of informal interviews and discussions were held prior to,
during, and after the main survey in 1976. These involved
local government officers, teachers, social workers,
police, local politicians, community activists of all
kinds, representatives of official agencies such as the
CRC, RRB, and members of local religious bodies. The educational component of the research was often tackled using
more explicitly ethnographic techniques.

Many of the substantive and theoretical ideas which
emerged during the initial phases of fieldwork in 1974 and
1975 helped to give the research a clearer focus and guide
the formal questionnaire through its lengthy period of development (see Appendix 2 for the final version). Given
that the early stages of the work were so productive, one
could legitimately ask why it was deemed necessary to
invest a massive amount of time, money and effort in a
large-scale survey. Was it the case as with some researchers, for example Willmott (1966; see especially his
Introduction), that we were implicitly 'pressurised' to
produce something which was more 'scientifically' acceptable? The answer quite simply is 'No'. Willmott, re-
searching in the late 1950s and early 1960s, found himself
surrounded by the proponents of the then dominant research
paradigm in British sociology, i.e., survey research. His
'observational' work was apparently deemed to be 'interesting' but lacking in 'hard facts' (to use his term). We
had no such problems. If anything, the mood of British
sociologists in the 1970s had turned in favour of the more
ethnographic approach.

Why did we do it, then? The answer essentially rests, as it always should, on the nature of the research problem being tackled. We needed more than what Becker has described as 'quasi-statistics'. (See his paper on Problems of Inference and Proof in Participant Observation, first published in 'American Sociological Review', 23: pp. 652-60 and reprinted in Filstead (1970).) In studying the success (or failure) of British blacks in gaining equality of treatment in important spheres of life such as education, employment and housing we wanted to quantify distinctions between the various ethnic groups. This desire to quantify combined with restrictions on time almost inevitably ruled out ethnographic field research.

To be successful the study of a community in situ requires a major investment of the researcher's time (and requires a certain open-endedness on this issue). Gaining effective access to a particular social group requires in effect (in terms of prior planning) an unknowable commitment. Furthermore, the political tension between the various community groups is such that access to one would almost certainly preclude access to others. A major team of sociologists, rather than simply trained interviewers, would therefore have been required to perform an effective ethnographic study. Our aim was to maintain a certain measure of detachment from the various interest groups whilst communicating effectively with individual householders. By achieving the latter (as noted above) we hoped to estimate the volume of disquiet about racial tensions, the frequency of discriminatory treatment, the relative distributions of work roles, statuses and so on, in addition to gaining a set of qualitative 'collages' of local Handsworth residents.

SAMPLING CONSIDERATIONS

Having decided that a formal sample survey would constitute the central source of data on individual households, we were faced with the usual barrage of questions. Many, predictably, are highly inter-related but for ease of presentation we shall attempt to delineate the major issues.

First, there is the question of defining the survey area. The stated aim of the research was to examine the black experience in a major British city, something which would appear to entail the coverage of a city (in our case Birmingham) in toto. To have attempted this, however, would have been to stretch our resources beyond their limits. We might ask, in any case, whether such an exercise was necessary, even if feasible. As pointed out early in the book, black immigrants tend to be found in particular parts of the city. It would, therefore, seem sensible to concentrate one's resources on such an area (or areas) and use other data to explain why it was that the given spatial patterns exist.

In the light of these considerations, we chose for our study the area popularly known as Handsworth. This would enable us to study one densely populated multi-racial and poly-ethnic area in depth. Using figures from the (admittedly slightly out of date) 1971 Census, we drew our survey area boundary on the basis of the 128 enumeration districts with the highest proportions of New Commonwealth residents. The implications for the research were therefore clear. We would be focusing on the experience of black and white citizens in an inner-city (or strictly middle-ring) context. We would be able to say little, for example, about those who had managed to escape such a fate. On the other hand, as pointed out in the text, the vast majority of blacks, not just in Birmingham but in Britain as a whole, had already been located in the inner-city zones. Because of this, our research would, we hoped, reflect the experiences of the 'average' immigrant, and the reactions of the indigenous population to his presence.

Having defined the survey area, we then had to decide on whether the focus of our fieldwork would be the household or simply the householder, and whether first-generation immigrants, rather than, say, first plus second and third generation would be interviewed. In the event, we felt that the best strategy would be to concentrate on first-generation householders for the immigrant component of the sample. Information about an individual's family was therefore collected through a third party, i.e., the head of household. To have interviewed every member of a household would have presented intractable practical problems, principally the need for interpreters, for more than one basic questionnaire and for more resources in terms of time and money. Analytical problems would also have presented the research team with an unenviable task.

Given the complexities of any study of race relations, it was felt that we should follow the most straightforward approach. We could, and did, complement the main study with a series of interviews with a small number (50) of second-generation immigrants (as was reported in Chapter 6, and, in more detail, by Rex and Tomlinson, 1979). But the latter were chosen (using systematic random sampling) from the sampling frame composed of boys and girls aged 16 to 21 who were living within households whose head had al-

ready been interviewed. This and the points raised earlier inevitably had important implications for the research
which should perhaps be spelt out at this point.

Since we concentrated on one particular middle-ring
area, a number of issues are raised. As noted earlier, it
means that we have automatically excluded blacks who have
moved away from (or never lived in) such an area. Importantly also, we are comparing their experiences with
what, in some ways, was a rather unusual 'control group':
a group of mainly ageing white residents. (The implications of this perhaps do not need to be restated here as
they have often been raised explicitly and implicitly in
the text.) A further, and inevitable, problem is that we
could only speak to those who were willing to be interviewed by our (mainly white) fieldwork team (see the
section on interviewing below). Thus, in technical terms,
we have a confounding of methodological and substantive
issues. We have an additional problem in the case of the
second-generation blacks. As noted in the previous paragraph, we spoke only to those who were still living with
their families. This clearly means that those who had
left home for whatever reason (conflict with parents,
marriage, work, and so on) were excluded. What I have
attempted to do in this book is to fill some of these gaps
by using empirical and other material from as many additional sources as possible. (These included official
statistical material, research reports, observational data
and, of course, the unstructured interviews mentioned earlier in this Appendix.)

SAMPLE DESIGN

The main sample was, then, to be based on the first-generation immigrant and indigenous householders in the 128
enumeration districts in 'Handsworth'. This seemed satis-
factory in most respects, with one notable exception. The
area as defined contained few council properties and none
which were purpose-built. As this would have left a
massive gap in the analysis of immigrant housing it was
decided to add the Newtown council estate to the survey
area. (It was, in any case, contiguous to it.) As the
method of sample selection in these two sectors was quite
different, however, we now discuss them separately.

(i)   The main sample (excluding Newtown)

The principal comparisons we wished to make in the analysis related to three major ethnic groups: West Indians, Asians and British (indigenous whites).   It was immediately clear, however, that one cannot talk sensibly about, for example, 'Asians' as a single homogeneous body of people in terms of, say, religious and cultural traditions.   This meant that we needed a sample size which was large enough for comparisons to be made between the various distinct sub-groups.   We therefore decided to aim for the maximum practical sample size: 300 from each of the major ethnic groups.

We now reached a critical stage.   How exactly were the 900 householders to be chosen?   Clearly, given the aims stated earlier (namely, the desire to quantify certain features of our sample), some form of random sampling would be highly desirable.   In fact, even if we had not wished to analyse the data in such a form an 'objective' selection procedure would have been theoretically necessary.   The problem is, however, that there was no sampling frame which would enable one to identify an individual's birthplace.   To achieve a random selection of people on this basis would have therefore required some form of post-stratification (see Moser and Kalton, 1971).   We would have needed to select householders from, say, the register of electors and then (at the fieldwork stage) correct for the inevitable imbalance between the different ethnic groups by a process of random deletion.   Desirable though this procedure might have been, we simply did not have the time nor the resources to perform a study on this basis.

The only option effectively open to us was a form of quota sample.   For each of the major ethnic groups we produced a sample stratified by enumeration districts (e.d.) using proportionate (non-random) selection of householders within these districts.   In other words, once the overall proportion of, say, Asian households was determined (by dividing 300 by the estimated number of Asian households in the survey area as a whole) this proportion was applied uniformly across e.d.s to determine stratum sample sizes.   (Given the stability or 'robustness' of stratum sample size, it is highly unlikely that estimation errors had a significant effect on the distribution of households between e.d.s.)   This has the practical effect of simplifying the analysis in that re-weighting is unnecessary.

The major problem with the quota sample, of course, is that, despite the valuable contribution of Stephen and McCarthy (1958), sampling errors cannot theoretically be estimated. This means, in layman's terms, that we have no idea about the likely representativeness of our final sample. It does appear, however, on the basis of the few external data checks which are available, that the more obvious types of bias are absent. Our careful briefing of interviewers seems to have shown positive results in this respect. Overall, then, we are confident that, despite having been forced to rule out the use of random sampling, our final sample represents a broad cross-section of Handsworth residents.

(ii)   The Newtown council estate sample

As noted above, it was seen by the research team as essential to include a group of council tenants in our final sample. The Birmingham Corporation Housing Department came to our assistance here by providing us with a list of 200 tenants on the Newtown estate: 100 British (i.e., white) tenants, 95 West Indians, and 5 Asians. Two points arise directly from this. First, it is rather unclear exactly how this list was compiled; though it is likely that purposive rather than random selection methods were used. (One possible outcome of this might have been the selection of relatively docile rather than hostile residents. Our results suggest that this is unlikely.) Second, although the small number of Asians reflects fairly accurately the lack of penetration of the group in the public sector, West Indians are greatly over-represented vis-à-vis white tenants. (At most one in eight tenants on the estate is black.) So long as comparisons are between white and black Newtown residents, this over-representation is not of major significance. Where this and the selection problem become critical is when one attempts to produce a hybrid sample by combining this group of 200 council tenants with the 900 in the main sample. There are essentially three ways of dealing with this problem:

1 Separate presentation of data: Throughout the book we could have presented the data from the two samples separately. The problem with this 'solution' is that it would inevitably have led to an extremely large and cumbersome set of tables which would have been both difficult and tedious to interpret. Rather more importantly, it would have given undue prominence throughout the analysis to one variable, i.e., housing tenure.

The corollary of this would seem to be a policy of ignoring the council sample except when housing was being discussed (and then presenting the material separately).

If we had done this, we would effectively have been throwing away the best part of 200 interview schedules, an appalling waste of money and effort.

2 Ignore the problem: One way out of this impasse is to treat the samples as if they had been drawn in exactly the same fashion and simply combine the results. This was the 'solution' adopted by Rex and Tomlinson (1979). They clearly acknowledge their assumptions and state quite correctly that in most cases the data from the two samples viewed as a whole are not of a markedly different nature.

3 Re-weight and combine into one composite sample: A rather more sophisticated solution to the two-sample problem is to use re-weighting. This essentially involves a comparison between the number of households actually studied in particular e.d.s on the Newtown estate and the number who would have been studied if we had adopted the same sampling scheme as in the main sample. Expressed simply this means that if we had interviewed 4 householders in e.d.A, say, where we 'should' only have interviewed 2, a weighting factor of $\frac{1}{2}$ was applied to the data for that e.d. The data transformation facility in SPSS (Statistical Packages for the Social Sciences) proved extremely useful in this respect.

The question, now, is this. Are we justified in presenting the data solely in their re-weighted form? The answer is far from clear cut. Had both samples involved random sampling we would have clearly said 'yes'. Unfortunately, in this case we have two non-random samples whose mode of selection was of an entirely different nature.

The solution adopted in this book, then, has been to present both weighted and unweighted figures. We feel that this apparently cumbersome procedure is justified by the uncertainties involved.

THE INTERVIEW IN RACE RELATIONS RESEARCH

The problems of formal interviewing in sociological research are well documented elsewhere (see, for example, Hyman, 1954; Cicourel, 1964; and Phillips, 1971). It would consequently be rather tedious to raise the points again here. On the other hand, there is one issue which was noted throughout the book as being in some sense a problem.

We have argued that many first-generation Asians appeared somewhat reluctant to indulge in critical reflections on their life in Britain. To say they were 'reluctant', however, implies that 'in reality' their views were not as expressed. We must ask ourselves, therefore, whether we as researchers are imposing our own value system on the data by casting doubt on the evidence as it stands. At least one reviewer of Rex and Tomlinson's book accused the authors of wishing to do just that. Although writing largely in ignorance of the book's contents, the 'Daily Telegraph's columnist nevertheless indulged in a general criticism of sociologists in that they were inclined to sow the seeds of unrest amongst people who were perfectly contented with their lot.

To answer this criticism and the general principle itself, we need to look first of all at how the fieldwork was undertaken. It was clear from the outset that the research team itself could not cope with the number of interviews involved. Tenders were invited, and NOP Ltd were contracted to provide the fieldwork team. As Rex and Tomlinson point out (1979, p.325) the use of ethnically matched interviewers was rejected, with the exception of 105 Asians who were interviewed by fellow Asians. We have to bear in mind, therefore, that the vast majority of interviews were conducted by NOP's standard source of employee: middle-aged white women.

Bearing this in mind, we now look at the researcher's perspective. Central here are the theories which he/she brings to a study of race relations. Almost inevitably these will entail the belief that institutionalised racism is a 'fact of life' for the black man or woman in Britain today. It would perhaps not be surprising to find that even if this is subjectively meaningful to the actor involved, it would not be communicated to a stranger and particularly to a white stranger who may be seen as representing the source of his oppression. This would not explain, however, (a) why West Indians in objectively similar circumstances to Asians tended to be much more forthright in their responses, or (b) why the pattern of Asian responses differed little when the workloads of Asian and British interviewers were compared. (Further discussion of this issue will be found in a future publication by the present author.)

What makes the form of analysis in this book rather different from most which are ostensibly similar is that interviews are always seen as total entities. This de-emphasis of isolated 'face-sheet variables' has given us a clue to the queries of the previous paragraph. It appears that among all minority groups there were a sizeable number who saw themselves as permanent British citizens and did their best to ignore 'the race issue' in their everyday lives. Point (a) above seems to be best explained by a much higher level of interaction with the

white community and a greater identification with Britain
and certain aspects of British culture. Racism undermines
such an orientation. Given the strength and cohesiveness
of the primary community among Asians, the lack of interaction between many first-generation Asians and local
whites, the strength of their traditional culture (and
corresponding lack of identification with indigenous cultural norms), point (b) is fairly easily explicable. Certainly these factors help to explain the slight unease
often felt by Asians and interviewers alike in the face-
to-face situation. The Asian interviewer (as well as his
white counterpart) is very much an outsider and as such
regarded with a measure of suspicion.

In conclusion, then, we must assess the data first in
the light of the interview situation itself (as argued by
Phillips, 1971) and, second, against the prevailing social
and political climate.

As we have now seen, the research reported in this book
is particularly intriguing in that the issues were very
closely intertwined. Whilst no researcher can rid himself
of his values, beliefs and attitudes, he can, by subtle
handling of his subject in both fieldwork and analysis,
avoid the most obvious pitfalls. Much consideration in
the present context, for example, was given to the construction of a questionnaire which did not suggest to a
respondent that 'race' was the principal focus of the
study (hence the title of the document) (see Appendix 2).
It is for the reader to judge by examining the questionnaire in conjunction with the substantive analysis in the
text, whether or not we have achieved a credible reflection of the experience of Handsworth residents.

Appendix 2 The interview schedule

NOP/9263   Serial No. _____
                                              (1 - 4)

BIRMINGHAM HOUSEHOLD SURVEY

NAME: _____

ADDRESS: _____
_____

ENUMERATION DISTRICT NUMBER: ┌──┬──┬──┐
                                                └──┴──┴──┘
                                                (5) (6) (7)

Good morning/afternoon/evening.
I am from NOP Market Research Limited and we are conducting a survey in this
area. I am interviewing a cross-section of people of different nationalities
who live around here asking their likes and dislikes about this area, their
housing and the jobs they do.

1. ESTABLISH COUNTRY OF BIRTH OF HEAD OF HOUSEHOLD

2. IF HEAD OF HOUSEHOLD FITS YOUR QUOTA CARRY OUT THE INTERVIEW

3. IF HEAD OF HOUSEHOLD DOES NOT FIT QUOTA ENQUIRE ABOUT ANY OTHER
    HOUSEHOLDS THAT MAY SHARE THE BUILDING.

HEAD OF HOUSEHOLDS COUNTRY OF BIRTH
                                                 (8)
             West Indies ------------------ 1   IF IN QUOTA
             Indian sub-continent --------   2   GO TO
             Other 'Asian' ---------------   3   LOCAL AREA
             Great Britain ---------------   4   SECTION
             Elsewhere -------------------   N   DO NOT INTERVIEW   (9)①

CHECKING RECORD			INTERVIEWER No. _____
	INITIAL	DATE	(10 - 13)
INTERVIEWER			LENGTH OF
ACCOMPANY/ SUPERVISE			INTERVIEW: ┌──┬──┬──┐ mins.
EDIT			(14 - 16)
CODING			DATE: Day Month
OTHER			(17)(18) (19)(20)

SIGNATURE: ....

SUMMARY OF INTERVIEW - PROBLEMS - NOTES

LOCAL AREA SECTION
ASK ALL

Firstly, I would like to ask you some general questions about this local area.

Q.1 In general, would you say you like or dislike living in this area of Birmingham?

```
                                    Like ------------------------------------- 1
                                    Neither like nor dislike ----------------- 2
                                    Dislike ---------------------------------- 3
                                    Don't know ------------------------------- 4    (21)
```

Q.2 What are the things you like most about living in this area? (WRITE IN)

_____   (22)

PROBE: What else? _____   (23)

_____   (24)

IF MORE THAN ONE THING MENTIONED AT Q.2. ASK Q.3.   OTHERS GO TO Q.4.

Q.3 And what would you say is the <u>one</u> thing you most like about living in this area? (WRITE IN)

_____   (25)

_____   (26)

ALL
Q.4 What are the main things you do not like about living in this area? (WRITE IN)

_____   (27)

_____   (28)

PROBE: What else? _____   (29)

IF MORE THAN ONE THING MENTIONED AT Q.4. ASK Q.5.   OTHERS GO TO Q.6.

Q.5 And what would you say is the <u>one</u> thing you most dislike about living in this area? WRITE IN

_____   (30)

_____   (31)

ASK ALL

Q.6 If you wanted to complain or get something done about a local problem who would you go to?
DO NOT PROMPT   RECORD BELOW

	1st mention (32)	2nd mention (33)	3rd mention (34)
Local Councillor	1	1	1
Local Authority (Council)	2	2	2
Local M.P.	3	3	3
Local Community Group	4	4	4
Local Newspaper or Radio	5	5	5
Church Minister/Priest	6	6	6
Friend/Relative	7	7	7
Citizens Advice Bureau	8	8	8
Other (WRITE IN AND RING)	9	9	9

```
_____

_____
```
(32 - 34)

```
Don't know ----------------------------------------- 0
```

Q.7 How would you rate this area for ..... a) shopping facilities .... would you say it is
very good, good, bad or very bad for shopping facilities? RECORD BELOW. REPEAT FOR ITEMS B-E.

	Very good	Good	Bad	Very bad	Don't know	
a) Shopping facilities	1	2	3	4	5	(35)
b) Public Transport Services	1	2	3	4	5	(36)
c) Quietness	1	2	3	4	5	(37)
d) Schools	1	2	3	4	5	(38)
e) Safety from violence	1	2	3	4	5	(39)

3.

Q.8 How long have you lived in the Birmingham area? RECORD BELOW
Q.9 and how long have you lived at this address?

	Q.8 (40)	Q.9 (41)	
Less than one year ----------------------	1	1	
One year but less than 2 years ----------	2	2	ASK Q.10
2 years but less than 3 years -----------	3	3	
3 years but less than 5 years -----------	4	4	
5 years but less than 7 years -----------	5	5	GO TO Q.11
7 years but less than 10 years ----------	6	6	
10 years but less than 15 years ---------	7	7	GO TO
15 years but less than 20 years ---------	8	8	Q.22 ON
20 years or more ------------------------	9	9	PAGE 4
Don't know/Can't remember ---------------	0	0	

(40/41)

Q.10 How many times have you moved house in the last five years? (Not counting moves outside U.K. or temporary moves)

Once -------------------------- 1
Twice ------------------------- 2
Three times ------------------- 3
Four times -------------------- 4
Five or more times ------------ 5
Don't know/Can't remember ----- 6

(42)

Q.11 What was your last address? (WRITE IN DETAILS AND CODE BELOW)   (45)

(43)
(44)

TOWN/CITY/COUNTY _____

IF BIRMINGHAM - DISTRICT _____

Birmingham -------- 1   ASK Q.12
U.K. but not Birmingham -------- 2
Outside U.K. ------ 3   GO TO Q.22

(45)

IF LAST ADDRESS WAS NOT IN U.K. GO TO Q.22 ON PAGE 4

Q.12 How long did you live there?

Less than one year ------------------------ 1
One year but less than 2 years ----------- 2
2 years but less than 3 years ----------- 3
3 years but less than 5 years ----------- 4
5 years but less than 7 years ----------- 5
7 years but less than 10 years ----------- 6
10 years but less than 15 years ----------- 7
15 years but less than 20 years ----------- 8
20 years or more -------------------------- 9
Don't know/Can't remember ----------------- 0

(46)

Q.13 Did you personally own it or rent it or was there some other arrangement? PROMPT IF NECESSARY

Owned/was buying --------------------- 1
Rented - furnished from relative ---- 2
Rented - furnished from other ------- 3   ASK Q.14
Rented - unfurnished from relative -- 4
Rented - unfurnished from other ----- 5
Rented - Council -------------------- 6
Lived with parents ------------------ 7   GO TO Q.20
Other (Write in and ring) ----------- 8   ASK Q.14

(47)

Q.14 What sort of accommodation did you have at your last address? PROMPT IF NECESSARY EMPHASISE LAST ADDRESS

Whole house detached ------------------------ 1
Whole house semi-detached ------------------- 2
Whole house terraced ------------------------ 3
Purpose built flat/maisonette --------------- 4
Other flat/maisonette/rooms ----------------- 5
Dwelling with business premises ------------- 6
Other (Write in and ring) ------------------- 7

(48)

Q.15 Did all the people in your household now, live with you at your last address?

Yes --------------------------------- 1   GO TO Q.17
No ---------------------------------- 2   ASK Q.16

(49)

Q.16 Which members of your present household did not live with you at your previous address? WRITE IN DETAILS

(50)
(51)
(52)

Q.17 How many rooms did your household have there? PROBE: Bedrooms, living rooms, kitchen EXCLUDE lavatories, bathrooms, garages rooms used entirely for business purposes.

N.B. [9][9] = Don't know/Can't remember/Refused

(53)(54)
WRITE IN BOXES [ ][ ] rooms

(53/54)

4.

Q.18 Did you sub-let any of these rooms?

Yes ------------------- 1 ASK Q.19
No -------------------- 2 GO TO Q.20   (55)

Q.19 How many?   WRITE IN BOXES   (56) (57)

rooms   (56/57)

Q.20 Why did you move from your last house/flat?

	First mention (58)	Second mention (60)	Third mention (62)
Comments about house			
House to be demolished or condemned ----------------------	1	1	1
House in poor repair -------------------------------------	2	2	2
House in poor area ---------------------------------------	3	3	3
House too large --	4	4	4
House too small --	5	5	5
Wanted to buy (rent) i.e. change tenure ------------------	6	6	6
Comments on general dislikes about the previous area ---------	7	7	7

(58/63)

	(59)	(61)	(63)
Changes in circumstances			
Changed/new job --	1	1	1
Marriage ---	2	2	2
Wanted to live with relations ---------------------------	3	3	3
Wanted to live away from relations ----------------------	4	4	4
Wanted to be near friends/relations ---------------------	5	5	5
Other answers (Write in and ring) -----------------------	6		

_____._____   6

_____   6

Don't know --- 7

Q.21 When you last moved house, what decided you to come and live in this area rather than any other part of Birmingham? (WRITE IN)

_____   (64)
_____   (65)
_____   (66)
PROBE: What else? _____   (67)
_____   (68)
_____   (69)

ASK ALL

Q.22 Are you thinking about moving from this area?

Yes ------------------- 1 ASK Q.23
No -------------------- 2 GO TO EDUCATION
SECTION PAGE 5   (70)

Q.23 Have you done anything about moving?

	First mention (71)	Second mention (72)	Third mention (73)
Nothing -----------------------------------	1		
Put name on Council waiting list -------------	2	2	2
Applied for transfer ------------------------	3	3	3
Looked in newspapers ------------------------	4	4	4
Looked in estate agents ---------------------	5	5	5
Other (Please specify)	6		

(71/73)

_____   6

_____   6

Q.24 Why would you want to move from this area? WRITE IN

_____   (74)
_____   (75)
_____   (76)
_____   (77)

Q.25 Where would you like to move to?

(78)
In Birmingham (Write in & ring) _____ 1
Elsewhere in Midlands -- 2   (78)
Other answers (Write in & ring) _____ 3
No preference --- 4   (79)
Don't know -- 5   (80)

NOW GO TO EDUCATION SECTION ON PAGE 5

DUPLICATE COLS. 1-8
(9) (2)

EDUCATION SECTION

IF BORN IN G.B. ASK Q.1 OTHERS START AT Q.11

IF BORN IN G.B.

Q.1 What type of secondary school did you last attend full-time?

Maintained School
{ Grammar/Senior Secondary -------------------------------------- 1
{ Technical -- 2
{ Secondary Modern/Elementary/Junior Secondary --------------- 3
{ Comprehensive (include bilateral, multilateral ------------- 4

Direct grant -- 5
Independent --- 6
Special school -- 7
School outside U.K. --- 8
Other (Write in and ring) -------------------------------------- 9   (16)

Q.2 Did you attend any college or university as a full time student after leaving secondary school?
Yes --------------- 1 ASK Q.3
No ---------------- 2 GO TO Q.4   (17)

Q.3 What type of college did you last attend?

Technical/Commercial College/Central Institution ------------------- 1
College of Advanced Technology/Polytechnic ----------------------- 2
College or School of Art, Music, Drama --------------------------- 3
College of Education/Teacher Training College -------------------- 4
University --- 5
College/University outside U.K. ---------------------------------- 6
Other (Write in and ring) -- 7   (18)

Q.4 How old were you when you finished your full time education?
Under 15 years ------------------ 1
15 years ------------------------ 2
16 years ------------------------ 3
17 - 20 years ------------------- 4
Over 20 years ------------------- 5
Continuing/still student -------- 6   (19)

Q.5 SHOWCARD 1 Have you passed any examinations or gained any qualifications of the types listed on this card?
None of these ----------------------- 1   (20)
Yes - School qualifications ---- 1   (21)
Yes - Higher Education ---- ---- 1   (22)
Yes — Work qualifications - ---- 1   (23)

IF NONE OF THESE GO TO Q.7. OTHERS ASK Q.6

Q.6 Which qualifications do you have? WRITE IN DETAILS   (24)
_____   (25)
_____   (26)

Q.7 Looking back on your education (so far), are you satisfied or dissatisfied with the education you have received?
Satisfied ----------------------- 1
Dissatisfied -- ---- ---- -- 2
Don't know ---------------------- 3   (27)

Q.8 Why do you say that? WRITE IN _____   (28)
_____   (29)
_____   (30)
_____   (31)
PROBE: What else? _____   (32)
_____   (33)

Q.9 Are you, at present, enrolled on any education course, full time, part time or evening?
Yes ------------ 1 ASK Q.10
No ------------- 2 GO TO OCCUPATION
                   SECTION ON PAGE 8   (34)

Q.10 IF YES RECORD DETAILS BELOW
Full time ----------------------- 1   (35)
Part time ----------------------- 1   (36)
WRITE IN DETAILS OF COURSES
Evening ------------------------- 1   (37)
NAME OF INSTITUTION _____
NAME OF COURSE _____   (38)
DOES IT LEAD TO A QUALIFICATION? WHAT? _____
FULL TIME, PART TIME, OR EVENING _____   (39)

NOW GO TO OCCUPATION SECTION ON PAGE 8

IF NOT BORN IN G.B. ASK Q.11

6.

Q.11 Since coming to the U.K. have you been a **full-time** pupil or student at a school or college in the U.K.?

Yes ------------------- 1 ASK Q.12
No -------------------- 2 GO TO Q.21   (10)

Q.12 At what age did you begin your full-time education in the U.K.? WRITE IN BOXES

(11)(12)
[ ][ ] years   (11/12)

Q.13 and at what age did you finish your full-time education in the U.K.? WRITE IN BOXES

N.B. [O][O] = Still student

(13)(14)
[ ][ ] years   (13/14)

Q.14 What type of school or college did you last attend in the U.K.?

Maintained Grammar --------------------- 1
Other maintained ---------------------- 2
Direct Grant/Independent --------------- 3
Other secondary school ---------------- 4
College of Further Education/
   Technical College ------------------ 5
College of Education/Teacher Training -- 6
University ---------------------------- 7
Other (Write in and ring) ------------- 8   (15)

SKIP TO COL 20

Q.15 SHOW CARD 1 Have you passed any examinations or gained any qualifications of the types listed on this card?

None of these --------------------------- 1   (20)
Yes - School Qualifications ------------- 1   (21)
Yes - Higher Education ----------------- 1   (22)
Yes - Work Qualifications -------------- 1   (23)

IF NONE OF THESE GO TO Q.17 OTHERS ASK Q.16

Q.16 Which qualifications do you have? (WRITE IN)

_____   (24)
_____   (25)
_____   (26)

Q.17 Looking back on your education in the U.K. are you satisfied or dissatisfied with the education you received?

Satisfied ------------------------------ 1
Dissatisfied --------------------------- 2   (27)
Don't know ----------------------------- 3

Q.18 Why do you say that? WRITE IN

_____   (28)
                                            (29)
PROBE: What else? _____ (30)
_____   (31)
_____   (32)
                                            (33)

Q.19 Are you at present enrolled on any education courses, full time, part time, or evening?

Yes ---------------- 1 ASK Q.20
No ----------------- 2 GO TO OCCUPATION
                       SECTION PAGE 8   (34)

Q.20 IF YES RECORD DETAILS BELOW

Full time ----------------------------- 1   (35)
Part time ----------------------------- 1   (36)
Evening ------------------------------- 1   (37)

WRITE IN DETAILS OF COURSE

NAME OF INSTITUTION _____

NAME OF COURSE _____   (38)

DOES IT LEAD TO A QUALIFICATION? WHAT? ____   (39)
_____

FULL TIME, PART TIME, OR EVENING _____

NOW GO TO OCCUPATION SECTION PAGE 8

7.

IF NEVER BEEN IN FULL TIME EDUCATION IN U.K. ASK Q.21

Q.21 How many years of schooling did you have before coming to the U.K.?
WRITE IN BOXES

(11)(12) □□ years (11/ 12)

IF NONE GO TO Q.25

Q.22 At what age did you finish your full time education?
WRITE IN BOXES

(13)(14) □□ years (13/ 14)
SKIP TO COL 20

Q.23 During your time at school (or college) did you gain any qualifications?

Yes ----------------- 2 ASK Q.24
No ----------------- 1 GO TO Q.25   (20)

Q.24 IF YES WRITE IN DETAILS OF QUALIFICATIONS

_____

(21)
(22)
(23)

Q.25 Have you any work qualifications such as apprenticeships, professional qualifications, examinations or other work skills?

Yes ----------------- 1 ASK Q.26
No ----------------- 2 GO TO Q.27   (24)

Q.26 What work qualifications do you have? (WRITE IN)

_____

(25)

(26)
SKIP TO COL 34

Q.27 Are you at present enrolled on any education courses, full time, part time or evening?

Yes ----------------- 1 ASK Q.28
No ----------------- 2 GO TO OCCUPATION SECTION ON PAGE 8   (34)

Q.28 IF YES RECORD DETAILS BELOW

Full time ----------------------- 1 (35)
Part time ----------------------- 1 (36)
Evening ----------------------- 1 (37)

WRITE IN DETAILS OF COURSE

NAME OF INSTITUTION _____

NAME OF COURSE _____

(38)

DOES IT LEAD TO A QUALIFICATION? WHAT? _____

(39)

FULL TIME, PART TIME, OR EVENING _____

NOW GO TO OCCUPATION SECTION ON P. 8

8.

```
┌─────────────────────────────┐
│     OCCUPATION SECTION       │
├─────────────────────────────┤
│          ASK ALL             │
└─────────────────────────────┘
```

I would now like to ask you about your work.

Q.1 At present do you work full time, part time or are you not working?
IF WORKING ASK Q.2.   OTHERS GO TO Q.3.

Q.2 Are you self-employed or an employee?

Self employed full time (30+ hrs per week) ----------- 1	GO TO
Self employed part time (less than 30 hrs per week) --- 2	WORKING
Employee full time (30+ hrs per week) ---------------- 3	SECTION
Employee part time (less than 30 hrs per week) ------- 4	ON P. 9
Not working --- 5	ASK Q.3

(40)

Q.3 **IF NOT WORKING PROBE FOR DETAILS**

Are you ....

waiting to take up job already planned --------------- 1	GO TO
out of employment looking for work ------------------- 2	NOT
off work through temporary illness (less than	WORKING
6 months) -- 3	SECTION
off work through illness or disability (of more	ON
than six months) ---------------------------------- 4	PAGE 12
temporarily laid off --------------------------------- 5	
	GO TO
Retired male --- 6	RETIRED
	SECTION
	PAGE 13
Non-working housewife -------------------------------- 7	GO TO
Full-time student ------------------------------------ 8	NOT
Other (Write in and ring) ---------------------------- 9	WORKING
_____	SECTION
	ON
_____	PAGE 12
	GO TO
Never worked --- 0	CHILDREN
	SECTION
	PAGE 15

(41)

9.

```
┌─────────────────────────────────────────┐
│            WORKING SECTION               │
│   ASK ALL IN FULL TIME/PART TIME         │
│   EMPLOYMENT AND SELF EMPLOYED           │
└─────────────────────────────────────────┘
```

Q.1 What is your main job at present?   __WRITE IN FULLY__

OCCUPATION _____   (42)

INDUSTRY _____   (43)

NAME OF FIRM _____   (44)

ADDRESS OF PLACE OF EMPLOYMENT _____

IF MANAGER/SUPERINTENDENT OR SELF EMPLOYED

Number of employees in the establishment

25 or more -------------------------- 1	
1 - 24 ------------------------------ 2	
None -------------------------------- 3	(45)

IF NOT MANAGER ETC. CODE HERE ------------------------------ 4

Q.2 In your present job, how many hours did you work in the last week? (Including any over-time)

N.B. [9] [9] = Can't remember/D.K./Refused

(46)(47)

WRITE IN BOXES [ ][ ] hours   (46/47)

Q.3 Do you ever do shift work as part of this job?

Yes -------------------- 1	ASK Q.4	(48)
No --------------------- 2	GO TO Q.5	

Q.4 Do you do a permanent or an occasional night shift on this job?

No nightshift ------------------------- 1	
Occasional night-shift ---------------- 2	(49)
Permanent night-shift ----------------- 3	

Q.5 How do you normally travel to work? (MAIN METHOD ONLY)

Walk ---------------------------------- 1	
Bus ----------------------------------- 2	
Car - shared -------------------------- 3	
Car - alone --------------------------- 4	
Train --------------------------------- 5	
Works bus ----------------------------- 6	
Cycle --------------------------------- 7	
Motor cycle --------------------------- 8	
Work at home -------------------------- 9	(50)
Other (Write in and ring) ------------- 0	

Q.6 How long does it usually take you to get to work?

0 - 5 minutes ------------- 1		
6 - 15 minutes ------------ 2		
16 - 30 minutes ----------- 3	ASK	
31 - 45 minutes ----------- 4	Q.7	
Over 45 minutes ----------- 5		
No fixed time ------------- 6	GO TO Q.8	(51)
Work at home -------------- 7		

Q.7 And roughly how far is that?

Less than ½ mile --------------------- 1	
Over 1 mile but less than 2 miles ----- 2	
Over 2 miles but less than 3 miles ---- 3	
Over 3 miles but less than 5 miles ---- 4	
Over 5 miles but less than 10 miles --- 5	
Over 10 miles ------------------------- 6	(52)
Don't know ---------------------------- 7	

ALL WORKING

Q.8 On the whole, would you say you are satisfied or dissatisfied with your present job?

Satisfied ----------------------------- 1	
Dissatisfied -------------------------- 2	
Don't know ---------------------------- 3	(53)

Q.9 Is there anything you would say you particularly like about the job you are doing at the moment? WRITE IN _____

(54)
(55)
(56)
(57)

PROBE: What else? _____

_____

10.

Q.10 Is there anything which you particularly dislike about the job you are doing at the moment? (WRITE IN)

_____ (58)

PROBE: What else? _____ (59)
_____ (60)
_____ (61)

Q.11 Are you looking for another job at the moment?

IF YES

Yes ---------------------- 1 ASK Q.12
No ----------------------- 2 GO TO Q.13   (62)

Q.12 What is your main reason for looking for another job? ONE ANSWER ONLY

More money ---------------------------- 1
Moved house --------------------------- 2
More responsibility ------------------- 3
More interesting work ----------------- 4
Better work conditions ---------------- 5
Redundancy ---------------------------- 6
Illness ------------------------------- 7
Transport problems -------------------- 8
Racial problem (Write in) ------------- 9

Other answer (Write in) -------------- 0   (63)

Don't know --------------------------- x

Q.13 IF EMPLOYEE: How long have you been working with your present employer?

IF SELF-EMPLOYED: How long have you been self-employed in your present line of work?

Less than 6 months ------- 1
6 mths but less than 1 yr - 2 ASK Q.14
1 yr. but less than 2 yrs. 3
2 yrs but less than 5 yrs. 4 SELF EMPLOYED GO
5 years and over --------- 5 TO TRADE UNION
SECTION P.14
EMPLOYEES GO TO
PROMOTIONS
SECTION ON P.13   (64)

Q.14 In the last 2 years how many employers have you worked for as a full-time employee? Not counting your present job.

None --------------------- 0 GO TO Q.17
One ---------------------- 1
Two ---------------------- 2
Three -------------------- 3 ASK Q.15
Four --------------------- 4
Five or more ------------- 5   (65)

Q.15 (Not counting your present job) what was the last full time job you had as an employee? (WRITE IN FULLY)

OCCUPATION _____

INDUSTRY _____   (66)

NAME OF FIRM _____   (67)

ADDRESS OF PLACE OF EMPLOYMENT _____   (68)

IF MANAGER/SUPERINTENDENT OR SELF-EMPLOYED

Number of employees in the establishment

25 or more --------------------------- 1
1 - 24 ------------------------------- 2
None --------------------------------- 3

IF NOT MANAGER ETC. CODE HERE ------------------------------------- 4   (69)

Q.16 What were your reasons for leaving that job? (WRITE IN)

	1st mention (70)	2nd mention (71)	3rd mention (72)
More money	1	1	1
Moved house	2	2	2
More responsibility	3	3	3
More interesting work	4	4	4
Better work conditions	5	5	5
Redundancy (PROBE FOR DETAILS)	6	6	6

_____

Illness	7	7	7
Transport problems	8	8	8
Racial problems (WRITE IN)	9	9	9

(71/72)

_____

Other (WRITE IN) _____ 0

_____ 0

_____ 0

Don't know ------------------------------- X   _____

Q.17 Have you been unemployed for a period of a week or more at any time during the last two years?

Yes --------------- 1   ASK Q.18
No ---------------- 2   GO TO PROMOTION SECTION ON PAGE 13   (73)

Q.18 What is the longest period you have been unemployed in the last two years?

1 week but less than 1 month	1
1 month but less than 3 months	2
3 months but less than 6 months	3
6 months but less than 1 year	4
1 year or more	5
Don't know/Refused	6

(74)

Q.19 Thinking about the last time you were unemployed how difficult was it for you to find a job?

Was it .... READ OUT .... Very difficult ------------ 1   ASK Q.20
Fairly difficult ----------- 2
Not very difficult --------- 3   GO TO
or not at all difficult ------- 4   PROMOTION
Don't know ---------------- 5   SECTION ON PAGE 13   (75)

Q.20 Why do you think you found it difficult to get a job? (WRITE IN)

_____ (76)

_____ (77)

_____ (78)

PROBE: What else: _____ (79)

_____ (80)

NOW GO TO PROMOTION SECTION ON P. 13

```
┌─────────────────────────────────┐
│        NOT WORKING SECTION       │  12.
│ ASK ALL NOT WORKING EXCEPT RETIRED│
└─────────────────────────────────┘
```

Q.1 When did you last work at a full time job?

Less than 1 week ago	1
1 week but less than 1 month	2
1 month but less than 3 mths	3 — ASK Q.2
3 mths but less than 6 mths	4
6 mths but less than 1 year	5
Between 1 - 2 years	6
Between 2 - 10 years	7 GO TO Q.4
Over 10 years	8 GO TO
Never worked full time	9 CHILDREN SECT. P 15

(62)

Q.2 On how many occasions during the last two years have you been unemployed for a week or more?

None	0 GO TO Q4
One	1
Two	2
Three	3 — ASK Q.3
Four or more	4
Don't know/Can't remember	5

(63)

Q.3 What is the longest period you have been unemployed in the last two years?

1 week but less than one month	1
1 mth but less than 3 mths	2
3 mths but less than 6 mths	3
6 mths but less than 1 year	4
One year or over	5
D.K./Refused/Can't remember	6

(64)

Q.4 Thinking now about your last full-time job, were you self employed or an employee?

Self employed	1
Employee	2

(65)

Q.5 What was your last full-time job? **WRITE IN FULLY**

OCCUPATION _____

INDUSTRY _____ (66)

NAME OF FIRM _____ (67)

ADDRESS OF PLACE OF EMPLOYMENT _____ (68)

IF MANAGER/SUPERINTENDENT OR SELF EMPLOYED
Number of employees in the establishment .....

25 or more	1
1 - 24	2
None	3

IF NOT MANAGER ETC., CODE HERE 4   (69)

Q.6 What were your reasons for leaving that job? **(WRITE IN)**

	1st mention (70)	2nd mention (71)	3rd mention (72)
More money	1	1	1
Moved house	2	2	2
More responsibility	3	3	3
More interesting work	4	4	4
Better work conditions	5	5	5
Redundancy (PROBE FOR DETAILS)	6	6	6
Illness	7	7	7
Transport problems	8	8	8
Racial problems (WRITE IN)	9	9	9
Other (Write in) _____	0		
_____		0	
			0
Don't know	X		

(70/72)

SKIP TO COL. 75

Q.7 How difficult do you think it will be for you to find another job? Will it be ....
(READ OUT)

Very difficult	1
Fairly difficult	2
Not very difficult	3
or not at all difficult	4
Don't know	5

(75)

Q.8 Why do you say that? (WRITE IN)

_____

PROBE: What else? _____

(76)
(77)
(78)
(79)
(80)

NOW GO TO PROMOTION SECTION ON PAGE 13

13.

```
┌────────────────────────────────────────────┐
│            RETIRED SECTION                   │
│  ALL WHO ARE RETIRED AT OCCUPATION SECTION   │
└────────────────────────────────────────────┘
```

Q.1 What was your main job before you retired?

	(42)
OCCUPATION _____	Employee ----------------- 1
	Self employed ------------ 2	(42)
INDUSTRY _____	

NAME OF FIRM _____   (43)
                                                            (44)
ADDRESS OF PLACE OF EMPLOYMENT _____   (45)

IF MANAGER/SUPERINTENDENT OR SELF EMPLOYED   (46)
Number of employees in the establishment .... 25 or more -------------- 1
                                                    1 - 24 ------------------- 2   (46)
                                                    None --------------------- 3   SKIP TO
IF NOT MANAGER ETC., CODE HERE --- 4   COL. 80

                              NOW GO TO CHILDREN SECTION ON P. 15   (80)

                                                               DUP. COLS.
                                                               1 - 8
```
┌────────────────────────────────────────────┐
│            PROMOTION SECTION                 │       (9)  ③
│  ALL EXCEPT: RETIRED, NEVER WORKED FULL TIME AND │
│    SELF EMPLOYED FOR MORE THAN FIVE YEARS    │
└────────────────────────────────────────────┘
```

IF FULL TIME EMPLOYEE

Q.1 During your present job have you ever been offered promotion of any kind or are you not
     interested in promotion? (CODE BELOW)

IF NOT FULL TIME EMPLOYEE

Q.1 In your last full time job were you ever offered promotion of any kind or were you not
     interested in promotion?

	Yes ------------------------ 1 ASK Q.2
	No ------------------------- 2 GO TO Q.4
IF YES	Not interested in promotion - 3 GO TO Q.6	(10)

Q.2 What was the promotion? (WRITE IN)   (11)
     _____   (12)
     _____   (13)
                                                               (14)

Q.3 Did you take the promotion?   Yes ------------------------- 1
                                        No -------------------------- 2 GO TO Q.6   (15)

IF NO AT Q.1

Q.4 Do you think that there are any particular   Yes ------------------- 1 ASK Q.5
     reasons why you haven't been (weren't)   No -------------------- 2 GO TO Q.6   (16)
     offered any promotion?

Q.5 What were these reasons? (WRITE IN)   (17)
     _____   (18)
     _____   (19)
                                                               (20)

Q.6 Generally, in your job/last job who is/was offered promotion? WRITE IN   (21)
     _____   (22)
     _____   (23)
                                                               (24)

Q.7 Have you ever been for an interview or   Yes ------------------------- 1 ASK Q.8
     been seen for a job and then not been   No -------------------------- 2 GO TO TRADE
     given it?   UNION SECT.
                                                                                ON PAGE 14   (25)

Q.8 Has this happened in the last five   Yes ------------------------- 1 ASK Q.9
     years?   No -------------------------- 2 GO TO TRADE
                                                                                UNION SECT.
                                                                                ON PAGE 14   (26)

Q.9 How many times, roughly, has this   Once ------------------------------- 1
     happened?   A few times (2 - 5 times) ---------- 2
                                               Quite often (6 - 10 times) --------- 3
                                               Very often (11+ times) ------------- 4   (27)
                                               Don't know ------------------------- 5

14.

Q.10 Thinking about the last occasion - do you think that there were any reasons in particular why you did not get the job? __WRITE IN__

_____ (28)

_____ (29)

PROBE: What else? _____ (30)

_____ (31)

```
┌─────────────────────────────────────────┐
│           TRADE UNION SECTION            │
├─────────────────────────────────────────┤
│  ASK ALL EXCEPT RETIRED, NEVER WORKED OR │
│       NOT WORKED IN LAST TEN YEARS       │
└─────────────────────────────────────────┘
```

Q.1 Do you, or have you ever, belonged to a Trade Union?

Yes - now -------------------- 1 ASK
Yes - used to belong ---------- 2 Q.2
No - never belonged ----------- 3 GO TO Q.6   (32)

Q.2 Which Union is that? WRITE IN

(33)
(34)

IF RESPONDENT IS NO LONGER A UNION MEMBER ASK Q.3.   OTHERS GO TO Q.4

Q.3 Why are you no longer a member of that Union? WRITE IN

(35)
(36)
(37)

IF UNION MEMBER   NOW GO TO CHILDREN SECTION ON PAGE 15

Q.4 What is the most important thing the Union does for people in your job or position? CODE ONE ANSWER

Negotiates pay rates ---------------- 1
Decides who does what --------------- 2
Other answer (WRITE IN AND RING) ----- 3   (38)

_____

_____

Don't know ------------------------- 4

Q.5 Is there anything you think the Union doesn't do but should do? WRITE IN DETAILS

(39)
(40)
(41)

NOW GO TO CHILDREN SECTION ON PAGE 15

IF NEVER A UNION MEMBER ASK Q.6.

Q.6 Is there any reason why you have never joined a Union? WRITE IN

(42)
(43)
(44)

NOW GO TO CHILDREN SECTION ON PAGE 15

15.

```
┌─────────────────────────┐
│    CHILDREN SECTION      │
│        ASK ALL           │
└─────────────────────────┘
```

CARD 3

Q.1 Are there any of your children in this household who are at present attending primary or secondary school?

Yes ------------------ 1 ASK Q.2
No ------------------- 2 GO TO Q.16   (45)

BY CONVERSATION FIND OUT:

a) does respondent have a boy at school?

Yes ------------------ 1
No ------------------- 2   (46)

b) IF YES name of eldest boy at school _____

c) Does respondent have a girl at school?

Yes ------------------ 1
No ------------------- 2

d) IF YES name of eldest girl at school? _____   (47)

Q.2 Have you ever been to the school(s) to talk to someone there about your child(ren)?

Yes ------------------ 1 ASK Q.3
No ------------------- 2 GO TO Q.4   (48)

Q.3 The last time you went .... PROBE FOR DETAILS

Who did you see (e.g. teachers, headmaster, etc.) _____   (49)

What was visit about? (which child)? _____

_____   (50)

When was that? _____   (51)

Q.4 In general, have you been satisfied or dissatisfied with the education your child(ren) is/are receiving?

Satisfied ----------- 1
Dissatisfied -------- 2
Don't know ---------- 3   (52)

Q.5 Why do you say that? (WRITE IN)

_____   (53)

_____   (54)

PROBE: What else? _____   (55)

IF RESPONDENT HAS A SON AT SCHOOL ASK Q.6. OTHERS GO TO FILTER AT Q.9.

Q.6 At what age would you like .... (eldest son) to finish at school?

Under 16 ---------------- -- 1
16 ---------------------- -- 2
17 ---------------------- -- 3
18 ------------------------ 4
19 ------------------------ 5
Over 19 ------------------- 6
Don't know ---------------- 7
Don't care/up to him ------- 8
Can't tell at moment ------- 9   (56)

Q.7 When .... (eldest son) leaves school would you prefer him to get a job or to stay on in full time education?

Get a job ------------------ 1
Stay on in education ------- 2
Up to him ------------------ 3
Don't know ----------------- 4
Don't care ----------------- 5   (57)

Q.8 (a) What kind of job would you like .... (eldest son) to have after he finishes his education (WRITE IN)

_____   (58)

_____   (59)

(b) What kind of job do you think (eldest son) wants to do when he has finished his education?

_____   (60)

_____   (61)

16.

IF RESPONDENT HAS DAUGHTER AT SCHOOL ASK Q.9.   OTHERS GO TO FILTER AT Q.12

Q.9   At what age would you like ....
       (eldest daughter to finish at school?

Under 16	1
16	2
17	3
18	4
19	5
Over 19	6
Don't know	7
Don't care/up to her	8
Can't tell at moment	9

(62)

Q.10 When .... (eldest daughter) leaves
       school would you prefer her to get a
       job or to stay on in full time
       education?

Get a job	1
Stay on in education	2
Up to her	3
Don't know	4
Don't care	5

(63)

Q.11 (a) What kind of job would you like ..... (eldest daughter) to have after she
            finishes her education? (WRITE IN)

(64)

       (b) and what kind of job do you think .... (eldest daughter) wants to do when
            she has finished her education? (WRITE IN)

(65)

(66)

(67)

IF RESPONDENT IS WEST INDIAN OR ASIAN ASK Q.12.   OTHERS GO TO Q.16.

Q.12 Do your children/does your child go to
       any of these types of school as well as
       their ordinary school? (SHOWCARD 2)

	Yes	No	
Black Saturday School	1	2	(68)
Black Holiday School	1	2	(69)
School at Mosque/Temple	1	2	(70)
Sunday School	1	2	(71)
Any other extra schooling	1	2	(72)
WRITE IN			

IF RESPONDENT IS ASIAN ASK Q.13.   OTHERS GO TO Q.16

Q.13 Did any of your children/did your child
       have any difficulty in speaking English
       when he/she/they started school in U.K.?

Yes ------------------------- 1 ASK Q.14
No ------------------------- 2 GO TO Q.16   (73)

Q.14 Were any special efforts made to help
       your child(ren) to speak English?

Yes ------------------------- 1 ASK Q.15
No ------------------------- 2 GO TO Q.16   (74)

Q.15 Could you tell me what special efforts were made and who made them? WRITE IN
       PROBE FOR SPECIAL EFFORTS BY PARENTS, SCHOOL, ETC.

(75)

(76)

(77)

(78)

ASK ALL

Q.16 Are there any children in your household
       who have left school but are in full time
       education in a college or university?

Yes ------------------- 1 ASK Q.17
No ------------------- 2 GO TO HOUSING
                              SECT. P. 17   (79)

Q.17 RECORD DETAILS OF CHILD/CHILDREN IN FURTHER EDUCATION

NAME OF COLLEGE/UNIVERSITY _____

NAME OF COURSE _____

QUALIFICATIONS BEING ATTEMPTED (USE SHOWCARD 1) _____

(80)

WHEN COURSE STARTED _____   WHEN EXPECTED TO FINISH _____

NOW GO TO HOUSING SECTION ON PAGE 17

17.

HOUSING SECTION
ASK ALL

Now I would like to move on to some questions about your accommodation here.

Q.1 Firstly, are there any aspects of your present accommodation with which you are not satisfied? If so, what are they?

	1st mention (10)	2nd mention (11)	3rd mention (12)
None	1	1	1
Poor physical condition (e.g. damp)	2	2	2
Layout of dwelling e.g. no hall/small kitchen	3	3	3
Lack of amenities (W.C./hot water etc.)	4	4	4
Type of dwelling (e.g. flat)	5	5	5
No/inadequate garden	6	6	6
House too big/small	7	7	7
High cost (rent/mortgage)	8	8	8
Noise	9	9	9
Neighbours	0	0	0
Racial problem (WRITE IN DETAILS)	X	X	X
Other answers (WRITE IN DETAILS)	Y	Y	Y

(10/12)

Q.2 I would like to ask about some of the basic amenities you have here: (ASK ALL)

A) Do you have the use of:

i) A fixed sink
ii) A fixed bath or shower
iii) A fixed hand basin other than the sink
iv) A toilet inside your house
v) A garden or yard

FOR EACH AMENITY RESPONDENT HAS ASK:
B) Does your household have the sole use of it, or do you share it with some other household?

FOR AMENITIES i), ii), iii) ASK:
C) Does it have piped hot and cold water, cold water only or no piped water at all?

	i) Fixed sink (13)	ii) Fixed bath or shower (16)	iii) Fixed hand-basin (19)	iv) Inside toilet (22)	v) Garden or yard (24)
A. Have amenity					
Yes	1	1	1	1	1
No	2	2	2	2	2
	(14)	(17)	(20)	(23)	(25)
B. Use					
Sole	1	1	1	1	1
Shared	2	2	2	2	2
	(15)	(18)	(21)		
C. Piped water					
Hot and cold	1	1	1	N	N
Cold only	2	2	2	N	N
None	3	3	3	N	N

(13/25)

Q.3 How many rooms does your household have here?
PROBE FOR: Bedrooms, living rooms etc. used solely by respondent's household
EXCLUDE Bathrooms, toilets, small kitchens less than 6ft x 6ft, closets, pantries, landings, halls, lobbies, recesses, store rooms, offices or shops used solely for business purposes, and sculleries not used for cooking.

CODE NUMBER OF ROOMS ------ 1 --- 2 --- 3 --- 4 --- 5 --- 6 --- 7 --- 8 --- 9 or more   (26)

Q.4 Do you have any other rooms here which you sub-let

Yes ------------ 1 ASK Q.5
No ------------ 2 GO TO Q.6   (27)

Q.5 How many?
CODE NUMBER SUB-LET ------ 1 --- 2 --- 3 --- 4 --- 5 --- 6 --- 7 --- 8 --- 9 or more   (28)

18.

Q.6 Do you own or rent your present accommodation? PROBE IF NECESSARY

Own/is buying	1	GO TO OWNERS SECTION BELOW
Rented privately furnished	2	GO TO RENTERS SECTION
Rented privately unfurnished	3	ON PAGE 19
Rented from Council	4	GO TO COUNCIL SECTION ON P.21
Other (WRITE IN AND RING)	5	GO TO HOUSING LIST SECTION ON PAGE 20

(29)

OWNERS SECTION
ALL WHO OWN/ARE BUYING PRESENT ACCOMMODATION

Q.1a Do you own this accommodation
leasehold or freehold?

Leasehold ------------- 1 ASK Q.1b
Freehold -------------- 2 GO TO Q.2
Don't know ------------ 3   (30)

Q.1b How much of your lease is left to run?
WRITE IN NUMBER OF YEARS   (31/32)
(31)(32)

Q.2 Do you own it on your own or jointly
with your wife or others?

Alone ------------------ 1
Joint with wife only --- 2
Joint with relatives --- 3
Joint with others ------ 4
Spouse owns house ------ 5   (33)

Q.3 Do you own it outright or are you buying
it with the help of a loan or mortgage?

Outright -------------- 1 GO TO Q.6
Mortgage -------------- 2 ASK Q.4a
Loan ------------------ 3
Other/Refused/D.K. ---- 4 GO TO Q.6   (34)

Q.4a From which business or person are you
borrowing the money? PROBE FOR DETAILS

_____

_____

_____   (35)

Q.4b Do you have a second mortgage?

Yes -------------------- 1 ASK Q.4c
No --------------------- 2 GO TO Q.5
Don't know ------------- 3   (36)

Q.4c Probe for details of second mortgage?
WRITE IN

_____

Q.5 What are your repayments on your loan/
mortgage(s)?   (37)(38)(39) (40)(41)
£   .
(42)   (42)
per month ------- 3   D.K. amount - 9   (37/43)
quarter ----- 4   D.K. period - 0
6 months ---- 5   (43)
year -------- 6   Exact ------- 1
Refused ----- 8   Estimate ---- 2

Q.6 Do you have to pay rates?

Yes ----------------- 1 ASK Q.7
No ------------------ 2 GO TO Q.10
Don't know ---------- 3   (44)

Q.7 How much do you pay in rates?
SEE NOTE AT Q.9.   (45)(46)(47) (48)(49)
£   .
per month ----- (50)   D.K. amount --- (50)
quarter ---- 4   D.K. period --- 9   (45/51)
6 months --- 5   (51)
year ------- 6   Exact -------- 1
Refused ---- 8   Estimate ----- 2

Q.8 Do you receive a rate rebate?

Yes ----------------- 1 ASK Q.9
No ------------------ 2
Don't know ---------- 3 GO TO
Refused ------------- 4 Q.10
Supplementary Benefit 5   (52)

Q.9 How much rate rebate do you receive?

INTERVIEWER: Make sure that amount at
Q.7 is full amount before deduction of
rebate. Change Q.7. if necessary.

(53)(54)(55) (56)(57)
£   .   p
(58)   (58)   (53/59)
per month ------ 3   D.K. amount -- 9
quarter ---- 4   D.K. period -- 0
6 months --- 5   (59)
year ------- 6   Exact -------- 1
Refused ------- 8   Estimate ----- 2

ALL OWNERS

Q.10 Do you own or are you buying any other
houses at present in Birmingham?

Yes -------------- 1 ASK Q.11
No --------------- 2 GO TO Q.13   (60)

Q.11 How many other houses do you own/are
you buying?

One ---------------- 1
Two ---------------- 2
Three -------------- 3   (61)
Four or more ------- 4

Q.12 Do you own them/it yourself or jointly
with other people?
WRITE IN DETAILS FOR OTHER HOUSE(S)

_____   (62)

_____

_____   (63)

19.

		Yes	No	Don't know	

ALL OWNERS
Q.13 Do you know if your house is now in one of the following areas .... READ OUT

a) is it in a Redevelopment area -- 1 -- 2 -- 3 (64)
b) is it in an Improvement area --- 1 -- 2 -- 3 (65)
c) is it in a Housing Action area - 1 -- 2 -- 3 (66)

IF YES TO a), b) OR c) ASK Q.14 OTHERS GO TO Q.15

Q.14 How do you think this might affect you? WRITE IN

_____ (67)

_____ (68)

_____ (69)

PROBE: How else? _____ (70)

ALL OWNERS

Q.15 Have you ever heard about housing improvement grants?

Yes ------------- 1 ASK Q.16
No/Don't know --- 2 GO TO Q.19 (71)

Q.16 Have you ever applied to the Council for an improvement grant for this house?

Yes ------------- 1 ASK Q.17
No -------------- 2 GO TO Q.18a (72)

Q.17 Could you tell me what for and what happened to the application? WRITE IN DETAILS

_____ (73)

(74)

IF NO AT Q.16 ASK Q.18a

NOW GO TO Q.19

Q.18a Do you know whether or not you are eligible for a grant?

Don't know ------------- 1 GO TO Q.19
Yes - eligible ---------- 2 GO TO Q.19
No - not eligible ------- 3 ASK Q.18b (75)

Q.18b Why are you not eligible for a grant? (WRITE IN DETAILS)

(76)

_____ (77)

Q.19 Do you belong to any residents associations locally?

Yes ----------------- 1 ASK Q.20
No ------------------ 2 GO TO HOUSING LIST SECT. P.20 (78)

Q.20 Could you tell me which one and what it does? (WRITE IN)

(79)

_____ (80)

NOW GO TO HOUSING LIST SECTION ON PAGE 20

DUPLICATE COLS. 1 - 8

(9) ⑤

RENTERS SECTION
ALL PRIVATE RENTERS

Q.1 Do you know who your landlord is? PROBE

No ------------------------- 1 GO TO Q.4
Yes - relative ------------- 2 ASK Q.2
Yes - other individual ----- 3
Yes - Housing Association -- 4
Yes - Property Agency ------ 5 GO TO Q.4
Yes - other Institution ---- 6 (10)

Q.2 Does your landlord live in this building?

Yes ------------------------- 1
No -------------------------- 2 (11)

Q.3 Do you know the nationality or country of birth of your landlord? (12)

Don't know -------------------- 1
British (born in G.B.) -------- 2
Asian (Indian) ---------------- 3
Asian(Pakistani) -------------- 4
Asian (Other) ----------------- 5
West Indian ---------------- 6
Irish ---------------------- 7
Other (Write in) ----------- 8 (12)

ALL RENTERS

Q.4 Do you know whether or not you are eligible for a council house in Birmingham at the moment?

No - I am not ------------- 1 ASK Q.5
Yes I am ------------------ 2 GO TO HOUSING
Don't know ---------------- 3 LIST SECTION ON PAGE 20 (13)

(14)
(15)
(16)

Q.5 Why are you not eligible for a council house at the moment? (WRITE IN)

HOUSING LIST SECTION
ALL EXCEPT COUNCIL TENANTS

20.

Q.1 Have you ever applied for a council house in Birmingham in the last ten years?

Yes ---------------------- 1 GO TO Q.3   (17)
No ----------------------- 2 ASK Q.2

Q.2 Are there any particular reasons why you have not applied? (WRITE IN)

_____ (18)

_____ (19)

_____ (20)

RENTERS GO TO RENT PAYMENTS SECTION ON P.22
NON-RENTERS GO TO PERSONAL DETAILS SECT. P.23

Q.3 When did you last apply?

1976 ---------------------- 1
1975 ---------------------- 2
1973-74 ------------------- 3
1970-72 ------------------- 4   (21)
1965-69 ------------------- 5
Don't know/Can't remember --- 6

Q.4 Why did you apply? (WRITE IN)

_____ (22)

_____ (23)

PROBE: What other reasons?

_____ (24)

Q.5 Did you ask anyone's advice about how to apply?

Yes ---------------------- 1 ASK Q.6
Ho ----------------------- 2 GO TO Q.7   (25)

Q.6 Who did you ask for advice? WRITE IN

_____ (26)

_____ (27)

Q.7 Did you get a visit from a Housing Visitor from the Council?

Yes ---------------------- 1 ASK Q.8
No ----------------------- 2
Don't know --------------- 3 GO TO Q.9   (28)

Q.8 Do you remember what sort of questions the Housing Visitor asked you? WRITE IN DETAILS

_____ (29)

_____ (30)

_____ (31)

Q.9 Did you ask for a Council house in any particular areas of Birmingham?

Yes ---------------------- 1 ASK Q.10
No ----------------------- 2
Don't know --------------- 3 GO TO Q.11   (32)

Q.10 Which area(s)? WRITE IN

_____ (33)

_____ (34)

Q.11 At present are you on the Council Housing List?

Yes ------------- 1 GO TO Q.13
No -------------- 2   (35)
Don't know ------ 3 ASK Q.12

Q.12 Was your last application .. READ OUT

a) refused -------------- 1 GO TO Q16
b) did you withdraw it
   voluntarily ---------- 2 GO TO Q17
c) are you still in proc
   process of applying -- 3 GO TO Q18   (36)
or d) never heard from
   Housing Department ---- 4 ASK Q13

Q.13 Have you been offered a house so far?
IF YES: Have you accepted it?

Yes - offered and accepted - 1 ASK Q14
Yes - offered but refused -- 2 GO TO Q15
Yes-now considering offer - 3   (37)
No - never offered ------- 4 GO TO Q18

IF OFFERED AND ACCEPTED AT Q.13
Q.14 Is the house in an area you want?

Yes ---------------------- 1 NOW GO
No ----------------------- 2 TO
Don't know --------------- 3 Q.18   (38)

IF OFFERED AND REFUSED AT Q.13
Q.15 Why did you refuse the offer? WRITE IN

_____ (39)

_____ (40)

NOW GO TO Q.18

Q.16 Why do you think your application was refused? WRITE IN

_____ (41)

_____ (42)

Q.17 Why did you withdraw your application? WRITE IN

_____ (43)

_____ (44)

ALL WHO HAVE APPLIED FOR A COUNCIL HOUSE

Q.18 In general are you satisfied or dissatisfied with the way your application for a council house was dealt with by the Housing Department?

Satisfied ----------------- 1
Dissatisfied -------------- 2   (45)
Don't know ---------------- 3

Q.19 Why do you say that? WRITE IN   (46)

_____ (47)

_____ (48)

PROBE: What else? _____ (49)

_____ (50)

_____ (51)

RENTERS GO TO RENT PAYMENTS SECTION ON P.22
NON RENTERS GO TO PERSONAL DETAILS SECT ON P23

21.

COUNCIL SECTION
ALL IN COUNCIL HOUSING

Q.1 Could I just check again. **Did you personally** rent a council house in **Birmingham** before you moved to this address?

Yes --------------------- 1 ASK Q.2   (52)
No ---------------------- 2 GO TO Q.3

Q.2 When did you first start renting a Council house in Birmingham?

This year --------------- 1
Last year --------------- 2   GO TO
2-3 years ago ----------- 3   Q.17
4-5 years ago ----------- 4
6-10 years ago ---------- 5   (53)
Over 10 years ago ------- 6
D.K./Can't remember ----- 7

Q.3 When did you first apply for a council house in Birmingham?

1975 - 1976 ----------------------- 1
1973 - 1974 ----------------------- 2
1970 - 1972 ----------------------- 3
1965 - 1969 ----------------------- 4
1960 - 1964 ----------------------- 5   (54)
Before 1960 ----------------------- 6
Can't remember -------------------- 7

Q.4 How long were you on the Housing List before you were allocated a Council House?

Up to 1 year --------------------- 1
Over 1 yr. but less than 2 years -- 2
Over 2 yrs but less than 3 years -- 3
Over 3 yrs but less than 5 years -- 4
Over 5 yrs but less than 7 years -- 5   (55)
Over 7 yrs but less than 10 years - 6
10 years or over ------------------ 7
Can't remember/Don't know --------- 8

Q.5 Did you ask anyone's advice on how to apply?

Yes --------------------- 1 ASK Q.6   (56)
No ---------------------- 2 GO TO Q.7

Q.6 Who or what organisation? WRITE IN   (57)

_____

   (58)

Q.7 Did you get a visit from a Housing Visitor from the Council?

Yes --------------------- 1 ASK Q.8   (59)
No ---------------------- 2 GO TO Q.10

Q.8 Do you remember what sort of questions you were asked? WRITE IN   (60)

_____

_____ (61)

_____

   (62)

Q.9 How helpful did you find this service? READ OUT   Was it ....

very helpful ---------------------- 1
fairly helpful -------------------- 2
not very helpful ------------------ 3
or not at all helpful ---------------- 4   (63)
Don't know ------------------------ 5
Can't remember -------------------- 6

Q.10 Did you ask for a council house in any particular areas of Birmingham?

Yes --------------------- 1 ASK Q.11   (64)
No ---------------------- 2 GO TO Q.12

Q.11 Which areas? WRITE IN   (65)

_____

   (66)

Q.12 Did you accept the first offer of a council house you were given?

Yes --------------------- 1 GO TO Q.15   (67)
No ---------------------- 2 ASK Q.13

Q.13 How many offers did you refuse?

One ---------------------------- 1
Two ---------------------------- 2
Other answer (WRITE IN AND RING) 3   (68)

IF ANY OFFERS REFUSED ASK Q.14. OTHERS GO TO Q.15

Q.14 a) Why did you refuse the first offer?
WRITE IN _____

   (69)

b) **IF SECOND OFFER REFUSED** Why did you refuse the second offer?
WRITE IN _____

   (70)

Q.15 In general, are you satisfied or dissatisfied with the way your application for a council house was dealt with by the Housing Department?

Satisfied ----------------------- 1
Dissatisfied -------------------- 2   (71)
Don't know ---------------------- 3

Q.16 Why do you say that? WRITE IN   (72)
_____   (73)
   (74)
   (75)
PROBE: What else? _____   (76)

ALL COUNCIL TENANTS
Q.17 Since coming to live at this address (or during the last 5 years - which ever is shorter) have you ever applied for a transfer to a council house in another part of Birmingham?

Yes --------- 1 ASK Q.18   (77)
No ---------- 2 GO TO Q.19

Q.18 Could you tell me when, and what happened? WRITE IN DETAILS

   (78)

_____

   (79)

ASK ALL
Q.19 Would you like to buy this council house or not?

Yes -------- 1   (80)
No --------- 2
Don't know - 3

GO TO RENT PAYMENTS SECTION P. 22

22.

RENT PAYMENTS SECTION
ALL RENTERS - PRIVATE AND COUNCIL

DUP.
COLS.
(9) ⑥

Q.1a Have you had any disputes with your landlord/the council about this accommodation in the last 2 years?

Yes ------------------- 1 ASK Q.1b
No -------------------- 2 GO TO Q.2   (10)

Q.1b What was the last dispute about? WRITE IN

_____   (11)
_____   (12)
_____   (13)

ASK ALL
Q.2 Do you have a rent book?   Yes ------ 1
                               No ------- 2   (14)

Q.3 How much rent do you pay altogether?
SEE NOTE AT Q.5 AND Q.12
(15)(16)(17) (18)(19)
£ [   ] p

                          (20)
per week ------ 1   D.K. amount --- 9   (15/
month ----- 3   D.K. period -- 0   24)
quarter --- 4
6 months -- 5   (21)
year ------ 6   Exact --------- 1
Rent free ---- 7   Estimate ------ 2
Refused ------- 8

Q.4 Do you receive a rent rebate or allowance?

Yes -------------------- 1 ASK Q.5
No --------------------- 2
Don't know ------------- 3 GO TO Q.6   (22)
Refused ---------------- 4
Supplementary Benefit -- 5
IF YES

Q.5 How much rebate or allowance do you receive? INTERVIEWER: MAKE SURE THAT FIGURE AT Q.3 IS THE FULL AMOUNT OF RENT BEFORE THE DEDUCTION OF RENT REBATE.
(23)(24)(25) (26)(27)
£ [   ] p

                          (28)
                    (28) Refused ------- 8   (23/
per week ------- 1   D.K. amount --- 9   29)
month ------ 3   D.K. period --- 0
quarter ---- 4   (29)
6 months --- 5   Exact --------- 1
year ------- 6   Estimate ------ 2
ASK ALL

Q.6 Do you pay rates in addition to your rent?

Yes -------------------- 1 ASK Q.7
No, rates included in rent -- 2 GO TO Q10
No, don't pay rates at all -- 3 GO TO   (30)
Don't know ------------------ 4 Q.13
IF YES

Q.7 How much do you pay in rates?
SEE NOTE AT Q.9
(31)(32)(33) (34)(35)
£ [   ] p

                          (36)
per week ----- 1   D.K. amount --- 9   (31/
month ---- 3   D.K. period --- 0   37)
quarter -- 4
6 months - 5   (37)
year ----- 6   Exact --------- 1
Refused ------- 8   Estimate ------ 2

Q.8 Do you receive a rate rebate?

Yes ------------------- 1 ASK Q.9
No --------------------- 2
Don't know ------------- 3
Refused ---------------- 4 GO TO Q.13   (38)
Supplementary Benefit -- 5
IF YES

Q.9 How much rate rebate do you receive?
INTERVIEWER: CHECK THAT THE FIGURE GIVEN AT Q.7 IS FULL AMOUNT PAID IN RATES BEFORE REBATE.

(39)(40)(41) (42)(43)
£ [   ] p

                          (44)
per week --- 1   Refused ---- 8 GO   (39/
month --- 3 GO   D.K. amount -- 9 TO   45)
quarter -- 4 TO   D.K. period - 0 Q13
6 months- 5 Q13   (45)
year ---- 6   Exact ------- 1
                       Estimate ---- 2

ASK Q.10 IF RATES INCLUDED IN RENT(Q.6)
OTHERS GO TO Q.13.

Q.10 How much of your total rent (from Q.3) is for rates? INTERVIEWER: BEFORE ACCEPTING "D.K." ASK TO SEE RENT BOOK.

(46)(47)(48) (49)(50)
£ [   ] p

                          (51)
per week ------- 1   D.K. amount --- 9   (46/
month ------ 3   D.K. period --- 0   52)
quarter ---- 4
6 months --- 5   (52)
year ------- 6   Exact --------- 1
Refused -------- 8   Estimate ------ 2

Q.11 Do you receive a rate rebate?

Yes -------------------- 1 ASK Q.12
No --------------------- 2
Don't know ------------- 3 GO TO
Refused ---------------- 4 Q.13   (53)
Supplementary Benefit -- 5
IF YES

Q.12 How much rate rebate do you receive?
INTERVIEWER: CHECK THAT FIGURE AT Q.10 IS FULL AMOUNT PAID FOR RATES BEFORE REBATE. ALSO MAKE SURE FIGURE AT Q.3 IS FULL AMOUNT FOR RENT AND RATES BEFORE ANY REBATES.

(54)(55)(56) (57)(58)
£ [   ] p

                          (59)
per week ------ 1   D.K. amount --- 9   (54/
month ----- 3   D.K. period --- 0   60)
quarter --- 4
6 months -- 5   (60)
year ------ 6   Exact --------- 1
Refused ------- 8   Estimate ------ 2

Q.13 Do you belong to a Tenant's Association locally?

Yes ----------- 1 ASK Q.14
No ------------ 2 GO TO PERSONAL DETAILS   (61)
                  SECTION ON PAGE 23
Q.14 Could you tell me which one and what it does?
                                          (62)

                                          (63)
NOW GO TO PERSONAL DETAILS SECTION ON P. 23

PERSONAL DETAILS SECTION
ASK ALL

Q.1a Thinking about Council housing in Birmingham. Do you think that Birmingham Council does or does not treat Asian and West Indian families differently to other families in the allocation of council housing?

Does treat them differently — 1 ASK Q1b
Doesnt treat them differently — 2 GO TO Q.2a
Don't know ---------------- 3   (64)

Q.1b In what way does the council treat Asian and West Indian families differently?
WRITE IN
(65)
(66)
(67)
PROBE: What else? (68)
(69)
(70)

ASK ALL
Q.2a In this area of Birmingham, there are a lot of people of different types and nationalities; do you think that on the whole, they get on well together or are there problems?

Get on well together -------------- 1
Get on well but some problems ----- 2   (71)
Problems ------------------------- 3
Don't know ----------------------- 4

Q.2b Why do you say that (WRITE IN)   (72)
(73)
(74)
PROBE: What else? _____

ASK ALL
Q.3 Now I would just like to ask you a few more questions about yourself. What is your religion?   (10)

DUP. COLS. 1 - 8 (9)⑦

Buddhist -------------------- 1
Muslim (specify sect) ------ 2

Hindu --------------------- 3
Sikh ---------------------- 4
Church of England --------- 5
Church of Scotland -------- 6
Baptist ------------------- 7   ASK
Methodist ----------------- 8   Q.4
Pentecostal --------------- 9
Other non-confirmist (Write) 0   (10)

(11)
Roman Catholic ------------- 1
Other Catholic ------------- 2
Jewish --------------------- 3
Other (Write in and ring) -- 4   (11)

No religion --------------- 5 GO TO Q5

Q.4 Generally how often do you go to a place of religious worship these days?

More than once a week ------------ 1
Once a week ---------------------- 2
Once a fortnight ----------------- 3
Once a month --------------------- 4   (12)
Less than once a month ----------- 5
Special occasions only ----------- 6
Never ---------------------------- 7

ASK ALL
Q.5 Which of the various political parties do you think does most for people like you?

Conservative -------------------------- 1
Labour -------------------------------- 2
Liberal ------------------------------- 3
Communist ----------------------------- 4
National Front ------------------------ 5
Other (Write in and ring) ------------- 6

None of them -------------------------- 7   (13)
Don't know ---------------------------- 8

Q.6 Are you a paid up member of any British political party?

Yes ----------------- 1 ASK Q.7   (14)
No ------------------ 2 GO TO Q.8

Q.7 Which Party?
Conservative ---------- 1
Labour ---------------- 2
Liberal --------------- 3
Communist ------------- 4
National Front -------- 5
Other (WRITE IN) ------ 6   (15)

ASK ALL   Refused -------------- 7

Q.8 Did you vote in the last General Election in October 1974? IF YES: Which party did you vote for? RECORD BELOW

Q.9 Did you vote in the last local elections in Birmingham early in May this year? IF YES: Which party did you vote for?

Q.8   Q.9
(16)   (17)
Can't remember if voted ------ 1 --- 1
Not eligible to vote --------- 2 --- 2
Did not vote ----------------- 3 --- 3
Voted - Conservative --------- 4 --- 4   (16/17)
Voted - Labour --------------- 5 --- 5
Voted - Liberal -------------- 6 --- 6
Voted - Communist ------------ 7 --- 7
Voted - National Front ------- 8 --- 8
Voted - Other Party (WRITE IN) 9 --- 9

Voted - Can't remember Party - 0 --- 0
Voted - Refused to tell Party- X --- X
Refused to answer question --- Y --- Y

Q.10 In what country was your father born?
WRITE IN   (18)

IF IN U.K. PROBE FOR TOWN/CITY
(19)

Q.11 What kind of job did your father do for most of his working life?

Don't know ---------------------- 1   (20)
Refused ------------------------- 2

OCCUPATION _____   (21)
(22)
INDUSTRY _____   (23)

Self employed ------------------- 1   (24)
Employee ------------------------ 2

IF MANAGER, SUPERINTENDENT OR SELF EMPLOYED
Number of employees .. 25 or more -- 1
1 - 24 ------- 2   (25)
None -------- 3
IF NOT MANAGER ETC. CODE HERE ------ 4

IF BORN IN G.B. GO TO HOUSEHOLD SECTION ON PAGE 25
OTHERS GO TO HOMELAND SECTION ON PAGE 24

HOMELAND SECTION
ALL NOT BORN IN U.K.

Now I would like to ask a few questions about your life before coming to Britain.

Q.1 **What sort of reasons did you have for leaving** .... (country of birth) and coming to Britain? WRITE IN

(26)
(27)
(28)
(29)

Q.2 What sort of job were you doing just before you came to Britain?
WRITE IN
OCCUPATION

At school ------------------ 1
Too young to work ---------- 2
Never worked before -------- 3   (30)

INDUSTRY   (31)
                                         (32)

IF ASIAN ASK Q.3 OTHERS GO TO Q.4   Employee -------------------- 1   (33)
Q.3 Which caste are you? (WRITE IN)   Self-employed -------------- 2   (34)

(35)

(36)

Q.4 Since coming to Britain have you found things here to be as you thought they would be or are they better or worse than you thought they would be?
Better -------------------- 1
Worse --------------------- 2
As thought they would be ---- 3
Don't know ---------------- 4   (37)

Q.5 Why do you say that? WRITE IN

(38)
(39)
(40)

PROBE: What else?   (41)
                                         (42)
                                         (43)

Q.6 Up to now have you been generally satisfied or dissatisfied with life in this country?
Satisfied ------------------ 1
Dissatisfied --------------- 2
Don't know ---------------- 3   (44)

Q.7 What sort of things do you like most about living in this country compared with .... (country of birth)? WRITE IN

(45)
(46)
(47)

PROBE: Anything else?   (48)
                                         (49)
                                         (50)

Q.8 What sort of things do you dislike most about living in this country compared with .... (country of birth)? WRITE IN

(51)
(52)
(53)

PROBE: Anything else?   (54)
                                         (55)
                                         (56)

Q.9 How interested are you in the news and politics in .... (country of birth)?
Very interested --------- 1
Fairly interested ------- 2 } GO TO Q.10
Not very interested ----- 3
Not at all interested --- 4 } GO TO Q.11
Don't know ------------- 5   (57)

Q.10 How do you keep in touch? WRITE IN PROBE IF NECESSARY: e.g. Newspapers?

(58)
(59)
(60)

25.

Q.11 Have you been back to .... (country of birth) since you came to live in Britain?

Yes ---------------------- 1
No ----------------------- 2   (61)

Q.12 Do you feel that you would like, at sometime, to go back and live permanently in .... (country of birth) or do you want to live permanently in Britain?

Want to go back ------------ 1 ASK Q.13
Want to live in Britain ---- 2
Don't know ----------------- 3 ASK Q.14   (62)

Q.13 Are you at present making any definite plans to go back permanently?
IF YES: Could you tell me about them?   WRITE IN

_____

_____

_____

(63)

(64)

(65)

(66)

Q.14 Finally, do you have any dependant relatives such as your parents, husband/wife or children who are not living in this household at the moment but may be living in other parts of the United Kingdom or abroad?

Yes ------------------------------- 1 ASK Q.15
No -------------------------------- 2 GO TO HOUSEHOLD SECTION BELOW   (67)

IF YES
Q.15 How many dependant relatives?

1 ----- 2 ----- 3 ----- 4 ----- 5 ----- 6 ----- 7 ----- 8 ----- 9 or more   (68)

Q.16 Details of dependant relatives.   WRITE IN BELOW   IF NOT IN G.B.

RELATIONSHIP TO HEAD OF HOUSEHOLD	SEX	AGE	COUNTRY OF BIRTH	PRESENT RESIDENCE (COUNTRY)	THINKING OF COMING TO BRITAIN Yes or No	
					1 --------- 2	(69)
					1 --------- 2	(70)
					1 --------- 2	(71)
					1 --------- 2	(72)
					1 --------- 2	(73)

DUP. COLS
1 - 8
(9) ⑨

HOUSEHOLD SECTION
ASK ALL

Q.1 Firstly, how many people are there in your household including children and yourself?

WRITE IN BOXES   (10) (11)   (10/11)

Q.2 How many adults aged 16+ are there?

WRITE IN BOXES   (12) (13)   (12/13)

Q.3 How many children under 16 are there?

WRITE IN BOXES   (14) (15)   (14/15)

INTERVIEWER: CHECK THAT NUMBERS AT Q.2 AND Q.3 ADD UP TO THE NUMBER AT Q.1

Q.4 FOR EACH MEMBER OF THE HOUSEHOLD COMPLETE DETAILS REQUIRED ON NEXT PAGE. START WITH HEAD OF HOUSEHOLD AS PERSON NUMBER 1. THEN WHERE POSSIBLE WORK THROUGH HOUSEHOLD FROM ELDEST TO YOUNGEST. DETAILS FOR HEAD OF HOUSEHOLD MUST BE THE SAME AS EARLIER IN QUESTIONNAIRE. DETAILS MUST BE COLLECTED FOR EVERY HOUSEHOLD MEMBER. IF NECESSARY USE SUPPLEMENTARY SHEETS.

26.

Person 1

PERSON NUMBER	SEX	AGE IN YRS.	MARITAL STATUS	RELATIONSHIP TO HEAD OF HOUSEHOLD	WRITE IN COUNTRY OF BIRTH	IF NOT BORN IN U.K.	WRITE IN NATIONALITY	WORKING STATUS	WRITE IN DETAILS OF PRESENT JOB OR LAST MAIN JOB OCCUPATION AND INDUSTRY OR NAME AND TYPE OF SCHOOL	SOCIAL CLASS	IF AT SCHOOL
1	M=1 F=2	N.B. 99 = Over 98 00 = Less than 1	Single -1 Married -2 Widowed -3 Divorced -4 Separated-5	Head -1 Spouse -2 Child of -3 Parent of -4 Bro/Sist. -5 Other relative -6 Other -7		DATE OF ARRIVAL IN U.K. WRITE IN YEAR		Full time -1 Part time -2 Unemployed -3 Not working -4 Retired -5 Student 16+ -6 At school -7 Pre school -8		A -1 B -2 C1 -3 C2 -4 D -5 E -6 Never worked-7	AGE STARTED SCHOOL IN ALL WRITE IN YEARS
(16)	(17)	(18)(19)	(20)	(21)		(22)(23)(24)		(25)	(26)(27)	(28)	(29)

Person 2

PERSON NUMBER	SEX	AGE IN YRS.	MARITAL STATUS	RELATIONSHIP TO HEAD OF HOUSEHOLD	WRITE IN COUNTRY OF BIRTH	IF NOT BORN IN U.K.	WRITE IN NATIONALITY	WORKING STATUS	WRITE IN DETAILS OF PRESENT JOB OR LAST MAIN JOB OCCUPATION AND INDUSTRY OR NAME AND TYPE OF SCHOOL	SOCIAL CLASS	IF AT SCHOOL
2	M=1 F=2	N.B. 99 = Over 98 00 = Less than 1	Single -1 Married -2 Widowed -3 Divorced -4 Separated-5	Head -1 Spouse -2 Child of -3 Parent of -4 Bro/Sist. -5 Other relative -6 Other -7		DATE OF ARRIVAL IN U.K. WRITE IN YEAR		Full time -1 Part time -2 Unemployed -3 Not working -4 Retired -5 Student 16+ -6 At school -7 Pre school -8		A -1 B -2 C1 -3 C2 -4 D -5 E -6 Never worked-7	AGE STARTED SCHOOL IN ALL WRITE IN YEARS

Person 3

PERSON NUMBER	SEX	AGE IN YRS.	MARITAL STATUS	RELATIONSHIP TO HEAD OF HOUSEHOLD	WRITE IN COUNTRY OF BIRTH	IF NOT BORN IN U.K.	WRITE IN NATIONALITY	WORKING STATUS	WRITE IN DETAILS OF PRESENT JOB OR LAST MAIN JOB OCCUPATION AND INDUSTRY OR NAME AND TYPE OF SCHOOL	SOCIAL CLASS	IF AT SCHOOL
3	M=1 F=2	N.B. 99 = Over 98 00 = Less than 1	Single -1 Married -2 Widowed -3 Divorced -4 Separated-5	Head -1 Spouse -2 Child of -3 Parent of -4 Bro/Sist. -5 Other relative -6 Other -7		DATE OF ARRIVAL IN U.K. WRITE IN YEAR		Full time -1 Part time -2 Unemployed -3 Not working -4 Retired -5 Student 16+ -6 At school -7 Pre school -8		A -1 B -2 C1 -3 C2 -4 D -5 E -6 Never worked-7	AGE STARTED SCHOOL IN ALL WRITE IN YEARS

(30) (31) (32) (33) (34) (35) (36) (37) (38) (39) (40) (41) (42) (43) (44) (45) (46) (47) (48) (49) (50)

Person 4

PERSON NUMBER	SEX	AGE IN YRS.	MARITAL STATUS	RELATIONSHIP TO HEAD OF HOUSEHOLD	WRITE IN COUNTRY OF BIRTH	IF NOT BORN IN U.K.	WRITE IN NATIONALITY	WORKING STATUS	WRITE IN DETAILS OF PRESENT JOB OR LAST MAIN JOB OCCUPATION AND INDUSTRY OR NAME AND TYPE OF SCHOOL	SOCIAL CLASS	IF AT SCHOOL
4	M=1 F=2	N.B. 39 = Over 98 00 = Less than 1	Single =1 Married =2 Widowed =3 Divorced =4 Separated=5	Head Spouse =2 Child of =3 Parent of =4 Bro/Sist.=5 Other relative =6 Other =7		DATE OF ARRIVAL IN U.K. WRITE IN YEAR		Full time 1 Part time =2 Unemployed =3 Not working =4 Retired =5 Student 16+ =6 At school =7 Pre school =8		A B C1 C2 D E Never Worked	AGE STARTED SCHOOL IN U.K. WRITE IN YEARS

Person 5

PERSON NUMBER	SEX	AGE IN YRS.	MARITAL STATUS	RELATIONSHIP TO HEAD OF HOUSEHOLD	WRITE IN COUNTRY OF BIRTH	IF NOT BORN IN U.K.	WRITE IN NATIONALITY	WORKING STATUS	WRITE IN DETAILS OF PRESENT JOB OR LAST MAIN JOB OCCUPATION AND INDUSTRY OR NAME AND TYPE OF SCHOOL	SOCIAL CLASS	IF AT SCHOOL
5	M=1 F=2	N.B. 99 = Over 98 00 = Less than 1	Single =1 Married =2 Widowed =3 Divorced =4 Separated=5	Head Spouse =2 Child of =3 Parent of =4 Bro/Sist.=5 Other relative =6 Other =7		DATE OF ARRIVAL IN U.K. WRITE IN YEAR		Full time =1 Part time =2 Unemployed =3 Not working =4 Retired =5 Student 16+ =6 At school =7 Pre school =8		A B C1 C2 D E Never Worked	AGE STARTED SCHOOL IN U.K. WRITE IN YEARS

Person 6

PERSON NUMBER	SEX	AGE IN YRS.	MARITAL STATUS	RELATIONSHIP TO HEAD OF HOUSEHOLD	WRITE IN COUNTRY OF BIRTH	IF NOT BORN IN U.K.	WRITE IN NATIONALITY	WORKING STATUS	WRITE IN DETAILS OF PRESENT JOB OR LAST MAIN JOB OCCUPATION AND INDUSTRY OR NAME AND TYPE OF SCHOOL	SOCIAL CLASS	IF AT SCHOOL
6	M=1 F=2	N.B. 99 = Over 98 00 = Less than 1	Single =1 Married =2 Widowed =3 Divorced =4 Separated=5	Head Spouse =2 Child of =3 Parent of =4 Bro/Sist.=5 Other relative =6 Other =7		DATE OF ARRIVAL IN U.K. WRITE IN YEAR		Full time =1 Part time =2 Unemployed =3 Not working =4 Retired =5 Student 16+ =6 At school =7 Pre school =8		A B C1 C2 D E Never worked	AGE STARTED SCHOOL IN U.K. WRITE IN YEARS

28.

INCOME SECTION
ASK ALL

Finally, I would like to ask just two more questions.

Q.1 Would you please give me the letter from this card (SHOWCARD 3) for the group in which you would place your **own personal** income before tax and other deductions?   RECORD BELOW

Q.2 And which letter on this card (SHOWCARD 4) is the group in which you would place your total family income from all sources before tax and other deductions?   RECORD BELOW

DUPLICATE COLUMNS
1 - 8
(9)(8)

	Per Week	Per Year	Q.1 (10)	Q.2 (11)
A.	Under £10	Under £500	1	1
B.	£10 - £19	£500 - £999	2	2
C.	£20 - £29	£1000 - £1499	3	3
D.	£30 - £39	£1500 - £1999	4	4
E.	£40 - £49	£2000 - £2499	5	5
F.	£50 - £59	£2500 - £2999	6	6
G.	£60 - £69	£3000 - £3499	7	7
H.	£70 - £89	£3500 - £4499	8	8
I.	£90 - £109	£4500 - £5499	9	9
J.	£110 or over	£5500 and over	0	0
Refused			X	X
Don't know			Y	Y

(10/ 11)

OTHER HOUSEHOLDS
ASK ALL

RING THE No. OF HOUSE-HOLDS IN DWELLING
(12)

		No. Adults (13)	No. chil-dren (14)	HEAD OF HOUSEHOLD BORN IN		
	FOR OTHER HOUSEHOLDS COMPLETE			West Indies / Asia / U.K. / Other	Don't know	
1						
2	Composition of 2nd household	(16)	(17)	(15) 1 --- 2 --- 3 --- 4 ---- 5		(12-15)
3	Composition of 3rd household	(19)	(20)	(18) 1 --- 2--- 3 ---- 4 ---- 5		(16-18)
4	Composition of 4th household	(22)	(23)	(21) 1 --- 2 --- 3 --- 4 --- 5		(19-21)
5	Composition of 5th household			(24) 1 --- 2 --- 3 --- 4 ---- 5		(22-24)
6+						

ACCOMMODATION
ASK ALL

Accommodation of Household   (25)
Whole house - detached ---------------- 1
Whole house - semi-detached ----------- 2
Whole house - terraced ---------------- 3
Purpose built flat/maisonette --------- 4
Other flat/maisonette/rooms ----------- 5
Dwelling with Business Premises ------- 6
Other (Write in) ---------------------- 7

Accommodation Level   (26)
Basement ------------------------- 1
Ground --------------------------- 2
First floor ---------------------- 3
Second floor --------------------- 4
Third floor ---------------------- 5
Fourth floor --------------------- 6
Fifth + -------------------------- 7

(25/ 26)

INTERVIEWER OBSERVATIONS
COMPLETE THIS BOX WHEN INTERVIEW IS OVER

Q.1 Did the respondent complete all or only part of the questionnaire?

All ---------------------- 1 GO TO Q.3
Part --------------------- 2 GO TO Q.2   (27)

IF ONLY PART
Q.2 What was the reason for partial completion?

Language problems --------------- 1
Deafness/other illness (Write in) - 2

Other reasons (WRITE IN) ---------- 3   (28)

ASK ALL
Q.3 In general, how did the respondent cope with answering the questionnaire?

Without any difficulty -------------- 1
With very little difficulty --------- 2
With a fair degree of difficulty ---- 3
With a great degree of difficulty --- 4   29)

Q.4 What was the general reaction of the respondent to being interviewed?

Very pleased ---------------------- 1
Fairly pleased -------------------- 2
Fairly displeased ----------------- 3
Very displeased ------------------- 4   30)

Notes

CHAPTER 1   THE SOCIOLOGY AND POLITICS OF MIGRATION

1   Throughout this book unweighted figures are presented
with weighted figures alongside. The distinction between the weighted and unweighted figures is discussed
in the next few paragraphs and in Appendix 1.
2   This issue is followed up in detail in Chapter 6 in
particular.
3   See, for example, Adorno, T.W., Sociology and Empirical Research, in 'The Positivist Dispute in German
Sociology'.
4   This concept is discussed in more detail in Chapter 5.
5   As will be noted in later chapters, this is a feature
as much of structural forces as it is of a natural
desire on the part of immigrants, for whatever reason,
to live in close proximity to one another.
6   In addition, Davison's relationship does not appear to
hold for Jamaicans, whom Peach (1968) describes (p.27)
as 'a weighty exception to the rule'.
7   Quoted from Hansard by Field, F. and Haikin, P.,
'Black Britons' (1971), p.9.
8   It is perhaps worth noting here that Lawrence, in attempting to answer the question of why people emigrated to the UK, separated this into two distinct
issues: (a) why they left the West Indies, say; (b)
why they came to the UK. Despite the appealing logic
of this procedure, it does have the serious inbuilt
weakness that in attempting to separate the 'push' and
'pull' factors, it is not possible to assess the major
determinant, and may be attempting to separate the in-
separable (Lawrence, D., 'Black Migrants: White
Natives', 1974).
9   Their fears are illustrated by the fact that the net
intake of Commonwealth immigrants rose very sharply in
1960 and the first half of 1962.

10 Lawrence, op.cit., p.22.
11 See, for example, Lawrence, op.cit.;   and Berger, J.
    and Mohr, J., 'A Seventh Man' (1975).
12 Lawrence, op.cit., p.40.
13 Ibid., p.40.
14 And the way in which he/she might react against and
    possibly reject his/her expected role.
15 This concept will be expanded upon in subsequent dis-
    cussion. Similar findings on the nature of restric-
    tions on de facto social status are reported in Rex,
    J. and Tomlinson, S., 'Colonial Immigrants in a
    British City' (1979).
16 This is a similar argument to the one adopted by
    Sivanandan, A., in Race, Class and the State: the
    Black Experience in Britain (1976).
17 Lawrence, op.cit., p.41.
18 Woods, R., Dynamic Urban Social Structure: A Study of
    Intra-urban Migration and the Development of Social
    Stress Areas in Birmingham (1975), p.iii. It must be
    stressed that this relates specifically to Birmingham.
    This point may not hold for other cities with immi-
    grant populations. The general issue of settlement
    patterns will be discussed in Chapter 2.
19 We restricted our sample to first-generation immi-
    grants and interviewed heads of household (see also
    Appendix 1).
20 They also arrived here, of course, at a time when the
    tide of political opinion in many quarters was turning
    against continuing immigration. This whole issue of
    difference in 'life-satisfaction' is followed up in
    much more detail in Chapter 6.
21 This point is discussed in particular in Chapter 4.
22 See, for example, Hiro, D., 'Black British, White
    British' (1973). It should perhaps be noted, on the
    other hand, that many Handsworth Asians saw these
    'sins' as strong factors in Britain's favour! This
    group (as we shall see shortly) tended to stress the
    importance of individual freedom, meaning freedom for
    the normative constraints of their homeland culture.
23 In Chapter 6 we focus on the second-generation Asians.
24 The chances of black children actually achieving such
    upward mobility are discussed in Chapter 6.
25 Lawrence, op.cit., p.43.
26 It is possible that sampling error plays a part in
    this differential, though this is not amenable to
    analysis by virtue of the sample design.
27 Research towards the degree of PhD in Sociology at the
    University of Warwick.
28 Cf. Banton, M., 'Racial Minorities' (1972), p.128.

29   Some of the former group may, in any case, be similar-
     ly constrained.
30   It is a moot point whether in the fullness of time
     they will still wish (or be able) to do so.
31   It should not be forgotten that the 1971 Immigration
     Act effectively prevents permanent immigration of
     blacks who are not in the dependency group, since the
     vast majority will find themselves defined as non-
     patrials.
32   Eversley, D. and Sudkeo F., 'The Dependants of the
     Coloured Population of England and Wales' (1969).
33   This is the total size of the 700 immigrant families
     studied.
34   It is highly likely that irrespective of immigration
     laws a number of these for various reasons would not
     come here.
35   We are talking here about 'natural increase' and not
     immigration.
36   The two from Pakistan came in 1958. One Indian ar-
     rived in 1960 and the other two Indians in 1962.

CHAPTER 2   HANDSWORTH: THE CHANGING FACE OF AN URBAN
            COMMUNITY

1   See note 2 of Table 2.1.
2   This issue will be treated in much greater detail in
    Chapter 4.
3   Report by the Liaison Officer for Commonwealth Immi-
    grants, BCC Pro. 21 May 1959, pp.16-20 (General Pur-
    poses Committee), reported in Sutcliffe and Smith
    (1974), p.376.
4   These are estimates based on the 5-14 age-range in
    Table 2.4. 'Black' here is equated with 'New Common-
    wealth origin'.
5   The figures for Sandwell and Newtown are significantly
    lower than those for the other two wards principally
    because the overall level of immigration in these
    areas has been smaller.
6   Hiro, D., 'Black British, White British' (1973), p.
    157. This is based on the findings of a study pub-
    lished in 'New Society' in 1968.
7   This issue will be discussed further in Chapter 4. It
    is worth noting here, however, that later discussion
    in this present chapter shows that the present Asians
    have largely adopted a nuclear household structure.
    This does not, of course, in itself imply that the
    'joint family' has disappeared. It may well be that
    families have bought a number of houses in close prox-
    imity.

8 The divergence between weighted and unweighted figures might have been expected, since this process affects the results of those interviewed in the Newtown council estate. The 'points' system adopted by councils in allocating their properties tends to produce a situation where large families are more likely to obtain accommodation. The comparable figures for the West Indians are very similar because the 'extreme value' effect on the mean is less pronounced.

9 Source: 'Birmingham Statistics', vol.18, 1973-5, Table 30.

10 It would be quite possible to compute the number of children per 'household' and reach an average figure which might be wildly in excess of 'true' figures ('true' in terms of births to constituent members of the joint family).

11 The rather smaller figures for the weighted sample are due to the fact that a greater proportion of single-parent black families have achieved council housing than have the general black population. As we shall see, however, this figure is still very low. Even the lower figure of 14.4 per cent is rather higher than the 13 per cent quoted by Smith for the PEP research (Smith, D.J., 'Racial Disadvantage in Britain', 1977, p.49).

12 Smith, op.cit., p.49.

13 Krausz, E., 'Ethnic Minorities in Britain' (1972), pp.14-15.

14 The broader implications of this issue will be discussed in subsequent chapters.

15 We assume implicitly here, as earlier, that single parenthood is negatively valued by the participants.

16 Smith, op.cit., p.49.

17 Ibid., p.49.

18 Hiro, op.cit., p.158.

19 Ibid., pp.158-9.

20 Smith, op.cit., p.48.

21 Ibid., pp.48-9.

22 He may also be better able to find his way around the British house financing system.

23 Smith, op.cit., p.49.

24 See Chapter 5 for further discussion of this finding.

25 The comparable figures for the West Indians are 4(5).

26 During 1977 this figure rose to well over 1.6 million. As we shall see in Chapter 5, there were no signs that the situation in Birmingham was easing.

27 By this term we mean post-partition India. It is, however, conceivable that despite careful fieldwork instructions, one or two errors may have been made.

28 It is still regarded as totally unacceptable for Sikh
    women to adopt this mode of behaviour (and particular-
    ly in public).
29 Strictly speaking, this practice is common throughout
    the Indian subcontinent. It is, however, traditional-
    ly enforced most rigidly by Moslems.
30 Banton, M., 'Racial Minorities' (1972), p.145.
31 Khan, V.S., 'The Pakistanis: Mirpuri Villagers at Home
    and in Bradford', in Watson (1977), pp.77-8.
32 Calley, M.J.C., 'God's People: West Indian Pentecostal
    Sects in England' (1965).
33 At least this is the case in areas which have a large
    black immigrant population.
34 Banton, op.cit., p.151.
35 This refers to a piece of research (as yet unpublish-
    ed) which was conducted as part of a PhD programme for
    the Sociology department at Warwick University.
36 Banton, op.cit., p.150.
37 Ibid., pp.150-1.
38 In this case important spatial clustering may exist,
    but be arbitrarily split up by wards. This problem
    may be diluted by rather more detailed analysis: for
    example, by looking at enumeration districts rather
    than wards.
39 This general finding is confirmed by a closer look at
    the available evidence. If we take the analysis down
    to the level of enumeration districts we see that the
    segregation of Sikhs and Hindus, for example, is quite
    marked. Although at the ward level the settlement
    pattern of these groups seems quite similar, within
    the enumeration districts a quite different picture
    emerges. Thus Indians and Pakistanis on the whole
    seem to have settled in different parts of Handsworth.
    In addition, among the Indian groups there is evidence
    of concentrations of Sikhs and Hindus in small groups
    within wards.
40 Millar, India (Anthropology) (1959), makes this point
    on p.431 where he argues that Sikhs 'reject among
    other things, caste ...'. Banton (op.cit., p.136)
    argues that 'nominally there are no castes among the
    Sikhs and Muslims' but that 'they maintain internal
    distinctions based on occupations'.
41 Banton, op.cit., p.137.
42 Interview screened on 12 September 1977; reported in
    'The Listener', 15 September 1977.
43 Such fears are usually heightened by reference to the
    racial disturbances in Britain. These eruptions of
    overt conflict will be discussed in Chapter 6.
44 Lawrence, D., 'Black Migrants: White Natives' (1974),
    p.114.

45 This issue of citizenship rights will be seen as critical to discussions of race both by the present author and by Rex, J. and Tomlinson, S., 'Colonial Immigrants in a British City' (1979).

46 See the relevant discussion of this issue in Chapter 3.

47 Or conceivably to some combination of both.

48 Professor Brass argued that in 1969 the average completed family in the general population was 'about three children per mother: by 1975 the three had been reduced to something under two. This is a dramatic fall, of the kind which has been going on all over Europe. But the change for the West Indian population was even more dramatic. An average family size, in 1969, of four was reduced to slightly over two in 1975' (reported in the 'Listener', 15 September 1977).

49 Professor Brass continued: 'If we look at the Asians in 1969 there is a very high rate of family building: about six children. This had decreased by 1975 to about four: proportionately much the same change as the average' ('Listener', 15 September 1977).

50 Another statistical trap! Crude fertility rates measure the number of live births per 1,000 of the 'at risk' population. They do not take into account differences in the age structure of the population. It follows, therefore, that such figures could be used as evidence of a 'population explosion' among black immigrants. In fact, they have been. We need therefore to look carefully at the age-specific fertility rates.

CHAPTER 3   IMAGES OF CONTEMPORARY HANDSWORTH

1 See, in particular, Rex, J. and Moore, R., 'Race, Community and Conflict' (1967), chapter 12.

2 An example of the unification of these elements is embodied in the notion of 'housing-class', as discussed in Rex and Moore, op.cit.

3 Approximately seven out of every ten white owner-occupiers in the Soho ward 'dislike' the area in which they live. In Newtown ward half of the whites interviewed said that they liked the area.

4 Many 'liberal' policies which suggest that immigrant groups should be dispersed (e.g., those noted by Smith, D.J., 'Racial Disadvantage in Britain', 1977, p.35) are thus missing the major issue here. We are dealing with a structural problem with much wider implications than those of housing. Until the black immigrant attains equality of treatment in this much

broader sense the whole question of dispersal is
rather academic.
5 Weighted figures in brackets.
6 This is so, even if we take account of the fact that
the open-ended nature of the question may in itself
have created analytical problems. In particular,
there are those which arise from exploring a 'taken-
for-granted' world.
7 It is not, of course, claimed that we as academic researchers have especially privileged access to this
level of 'knowledge'.
8 One could argue that there are too many people within
a particular physical space but not too many of one
particular social or ethnic group.
9 Grodzin, M., Metropolitan Segregation (1957).
10 As the concept of 'prejudice' has provoked a great
deal of shallow empirical research and is crucial to
the notion of 'understanding a race relations situation' we shall consider it at length later in the
present chapter.
11 The slight decline in the weighted percentage reflects
the finding that delinquency was seen as a problem
more frequently by the whites on the Newtown council
estate than by this group taken as a whole.
12 The reader should note here that the categories may
overlap in a substantive sense and also occasionally
contain the same respondents; i.e., the same respondent may give both answers.
13 The question of why there are so few members of the
minority groups in council housing will be raised
again in Chapter 4. It will be noted, in particular,
that the number of Asian tenants is almost negligible.
14 Furthermore, as noted in Chapter 1, many of the more
recent arrivals did not actually want to come here.
15 Adorno, T.W. et al. (1950), quoted in Rex and Moore,
op.cit., p.12.
16 We shall not follow up the problematic features of
this issue here, for example, the question of when
the personality is deemed to be fully 'developed'.
17 Rex and Moore, op.cit., p.12.
18 In Gould and Kolb (1964), and quoted by Deakin, N.,
'Colour, Citizenship and British Society' (1970),
p.317.
19 Deakin, op.cit., pp.317-34.
20 Ibid., p.317.
21 Cox, O.C., 'Caste, Class and Race' (1948), p.393;
quoted in Lawrence, D., 'Black Migrants: White
Natives' (1974), p.52.
22 Lawrence, op.cit., pp.52-3.

23 In the foreword to Deakin (op.cit.) it is stated that Alan Marsh 'produced the new version of chapter 12'.

24 Mills, C.Wright, 'The Sociological Imagination' (1959), chapter 3.

25 Lawrence, op.cit., p.50.

26 These represent the group of people who have given three or more hostile responses to the 'prejudice' questions.

27 Lawrence (op.cit., p.53) questions the reliability and validity of their measure of authoritarianism.

28 Deakin, op.cit., p.324.

29 Ibid., p.325.

30 Lawrence, op.cit., p.53, footnote (g).

31 Ibid., p.53.

32 Referred to in Deakin, op.cit., p.334.

33 Ibid., p.319.

34 It is naive, we feel, to talk about a single 'value system' in relation to British society.

35 Lawrence, op.cit., p.51.

36 Ibid., p.54.

37 This approach is implicit in some of the foregoing discussion of the works of Rose, Deakin and associates.

38 See the questionnaire in Appendix 2.

39 It is conceded that the interviewers were instructed to introduce themselves as members of a NOP team 'interviewing a cross section of people of different nationalities'. The possibility remains, therefore, that this might have influenced some respondents to think in terms of racial issues even in 'general' questions.

40 Layton-Henry, Z. and Taylor, S., Race at the Polls, in 'New Society', vol.41 (25 August 1977), p.392.

41 A few days before the Ladywood violence a National Front march in Lewisham was the scene of fierce battles between Front supporters and rival demonstrators composed predominantly of left-wing groups.

42 Lawrence, op.cit., pp.47-8.

43 Rex and Moore, op.cit., chapter 3, pp.59-83. This and the general lack of mobility are not, of course, particularly surprising. One would expect similar findings in many other working-class areas of Britain. They do, however, take on a special significance in the context of a multi-racial area such as Handsworth, as will be seen.

44 This relation to 'capital' in the form of property constitutes a central feature of the notion of 'housing class' (see Rex and Moore, op.cit.). The usefulness of this as an analytical tool will be reviewed in the next chapter.

45 These two groups do differ in size considerably
    (roughly in the ratio three to one). We must beware,
    therefore, of placing too much emphasis on any conclu-
    sions we make here.

46 The issue will be confronted a little later in the
    current chapter.

47 It should perhaps be noted here that we have, in tech-
    nical jargon, a 'confounding' of at least two vari-
    ables; 'Newtown/non-Newtown' and 'estate council/non-
    estate council'. This may or may not be of signifi-
    cance in substantive terms.

48 This is clearly one dimension of the concept of gener-
    al 'well-being', hypothesised as being conferred on
    the owner-occupier.

49 Discussed further in Chapter 4.

50 See, for example, Deakin, op.cit., p.318: 'Having es-
    tablished that simple proximity to coloured minorities
    (as opposed to face-to-face contacts) is not in itself
    a major element in shaping attitudes, it was decided
    to proceed to an intensive study conducted in areas of
    high immigrant settlement.'

51 This presents, in simplified form, the data contained
    in Table 20, p.321 of Deakin, op.cit.

52 In this instance the 'lower middle class' are being
    compared with three categories of workers whose defi-
    nition appears to match Deakin's 'Professional/
    Managerial', 'Skilled Working Class' and 'Other
    Working Class'.

53 See, for example, Rex and Moore, op.cit., chapter 3,
    pp.59-83.

54 This simplistic distinction was inserted as a short-
    hand form in lieu of a more general discussion of the
    ideological use of such a ploy. The author realises
    that inherent in this argument is the vexed question
    of subjectivity and value commitment.

55 Much public debate has surrounded the operationalisa-
    tion of this concept, at least by those who believe
    that such a discussion is ideologically acceptable.

56 This comprises part of the quote in Cox, op.cit.,
    p.393, referred to earlier in the present chapter.

57 Although in general in this book we include both
    Asians and West Indians in the term 'black', in this
    instance we are speaking almost exclusively of West
    Indian youth. Chapter 6 includes a discussion of why
    this is so.

58 See, for example, the report of a working party of the
    British Youth Council, 'Youth Unemployment: Causes and
    Cures' (March 1977), paras 31-5.

59 This distinction between the general and the specific

is of great theoretical importance. Many respondents who showed great hostility towards blacks in general displayed in other answers a total acceptance of particular black neighbours. Indeed, such families were often regarded as 'friends'. The significance of this lies in the extent to which particular experiences fail to modify racial stereotypes.

60 This alludes to the fact that 82 per cent of our Asian sample are owner-occupiers.

61 The centrality of the notion of 'access to housing' in the context of an analysis of 'class' and 'race relation situations' was stressed in Rex and Moore, op. cit. Chapter 4 in the present book will continue this debate.

62 This is not, of course, to imply that there are no means by which we may differentiate in terms of verbal hostility between a person with three answers exhibiting a measure of race hatred, and another who answers only one question, say, in this fashion.

63 This contains a slight over-simplification. For example, a number of those included in this category mentioned the presence of 'coloureds' as one thing they disliked about Handsworth. They are included here because they regarded the issue as only of secondary importance.

CHAPTER 4   HOUSING AND RACE

1 City of Birmingham Structure Plan, Report of Survey: Housing (February 1973), p.6.

2 At the time of the 1971 Census the total number of enumerated dwellings in the city was 330,190.

3 City of Birmingham Structure Plan, op.cit., p.7.

4 See, for example, Kendall, M.G. and Stuart, A., 'Advanced Theory of Statistics' (vol.3) 3rd edition (1977); or, for rather less technical accounts, Tyron, R.C. and Bailey, D.E., 'Cluster Analysis' (1970); and Everitt, B., 'Cluster Analysis' (1974).

5 The major elements of this cluster are as follows: more affluent, non-manual workers, owner-occupied housing and larger dwellings.

6 City of Birmingham Structure Plan, op.cit., p.37, para. 5.3.

7 Ibid., p.38.

8 Rex, J. and Moore, R., 'Race, Community and Conflict' (1967).

9 There is no space here to include a detailed critique. However, it is clear that at the level of data, two

major problems exist: (a) the question of which variables are selected, especially given the nature of
data available; i.e., one is limited to sample census
data; and (b) we are in a situation where a study of
inter-relationships at the level of individuals (or
individual households) is not possible. This caused
the confusion in the interpretation of results which
was noted above.

10   City of Birmingham Structure Plan, op.cit., p.37.

11   This is a reference to the remark in para. 5.3 that
'it is towards these (1b and 1c) areas that future
planning policies will therefore be largely directed'.

12   Gill, C., 'History of Birmingham' vol.1 (1952).

13   See, for example, the article in the 'Observer' of
11 December 1977 by George Brock: Police 'Dreadlock'
Report Starts a Row. The report referred to was
Brown, J., 'Shades of Grey' (1977).

14   Reports of the Housing Enquiry Committee, City of
Birmingham, 1914.

15   City of Birmingham Structure Plan, op.cit., p.47.

16   'Preferred' is placed in quotation marks because the
concept is, as we shall see, of much broader significance than it might at first appear. We are talking
about much more than environmental considerations.

17   Rex, J. and Tomlinson, S. ('Colonial Immigrants in a
British City', 1979), among others, are led to argue
in terms of the notion of blacks as an 'under-class',
or 'sub-proletariat'.

18   Community Relations Commission Report, 'Urban Deprivation, Racial Inequality and Social Policy' (1977),
p.15.

19   This is not intended to imply that the sole purpose of
the analysis is to generate empirical conclusions
based on the specific situational factors at work in
Birmingham. To do so would be to create an abstraction. It is hoped that the analysis will throw light
on conceptual issues of rather broader significance.

20   Woods, 'Dynamic Urban Social Structure' (1975), p.ii.

21   It should, perhaps be noted here that Woods was using
the 1971 Census data, whereas the Birmingham report
had to rely on what it admitted to be out-of-date
figures, namely, those of the 1966 Census.

22   See, for example, PEP, 'The Facts of Racial Disadvantage' (1976); CRC (1977), op.cit.

23   See, for example, PEP (1976), op.cit.; and Lawrence,
D., 'Black Migrants: White Natives' (1974), especially
pp.90ff.

24   Rex and Moore, op.cit., chapter 1.

25   See, for example, Lawrence, op.cit., chapter 4; and

Karn, V., A note on race, community and conflict (1967).

26 Rex and Moore, op.cit., p.36. Rex and Tomlinson (op. cit.) discuss the more radical criticism in their footnote 1 to page 127. This position is challenged by Lawrence (op.cit., p.87, footnote h), who argues that 'Rex and Moore's list of housing "classes" is essentially a list of levels in a given status hierarchy' and as such represents a misinterpretation of Weber. Whether or not this is the case, interesting though the academic point may be, it makes no difference, of course, to the theory derived from the analysis (as seen through Rex and Moore's definitional framework).

27 See, for example, the three works noted in notes 24 and 25, as well as Rex and Tomlinson, op.cit.

28 Rex and Moore, op.cit., p.41.

29 See Rex, J., 'The Sociology of a Zone of Transition', in Pahl (1968).

30 Throughout this chapter in particular it is the weighted figures which will be given prominence. This is due to the fact that disproportionately large numbers of both West Indians and British were chosen from the Newtown council estate (see Appendix 1).

31 This estimated projection is based on the relevant census material.

32 As noted below, according to the 1971 Census, 50 per cent of all householders in England and Wales were owner-occupiers.

33 Smith, D.J., 'Racial Disadvantage in Britain (1977), p.211.

34 Ibid., p.210.

35 Rex and Moore, op.cit., pp.36-7.

36 See Daniel, W.W., 'Racial Discrimination in England' (1968).

37 Lawrence, op.cit., p.90.

38 See, for example, the discussion of research material presented in Lawrence, pp.90-2.

39 Rex and Moore, op.cit., p.37.

40 It should perhaps be pointed out here that the Asians who enter the 'class' of owner-occupiers tend to do so at the bottom end of the market. This point will be discussed further in the current chapter.

41 Smith, op.cit., p.210.

42 Ibid., p.213. The remainder of his thesis will be tested later in the present chapter.

43 Smith finds that white-collar Asians are much more likely than their blue-collar counterparts to be found in privately rented accommodation (often in predomi-

nantly white areas). It appears that this is seen, as with many young whites, as a springboard to good-quality housing to be bought at a later date. Given the shortage of privately rented accommodation in Handsworth and the greater purchasing power of these individuals, many may be able to choose not to live in this area.

44 See Smith, op.cit., Table A.5.2, p.215.

45 There was considerable evidence that some tenants were being coerced into leaving properties prematurely.

46 An analysis of the 1971 Census figures reveals that this sharp decline is continuing. The appropriate figure over the 1961-71 period is 34.6 per cent.

47 City of Birmingham Structure Plan, op.cit., p.68.

48 It should perhaps be noted here that all the private rented property in our survey area lies in a Housing Action area, a Redevelopment area or a General Improvement area.

49 If the property is compulsorily improved it remains on the housing stock for thirty years, and the Housing Department has no obligation to rehouse people in council property.

50 City of Birmingham Structure Plan, op.cit., p.68.

51 Smith, D.J. and Whalley, A., 'Racial Minorities and Public Housing' (1975), p.12.

52 City of Birmingham Structure Plan, op.cit., p.68, para. 12.4.

53 See Table A.5.3 in Smith, op.cit., p.220.

54 Here we are referring to our own study and that reported by Smith, op.cit.

55 The Housing Department estimated that this figure was approximately 8 per cent.

56 Smith, op.cit., p.219.

57 Ibid., p.236.

58 Rex and Moore, op.cit., p.37.

59 See, for example, Table 3.5.

60 One family has rented its current accommodation (in the private sector) for over ten years and the other has also occupied the same council property for this period.

61 It is, of course, conceivable that many West Indians conform to Runciman's argument: namely, that the objectively deprived often have very limited horizons (Runciman, W.G., 'Relative Deprivation and Social Justice', 1966).

62 Smith, op.cit., p.224.

63 This contrasts sharply with the sample of West Indians, where 85 per cent of owner-occupiers have mortgages or loans to repay.

64 Smith and Whalley, op.cit., p.13.
65 See the discussion of this issue in Chapter 2.
66 See, for example, the discussion on this issue contained in Chapter 3.
67 It will be noticed here that the definition of the 'cake' is problematic. At least three interpretations have already been used, and will continue to be used for comparative purposes: the wards from which the sample was chosen, the City of Birmingham, and England and Wales.
68 Perhaps one point should be underlined here: to say that black immigrants are not uniformly spread throughout the country is not to imply that the majority live in inner-city areas.
69 'Inner Area Studies', consultants' final report (February 1977).
70 City of Birmingham Structure Plan, op.cit., p.81.
71 This distinction between 'sharing' and 'sub-letting' is vital for the subsequent analysis, given that it has important implications for the nature of the relationship between those who share a dwelling.
72 This group are noted as belonging to housing class 4. See Rex and Moore, op.cit., pp.36-8.
73 The qualification 'in physical terms' is vital here. Although not strictly an objective measure, since the classification results from the judgment of housing officials and other 'professionals', it is at least defined external to the residents themselves. We are not concerned at this stage with how residents feel about their property but with the implications in terms of housing market competition and ultimately housing policies.
74 See, for example, the Green Paper, 'Housing Policy, a Consultative Document', published in June 1977.
75 The idea was first mooted at parliamentary level in the Government White Paper of 1968, 'Our Older Houses'.
76 This means, briefly, that every property would be inspected, and under the 1969 Housing Act grants of 50 per cent for repair costs, up to a maximum of £1,000, would be given (£1,200 in the case of dwellings of more than three storeys) and up to 50 per cent, up to a maximum of £200, given for environmental improvements. For further details, see City of Birmingham Structure Plan, op.cit., pp.46-50.
77 Once again this appears to be a statement of theory rather than practice. Few of our survey respondents have in fact benefited under this scheme.
78 For the geographical location of these areas compare Figures 3 and 4.

79   Smith and Whalley, op.cit., and Smith, op.cit., argue
     that Asians, for example, once rehoused in council
     property, tend to remain tenants of the local authori-
     ty.   However, this does not imply that they are satis-
     fied with this state of affairs.   It may be that the
     progressive clearance reduces 'their' sector of the
     housing market, or that they fear buying a similar
     property in case the same thing happens again.

80   As Smith (op.cit., p.232) points out, 'There is a high
     level of owner-occupation among Asians and West
     Indians but they still tend to be badly housed.'

81   See Table 2.4 (p.36) of the City of Birmingham
     Structure Plan, op.cit.   This gives the individual
     percentages as follows: Handsworth 9.8 per cent and
     Soho 9.4 per cent.

82   For a note on definitional 'problems' see the foot-
     notes (ibid.) on pp.28 and 32.

83   Ibid., p.32.

84   Ibid., p.28.

85   It may well be that repayments are, in fact, larger
     than they might have been, since the owner borrowed
     £3,000 from the Julian Hodge Group to repay a council
     mortgage and to install central heating.   This may,
     perhaps, reflect the phenomenon noted by Valerie Karn,
     that many immigrants (particularly Asians) desire to
     avoid organisations whose conditions deter sub-letting
     and impose other requirements relating to, for
     example, the maintenance of property standards (Karn,
     V., The Financing of Owner-Occupation, 1978).

86   It is important to realise, however, that this does
     not necessarily imply that, at the time when the pro-
     perties were purchased, there was no element of com-
     pulsion.

87   See, for example, Duncan, S.S., 'Self-Help: the allo-
     cation of mortgages and the formation of sub-markets'
     (1976).   There is, however, a major flaw in the uni-
     versality assumption here: why is it, for example,
     that it is only the Asians, in the main, to whom the
     'starvation' applies?

88   It is, of course conceivable that some of those re-
     spondents who were designated as not sharing their
     house were in fact doing so.

89   Whereas in the early days of emigration from the
     Indian subcontinent male members of the family might
     come to the UK and live in cheap lodging-house type
     accommodation for a few years, in order to accumulate
     capital, it is likely that fear of a complete halt on
     immigration has speeded up the emigration process and
     thereby contributed significantly to the appalling
     overcrowding which is discussed above.

90 City of Birmingham Structure Plan, op.cit., p.73, para. 10.

91 Ibid., para. 12. Because of the possibility of confusion arising from the definition of overcrowding, it is, we feel, important to stress, as did the authors of this report, that:

> This measure of overcrowding should not be confused with the statutory definition of overcrowding contained in section 77 of the Housing Act 1957, which takes account of the age and sex of occupants and the floor area of rooms. The census measure of persons per room, on the other hand, treats every member of the household as one unit, irrespective of age or sex, and takes no account of room size.

92 This is not to argue, of course, that the whites were experiencing particularly good housing conditions. Table 4.6 shows, for example, that a significant minority were without some of the basic amenities.

93 By this we mean: in terms of the possession of the three basic amenities and the level of occupational density.

94 One problem of this analysis lies in the cross-sectional nature of the data. Patterns may well change over time. There is no way, for example, of predicting the way in which today's young families will behave in the future, or indeed of tracing the detailed housing history of older West Indian residents. The latter would have required a questionnaire in itself! See, however, Table 4.3A.

95 This 'finding' is, of course, far from novel. Many writers, including Rex and Moore, op.cit., and Smith, op.cit., have reported the existence of similar phenomena.

96 Smith, op.cit., p.228.

97 Ibid., p.228. He also notes that, if anything, leasehold tenure is less common among West Indians than in the general population. This appears to be corroborated by our Handsworth data.

98 As there are only 12 families in this category it is difficult to come to any firm conclusions about their position in the housing market. What we know, however, is that eight of these are owner-occupiers; all but one family has exclusive access to the basic amenities, and none live in overcrowded conditions. Furthermore, five have freehold tenure and the others have extremely long leases to run (40 years, 50 years and 75 years respectively).

99 See Rex and Tomlinson, op.cit., Table 7.2.

100   See, for example, McIntosh, N. and Smith, D.J., 'The
      Extent of Racial Discrimination' (1974).
101   Methodological problems always complicate the analy-
      sis of income statistics. Perhaps, in this instance,
      'accuracy of reporting' rather than the question of
      'gross or net income' or 'non-response' is the major
      problem, though the three are clearly related. We
      asked for gross income (i.e., income before deduc-
      tions), and hoped to keep misreporting to a minimum
      by using showcards with broad wage bands rather than
      asking for exact amounts.
102   This measure (mortgage repayments) suffers from the
      same problems as that of income. It is partly be-
      cause of this (though mainly due to the need for sim-
      plicity of presentation) that only approximate
      figures are given here.
103   Because of non-response on this issue (amounting to
      4 per cent among Asians, 11 per cent among West
      Indians and 15 per cent for the British sample), and
      also the effect of reporting and recording errors, we
      should perhaps treat these figures with some caution.
      We estimate, however, that the median monthly repay-
      ments are as follows: West Indians, £23.26; Asians,
      £29.29; and the British, £22.67.
104   Rex and Tomlinson, op.cit., chapter 7.
105   The corresponding figures for white and West Indian
      owner-occupiers who unknowingly live in a Housing
      Action Area are 14 per cent and 16 per cent respec-
      tively.
106   One must, however, beware of making firm inferences
      on the basis of what are extremely small sample
      sizes.
107   There is some evidence of this in the qualitative
      questionnaire material which, for reasons of space,
      has been omitted here.
108   Immigrant densities on more 'desirable' estates tend
      to be even smaller than 10 per cent.
109   These controls have been seen by some as a direct
      result of class conflict, and in particular as im-
      portant victories for the working class.
110   Thirty Asian families do, in fact, rent privately.
      Unfortunately, one respondent failed to give details
      of his landlord.
111   But see Table 4.8, note 2.
112   Rex and Moore, op.cit., pp.40-1.

CHAPTER 5   BLACK IMMIGRANTS AND THE LABOUR MARKET

1   From 'Slave Driver' by Bob Marley and the Wailers
    (1973), discussed in Jamaican Rebel Music by Linton
    Kwesi Johnson in 'Race and Class'.
2   The quoted figure is based on the potential working
    population in 1976 (this being the base figure used by
    the Birmingham Department of Employment).
3   This comprises the City of Birmingham, plus Broms-
    grove, Chelmsley Wood and Solihull.
4   Manpower Services Commission, Annual Report, 1974-5.
5   Ibid., inside cover.
6   See, for example, the 1978 Government White Paper.
7   Martin, R. and Fryer, R.H., 'Redundancy and Paternal-
    ist Capitalism', especially chapter 1.
8   Ibid., p.19.
9   See, for example, Smith, D.J., 'Racial Disadvantage in
    Employment' (1974).
10 See Mullard, C., 'Black Britain' (1973).
11 Smith, op.cit., chapter 11.
12 Brown, J., 'Shades of Grey' (1977).
13 British Youth Council, 'Youth Unemployment' (1977),
    page 12, para. 32.
14 See, however, the warning contained in note 2 to
    Table 5.1.
15 The figures essentially cover the 16–19 age-group.
16 See 'Department of Employment Gazette' (September
    1975), p.868.   This paper, entitled 'Unemployment
    among Workers from Racial Minority Groups', presents
    statistical evidence of the way in which heavy unem-
    ployment hits minority groups particularly hard.   It
    is argued, for example, that 'the proportionate in-
    crease in unemployment among minority group workers
    has been more than twice as large between November
    1973 and May 1975 as among the total male unemployed.'
17 Although this is not the place to extend discussion of
    this issue, it may be noted in passing that the direc-
    tion of association may be rather different from that
    which is implied here.   For example, Rastafarianism
    grew (in Kingston, Jamaica) out of the slums and among
    the unemployed.
18 Smith, op.cit., p.88.
19 Ibid., p.88.
20 'Department of Employment Gazette' (March 1976):
    'Racial Disadvantage - a PEP Report'.
21 See in particular the discussion of changes in minori-
    ty group unemployment by age, which shows clearly that
    black school-leavers, and in particular black men,
    suffered especially badly between February 1974 and
    February 1975.

22   Smith, D.J., 'Racial Disadvantage in Britain' (1977),
     p.71.
23   Source: Manpower Services Commission, Birmingham.
24   The actual figures as given by the 'Department of
     Employment Gazette' are as follows:

                  West Midlands   UK
     May 1974   45,100   561,600
     August 1977   156,000   1,635,800

25   It should be remembered here that some caution is
     necessary in interpreting the figures since Handsworth
     EEA is not synonymous with the 'Handsworth' of our
     survey.
26   As hinted earlier, this analysis might be repeated in
     terms of class, thus giving a new slant to the notion
     of relative job permanency (i.e., white-collar vis-à-
     vis blue-collar).
27   'Department of Employment Gazette' (September 1975),
     op.cit., p.871.
28   See Table 5.2 and note the definitional problem sur-
     sounding 'Handsworth'.
29   This comprises the total of those who are either in
     work, seeking work, or off work temporarily through
     sickness or industrial action (i.e., laid off because
     of dispute).
30   It must be remembered that these are not unemployment
     rates in the strict sense, since the base figures
     include the 'economically inactive'. For 'corrected'
     rates, see the body of Table 5.3B.
31   Unemployment among West Indian, Asian and British men
     in this age-group was running at 6(8) per cent, 10 per
     cent and 13(16) per cent respectively.
32   As only 11 British male heads of household were unem-
     ployed, it might be misleading to quote figures here.
     Bearing this qualification in mind, 7 out of this
     number had been unemployed for at least six months.
33   Nine respondents (4 West Indians and 5 Asians) did, in
     fact, specify 'racial discrimination' as the reason
     for arguing that it would be difficult to find another
     job. This reinforces the finding of Smith, op.cit.
     (1974), who examined closely the discriminatory prac-
     tices of employers.
34   This refers to the Standard Industrial Classification
     produced by the Central Statistical Office. Unless
     otherwise stated, the 1968 edition will be used
     throughout this chapter.
35   There is indeed some evidence to support this sug-
     gestion in the main body of the questionnaires. It is
     likely that, as a result, unemployment among the
     'next' generation of whites would tend to be somewhat
     lower than that for either of the immigrant groups.

36   Of the women registered as unemployed in the Hands-
     worth EEA in May 1976 53.3 per cent were of New
     Commonwealth origin (i.e., born in, or having at least
     one parent born in, the New Commonwealth or Pakistan).
37   See, for example, Smith, op.cit. (1977), pp.65-7.
38   This is confirmed by Smith's analysis (see Smith, op.
     cit., 1977, p.71).
39   Source: Hospital Domestic Survey 1968, quoted in 'The
     Role of Immigrants in the Labour Market', Department
     of Employment (1976).
40   Source: Figures at 31 December 1975 compiled by the
     DHSS Statistics and Research Division.
41   See, for example, Department of Employment, op.cit.
     (1976), p.132, Table F12.
42   Ibid., Table 6.5, p.145.
43   City of Birmingham, 'A New Plan for the City - Employ-
     ment and Industry' (1973), p.13, para. 2.6.1.
44   Ibid., p.13.
45   Strictly speaking this is only an estimate of the
     actual figure, since the enumeration procedure covered
     only 10 per cent of households, and the figure for
     economically active includes those who are out of work
     and those who are off work temporarily through sick-
     ness.
46   See, for example, Department of Employment, Institute
     of Manpower Studies, 'The Role of Immigrants in the
     Labour Market' (1976); Smith, op.cit. (1977); and
     Rose, E.J.B. et al., 'Colour and Citizenship' (1969).
47   Department of Employment, Institute of Manpower
     Studies, op.cit. (1976), Table G.5, p.145.
48   This is not, of course, to argue that Asians achieve
     high-status jobs within the profession: indeed, we
     noted earlier that this is generally not the case. In
     addition, recent research by Stacey and Lambrou (as
     yet unpublished) suggests that some doctors from the
     Indian subcontinent find difficulty in obtaining high-
     quality training in the UK.
49   Forester, T., Asians in Business, 'New Society', 23
     February (1978).
50   Department of Employment, Institute of Manpower
     Studies, op.cit. (1976), p.75.
51   Phillips, M., 'West Indian Businessmen', 'New
     Society', 18 May (1978), pp.354-6.
52   Ibid., p.356.
53   It is interesting here to note the remarks of a black
     social worker, brought up and living in Handsworth,
     concerning the traditional distaste for merchants and
     commerce among some West Indians. See All Faiths For
     One Race, 'Talking Blues' (1978), p.7.

54   Ibid.
55   Ibid., p.8.
56   Department of Employment, Institute of Manpower
     Studies, op.cit. (1976), pp.145-6.
57   Wright, P.L., 'The Coloured Worker in British
     Industry' (1968), p.84. See para. 3 in particular.
58   Of course, the whole concept of 'reality' is, to some
     extent, illusory. 'Reality' here is socially condi-
     tioned, depending as it does on the subjective per-
     ceptions of blacks in a white-dominated labour market.
59   Wright, op.cit., p.159.
60   Banton's picture of the West Indian worker was that of
     a person who changed jobs regularly in the hope of
     eventually finding the right job. (Banton, M., 'The
     Coloured Quarter', 1955.)
61   Wright, op.cit., p.159.
62   These references are to the stated (and well-publi-
     cised) views of Enoch Powell and Margaret Thatcher
     respectively.
63   Lawrence, D., 'Black Migrants: White Natives' (1974),
     p.114.
64   Kohler, D.F., 'The Employment of Black People in a
     London Borough' (1974), p.15.
65   Lawrence, op.cit., p.117.
66   Wright, op.cit., p.83.
67   This remark was contained in a seminar paper presented
     to the Sociology Department at Warwick University in
     1977.
68   Wright, op.cit., pp.75-6.
69   Ibid., p.76.
70   See, for example, Table G.5 in Department of Employ-
     ment, Institute of Manpower Studies, op.cit. (1976)
     which was referred to earlier in the present chapter.
71   Wright, op.cit., p.78.
72   These arguments point to the genetic intellectual
     inferiority of some racial groups.
73   Stouffer, S., 'The American Soldier' (1949).
74   For a more detailed discussion of this material the
     reader is referred to Rex, J. and Tomlinson, S.,
     'Colonial Immigrants in a British City' (1979).
75   See Smith, op.cit. (1977), chapter 2.
76   See Rimmer, M., 'Race and Industrial Conflict' (1972),
     chapter 4.
77   Ibid., p.30.
78   Ibid., p.59.
79   In this context Brown's 'Shades of Grey' takes on a
     rather different meaning.
80   We do not, of course, know whether or not this was a
     positive decision. Earnings in the construction in-

dustry are good, however, and it may therefore be a relatively difficult sector for the black worker to enter. It may be significant that only a handful of West Indians without prior experience of this type of work in the Caribbean had obtained such a job here.

81 See his discussion of the 1951 Agrarian Census of India.

82 Interview notes suggest that this is, in most cases, a fair supposition.

83 Rimmer suggests (p.30) that the majority of immigrants in the Midlands foundries he studied were Punjabis.

84 Padrun, R. and Guyot, J. (eds), 'Migrant Women Speak' (1978).

85 This was an Indian lady who was continuing the medical career she had begun in India.

86 Sutcliffe, A. and Smith, R., 'Birmingham 1939-70' (1974), p.154.

87 Timmins, S., 'The Industrial History of Birmingham' (1866), p.208.

88 Sutcliffe and Smith, op.cit., p.158.

89 Ibid., p.162.

90 The 1971 Census figures quoted by Rex and Tomlinson (op.cit., Table 5.5) show that 40.5 per cent of Indian men are employed in metal manufacture compared with 11.0 per cent of the general male population.

91 City of Birmingham, op.cit., p.47.

92 Smith, op.cit. (1977), p.80.

93 Ibid., p.81.

94 Ignoring (by necessity) the problem of sampling error.

95 Smith, op.cit. (1977), p.81.

96 Care should be taken in interpreting this finding because of the small sample size.

97 Ten out of the thirteen West Indian girls who said that they worked shifts (and all those who worked nights) were nurses.

98 Smith, op.cit. (1977), p.86.

99 Unweighted figures alone have been given here since the differences concerned are a matter of only a few pence.

100 We should perhaps be slightly wary of these and later income figures for a number of reasons:

(a) Response error tends to be relatively high on a question such as this, and there may be differential misreporting among the ethnic groups.

(b) Refusal rates were fairly high: 10, 17, 19 and 21 per cent for the British, Indians, Pakistanis and West Indians respectively.

      (c) Sample sizes among a few of the occupational sub-groups were rather small, particularly among those from Pakistan.

101 However, see the discussion of female job status earlier in this chapter.

102 Smith, op.cit. (1977), p.191.

103 Ibid., p.199.

104 See also Banton, op.cit., p.365.

105 Sivanandan, A., 'Race, Class and the State' (1976), pp.138-42.

106 Rimmer, op.cit., p.46.

107 See Appendix 1.

CHAPTER 6   RACISM AND THE FUTURE OF HANDSWORTH

1 'Asians in Britain: Problem or Opportunity', televised on 19 July 1978 as the third in a series of public lectures entitled 'Multi-Racial Britain'.

2 The Asian Resource Centre recently announced the opening of such a hostel in Handsworth.

3 In this constituency in August 1977 Layton-Henry estimates that 35 to 40 per cent of the electorate were Asian or West Indian (Layton-Henry, Z., Race and Politics in Ladywood, 1977-8, p.130).

4 Ibid., p.133.

5 Quoted in Taylor, S., Race and Politics in Ladywood (1977-8), p.135.

6 Lawrence, D., 'Black Migrants: White Natives' (1974), p.135. The data contained in our Table 6.1 suggest that under-registration in Handsworth was not so common.

7 Katznelson, I., 'The Politics of Racial Buffering in Nottingham 1954-68' (1970); quoted in Lawrence, op. cit., p.132.

8 See, for example, Deakin's articles of 1966 and 1970.

9 Lawrence, op.cit., p.134.

10 The reader will recall the discussion of this issue in the previous chapter.

11 One problem here is that, because of the very nature of Handsworth, few white-collar immigrants were interviewed. The evidence of Taylor's research quoted below does, however, corroborate this point.

12 Taylor, op.cit.

13 It is not, of course, argued that the converse holds, i.e., that voting per se implies a high level of commitment to a particular party.

14 See, for example, Lawrence, op.cit., p.134.

15 Layton-Henry, op.cit., p.135.

16 Mullard, C., 'Black Britain' (1973), p.174.
17 Ibid., p.175.
18 BBC TV lecture; see note 1.
19 The reader will recall that in Chapter 5 we looked at this group from the point of view of unemployment.
20 See Peter Winch's critique of J.S.Mill in his 'Idea of a Social Science' (1958), p.71ff.
21 This, of course, is very much a function of the rather conservative (with large and small 'c') orientation of the media.
22 Smith, op.cit. (1977), p.311.
23 Ibid., p.316.
24 Ibid., p.317.
25 See Mullard, op.cit., chapter 7.
26 Mullard's chapter 7 contains a detailed discussion of the internal working of the RRB and the important implications which inefficiency has in this particular case.
27 This is in accord with Smith's remarks: see Smith, op.cit. (1977), p.310. Given his findings on the level of ignorance of the existence of the RRB, however, we shall see this rejection of political tactics in terms of a rather small group of militant blacks. Hence Mullard's statement concerning the alienation of blacks from the legal machinery should be viewed in a slightly new light.
28 Smith, op.cit. (1977), p.317.
29 It is, of course, plausible that a number of people could be referred to a body which they had never heard of by some of the social agencies discussed later in this chapter.
30 Smith, op.cit. (1977), p.317.
31 This is not the only cause of disquiet in the area of public sector funding. There is some evidence of a lack of monitoring of schemes such as the 'Work Experience Programmes' where some employers are suspected of using publicly funded labour as a form of 'labour subsidy'.
32 This has also come to be seen as a form of 'Jamaican talk'. See, for example, Cassidy, F.G. (1961).
33 The Rastafarian is referred to as 'he' in this context on the grounds, first, that women appear to play only a subordinate role in the movement's political sphere, and, second, that white society tends to focus on the male Rastafarian as the major 'concern'.
34 'Birmingham Evening Post', 3 November 1977.
35 The implication being that this is a fact of common-sense knowledge!
36 Barrett, L.E., 'The Rastafarians' (1977), p.1.

37 This is the theme of a song on the first LP of the Handsworth group 'Steel Pulse'. This West Indian band have called their LP, rather significantly, 'Handsworth Revolution'.

38 Frith has rightly argued that 'punk' is more akin to the 'pop art' phenomenon of the 1950s than to any manifestation of contemporary working-class pop culture (Frith, S., The Punk Bohemians, 1978).

39 We have also had to exclude discussions of a vast array of other (probably less significant) West Indian organisations in Handsworth. See, for example, Rex, J. and Tomlinson, S., 'Colonial Immigrants in a British City' (1979).

40 Layton-Henry, op.cit., p.134.

41 Ibid., p.135.

42 See, for example, AFFOR, 'Talking Blues' (1978).

43 It must therefore be borne in mind that we do not include those who have left home for any reason: work, marriage, to live with friends, etc. Cases of extreme inter-generational conflict may therefore be conspicuous by their absence.

44 See the results quoted by Department of Employment, Institute of Manpower Studies, 'The Role of Immigrants in the Labour Market' (1976), p.203, para. 23; and Table 3, p.209.

45 See, for example, Allen, S. and Smith, S., Minority group experience of the transition from education to work (1975).

46 Fowler, B. et al., 'Immigrant School-leavers and the Search for Work' (1977).

47 The interviews were conducted during February 1977 by Sally Tomlinson and David Hearnden.

48 Four of the children had not received any education in the UK.

49 This applied particularly to the girls, whose level of unemployment was much higher than that of the boys. Approximately half of both the West Indian and Asian girls were out of work at the time of the interview.

50 It will be remembered here that females have little place in the Rastafarian movement (see note 33, Chapter 6). This may have influenced the answer.

51 A few West Indians still, however, make this suggestion.

52 We must bear in mind at this point the fact that we asked the parents what they thought their children wanted to do, rather than asking the children themselves.

Bibliography

ADORNO, T.W. et al. (1950), 'The Authoritarian Personality', New York, Harper.
ADORNO, T.W. (1976), Sociology and Empirical Research, in 'The Positivist Dispute in German Sociology', London, Heinemann.
ALL FAITHS FOR ONE RACE (1978), 'Talking Blues: The black community speaks about its relationship with the police', Birmingham, AFFOR.
ALLEN, S. and SMITH, S. (1975), Minority group experience of the transition from education to work, in 'Entering the World of Work: Some Sociological Perspectives', ed. P. Brannen, London, Department of Education, HMSO.
BANKS, J.A. (1954), 'Prosperity and Parenthood', London, Routledge & Kegan Paul.
BANTON, M. (1955), 'The Coloured Quarter; Negro Immigrants in an English City', London, Cape.
BANTON, M. (1972), 'Racial Minorities', London, Fontana.
BARRETT, L.E. (1977), 'The Rastafarians', London, Heinemann.
BERGER, J. and MOHR, J. (1975), 'A Seventh Man', Harmondsworth, Penguin.
Birmingham CDP (1977), 'People in Paper Chains', Birmingham Community Development Project, Final Report no.3: Immigration and the State.
BOSANQUET, N. and DOERINGER, P. (1973), Is there a dual labour market in Britain?, 'Economic Journal', vol.83, July, pp.421-35.
BRASS, W. (1977), Article in the 'Listener', 15 September.
British Youth Council (1977), 'Youth Unemployment: Causes and Cures', BYC, March.
BROCK, G. (1977), Police 'dreadlock' report starts a row, in 'Observer', 11 December.
BROOKS, D. (1969), Who will go back?, in 'Race Today', vol.1, no.5.

BROOKS, D. (1975), 'Race and Labour in London Transport', London, Oxford University Press for the Institute of Race Relations and the Action Society Trust.

BROWN, J. (1977), 'Shades of Grey: Police - West Indian Relations in Handsworth', Cranfield, Cranfield Police Studies.

CALLEY, M.J.C. (1965), 'God's People: West Indian Pentecostal Sects in England', London, Oxford University Press for the Institute of Race Relations.

CASSIDY, F.G. (1961), 'Jamaican Talk: Three Hundred Years of the English Language in Jamaica', London, Macmillan.

CASTELLS, M. (1977), 'The Urban Question: A Marxist Approach', London, Edward Arnold.

CASTLES, S. and KOSACK, G. (1973), 'Immigrant Workers and the Class Structure', London, Oxford University Press for the Institute of Race Relations.

CICOUREL, A. (1964), 'Method and Measurement in Sociology', New York, The Free Press.

City of Birmingham (1973), 'A New Plan for the City: Report of Survey: (1) Housing; (2) Employment and Industry' Birmingham, Office of City Engineer and Planning Officer.

Community Relations Commission (1973), 'East Comes West: A background to some Asian faiths', London, CRC.

Community Relations Commission (1977), 'Urban Deprivation, Racial Inequality and Social Policy', London, HMSO.

COX, O.C. (1948), 'Caste, Class and Race', New York, Doubleday.

DAHYA, Z. (1965), Pakistani Wives in Britain, in 'Race', vol.6.

DANIEL, W.W. (1968), 'Racial Discrimination in England', Harmondsworth, Penguin.

DAVISON, R.B. (1962), 'West Indian Migrants: Social and Economic Facts of Migration from the West Indies', London, Oxford University Press for the Institute of Race Relations.

DAVISON, R.B. (1966), 'Black British', London, Oxford University Press for the Institute of Race Relations.

DEAKIN, N. et al. (1966), Colour and the 1966 General Election, 'Race', vol.8, no.1, July.

DEAKIN, N. (1970), 'Colour, Citizenship and British Society', London, Panther.

DEAKIN, N. (1970a), The minorities and the General Election, 1970, 'Race Today', vol.2, no.7, July.

Department of Employment (1975), Unemployment among workers from racial minority groups, 'Department of Employment Gazette', vol.83, no.9, September.

Department of Employment (1976), Racial Disadvantage - a PEP report, in 'Department of Employment Gazette', vol.74, no.3, March.

Department of Employment, Institute of Manpower Studies (1976), 'The Role of Immigrants in the Labour Market', London, Department of Employment.

DESAI, R. (1963), 'Indian Immigrants in Britain', London, Oxford University Press for the Institute of Race Relations.

DUNCAN, S.S. (1976), Self-Help: the allocation of mortgages and the formation of sub-markets, in 'Area', vol.8, no.4, pp.307-16.

EVERITT, B. (1974), 'Cluster Analysis', London, Heinemann.

EVERSLEY, D. and SUDKEO, F. (1969), 'The Dependants of the Coloured Population of England and Wales', London, Institute of Race Relations Special Series.

FIELD, F. and HAIKIN, P. (1971), 'Black Britons', London, Oxford University Press.

FILSTEAD, W.J. (ed.) (1970), 'Qualitative Methodology', Chicago, Markham.

FORESTER, T. (1978), Asians in Business, in 'New Society', 23 February.

FOWLER, B. et al. (1975), 'Immigrant School-leavers and the Search for Work', Discussion Paper no.12, Discussion Papers in Social Research, University of Glasgow.

FRITH, S. (1978), The Punk Bohemians, in 'New Society', vol.43, 9 March.

GILL, C. (1952), 'History of Birmingham, vol.1: Man and Borough to 1865', Oxford University Press for Birmingham City Council.

GLASER, B. and STRAUSS, A. (1968), 'The Discovery of Grounded Theory: Strategies for Qualitative Research', London, Allen & Unwin.

GLASS, R. (1960), 'The Newcomers', London, Allen & Unwin.

GOULD, J. and KOLB, W.L. (1964), 'A Dictionary of the Social Sciences', London, Tavistock.

GRODZIN, M. (1957), Metropolitan Segregation, in 'Scientific American', October.

HADDON, R. (1970), A Minority in a Welfare State Society: Location of West Indians in the London Housing Market, in 'New Atlantis', vol.2, no.1.

HILL, C. (1971), Pentecostalist Growth - result of racialism?, in 'Race Today', 3.

HINDESS, B. (1973), 'The Use of Official Statistics in Sociology: A Critique of positivism and ethnomethodology', London, Macmillan.

HIRO, D. (1973), 'Black British, White British', Harmondsworth, Penguin.

HYMAN, H. et al. (1954), 'Interviewing in Social Research', Chicago, University of Chicago Press.

JENKINS, S. (1971), 'Here to live: a study of race relations in an English town', Runnymede Trust.

JOHNSON, L.K. (1976), Jamaican Rebel Music, in 'Race and Class', vol.17, no.4, Spring.

KARN, V. (1967), A note on race, community and conflict: a study of Sparkbrook, 'Race', vol.9, no.1, July.

KARN, V. (1977/8), The Financing of Owner-Occupation and its impact on ethnic minorities, in 'New Community', vol.6, nos 1 and 2, Winter.

KATZNELSON, I. (1970), The Politics of Racial Buffering in Nottingham 1954-68, in 'Race', vol.2, no.4, April.

KENDALL, M.G. and STUART, A. (1977), 'Advanced Theory of Statistics, vol.3' (3rd edition), London, Griffin.

KHAN, V.S. (1977), 'The Pakistanis: Mirpuri Villagers at home and in Bradford', in Watson (1977).

KOHLER, D.F. (1974), 'The Employment of Black People in a London Borough', London, CRC.

KRAUSZ, E. (1972), 'Ethnic Minorities in Britain', London, Paladin.

LAWRENCE, D. (1974), 'Black Migrants: White Natives: A Study of Race Relations in Nottingham', London, Cambridge University Press.

LAYTON-HENRY, Z. (1977/8), Race and Politics in Ladywood: 1. The Parties and the Campaign, in 'New Community', vol.6, nos 1 and 2, Winter.

LAYTON-HENRY, Z. and TAYLOR, S. (1977), Race at the Polls, in 'New Society', vol.41, 25 August.

Manpower Services Commission (1975), Annual Report 1974-5, London, HMSO.

MARSH, P. (1967), 'The Anatomy of a Strike', Institute of Race Relations Special Research Series.

MARTIN, D. (1967), 'A Sociology of English Religion', London, Heinemann.

MARTIN, R. and FRYER, R.H. (1973), 'Redundancy and Paternalist Capitalism', London, Allen & Unwin.

McINTOSH, N. and SMITH, D.J. (1974), 'The Extent of Racial Discrimination', PEP Broadsheet, no.547, vol.40.

MILL, J.S. (1842-91), 'System of Logic', London.

MILLAR, E.J. (1959), India (Anthropology), in 'Chambers's Encyclopaedia', vol.7, London, George Newnes, p.430.

MILLS, C.WRIGHT (1959), 'The Sociological Imagination', Harmondsworth, Penguin.

MOSER, C.A. and KALTON, G.G.W. (1971), 'Survey Methods in Social Investigation', London, Heinemann.

MULLARD, C. (1973), 'Black Britain', London, Allen & Unwin.

NAIR, K. (1961), 'Blossoms in the Dust', London, Duckworth.

PADRUN, R. and GUYOT, J. (eds) (1978), 'Migrant Women Speak', London, Search Press.

PAHL, R.E. (1968), 'Readings in Urban Sociology', Oxford, Pergamon.

PARK, R.E. et al. (1923), 'The City', Chicago, Chicago University Press.

PATTERSON, S. (1963), 'Dark Strangers: A study of West Indians in London', London, Tavistock.

PEACH, C. (1968), 'West Indian Migration to Britain: A Social Geography', London, Oxford University Press for the Institute of Race Relations.

PHILLIPS, D.L. (1971), 'Knowledge from What? Theories and Methods in Social Research', Chicago, Rand McNally.

PHILLIPS, M. (1978), West Indian Businessmen, in 'New Society', 18 May.

RATCLIFFE, P.B. (1971), Housing in Wandsworth, unpublished BSc(Econ) dissertation, University of London.

REX, J. (1968), 'The Sociology of a Zone of Transition', in Pahl (1968).

REX, J. (1970), 'The Concept of Race in Sociological Theory', in Zubaida (1970).

REX, J. and MOORE, R. (1967), 'Race, Community and Conflict: A study of Sparkbrook', London, Oxford University Press for the Institute of Race Relations (1969 edition referred to in text).

REX, J. and TOMLINSON, S. (1979), 'Colonial Immigrants in a British City: A Class Analysis', London, Routledge & Kegan Paul.

RIMMER, M. (1972), 'Race and Industrial Conflict: A Study of a group of Midland Foundries', London, Heinemann.

ROSE, E.J.B. et al. (1969), 'Colour and Citizenship: A Report on British Race Relations', London, Oxford University Press for the Institute of Race Relations.

RUNCIMAN, W.G. (1966), 'Relative Deprivation and Social Justice: A study of attitudes to social inequality in twentieth-century England', London, Routledge & Kegan Paul.

SHARMA, U. (1971), 'Rampal and his family', London, Collins.

SIVANANDAN, A. (1976), Race, Class and the State: the black experience in Britain, in 'Race and Class', vol.17, no.4, Spring.

SMITH, D.J. (1974), 'Racial Disadvantage in Employment', PEP Broadsheet, no.544.

SMITH, D.J. (1976), 'The Facts of Racial Disadvantage', PEP Broadsheet, no.560.

SMITH, D.J. (1977), 'Racial Disadvantage in Britain', Harmondsworth, Penguin.

SMITH, D.J. and WHALLEY, A. (1975), 'Racial Minorities and Public Housing', PEP Broadsheet, no.556 (vol.41).

STACEY, M. and LAMBROU, Y. (1978), Why do they fail? unpublished research paper, University of Warwick.

Steel Pulse (1978), 'Handsworth Revolution', long-playing record from Island Records.

STEPHEN, F.F. and McCARTHY, P.J. (1958), 'Sampling Opinions: an analysis of survey procedure', New York, Wiley.

STOUFFER, S. (1949), 'The American Soldier', 4 vols, Princeton University Press.

SUTCLIFFE, A. and SMITH, R. (1974), 'History of Birmingham, vol.3: Birmingham 1939-1970', London, Oxford University Press for Birmingham City Council.

TAYLOR, S. (1977/8), Race and Politics in Ladywood, 2: Race and the result, in 'New Community', vol.6, nos 1 and 2, Winter.

THOMAS, W.I. and ZNANIECKI, F. (1927), 'The Polish Peasant in Europe and America', New York, Knopf.

TIMMINS, S. (1866), 'The Resources, Products and Industrial History of Birmingham and the Midland hardware district', London, Robert Hardwicke (latest edition 1967, F.Cass).

TYRON, R.C. and BAILEY, D.E. (1970), 'Cluster Analysis', New York, McGraw-Hill.

WATSON, J.L. (ed.) (1977), 'Between Two Cultures: Migrants and Minorities in Britain', Oxford, Blackwell.

WILLMOTT, P. (1966), 'Adolescent Boys of East London', Harmondsworth, Penguin.

WINCH, P. (1958), 'The Idea of a Social Science', London, Routledge & Kegan Paul.

WOODS, R. (1975), Dynamic Urban Social Structure: A Study of Intra-urban Migration and the Development of Social Stress Areas in Birmingham, unpublished DPhil thesis, University of Oxford.

WRIGHT, P.L. (1968), 'The Coloured Worker in British Industry', London, Oxford University Press for the Institute of Race Relations.

ZUBAIDA, S. (ed.) (1970), 'Race and Racialism', London, Tavistock.

Index

Routledge Social Science Series

Routledge & Kegan Paul   London, Henley and Boston

39 Store Street,
London WC1E 7DD
Broadway House,
Newtown Road,
Henley-on-Thames,
Oxon RG9 1EN
9 Park Street,
Boston, Mass. 02108

Contents

*Authors wishing to submit manuscripts for any series
in this catalogue should send them to the Social Science Editor,
Routledge & Kegan Paul Ltd, 39 Store Street,
London WC1E 7DD.*
● *Books so marked are available in paperback.*
○ *Books so marked are available in paperback only.*
*All books are in metric Demy 8vo format (216 × 138mm approx.)
unless otherwise stated.*

International Library of Sociology
General Editor John Rex

GENERAL SOCIOLOGY

Barnsley, J. H. The Social Reality of Ethics. *464 pp.*
Brown, Robert. Explanation in Social Science. *208 pp.*
● Rules and Laws in Sociology. *192 pp.*
Bruford, W. H. Chekhov and His Russia. *A Sociological Study. 244 pp.*
Burton, F. and Carlen, P. Official Discourse. *On Discourse Analysis, Government Publications, Ideology. About 140 pp.*
Cain, Maureen E. Society and the Policeman's Role. *326 pp.*
● Fletcher, Colin. Beneath the Surface. *An Account of Three Styles of Sociological Research. 221 pp.*
Gibson, Quentin. The Logic of Social Enquiry. *240 pp.*
Glassner, B. Essential Interactionism. *208 pp.*
Glucksmann, M. Structuralist Analysis in Contemporary Social Thought. *212 pp.*
Gurvitch, Georges. Sociology of Law. *Foreword by Roscoe Pound. 264 pp.*
Hinkle, R. Founding Theory of American Sociology 1881–1913. *About 350 pp.*
Homans, George C. Sentiments and Activities. *336 pp.*
Johnson, Harry M. Sociology: *A Systematic Introduction. Foreword by Robert K. Merton. 710 pp.*
● Keat, Russell and Urry, John. Social Theory as Science. *278 pp.*
Mannheim, Karl. Essays on Sociology and Social Psychology. *Edited by Paul Keckskemeti. With Editorial Note by Adolph Lowe. 344 pp.*
Martindale, Don. The Nature and Types of Sociological Theory. *292 pp.*
● Maus, Heinz. A Short History of Sociology. *234 pp.*
Myrdal, Gunnar. Value in Social Theory: *A Collection of Essays on Methodology. Edited by Paul Streeten. 332 pp.*
Ogburn, William F. and Nimkoff, Meyer F. A Handbook of Sociology. *Preface by Karl Mannheim. 656 pp. 46 figures. 35 tables.*
Parsons, Talcott and Smelser, Neil J. Economy and Society: *A Study in the Integration of Economic and Social Theory. 362 pp.*
Payne, G., Dingwall, R., Payne, J. and Carter, M. Sociology and Social Research. *About 250 pp.*
Podgórecki, A. Practical Social Sciences. *About 200 pp.*
Podgórecki, A. and Łos, M. Multidimensional Sociology. *268 pp.*
Raffel, S. Matters of Fact. *A Sociological Inquiry. 152 pp.*
● Rex, John. Key Problems of Sociological Theory. *220 pp.*
Sociology and the Demystification of the Modern World. *282 pp.*
● Rex, John. (Ed.) Approaches to Sociology. *Contributions by Peter Abell, Frank Bechhofer, Basil Bernstein, Ronald Fletcher, David Frisby, Miriam Glucksmann, Peter Lassman, Herminio Martins, John Rex, Roland Robertson, John Westergaard and Jock Young. 302 pp.*
Rigby, A. Alternative Realities. *352 pp.*
Roche, M. Phenomenology, Language and the Social Sciences. *374 pp.*
Sahay, A. Sociological Analysis. *220 pp.*
Strasser, Hermann. The Normative Structure of Sociology. *Conservative and Emancipatory Themes in Social Thought. About 340 pp.*
Strong, P. Ceremonial Order of the Clinic. *267 pp.*
Urry, John. Reference Groups and the Theory of Revolution. *244 pp.*
Weinberg, E. Development of Sociology in the Soviet Union. *173 pp.*

FOREIGN CLASSICS OF SOCIOLOGY

● Gerth, H. H. and Mills, C. Wright. From Max Weber: *Essays in Sociology. 502 pp.*

● **Tönnies, Ferdinand.** Community and Association *(Gemeinschaft und Gesell-schaft).\Translated and Supplemented by Charles P. Loomis. Foreword by Pitirim A. Sorokin. 334 pp.*

SOCIAL STRUCTURE

Andreski, Stanislav. Military Organization and Society. *Foreword by Professor A. R. Radcliffe-Brown. 226 pp. 1 folder.*

Broom, L., Lancaster Jones, F., McDonnell, P. and **Williams, T.** The Inheritance of Inequality. *About 180 pp.*

Carlton, Eric. Ideology and Social Order. *Foreword by Professor Philip Abrahams. About 320 pp.*

Clegg, S. and **Dunkerley, D.** Organization, Class and Control. *614 pp.*

Coontz, Sydney H. Population Theories and the Economic Interpretation. *202 pp.*

Coser, Lewis. The Functions of Social Conflict. *204 pp.*

Crook, I. and **D.** The First Years of the Yangyi Commune. *304 pp., illustrated.*

Dickie-Clark, H. F. Marginal Situation: *A Sociological Study of a Coloured Group. 240 pp. 11 tables.*

Giner, S. and **Archer, M. S.** (Eds) Contemporary Europe: *Social Structures and Cultural Patterns, 336 pp.*

● **Glaser, Barney** and **Strauss, Anselm L.** Status Passage: *A Formal Theory. 212 pp.*

Glass, D. V. (Ed.) Social Mobility in Britain. *Contributions by J. Berent, T. Bottomore, R. C. Chambers, J. Floud, D. V. Glass, J. R. Hall, H. T. Himmelweit, R. K. Kelsall, F. M. Martin, C. A. Moser, R. Mukherjee and W. Ziegel. 420 pp.*

Kelsall, R. K. Higher Civil Servants in Britain: *From 1870 to the Present Day. 268 pp. 31 tables.*

● **Lawton, Denis.** Social Class, Language and Education. *192 pp.*

McLeish, John. The Theory of Social Change: *Four Views Considered. 128 pp.*

● **Marsh, David C.** The Changing Social Structure of England and Wales, 1871–1961. *Revised edition. 288 pp.*

Menzies, Ken. Talcott Parsons and the Social Image of Man. *About 208 pp.*

● **Mouzelis, Nicos.** Organization and Bureaucracy. *An Analysis of Modern Theories. 240 pp.*

● **Ossowski, Stanislaw.** Class Structure in the Social Consciousness. *210 pp.*

● **Podgórecki, Adam.** Law and Society. *302 pp.*

Renner, Karl. Institutions of Private Law and Their Social Functions. *Edited, with an Introduction and Notes, by O. Kahn-Freud. Translated by Agnes Schwarzschild. 316 pp.*

Rex, J. and **Tomlinson, S.** Colonial Immigrants in a British City. *A Class Analysis. 368 pp.*

Smooha, S. Israel: Pluralism and Conflict. *472 pp.*

Wesolowski, W. Class, Strata and Power. *Trans. and with Introduction by G. Kolankiewicz. 160 pp.*

Zureik, E. Palestinians in Israel. *A Study in Internal Colonialism. 264 pp.*

SOCIOLOGY AND POLITICS

Acton, T. A. Gypsy Politics and Social Change. *316 pp.*

Burton, F. Politics of Legitimacy. *Struggles in a Belfast Community. 250 pp.*

Crook, I. and **D.** Revolution in a Chinese Village. *Ten Mile Inn. 216 pp., illustrated.*

Etzioni-Halevy, E. Political Manipulation and Administrative Power. *A Comparative Study. About 200 pp.*

Fielding, N. The National Front. *About 250 pp.*

● **Hechter, Michael.** Internal Colonialism. *The Celtic Fringe in British National Development, 1536–1966. 380 pp.*

Kornhauser, William. The Politics of Mass Society. *272 pp. 20 tables.*

Korpi, W. The Working Class in Welfare Capitalism. *Work, Unions and Politics in Sweden. 472 pp.*

Kroes, R. Soldiers and Students. *A Study of Right- and Left-wing Students. 174 pp.*

Martin, Roderick. Sociology of Power. *About 272 pp.*

Merquior, J. G. Rousseau and Weber. *A Study in the Theory of Legitimacy. About 288 pp.*

Myrdal, Gunnar. The Political Element in the Development of Economic Theory. *Translated from the German by Paul Streeten. 282 pp.*

Varma, B. N. The Sociology and Politics of Development. *A Theoretical Study. 236 pp.*

Wong, S.-L. Sociology and Socialism in Contemporary China. *160 pp.*

Wootton, Graham. Workers, Unions and the State. *188 pp.*

CRIMINOLOGY

Ancel, Marc. Social Defence: *A Modern Approach to Criminal Problems. Foreword by Leon Radzinowicz. 240 pp.*

Athens, L. Violent Criminal Acts and Actors. *104 pp.*

Cain, Maureen E. Society and the Policeman's Role. *326 pp.*

Cloward, Richard A. and **Ohlin, Lloyd E.** Delinquency and Opportunity: *A Theory of Delinquent Gangs. 248 pp.*

Downes, David M. The Delinquent Solution. *A Study in Subcultural Theory. 296 pp.*

Friedlander, Kate. The Psycho-Analytical Approach to Juvenile Delinquency: *Theory, Case Studies, Treatment. 320 pp.*

Gleuck, Sheldon and **Eleanor.** Family Environment and Delinquency. *With the statistical assistance of Rose W. Kneznek. 340 pp.*

Lopez-Rey, Manuel. Crime. *An Analytical Appraisal. 288 pp.*

Mannheim, Hermann. Comparative Criminology: *A Text Book. Two volumes. 442 pp. and 380 pp.*

Morris, Terence. The Criminal Area: *A Study in Social Ecology. Foreword by Hermann Mannheim. 232 pp. 25 tables. 4 maps.*

Rock, Paul. Making People Pay. *338 pp.*

● **Taylor, Ian, Walton, Paul** and **Young, Jock.** The New Criminology. *For a Social Theory of Deviance. 325 pp.*

● **Taylor, Ian, Walton, Paul** and **Young, Jock.** (Eds) Critical Criminology. *268 pp.*

SOCIAL PSYCHOLOGY

Bagley, Christopher. The Social Psychology of the Epileptic Child. *320 pp.*

Brittan, Arthur. Meanings and Situations. *224 pp.*

Carroll, J. Break-Out from the Crystal Palace. *200 pp.*

● **Fleming, C. M.** Adolescence: Its Social Psychology. *With an Introduction to recent findings from the fields of Anthropology, Physiology, Medicine, Psychometrics and Sociometry. 288 pp.*

● The Social Psychology of Education: *An Introduction and Guide to Its Study. 136 pp.*

Linton, Ralph. The Cultural Background of Personality. *132 pp.*

● **Mayo, Elton.** The Social Problems of an Industrial Civilization. *With an Appendix on the Political Problem. 180 pp.*

Ottaway, A. K. C. Learning Through Group Experience. *176 pp.*

Plummer, Ken. Sexual Stigma. *An Interactionist Account. 254 pp.*

● **Rose, Arnold M.** (Ed.) Human Behaviour and Social Processes: *an Interactionist Approach. Contributions by Arnold M. Rose, Ralph H. Turner, Anselm Strauss, Everett C. Hughes, E. Franklin Frazier, Howard S. Becker et al. 696 pp.*

Smelser, Neil J. Theory of Collective Behaviour. *448 pp.*

Stephenson, Geoffrey M. The Development of Conscience. *128 pp.*

Young, Kimball. Handbook of Social Psychology. *658 pp. 16 figures. 10 tables.*

SOCIOLOGY OF THE FAMILY

Bell, Colin R. Middle Class Families: *Social and Geographical Mobility. 224 pp.*
Burton, Lindy. Vulnerable Children. *272 pp.*
Gavron, Hannah. The Captive Wife: *Conflicts of Household Mothers. 190 pp.*
George, Victor and **Wilding, Paul.** Motherless Families. *248 pp.*
Klein, Josephine. Samples from English Cultures.
    1. Three Preliminary Studies and Aspects of Adult Life in England. *447 pp.*
    2. Child-Rearing Practices and Index. *247 pp.*
Klein, Viola. The Feminine Character. *History of an Ideology. 244 pp.*
McWhinnie, Alexina M. Adopted Children. *How They Grow Up. 304 pp.*
● **Morgan, D. H. J.** Social Theory and the Family. *About 320 pp.*
● **Myrdal, Alva** and **Klein, Viola.** Women's Two Roles: *Home and Work. 238 pp.*
    27 tables.
Parsons, Talcott and **Bales, Robert F.** Family: Socialization and Interaction Process. *In collaboration with James Olds, Morris Zelditch and Philip E. Slater. 456 pp. 50 figures and tables.*

SOCIAL SERVICES

Bastide, Roger. The Sociology of Mental Disorder. *Translated from the French by Jean McNeil. 260 pp.*
Carlebach, Julius. Caring For Children in Trouble. *266 pp.*
George, Victor. Foster Care. *Theory and Practice. 234 pp.*
    Social Security: *Beveridge and After. 258 pp.*
George, V. and **Wilding, P.** Motherless Families. *248 pp.*
● **Goetschius, George W.** Working with Community Groups. *256 pp.*
Goetschius, George W. and **Tash, Joan.** Working with Unattached Youth. *416 pp.*
Heywood, Jean S. Children in Care. *The Development of the Service for the Deprived Child. Third revised edition. 284 pp.*
King, Roy D., Ranes, Norma V. and **Tizard, Jack.** Patterns of Residential Care. *356 pp.*
Leigh, John. Young People and Leisure. *256 pp.*
● **Mays, John.** (Ed.) Penelope Hall's Social Services of England and Wales. *368 pp.*
Morris, Mary. Voluntary Work and the Welfare State. *300 pp.*
Nokes, P. L. The Professional Task in Welfare Practice. *152 pp.*
Timms, Noel. Psychiatric Social Work in Great Britain (1939–1962). *280 pp.*
●   Social Casework: *Principles and Practice. 256 pp.*

SOCIOLOGY OF EDUCATION

Banks, Olive. Parity and Prestige in English Secondary Education: a Study in Educational Sociology. *272 pp.*
● **Blyth, W. A. L.** English Primary Education. *A Sociological Description.*
    2. Background. *168 pp.*
Collier, K. G. The Social Purposes of Education: *Personal and Social Values in Education. 268 pp.*
Evans, K. M. Sociometry and Education. *158 pp.*
● **Ford, Julienne.** Social Class and the Comprehensive School. *192 pp.*
Foster, P. J. Education and Social Change in Ghana. *336 pp. 3 maps.*
Fraser, W. R. Education and Society in Modern France. *150 pp.*
Grace, Gerald R. Role Conflict and the Teacher. *150 pp.*
Hans, Nicholas. New Trends in Education in the Eighteenth Century. *278 pp.*
    19 tables.
●   Comparative Education: *A Study of Educational Factors and Traditions. 360 pp.*
● **Hargreaves, David.** Interpersonal Relations and Education. *432 pp.*
●   Social Relations in a Secondary School. *240 pp.*
    School Organization and Pupil Involvement. *A Study of Secondary Schools.*

● **Mannheim, Karl** and **Stewart, W. A. C.** An Introduction to the Sociology of
　　Education. *206 pp.*
● **Musgrove, F.** Youth and the Social Order. *176 pp.*
● **Ottaway, A. K. C.** Education and Society: An Introduction to the Sociology of
　　Education. *With an Introduction by W. O. Lester Smith. 212 pp.*
　Peers, Robert. Adult Education: *A Comparative Study. Revised edition. 398 pp.*
　Stratta, Erica. The Education of Borstal Boys. *A Study of their Educational
　　Experiences prior to, and during, Borstal Training. 256 pp.*
● **Taylor, P. H., Reid, W. A.** and **Holley, B. J.** The English Sixth Form. *A Case Study in
　　Curriculum Research. 198 pp.*

SOCIOLOGY OF CULTURE

Eppel, E. M. and **M.** Adolescents and Morality: *A Study of some Moral Values and
　　Dilemmas of Working Adolescents in the Context of a changing Climate of
　　Opinion. Foreword by W. J. H. Sprott. 268 pp. 39 tables.*
● **Fromm, Erich.** The Fear of Freedom. *286 pp.*
●　The Sane Society. *400 pp.*
　Johnson, L. The Cultural Critics. *From Matthew Arnold to Raymond Williams.
　　233 pp.*
　Mannheim, Karl. Essays on the Sociology of Culture. *Edited by Ernst Mannheim in
　　co-operation with Paul Kecskemeti. Editorial Note by Adolph Lowe. 280 pp.*
　Merquior, J. G. The Veil and the Mask. *Essays on Culture and Ideology. Foreword
　　by Ernest Gellner. 140 pp.*
　Zijderfeld, A. C. On Clichés. *The Supersedure of Meaning by Function in Modernity.
　　150 pp.*

SOCIOLOGY OF RELIGION

Argyle, Michael and **Beit-Hallahmi, Benjamin.** The Social Psychology of Religion.
　　256 pp.
Glasner, Peter E. The Sociology of Secularisation. *A Critique of a Concept.
　　146 pp.*
Hall, J. R. The Ways Out. *Utopian Communal Groups in an Age of Babylon. 280 pp.*
Ranson, S., Hinings, B. and **Bryman, A.** Clergy, Ministers and Priests. *216 pp.*
Stark, Werner. The Sociology of Religion. *A Study of Christendom.*
　Volume II. *Sectarian Religion. 368 pp.*
　Volume III. *The Universal Church. 464 pp.*
　Volume IV. *Types of Religious Man. 352 pp.*
　Volume V. *Types of Religious Culture. 464 pp.*
Turner, B. S. Weber and Islam. *216 pp.*
Watt, W. Montgomery. Islam and the Integration of Society. *320 pp.*

SOCIOLOGY OF ART AND LITERATURE

Jarvie, Ian C. Towards a Sociology of the Cinema. *A Comparative Essay on the
　　Structure and Functioning of a Major Entertainment Industry. 405 pp.*
Rust, Frances S. Dance in Society. *An Analysis of the Relationships between the Social
　　Dance and Society in England from the Middle Ages to the Present Day. 256 pp.
　　8 pp. of plates.*
Schücking, L. L. The Sociology of Literary Taste. *112 pp.*
Wolff, Janet. Hermeneutic Philosophy and the Sociology of Art. *150 pp.*

SOCIOLOGY OF KNOWLEDGE

Diesing, P. Patterns of Discovery in the Social Sciences. *262 pp.*

● **Douglas, J. D.** (Ed.) Understanding Everyday Life. *370 pp.*
● **Hamilton, P.** Knowledge and Social Structure. *174 pp.*
Jarvie, I. C. Concepts and Society. *232 pp.*
Mannheim, Karl. Essays on the Sociology of Knowledge. *Edited by Paul Kecskemeti. Editorial Note by Adolph Lowe. 353 pp.*
Remmling, Gunter W. The Sociology of Karl Mannheim. *With a Bibliographical Guide to the Sociology of Knowledge, Ideological Analysis, and Social Planning. 255 pp.*
Remmling, Gunter W. (Ed.) Towards the Sociology of Knowledge. *Origin and Development of a Sociological Thought Style. 463 pp.*
Scheler, M. Problems of a Sociology of Knowledge. *Trans. by M. S. Frings. Edited and with an Introduction by K. Stikkers. 232 pp.*

URBAN SOCIOLOGY

Aldridge, M. The British New Towns. *A Programme Without a Policy. 232 pp.*
Ashworth, William. The Genesis of Modern British Town Planning: *A Study in Economic and Social History of the Nineteenth and Twentieth Centuries. 288 pp.*
Brittan, A. The Privatised World. *196 pp.*
Cullingworth, J. B. Housing Needs and Planning Policy: *A Restatement of the Problems of Housing Need and 'Overspill' in England and Wales. 232 pp. 44 tables. 8 maps.*
Dickinson, Robert E. City and Region: *A Geographical Interpretation. 608 pp. 125 figures.*
The West European City: *A Geographical Interpretation. 600 pp. 129 maps. 29 plates.*
Humphreys, Alexander J. New Dubliners: *Urbanization and the Irish Family. Foreword by George C. Homans. 304 pp.*
Jackson, Brian. Working Class Community: *Some General Notions raised by a Series of Studies in Northern England. 192 pp.*
● **Mann, P. H.** An Approach to Urban Sociology. *240 pp.*
Mellor, J. R. Urban Sociology in an Urbanized Society. *326 pp.*
Morris, R. N. and **Mogey, J.** The Sociology of Housing. *Studies at Berinsfield. 232 pp. 4 pp. plates.*
Mullan, R. Stevenage Ltd. *About 250 pp.*
Rex, J. and **Tomlinson, S.** Colonial Immigrants in a British City. *A Class Analysis. 368 pp.*
Rosser, C. and **Harris, C.** The Family and Social Change. *A Study of Family and Kinship in a South Wales Town. 352 pp. 8 maps.*
● **Stacey, Margaret, Batsone, Eric, Bell, Colin** and **Thurcott, Anne.** Power, Persistence and Change. *A Second Study of Banbury. 196 pp.*

RURAL SOCIOLOGY

Mayer, Adrian C. Peasants in the Pacific. *A Study of Fiji Indian Rural Society. 248 pp. 20 plates.*
Williams, W. M. The Sociology of an English Village: *Gosforth. 272 pp. 12 figures. 13 tables.*

SOCIOLOGY OF INDUSTRY AND DISTRIBUTION

Dunkerley, David. The Foreman. *Aspects of Task and Structure. 192 pp.*
Eldridge, J. E. T. Industrial Disputes. *Essays in the Sociology of Industrial Relations. 288 pp.*
Hollowell, Peter G. The Lorry Driver. *272 pp.*
● **Oxaal, I., Barnett, T.** and **Booth, D.** (Eds) Beyond the Sociology of Development.

8

Economy and Society in Latin America and Africa. 295 pp.

Smelser, Neil J. Social Change in the Industrial Revolution: *An Application of Theory to the Lancashire Cotton Industry, 1770–1840. 468 pp. 12 figures. 14 tables.*

Watson, T. J. The Personnel Managers. *A Study in the Sociology of Work and Employment, 262 pp.*

ANTHROPOLOGY

Brandel-Syrier, Mia. Reeftown Elite. *A Study of Social Mobility in a Modern African Community on the Reef. 376 pp.*

Dickie-Clark, H. F. The Marginal Situation. *A Sociological Study of a Coloured Group. 236 pp.*

Dube, S. C. Indian Village. *Foreword by Morris Edward Opler. 276 pp. 4 plates.* India's Changing Villages: *Human Factors in Community Development. 260 pp. 8 plates. 1 map.*

Fei, H.-T. Peasant Life in China. *A Field Study of Country Life in the Yangtze Valley. With a foreword by Bronislaw Malinowski. 328 pp. 16 pp. plates.*

Firth, Raymond. Malay Fishermen. *Their Peasant Economy. 420 pp. 17 pp. plates.*

Gulliver, P. H. Social Control in an African Society: a Study of the Arusha, Agricultural Masai of Northern Tanganyika. *320 pp. 8 plates. 10 figures.* Family Herds. *288 pp.*

Jarvie, Ian C. The Revolution in Anthropology. *268 pp.*

Little, Kenneth L. Mende of Sierra Leone. *308 pp. and folder.* Negroes in Britain. *With a New Introduction and Contemporary Study by Leonard Bloom. 320 pp.*

Tambs-Lyche, H. London Patidars. *About 180 pp.*

Madan, G. R. Western Sociologists on Indian Society. *Marx, Spencer, Weber, Durkheim, Pareto. 384 pp.*

Mayer, A. C. Peasants in the Pacific. *A Study of Fiji Indian Rural Society. 248 pp.*

Meer, Fatima. Race and Suicide in South Africa. *325 pp.*

Smith, Raymond T. The Negro Family in British Guiana: *Family Structure and Social Status in the Villages. With a Foreword by Meyer Fortes. 314 pp. 8 plates. 1 figure. 4 maps.*

SOCIOLOGY AND PHILOSOPHY

Adriaansens, H. Talcott Parsons and the Conceptual Dilemma. *About 224 pp.*

Barnsley, John H. The Social Reality of Ethics. *A Comparative Analysis of Moral Codes. 448 pp.*

Diesing, Paul. Patterns of Discovery in the Social Sciences. *362 pp.*

● **Douglas, Jack D.** (Ed.) Understanding Everyday Life. *Toward the Reconstruction of Sociological Knowledge. Contributions by Alan F. Blum, Aaron W. Cicourel, Norman K. Denzin, Jack D. Douglas, John Heeren, Peter McHugh, Peter K. Manning, Melvin Power, Matthew Speier, Roy Turner, D. Lawrence Wieder, Thomas P. Wilson and Don H. Zimmerman. 370 pp.*

Gorman, Robert A. The Dual Vision. *Alfred Schutz and the Myth of Phenomenological Social Science. 240 pp.*

Jarvie, Ian C. Concepts and Society. *216 pp.*

Kilminster, R. Praxis and Method. *A Sociological Dialogue with Lukács, Gramsci and the Early Frankfurt School. 334 pp.*

● **Pelz, Werner.** The Scope of Understanding in Sociology. *Towards a More Radical Reorientation in the Social Humanistic Sciences. 283 pp.*

Roche, Maurice. Phenomenology, Language and the Social Sciences. *371 pp.*

Sahay, Arun. Sociological Analysis. *212 pp.*

● **Slater, P.** Origin and Significance of the Frankfurt School. *A Marxist Perspective. 185 pp.*

Spurling, L. Phenomenology and the Social World. *The Philosophy of Merleau-Ponty and its Relation to the Social Sciences. 222 pp.*

Wilson, H. T. The American Ideology. *Science, Technology and Organization as Modes of Rationality. 368 pp.*

International Library of Anthropology
General Editor   Adam Kuper

● Ahmed, A. S. Millennium and Charisma Among Pathans. *A Critical Essay in Social Anthropology. 192 pp.*

Pukhtun Economy and Society. *Traditional Structure and Economic Development. About 360 pp.*

Barth, F. Selected Essays. *Volume I. About 250 pp.* Selected Essays. *Volume II. About 250 pp.*

Brown, Paula. The Chimbu. *A Study of Change in the New Guinea Highlands. 151 pp.*

Foner, N. Jamaica Farewell. *200 pp.*

Gudeman, Stephen. Relationships, Residence and the Individual. *A Rural Panamanian Community. 288 pp. 11 plates, 5 figures, 2 maps, 10 tables.*

The Demise of a Rural Economy. *From Subsistence to Capitalism in a Latin American Village. 160 pp.*

Hamnett, Ian. Chieftainship and Legitimacy. *An Anthropological Study of Executive Law in Lesotho. 163 pp.*

Hanson, F. Allan. Meaning in Culture. *127 pp.*

Hazan, H. The Limbo People. *A Study of the Constitution of the Time Universe Among the Aged. About 192 pp.*

Humphreys, S. C. Anthropology and the Greeks. *288 pp.*

Karp, I. Fields of Change Among the Iteso of Kenya. *140 pp.*

Lloyd, P. C. Power and Independence. *Urban Africans' Perception of Social Inequality. 264 pp.*

Parry, J. P. Caste and Kinship in Kangra. *352 pp. Illustrated.*

Pettigrew, Joyce. Robber Noblemen. *A Study of the Political System of the Sikh Jats. 284 pp.*

Street, Brian V. The Savage in Literature. *Representations of 'Primitive' Society in English Fiction, 1858–1920. 207 pp.*

Van Den Berghe, Pierre L. Power and Privilege at an African University. *278 pp.*

International Library of Phenomenology and Moral Sciences
General Editor   John O'Neill

Apel, K.-O. Towards a Transformation of Philosophy. *308 pp.*

Bologh, R. W. Dialectical Phenomenology. *Marx's Method. 287 pp.*

Fekete, J. The Critical Twilight. *Explorations in the Ideology of Anglo-American Literary Theory from Eliot to McLuhan. 300 pp.*

Medina, A. Reflection, Time and the Novel. *Towards a Communicative Theory of Literature. 143 pp.*

International Library of Social Policy
General Editor   Kathleen Jones

Bayley, M. Mental Handicap and Community Care. *426 pp.*

Bottoms, A. E. and McClean, J. D. Defendants in the Criminal Process. *284 pp.*

Bradshaw, J. The Family Fund. *An Initiative in Social Policy. About 224 pp.*

Butler, J. R. Family Doctors and Public Policy. *208 pp.*

Davies, Martin. Prisoners of Society. *Attitudes and Aftercare. 204 pp.*

Gittus, Elizabeth. Flats, Families and the Under-Fives. *285 pp.*

Holman, Robert. Trading in Children. *A Study of Private Fostering. 355 pp.*

Jeffs, A. Young People and the Youth Service. *160 pp.*

Jones, Howard and Cornes, Paul. Open Prisons. *288 pp.*

Jones, Kathleen. History of the Mental Health Service. *428 pp.*

Jones, Kathleen with **Brown, John, Cunningham, W. J., Roberts, Julian** and **Williams, Peter.** Opening the Door. *A Study of New Policies for the Mentally Handicapped. 278 pp.*

Karn, Valerie. Retiring to the Seaside. *400 pp. 2 maps. Numerous tables.*

King, R. D. and **Elliot, K. W.** Albany: Birth of a Prison—End of an Era. *394 pp.*

Thomas, J. E. The English Prison Officer since 1850: *A Study in Conflict. 258 pp.*

Walton, R. G. Women in Social Work. *303 pp.*

● **Woodward, J.** To Do the Sick No Harm. *A Study of the British Voluntary Hospital System to 1875. 234 pp.*

International Library of Welfare and Philosophy
General Editors   Noel Timms and David Watson

● **McDermott, F. E.** (Ed.) Self-Determination in Social Work. *A Collection of Essays on Self-determination and Related Concepts by Philosophers and Social Work Theorists. Contributors: F. P. Biestek, S. Bernstein, A. Keith-Lucas, D. Sayer, H. H. Perelman, C. Whittington, R. F. Stalley, F. E. McDermott, I. Berlin, H. J. McCloskey, H. L. A. Hart, J. Wilson, A. I. Melden, S. I. Benn. 254 pp.*

● **Plant, Raymond.** Community and Ideology. *104 pp.*

Ragg, Nicholas M. People Not Cases. *A Philosophical Approach to Social Work. 168 pp.*

● **Timms, Noel** and **Watson, David.** (Eds) Talking About Welfare. *Readings in Philosophy and Social Policy. Contributors: T. H. Marshall, R. B. Brandt, G. H. von Wright, K. Nielsen, M. Cranston, R. M. Titmuss, R. S. Downie, E. Telfer, D. Donnison, J. Benson, P. Leonard, A. Keith-Lucas, D. Walsh, I. T. Ramsey. 320 pp.*

● Philosophy in Social Work. *250 pp.*

● **Weale, A.** Equality and Social Policy. *164 pp.*

Library of Social Work
General Editor   Noel Timms

● **Baldock, Peter.** Community Work and Social Work. *140 pp.*

○ **Beedell, Christopher.** Residential Life with Children. *210 pp. Crown 8vo.*

● **Berry, Juliet.** Daily Experience in Residential Life. *A Study of Children and their Care-givers. 202 pp.*

○ Social Work with Children. *190 pp. Crown 8vo.*

● **Brearley, C. Paul.** Residential Work with the Elderly. *116 pp.*

● Social Work, Ageing and Society. *126 pp.*

● **Cheetham, Juliet.** Social Work with Immigrants. *240 pp. Crown 8vo.*

● **Cross, Crispin P.** (Ed.) Interviewing and Communication in Social Work. *Contributions by C. P. Cross, D. Laurenson, B. Strutt, S. Raven. 192 pp. Crown 8vo.*

● **Curnock, Kathleen** and **Hardiker, Pauline.** Towards Practice Theory. *Skills and Methods in Social Assessments. 208 pp.*

● **Davies, Bernard.** The Use of Groups in Social Work Practice. *158 pp.*

● **Davies, Martin.** Support Systems in Social Work. *144 pp.*

Ellis, June. (Ed.) West African Families in Britain. *A Meeting of Two Cultures. Contributions by Pat Stapleton, Vivien Biggs. 150 pp. 1 Map.*

● **Hart, John.** Social Work and Sexual Conduct. *230 pp.*

● **Hutten, Joan M.** Short-Term Contracts in Social Work. *Contributions by Stella M. Hall, Elsie Osborne, Mannie Sher, Eva Sternberg, Elizabeth Tuters. 134 pp.*

Jackson, Michael P. and **Valencia, B. Michael.** Financial Aid Through Social Work. *140 pp.*

● **Jones, Howard.** The Residential Community. *A Setting for Social Work. 150 pp.*

● (Ed.) Towards a New Social Work. *Contributions by Howard Jones, D. A. Fowler, J. R. Cypher, R. G. Walton, Geoffrey Mungham, Philip Priestley, Ian Shaw, M. Bartley, R. Deacon, Irwin Epstein, Geoffrey Pearson. 184 pp.*

Jones, Ray and **Pritchard, Colin.** (Eds) Social Work With Adolescents. *Contributions by Ray Jones, Colin Pritchard, Jack Dunham, Florence Rossetti, Andrew Kerslake, John Burns, William Gregory, Graham Templeman, Kenneth E. Reid, Audrey Taylor. About 170 pp.*

○ **Jordon, William.** The Social Worker in Family Situations. *160 pp. Crown 8vo.*

● **Laycock, A. L.** Adolescents and Social Work. *128 pp. Crown 8vo.*

● **Lees, Ray.** Politics and Social Work. *128 pp. Crown 8vo.*

● Research Strategies for Social Welfare. *112 pp. Tables.*

○ **McCullough, M. K.** and **Ely, Peter J.** Social Work with Groups. *127 pp. Crown 8vo.*

● **Moffett, Jonathan.** Concepts in Casework Treatment. *128 pp. Crown 8vo.*

Parsloe, Phyllida. Juvenile Justice in Britain and the United States. *The Balance of Needs and Rights. 336 pp.*

● **Plant, Raymond.** Social and Moral Theory in Casework. *112 pp. Crown 8vo.*

Priestley, Philip, Fears, Denise and **Fuller, Roger.** Justice for Juveniles. *The 1969 Children and Young Persons Act: A Case for Reform? 128 pp.*

● **Pritchard, Colin** and **Taylor, Richard.** Social Work: Reform or Revolution? *170 pp.*

○ **Pugh, Elisabeth.** Social Work in Child Care. *128 pp. Crown 8vo.*

● **Robinson, Margaret.** Schools and Social Work. *282 pp.*

○ **Ruddock, Ralph.** Roles and Relationships. *128 pp. Crown 8vo.*

● **Sainsbury, Eric.** Social Diagnosis in Casework. *118 pp. Crown 8vo.*

● Social Work with Families. *Perceptions of Social Casework among Clients of a Family Service. 188 pp.*

Seed, Philip. The Expansion of Social Work in Britain. *128 pp. Crown 8vo.*

● **Shaw, John.** The Self in Social Work. *124 pp.*

Smale, Gerald G. Prophecy, Behaviour and Change. *An Examination of Self-fulfilling Prophecies in Helping Relationships. 116 pp. Crown 8vo.*

Smith, Gilbert. Social Need. *Policy, Practice and Research. 155 pp.*

● Social Work and the Sociology of Organisations. *124 pp. Revised edition.*

● **Sutton, Carole.** Psychology for Social Workers and Counsellors. *An Introduction. 248 pp.*

● **Timms, Noel.** Language of Social Casework. *122 pp. Crown 8vo.*

● Recording in Social Work. *124 pp. Crown 8vo.*

● **Todd, F. Joan.** Social Work with the Mentally Subnormal. *96 pp. Crown 8vo.*

● **Walrond-Skinner, Sue.** Family Therapy. *The Treatment of Natural Systems. 172 pp.*

● **Warham, Joyce.** An Introduction to Administration for Social Workers. *Revised edition. 112 pp.*

● An Open Case. *The Organisational Context of Social Work. 172 pp.*

○ **Wittenberg, Isca Salzberger.** Psycho-Analytic Insight and Relationships. *A Kleinian Approach. 196 pp. Crown 8vo.*

Primary Socialization, Language and Education
General Editor Basil Bernstein

Adlam, Diana S., *with the assistance of Geoffrey Turner and Lesley Lineker.* Code in Context. *272 pp.*

Bernstein, Basil. Class, Codes and Control. *3 volumes.*
- 1. *Theoretical Studies Towards a Sociology of Language. 254 pp.*
  2. *Applied Studies Towards a Sociology of Language. 377 pp.*
- 3. *Towards a Theory of Educational Transmission. 167 pp.*

Brandis, W. and **Bernstein, B.** Selection and Control. *176 pp.*

Brandis, Walter and **Henderson, Dorothy.** Social Class, Language and Communication. *288 pp.*

Cook-Gumperz, Jenny. Social Control and Socialization. *A Study of Class Differences in the Language of Maternal Control. 290 pp.*

- **Gahagan, D. M.** and **G. A.** Talk Reform. *Exploration in Language for Infant School Children. 160 pp.*

Hawkins, P. R. Social Class, the Nominal Group and Verbal Strategies. *About 220 pp.*

Robinson, W. P. and **Rackstraw, Susan D. A.** A Question of Answers. *2 volumes. 192 pp. and 180 pp.*

Turner, Geoffrey J. and **Mohan, Bernard A.** A Linguistic Description and Computer Programme for Children's Speech. *208 pp.*

Reports of the Institute of Community Studies

Baker, J. The Neighbourhood Advice Centre. A Community Project in Camden. *320 pp.*

- **Cartwright, Ann.** Patients and their Doctors. *A Study of General Practice. 304 pp.*

Dench, Geoff. Maltese in London. *A Case-study in the Erosion of Ethnic Consciousness. 302 pp.*

Jackson, Brian and **Marsden, Dennis.** Education and the Working Class: *Some General Themes Raised by a Study of 88 Working-class Children in a Northern Industrial City. 268 pp. 2 folders.*

Marris, Peter. The Experience of Higher Education. *232 pp. 27 tables.*
- Loss and Change. *192 pp.*

Marris, Peter and **Rein, Martin.** Dilemmas of Social Reform. *Poverty and Community Action in the United States. 256 pp.*

Marris, Peter and **Somerset, Anthony.** African Businessmen. *A Study of Entrepreneurship and Development in Kenya. 256 pp.*

Mills, Richard. Young Outsiders: *a Study in Alternative Communities. 216 pp.*

Runciman, W. G. Relative Deprivation and Social Justice. *A Study of Attitudes to Social Inequality in Twentieth-Century England. 352 pp.*

Willmott, Peter. Adolescent Boys in East London. *230 pp.*

Willmott, Peter and **Young, Michael.** Family and Class in a London Suburb. *202 pp. 47 tables.*

Young, Michael and **McGeeney, Patrick.** Learning Begins at Home. *A Study of a Junior School and its Parents. 128 pp.*

Young, Michael and **Willmott, Peter.** Family and Kinship in East London. *Foreword by Richard M. Titmuss. 252 pp. 39 tables.*
The Symmetrical Family. *410 pp.*

Reports of the Institute for Social Studies in Medical Care

Cartwright, Ann, Hockey, Lisbeth and **Anderson, John J.** Life Before Death. *310 pp.*
Dunnell, Karen and **Cartwright, Ann.** Medicine Takers, Prescribers and Hoarders. *190 pp.*
Farrell, C. My Mother Said. . . *A Study of the Way Young People Learned About Sex and Birth Control. 288 pp.*

Medicine, Illness and Society
General Editor W. M. Williams

Hall, David J. Social Relations & Innovation. *Changing the State of Play in Hospitals. 232 pp.*
Hall, David J. and **Stacey, M.** (Eds) Beyond Separation. *234 pp.*
Robinson, David. The Process of Becoming Ill. *142 pp.*
Stacey, Margaret *et al.* Hospitals, Children and Their Families. *The Report of a Pilot Study. 202 pp.*
Stimson, G. V. and **Webb, B.** Going to See the Doctor. *The Consultation Process in General Practice. 155 pp.*

Monographs in Social Theory
General Editor Arthur Brittan

- ● **Barnes, B.** Scientific Knowledge and Sociological Theory. *192 pp.*
  Bauman, Zygmunt. Culture as Praxis. *204 pp.*
- ● **Dixon, Keith.** Sociological Theory. *Pretence and Possibility. 142 pp.*
  The Sociology of Belief. *Fallacy and Foundation. About 160 pp.*
  Goff, T. W. Marx and Mead. *Contributions to a Sociology of Knowledge. 176 pp.*
  Meltzer, B. N., Petras, J. W. and **Reynolds, L. T.** Symbolic Interactionism. *Genesis, Varieties and Criticisms. 144 pp.*
- ● **Smith, Anthony D.** The Concept of Social Change. *A Critique of the Functionalist Theory of Social Change. 208 pp.*

Routledge Social Science Journals

The British Journal of Sociology. *Editor – Angus Stewart; Associate Editor – Leslie Sklair. Vol. 1, No. 1 – March 1950 and Quarterly. Roy. 8vo. All back issues available. An international journal publishing original papers in the field of sociology and related areas.*
Community Work. *Edited by David Jones and Marjorie Mayo. 1973. Published annually.*
Economy and Society. *Vol. 1, No. 1. February 1972 and Quarterly. Metric Roy. 8vo. A journal for all social scientists covering sociology, philosophy, anthropology, economics and history. All back numbers available.*

Social and Psychological Aspects of Medical Practice
Editor   Trevor Silverstone

Printed and bound in Great Britain by
Redwood Burn Limited, Trowbridge & Esher